Front cover
Great Mosque, Domes, 1400, Bayezid I, Bursa.

Museum With No Frontiers *Exhibition Trails*

ISLAMIC ART IN THE MEDITERRANEAN | TURKEY

Early Ottoman Art

The Legacy of the Emirates

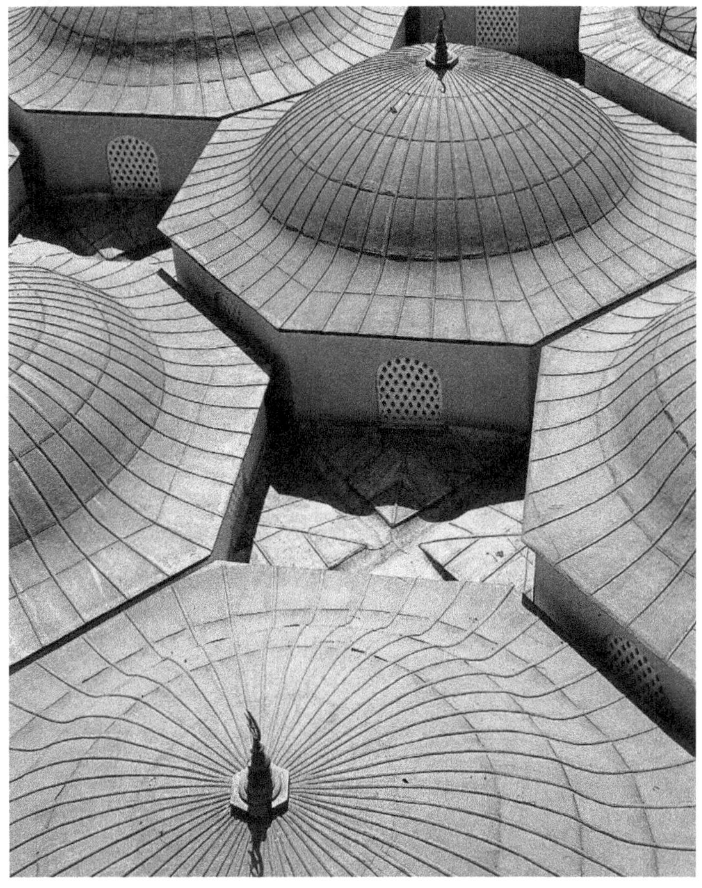

Museum With No Frontiers

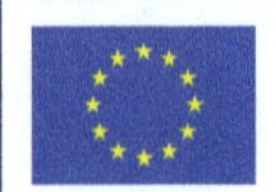
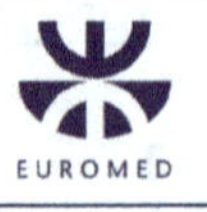

EUROPEAN UNION
Euromed Heritage

The realisation of the MWNF Exhibition Trail
EARLY OTTOMAN ART: The Legacy of the Emirates
has been co-financed by the **European Union** within the framework of the **Euromed Heritage** programme
and has received the support of the following Turkish institutions:

Ministry of Culture
Republic of Turkey, İstanbul

Ministry of Culture, Republic of Turkey, İstanbul

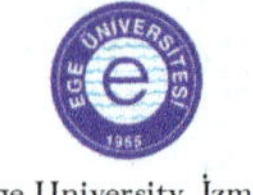

Ege University, İzmir

Ege University, İzmir

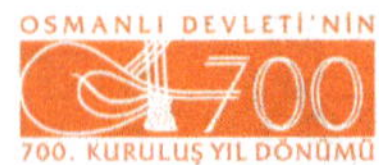

Celebration Committee
for the 700th anniversary of the Foundation of the Ottoman State

ISBN: 978-3-902782-20-5

Information
www.museumwnf.org
www.mwnfbooks.net

Museum With No Frontiers
Idea and overall concept
Eva Schubert

Head of project
Prof. Dr. Gönül Öney, İzmir

Curatorial Committee
Lale Bulut,
Ege University, İzmir
Şakir Çakmak,
Ege University, İzmir
Ertan Daş,
Ege University, İzmir
Aydoğan Demir,
Ege University, İzmir
Yekta Demiralp,
Ege University, İzmir
İnci Kuyulu,
Ege University, İzmir
Gönül Öney,
Ege University, İzmir
Rahmi H. Ünal,
Ege University, İzmir

Catalogue

Introductions
Gönül Öney
Aydoğan Demir

Presentation of the Itineraries
Curatorial Committee

Scientific Editors
Gönül Öney
Rahmi H. Ünal

Revision of the Itineraries
Inci Türkoglu

Technical Advisor
Pier Paolo Racioppi

Technical Editing
Mehmet Kahyaoğlu
Yavuz Tuna

Photographs
Ertan Daş, İzmir
Österreichische Nationalbibliothek, Vienna
İş Bank Collection, İstanbul
Library of Topkapı Palace, İstanbul

General map
Yekta Demiralp, İzmir

Monuments plans and Sketches
Şakir Çakmak, İzmir
Yekta Demiralp, İzmir

General introduction
Islamic Art in the Mediterranean

Text
Jamila Binous, Tunis
Mahmoud Hawari, East Jerusalem
Manuela Marín, Madrid
Gönül Öney, İzmir

Maps
Şakir Çakmak, İzmir
Ertan Daş, İzmir
Yekta Demiralp, İzmir

Translation
Sarah Walker, Madrid

Copy editors
Mandi Gomez, London
Sarah Walker, Madrid

Layout and design
Augustina Fernández,
Electa España, Madrid
Christian Eckart,
MWNF, Vienna (2nd edition)

Local coordination

Production Managers
Mehmet Kahyaoğlu, İzmir
Yavuz Tuna, İzmir

International coordination

Overall coordination
Eva Schubert

Curatorial committees, translations, editing and production of the catalogues (1st edition)
Sakina Missoum, Madrid

Acknowledgements

We thank the following institutions and people for their support:

Republic of Turkey, Ministry of Culture
Republic of Turkey, Prime Ministry General Directorate of the Foundations
Republic of Turkey, Prime Ministry Department of Religious Affairs
Republic of Turkey, Prime Ministry Promotion Fund
Celebration Committee for the 700th Anniversary of the Foundation of the Ottoman State
Austrian Culture Office, İstanbul
Topkapı Palace Museum Directorate, İstanbul
Türkiye İş Bankası, İstanbul
Österreichische Nationalbibliothek, Vienna
Kıymet Giray
Üstün Erek

We would also like to thank:

The Spanish Ministry of Foreign Affairs and Cooperation, Spanish Agency for International Development Cooperation
The Spanish Ministry of Culture

The Federal Ministry of Foreign and European Affairs, Austria
The Ministry of Cultural Heritage and Cultural Activities (National Museum for Oriental Arts, Rome), Italy
The Secretary of State for Tourism, Portugal
The Museum of Mediterranean and Near-Eastern Antiquities, Stockholm, Sweden

as well as
The Regional Government of Tyrol (Austria), where the MWNF Exhibition Trails pilot project was set up

Photographic references

See page 5, as well as
Österreichische Nationalbibliothek, Vienna (pages 84, 156, 159, 178, 190, 205 & 206)
Library of Topkapı Palace, İstanbul (page 40, 41, 42, 153, 157, 158, 177, 228 & 230)

General introduction Islamic Art in the Mediterranean
Ann & Peter Jousiffe, London, page 20 (Aleppo)
Archives of Oronoz Photographs, Madrid, page 23 (Alhambra, Granada)

Plan references

Ayverdi, E. H. (İstanbul, 1989), page 53 (Bedesten, Edirne), page 54 (Issız Han, Ulubat)
Çakmak, Ş. (İzmir, 1999), page 43 (Decoration on portal of Great Mosque, Bursa), page 68 (Decoration on portal of Yeşil Mosque, İznik), page 135 (Decoration on portal of Yeşil Mosque, Bursa)
Daş, E. (İzmir, 1998), page 52 (Saadet Hatun Hamamı, Selçuk)
Demiralp, Y. (Ankara, 1999), page 147 (Decoration on the *iwan* facade of Muradiye Madrasa, Bursa), page 50 (Yıldırım Madrasa, Bursa)
Demiriz, Y. (İstanbul, 1979), page 165 (Nilüfer Hatun İmaret, İznik)
Durukan, A. (Ankara, 1988), page 44 (İlyas Bey Mosque, Balat)
Emir, S. (İzmir, 1994), page 184 (Postinpuş Baba Zawiya, Yenişehir)
Sönmez, Z. (Ankara, 1995), page 45 (Eski Mosque, Edirne), page 47 (İsa Bey Mosque, Selçuk), page 48 (Firuz Bey Mosque, Milas), page 49 (Üç Şerefeli Mosque, Edirne), page 51 (Yeşil Türbe, Bursa), page 119 (Great Mosque, Manisa), page 136 (Yeşil Mosque, Bursa)
Ünal, R. H., page 46 (Great Mosque, Birgi), page 105 (Aydınoğlu Mehmed Bey Türbesi, Birgi)

General introduction Islamic Art in the Mediterranean
Ettinghaussen, R. and Grabar, O. (Madrid, I, 1997), page 26 (Damascus Mosque) and page 30 (Qasr al-Khayr al-Sharqi)
Blair, S. S. and Bloom, J. M. (Madrid, II, 1999), Page 29 (Sultan Hassan Madrasa)
Kuran, A. (İstanbul, 1986), page 31 (Sultan Khan Aksaray)
Sönmez, Z. (Ankara, 1995), page 27 (Mosques of Divriği & İstanbul) and page 28 (Mosque of Sivas)
Viguera, S. (Madrid), page 28 (Minaret types)

Preface

In 1996 Museum With No Frontiers (MWNF) initiated a comprehensive programme to research, document and increase knowledge and public awareness of the history and cultural legacy of Islam in the countries surrounding the Mediterranean basin. This book is one of the outcomes of this programme, which involves hundreds of scholars and is carried out in cooperation with institutions from all the countries concerned. Important initial funding from the European Union made it possible to set the basis for a sustainable network of public and private partners implementing attractive projects in the field of culture, education and tourism.

When the MWNF programme was first launched, the topic of Islamic art and architecture was familiar only to experts and there was an implicit understanding that cultural heritage in the Mediterranean meant the legacy of the classical civilisations. Thanks to the launch coinciding with the establishment at the end of 1995 of the Euro-Mediterranean Partnership, a joint initiative of the European Union and its Mediterranean neighbours, the MWNF programme took off quickly and became a pioneering venture to disseminate knowledge about the world contribution of Islam.

The initial focus on the Mediterranean region was determined by its place at the centre stage of Islamic history and the economic and cultural interdependence of its shores throughout that history. However, we look forward to extending the programme to other areas of the Islamic and Arab world.

In connection with our Exhibition Trails and related thematic guides, MWNF also offers the possibility to participate in themed tours organised in cooperation with specialised local travel agencies in each country. For further details and virtual tours to the Exhibition Trails please visit *www.mwnftravels.net*.

Our Virtual Museum – *www.discoverislamicart.org* – offers access to a large collection of Islamic artefacts and monuments, with descriptions for all items regularly updated in Arabic, English, French and Spanish. A series of Virtual Exhibitions enables visitors to locate the topics of the Exhibition Trails within the relevant regional context.

All MWNF publications are compiled, written and illustrated by scholars and photographers from the country concerned and convey the cultural and historical context of the featured sites from a local perspective. 'We appreciate only what we see and we understand only what we know.' It was with this idea in mind that our Egyptian colleagues who designed the visit and wrote the text for this book paid particular attention to providing information that usually remains undisclosed to tourists.

On behalf of the whole MWNF team I wish you an enjoyable visit to Early Ottoman Anatolia and Trace and look forward to meeting you soon in another part of our Euro-Mediterranean museum with no frontiers.

Eva Schubert
Chairperson and CEO
Museum With No Frontiers

Some preliminary words

The *EARLY OTTOMAN ART: The Legacy of the Emirates* Exhibition Trail has been realised by the joint work of the European Commission, the Ministry of Culture of the Republic of Turkey and Ege University. For Turkey, this is the first time this kind of work has been realised. We believe that similar exhibitions covering different periods will be very helpful for the presentation of a common Mediterranean heritage.

I hereby take the opportunity to thank members of the Scientific Committee, Production Managers, our Rector Prof. Dr. Refet Saygılı, who has provided us with the help and facilities of the University, and Mr. İstemihan Talay, Minister of Culture of the Republic of Turkey who has supported us in many ways.

I would like to thank the head of the Celebration Committee of the 700th anniversary of the foundation of the Ottoman State, Mr. Fikret Ünlü, Minister of State of the Republic of Turkey and Mrs. Füsun Koroğlu, the assistant undersecretary for the Prime Ministry of the Republic of Turkey.

I would also like to thank the following people who have helped us overcome all kinds of difficulties: Mr. Fikret Üçcan, under-secretary of the Ministry of Culture, Mr. Tekin Aybaş the ex-undersecretary of the Ministry of Culture, Mr. Alpay Pasinli General Director of Monuments and Antiquities, Mr. Kenan Yurttagül Acting General Director of Monuments and Antiquities, and the Ministry of Culture, Mrs. Nilüfer Ertan Director of the Cultural Activities Department in the Ministry of Culture.

The extraordinary efforts of Eva Schubert have been key to overcoming the problems we encountered and for the final realisation of the Exhibition Trail. On behalf of the Turkish team I congratulate her and give her my special thanks.

Prof. Dr. Gönül ÖNEY
Head of the Turkish Exhibition

Practical advice

The MWNF Exhibition Trail in Turkey *EARLY OTTOMAN ART: The Legacy of the Emirates* contains eight itineraries, which take nine days to visit. The itineraries in the catalogue are given Roman numbers, whereas the cities/centres within each itinerary are given cardinal numbers and the monuments are given letters. Before each itinerary there is a sketch in which the location and the types of monuments are shown. The aim of these sketches is to orient the visitor. The visitor will need a more detailed map and city plan to travel from one place to the another. Turkey has a very practical public transport system of "*dolmush*" minibuses and intercity buses, yet it is always necessary to inquire about the timings beforehand.

A signposting system has been established along the itineraries consisting of various elements. These signs lead visitors to the monuments and the Info-towers in the town centres, while brief information is given about each place. Besides the signposting elements, each monument included in the exhibition has a panel at the entrance for easier identification. Moreover, on the main roads there are brown signs for the major venues.

On the sketches the main route is indicated with a black line. Some monuments within the itineraries, which are indicated by grey circles, are optional; hence the grey routes are the way to these optional monuments. There are two types of icons in the sketches: the bigger ones are for the primary monuments and the smaller ones are for the optionalones. Right after the name of the monuments some technical information is given (for example the address, the opening/closing hours, etc.). Museum With No Frontiers is not responsible for any changes that may occur after publication of this catalogue.

In the catalogue some additional information on the other attractions of the region/town is given in a frame with a beige background.

Some sites are not open to the public; Museum With No Frontiers continues to negotiate with the authorities to have these sites opened.

The religious monuments included in the exhibition should not be visited during religious services. Since some mosques are open only for prayer, they can be visited shortly before or after prayers. Visitors should be appropriately dressed. For these visits please make sure you do not wear shorts and you have your shoulders covered. Women visitors are asked to wear a scarf to cover their hair.

Generally speaking Turkish museums to not allow photographs to be taken with a flash, and they do not allow tripods. Taking photographs or filming on or around military areas is strictly prohibited.

We have retained standard spelling for Turkish words in common use and included in the English dictionary. We have used spellings for the names as provided by the authors themselves, as well as the Turkish spelling of the localities. Words in italic in the text without an accompanying translation or explanation can be found in the glossary.

Museum With No Frontiers is not responsible for any accident, theft, etc. that may occur during your visit.

Mehmet Kahyaoğlu
Yavuz Tuna
Production Managers

INDEX

ISLAMIC DYNASTIES IN THE MEDITERRANEAN

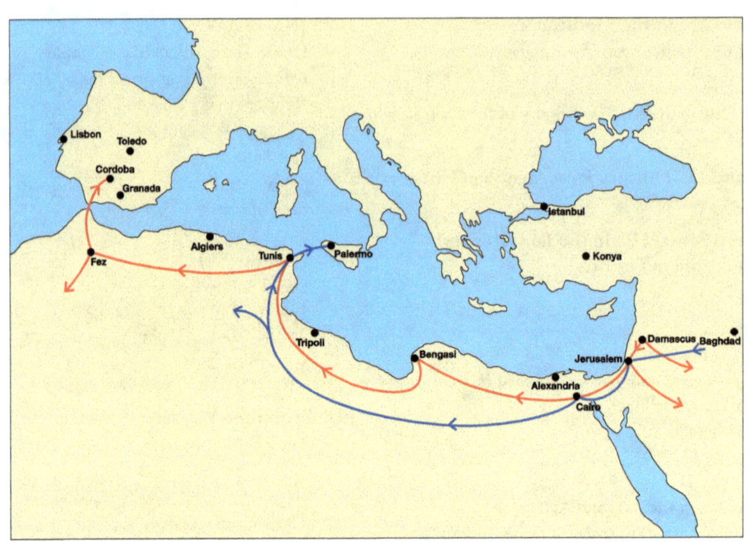

The Umayyads (41/661-132/750) Capital: Damascus
The Abbasids (132/750-656/1258) Capital: Baghdad

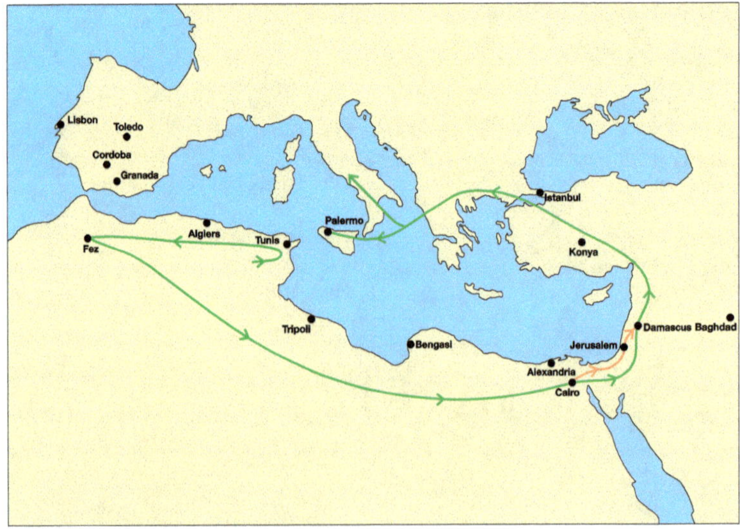

The Fatimids (296/909-567/1171) Capital: Cairo
The Mamluks (648/1250-923/1517) Capital: Cairo

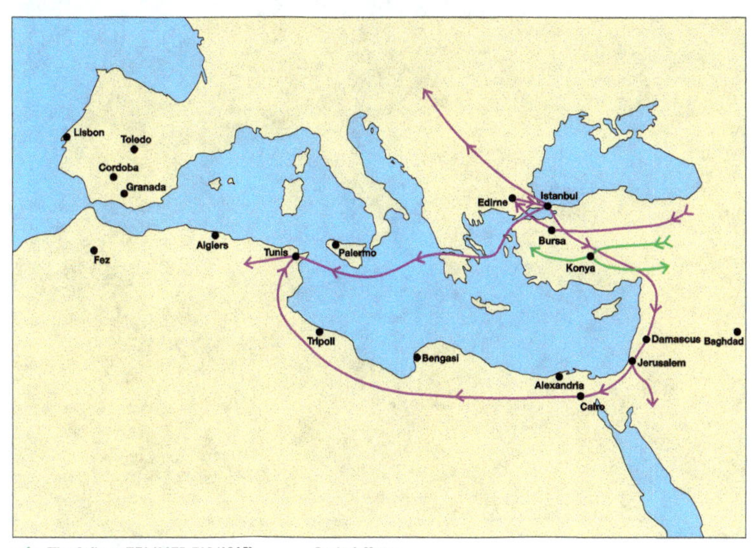

The Seljuqs (571/1075-718/1318) **Capital: Konya**
The Ottomans (699/1299-1340/1922) **Capital: Istanbul**

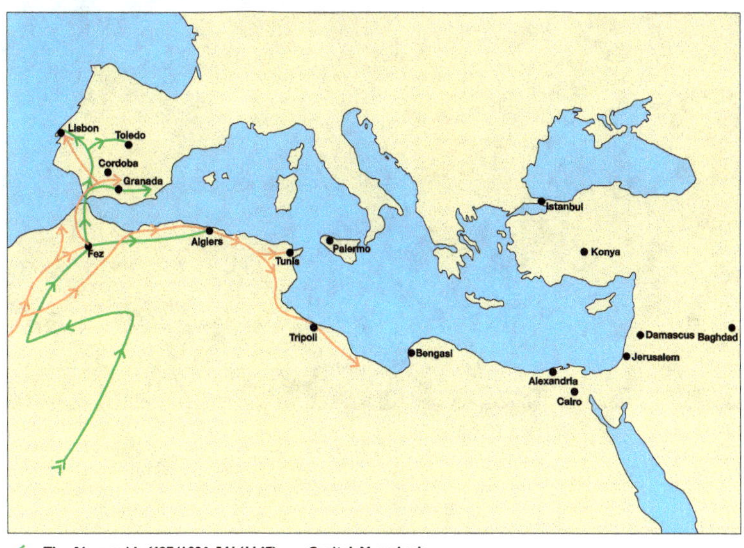

The Almoravids (427/1036-541/1147) **Capital: Marrakesh**
The Almohads (515/1121-667/1269) **Capital: Marrakesh**

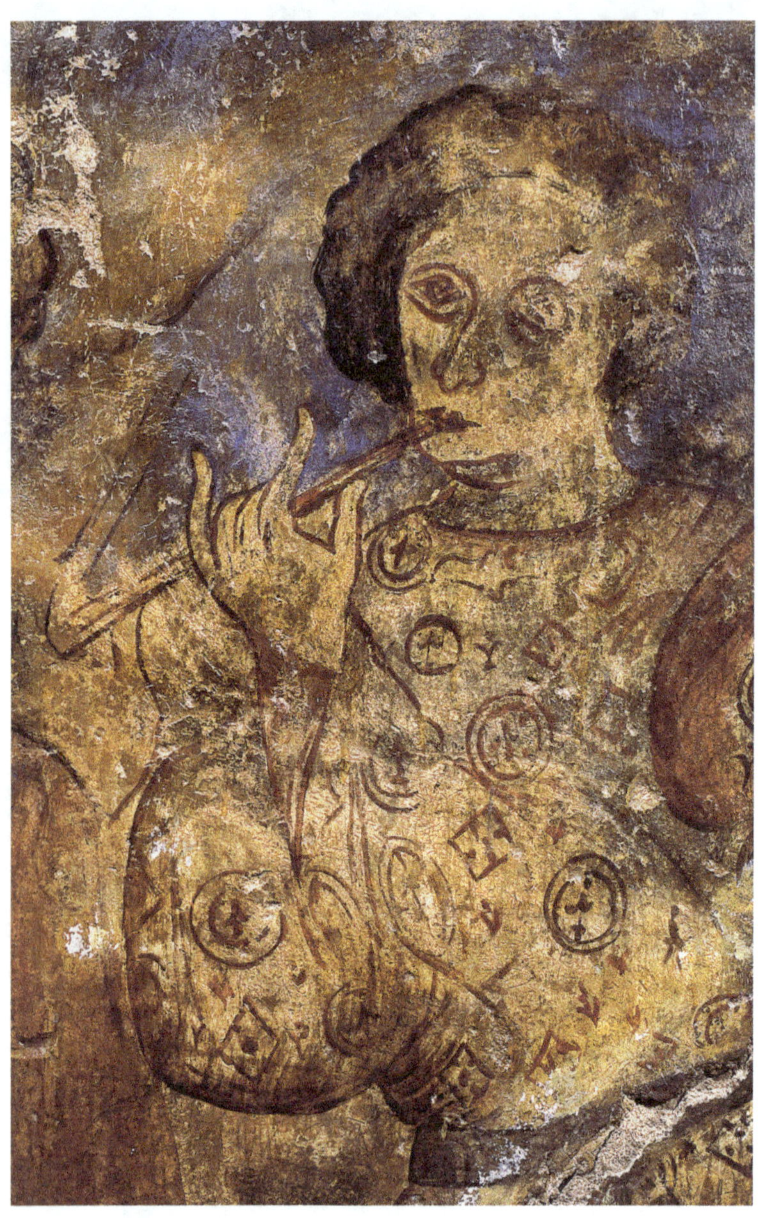

Qusayr 'Amra, mural in the Audience Hall, Badiya of Jordan.

ISLAMIC ART IN THE MEDITERRANEAN

Jamila Binous
Mahmoud Hawari
Manuela Marín
Gönül Öney

The Legacy of Islam in the Mediterranean

Since the first half of the 1st/7th century, the history of the Mediterranean Basin has belonged, in remarkably similar proportion, to two cultures, Islam and the Christian West. This extensive history of conflict and contact has created a mythology that is widely diffused in the collective imagination, a mythology based on the image of the other as the unyielding enemy, strange and alien, and as such, incomprehensible. It is of course true that battles punctuated those centuries from the time when the Muslims spilled forth from the Arabian Peninsula and took possession of the Fertile Crescent, Egypt, and later, North Africa, Sicily, and the Iberian Peninsula, penetrating into Western Europe as far as the south of France. At the beginning of the 2nd/8th century, the Mediterranean came under Islamic control.

This drive to expand, of an intensity seldom equalled in human history, was carried out in the name of a religion that considered itself then heir to its two immediate antecedents: Judaism and Christianity. It would be a gross oversimplification to explain the Islamic expansion exclusively in religious terms. One widespread image in the West presents Islam as a religion of simple dogmas adapted to the needs of the common people, spread by vulgar warriors who poured out from the desert bearing the *Qur'an* on the blades of their swords. This coarse image does away with the intellectual complexity of a religious message that transformed the world from the moment of its inception. It identifies this message with a military threat, and thus justifies a response on the same terms. Finally, it reduces an entire culture to only one of its elements, religion, and in doing so, deprives it of the potential for evolution and change.

The Mediterranean countries that were progressively incorporated into the Muslim world began their journeys from very different starting points. Forms of Islamic life that began to develop in each were quite logically different within the unity that resulted from their shared adhesion to the new religious dogma. It is precisely the capacity to assimilate elements of previous cultures (Hellenistic, Roman, etc.), which has been one of the defining characteristics of Islamic societies. If one restricts one's observations to the geographical area of the Mediterranean, which was extremely diverse culturally at the time of the emergence of Islam, one will discern quickly that this initial moment does not represent a break with previous history in the least. One comes to realise that it is impossible to imagine a monolithic and immutable Islamic world, blindly following an inalterable religious message.

If anything can be singled out as the *leitmotiv* running through the area of the Mediterranean, it is diversity of expression combined with harmony of sentiment, a sentiment more cultural than religious. In the Iberian Peninsula – to begin with the western perimeter of the Mediterranean – the presence of Islam, initially brought about by military conquest, produced a society clearly differentiated from, but in permanent contact with Christian society. The importance of the cultural expression of this Islamic society was felt even after it ceased to exist as such, and gave rise to perhaps one of the most original components of Spanish culture, Mudejar art. Portugal maintained strong Mozarab traditions throughout the Islamic period and there are many imprints from this time that are still clearly visible today. In Morocco and Tunisia, the legacy of al-Andalus was assimilated into the local forms and continues to be evident to this day. The western Mediterranean produced original forms of expression that reflected its conflicting and plural historical evolution.

Lodged between East and West, the Mediterranean Sea is endowed with terrestrial enclaves, such as Sicily, that represent centuries-old key historical locations. Conquered by the Arabs established in Tunisia, Sicily has continued to perpetuate the cultural and historical memory of Islam long after the Muslims ceased to have any political presence on the island. The presence of Sicilian-Norman aesthetic forms preserved in architectural monuments clearly demonstrates that the history of these regions cannot be explained without an understanding of the diversity of social, economic and cultural experiences that flourished on their soil.

In sharp contrast, then, to the immutable and constant image alluded to at the outset, the history of Mediterranean Islam is characterised by surprising diversity. It is made up of a mixture of peoples and ethnicities, deserts and fertile lands. As the major religion has been Islam since the early Middle Ages, it is also true that religious minorities have maintained a presence historically. The Classical Arabic language of the *Qur'an,* has coexisted side-by-side with other languages, as well as with other dialects of Arabic. Within a setting of undeniable unity (Muslim religion, Arabic language and culture), each society has evolved and responded to the challenges of history in its own characteristic manner.

The Emergence and Development of Islamic Art

Throughout these countries, with ancient and diverse civilisations, a new art permeated with images from the Islamic faith emerged at the end of the $2^{nd}/8^{th}$ century, which successfully imposed itself in a period of less than 100 years. This art, in its own particular manner, gave rise to creations and innovations based on unifying regional formulas and architectural and decorative processes, and was simultaneously inspired by the artistic traditions that proceeded it: Greco-Roman and Byzantine, Sasanian, Visigothic, Berber or even Central Asian.

The initial aim of Islamic art was to serve the needs of religion and various aspects of socio-economic life. New buildings appeared for religious purposes such as mosques and sanctuaries. For this reason, architecture played a central role in Islamic art because a whole series of other arts are dependent on it. Apart from architecture a whole range of complimentary minor arts found their artistic expressions in a variety of materials, such as wood, pottery, metal, glass, textiles and paper. In pottery, a great variety of glaze techniques were employed and among these distinguished groups are the lustre and polychrome painted wares. Glass of great beauty was manufactured, reaching excellence with the type adorned with gold and bright enamel colours. In metal work, the most sophisticated technique is inlaying bronze with silver or copper. High-quality textiles and carpets, with geometric, animal and human designs, were made. Illuminated manuscripts with miniature paintings represent a spectacular achievement in the arts of the book. These types of minor arts serve to attest the brilliance of Islamic art.

Figurative art, however, is excluded from the Islamic liturgical domain, which means it is ostracised from the central core of Islamic civilisation and that it is tolerated only at its periphery. Relief work is rare in the decoration of monuments and sculptures are almost flat. This deficit is compensated with a richness in ornamentation on the lavish carved plaster panelling, sculpted wooden panelling, wall tiling and glazed mosaics, as well as on the stalactite friezes, or *muqarnas*. Decorative elements taken from nature, such as leaves, flowers and branches, are generally stylised to the extreme and are so complicated that they rarely call to mind their sources of origin. The intertwining and combining of geometric motifs such as rhombus and etiolated polygons, form interlacing networks that completely cover the surface, resulting in shapes often called arabesques. One innovation within the decorative repertoire is the introduction of epigraphic elements

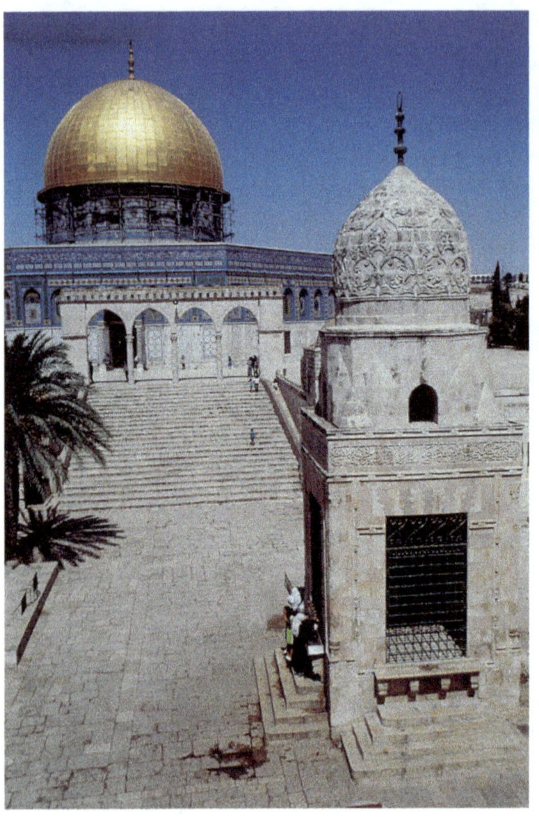

Dome of the Rock, Jerusalem.

in the ornamentation of monuments, furniture and various other objects. Muslim craftsmen made use of the beauty of Arabic calligraphy, the language of the sacred book, the *Qur'an*, not only for the transcription of the Qur'anic verses, but in all of its variations simply as a decorative motif for the ornamentation of stucco panelling and the edges of panels.

Art was also at the service of rulers. It was for patrons that architects built palaces, mosques, schools, hospitals, bathhouses, *caravanserais* and mausoleums, which would sometimes bear their names. Islamic art is, above all, dynastic art. Each one contributed tendencies that would bring about a partial or complete renewal of artistic forms, depending on historical conditions, the prosperity enjoyed by their states, and the traditions of each people. Islamic art, in spite of its relative unity, allowed for a diversity that gave rise to different styles, each one identified with a dynasty.

The Umayyad Dynasty (41/661-132/750), which transferred the capital of the caliphate to Damascus, represents a singular achievement in the history of Islam. It absorbed and incorporated the Hellenistic and Byzantine legacy in such a way that the classical tradition of the Mediterranean was recast in a new and innovative mould. Islamic art, thus, was formed in Syria, and the architecture, unmistakably Islamic due to the personality of the founders, would continue to bear a relation to Hellenistic and Byzantine art as well. The most important of these monuments are the Dome of the Rock in Jerusalem, the earliest existing monumental Islamic sanctuary, the Great Mosque of Damascus, which served as a model for later mosques, and the desert palaces of Syria, Jordan and Palestine.

When the Abbasid caliphate (132/ 750-656/1258) succeeded the Umayyads, the political centre of Islam was moved from the Mediterranean to Baghdad in Mesopotamia. This factor would influence the development of Islamic civilisation and the entire range of culture, and art would bear the mark of that change. Abbasid art and architecture were influenced by three major traditions: Sassanian, Central Asian and Seljuq. Central Asian influence was already present in Sassanian architecture, but at Samarra this influence is represented by the stucco style with its arabesque ornamentation that would rapidly spread throughout the Islamic world. The influence of Abbasid monuments can be observed in the buildings constructed during this period in the other regions of the empire, particularly Egypt and Ifriqiya. In Cairo, the Mosque of Ibn Tulun (262/876-265/879) is a masterpiece, remarkable for its plan and unity of conception. It was modelled after the Abbasid Great Mosque of Samarra, particularly its spiral minaret. In Kairouan, the capital of Ifriqiya, vassals of the Abbasid caliphs, the Aghlabids (184/800-296/909) expanded the Great Mosque of Kairouan, one of the most venerable congregational mosques in the Maghrib. Its *mihrab* was covered by ceramic tiles from Mesopotamia.

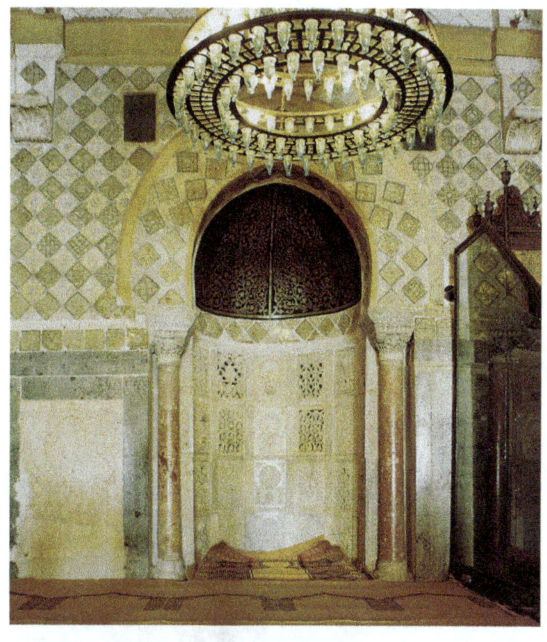

Kairouan Mosque, mihrab, Tunisia.

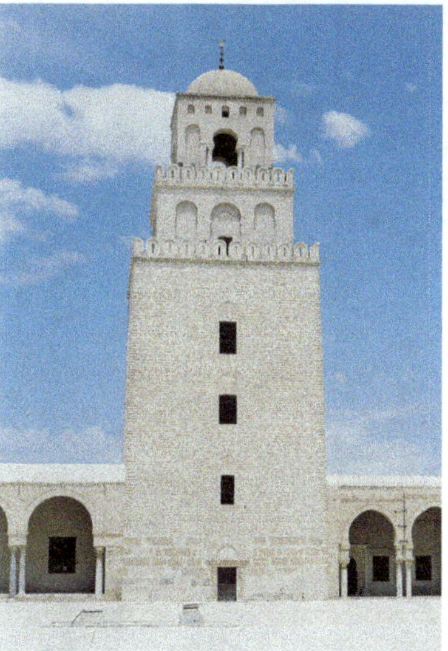

Kairouan Mosque, minaret, Tunisia.

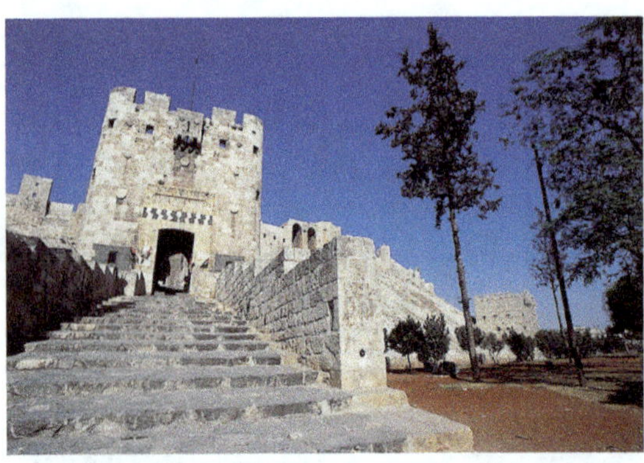

Citadel of Aleppo, view of the entrance, Syria.

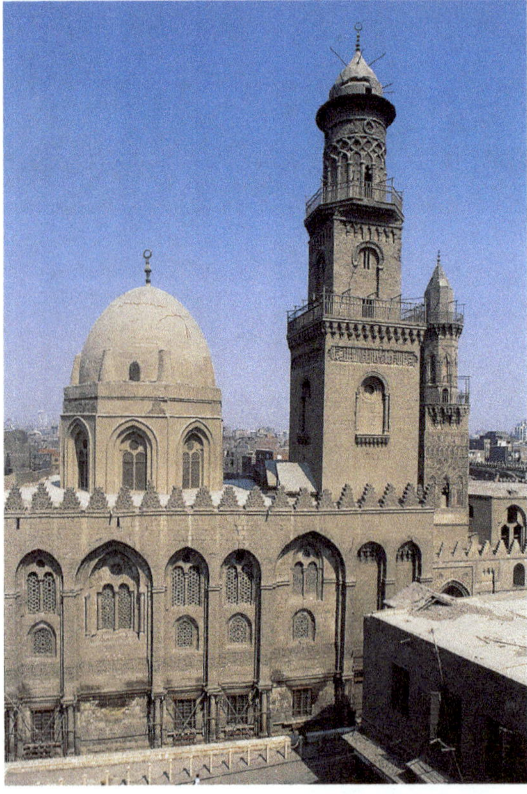

Complex of Qaluwun, Cairo, Egypt.

The reign of the Fatimids (297/909-567/1171) represents a remarkable period in the history of the Islamic countries of the Mediterranean: North Africa, Sicily, Egypt and Syria. Of their architectural constructions, a few examples remain that bear witness to their past glory. In the central Maghrib the Qal'a of the Bani Hammad and the Mosque of Mahdiya; in Sicily, the Cuba (*Qubba*) and the Zisa (*al-'Aziza*) in Palermo, constructed by Fatimid craftsmen under the Norman King William II; in Cairo, the Azhar Mosque is the most prominent example of Fatimid architecture in Egypt.

The Ayyubids (567/1171-648/1250), who overthrew the Fatimid Dynasty in Cairo, were important patrons of architecture. They established religious institutions *(madrasas, khanqas)* for the propagation of *Sunni* Islam, mausoleums and welfare projects, as well as awesome fortifications pertaining to the military conflict with the Crusaders. The Citadel of Aleppo in Syria is a remarkable example of their military architecture.

The Mamluks (648/1250-923/1517) successors of the Ayyubids, successfully resisted the Crusades and the Mongols, achieved the unity of Syria and Egypt and created a formidable empire. The wealth and luxury of the Mamluk Sultan's court in Cairo motivated artists and architects to achieve an extraordinarily elegant style of architecture. For the world of Islam, the Mamluk period marked a rebirth and renaissance. The enthusiasm for establishing religious foundations and reconstructing existing ones place the Mamluks among the greatest patrons of art and architecture in the history of Islam. The Mosque of Hassan (757/1356), a funerary mosque built with a cruciform plan in which the four arms of the cross were formed by four *iwans* of the building around a central courtyard, was typical of the era.

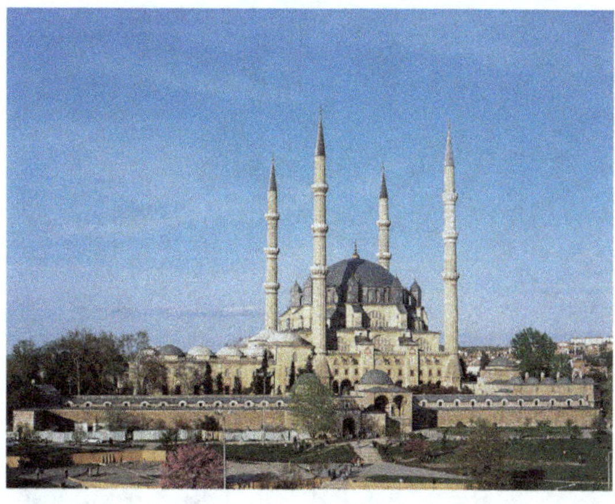

Selimiye Mosque, general view, Edirne, Turkey.

Anatolia was the birthplace of two great Islamic dynasties: the Seljuqs (571/1075-718/1318), who introduced Islam to the region; and the Ottomans (699/1299-1340/1922), who brought about the end of the Byzantine Empire upon capturing Constantinople, and asserted their hegemony throughout the region.

A distinctive style of Seljuq art and architecture flourished with influences from Central Asia, Iran, Mesopotamia and Syria, which merged with elements deriving from Anatolian Christian and antiquity heritage. Konya, the new capital in Central Anatolia, as well as other cities, were enriched with buildings in the newly developed Seljuq style. Numerous mosques, *madrasas, turbes* and *caravanserais,* which were richly decorated by stucco and tiling with diverse figural representations, have survived to our day.

Tile of Kubadabad Palace, Karatay Museum, Konya, Turkey.

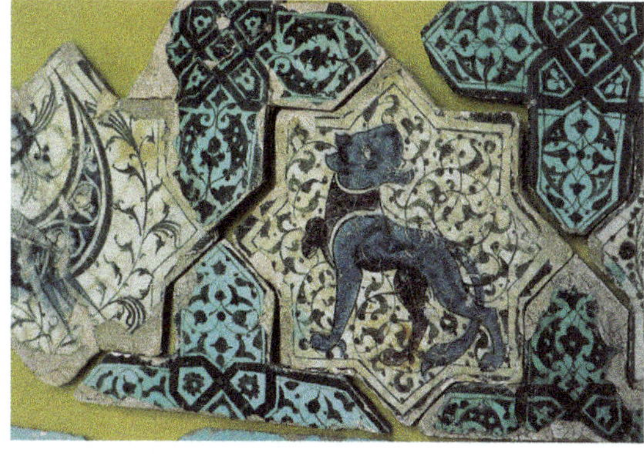

As the Seljuq Emirates disintegrated and Byzantium declined, the Ottomans expanded their territory swiftly changing their capital from Iznik to Bursa and then again to Edirne. The conquest of Constantinople in 858/1453 by Sultan Mehmet II provided the necessary impetus for the transition of an emerging state into a great empire. A superpower that extended its boundaries to Vienna including the Balkans in the West and to Iran in the East, as well

Great Mosque of Cordoba, mihrab, Spain.

Madinat al-Zahra', Dar al-Yund, Spain.

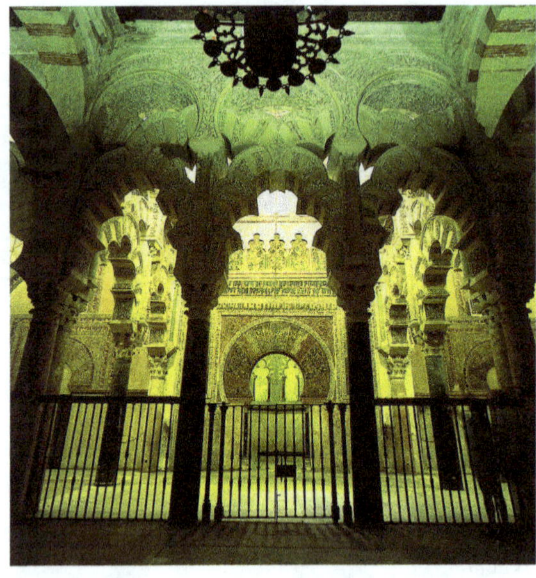

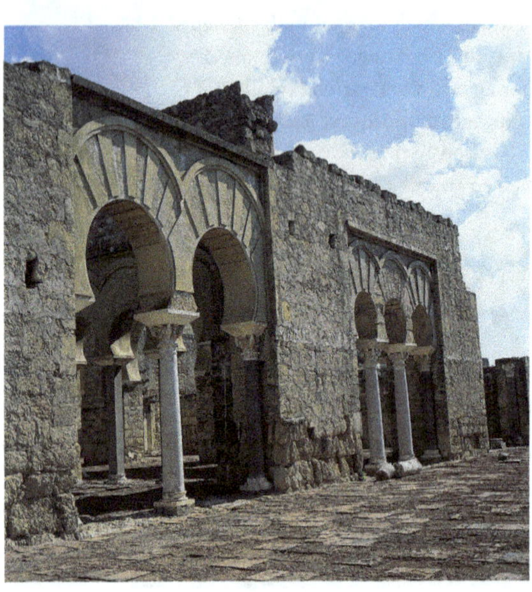

as North Africa from Egypt to Algeria, turning the Eastern Mediterranean into an Ottoman sea. The race to surpass the grandeur of the inherited Byzantine churches, exemplified by the Hagia Sophia, culminated in the construction of great mosques in Istanbul. The most significant one is the Mosque of Süleymaniye, built in the $10^{th}/16^{th}$ century by the famous Ottoman architect Sinan, it epitomises the climax in architectural harmony in domed buildings. Most major Ottoman mosques were part of a large building complex called *kulliye* that also consisted several *madrasas*, a *Qur'an* school, a library, a hospital (*darussifa*), a hostel (*tabhane*), a public kitchen, a *caravanserai* and mausoleums (*turbes*). From the beginning of the $12^{th}/18^{th}$ century, during the so-called Tulip Period, Ottoman architecture and decorative style reflected the influence of French Baroque and Rococo, heralding the Westernisation period in arts and architecture.

Al-Andalus at the western part of the Islamic world became the cradle of a brilliant artistic and cultural expression. 'Abd al-Rahman I established an independent Umayyad caliphate (138/750-422/1031) with Cordoba as its capital. The Great Mosque of Cordoba would pioneer innovative artistic tendencies such as the double-tiered arches with two alternating colours and panels with vegetal ornamentation which would become part of the repertoire of al-Andalus artistic forms.

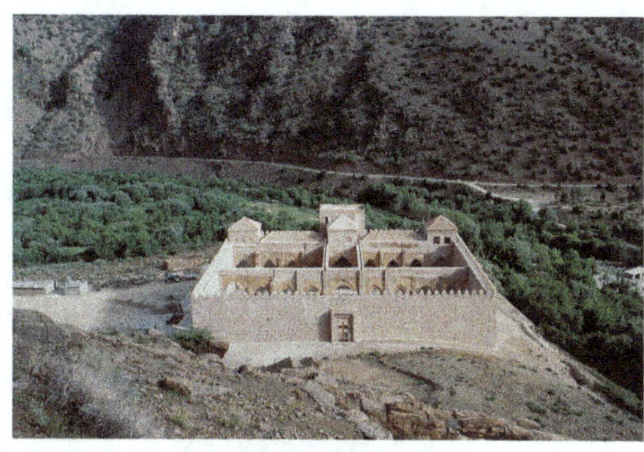

Tinmal Mosque, aerial view, Morocco.

In the $5^{th}/11^{th}$ century, the caliphate of Cordoba broke up into a score of principalities incapable of preventing the progressive advance of the reconquest initiated by the Christian states of the Northwestern Iberian Peninsula. These petty kings, or Taifa Kings, summoned the Almoravids in 479/1086 and the Almohads in 540/1145 in order to repel the Christians and re-established partial unity in al-Andalus.

Through their intervention in the Iberian Peninsula, the Almoravids (427/1036-541/1147) came into contact with a new civilisations and were captivated quickly by the refinement of al-Andalus art as reflected in their capital, Marrakesh, where they built a grand mosque and palaces. The influence of the architecture of Cordoba and other capitals such as Seville would be felt in all of the Almoravid monuments from Tlemcen, Algiers to Fez.

Under the rule of the Almohads (515/1121-667/1269), who expanded their hegemony as far as Tunisia, Western Islamic art reached its climax. During this period, artistic creativity that originated with the Almoravid rulers was renewed and masterpieces of Islamic art were created. The Great Mosque of Seville with its minaret the Giralda, the Kutubiya in Marrakesh, the Mosque of Hassan in Rabat and the Mosque of Tinmal high in the Atlas Mountains in Morocco are notable examples.

Upon the dissolution of the Almohad Empire, the Nasrid Dynasty (629/1232-897/1492) installed itself in Granada and was to experience a period of splendour in the $8^{th}/14^{th}$ century. The civilisation of Granada would become a cultural

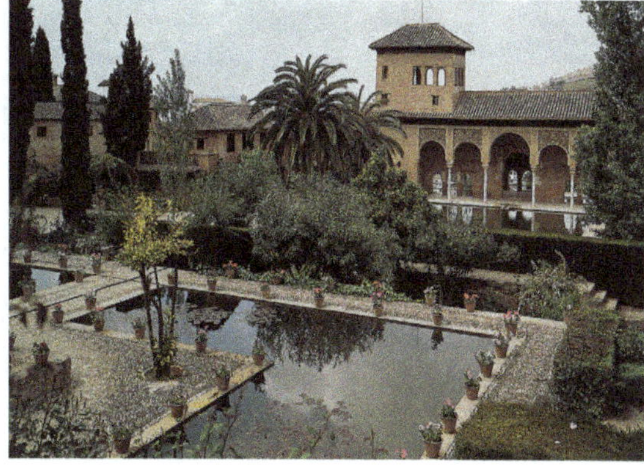

Ladies Tower and Gardens, Alhambra, Granada, Spain.

Mertola, general view, Portugal.

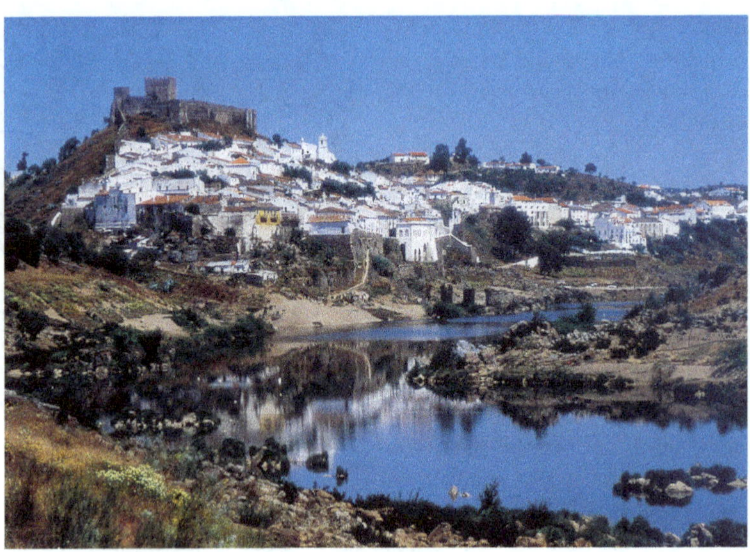

model in future centuries in Spain (Mudejar Art) and particularly in Morocco, where this artistic tradition enjoyed great popularity and would be preserved until the present day in the areas of architecture and decoration, music and cuisine. The famous palace and fort of *al-Hamra'* (the Alhambra) in Granada marks the crowning achievement of al-Andalus art, with all features of its artistic repertoire.

At the same time in Morocco, the Merinids (641/1243-876/1471) replaced the Almohads, while in Algeria the 'Abd al-Wadid's reigned (633/1235-922/1516), as did the Hafsids (625/1228-941/1534) in Tunisia. The Merinids perpetuated al-Andalus art, enriching it with new features. They embellished their capital Fez with an abundance of mosques, palaces and *madrasas*, with their clay mosaic and *zellij* panelling in the wall decorations, considered

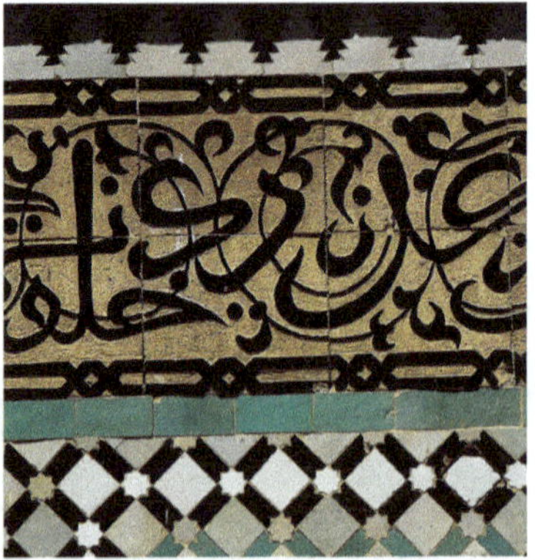

Decoration detail, Abu Inan Madrasa, Meknes, Morocco.

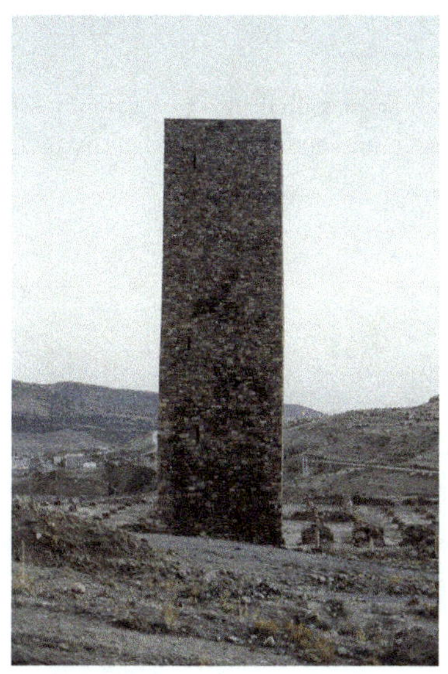

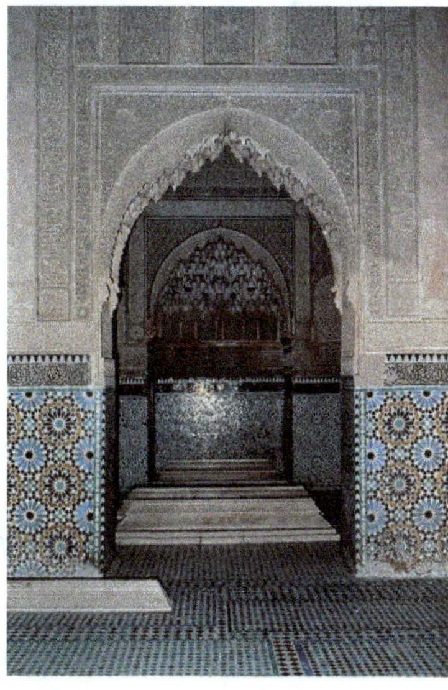

Qal'a of the Bani Hammad, minaret, Algeria.

Sa'adian Tomb Marrakesh, Morocco.

to be the most perfect works of Islamic art. The later Moroccan dynasties, the Sa'adians (933/1527-1070/1659) and the 'Alawite (1077/1659 – until the present day), carried on the artistic tradition of al-Andalus that was exiled from its native soil in 897/1492. They continued to build and decorate their monuments using the same formulas and the same decorative themes as had the preceding dynasties, adding innovative touches characteristic of their creative genius. In the early 11th/17th century, emigrants from al-Andalus (the *Moriscos*), who took up residence in the northern cities of Morocco, introduced numerous features of al-Andalus art. Today, Morocco is one of the few countries that has kept traditions of al-Andalus alive in its architecture and furniture, at the same time modernising them as they incorporated the architectural techniques and styles of the 15th/20th century.

ARCHITECTURAL SUMMARY

In general terms, Islamic architecture can be classified into two categories: religious, such as mosques, *madrasas*, mausoleums, and secular, such as palaces, *caravanserais*, fortifications, etc.

Religious Architecture

Mosques

The mosque for obvious reasons lies at the very heart of Islamic architecture. It is an apt symbol of the faith that it serves. That symbolic role was understood by Muslims at a very early stage, and played an important part in the creation of suitable visual markers for the building: minaret, dome, *mihrab*, *minbar*, etc.

The first mosque in Islam was the courtyard of the Prophet's house in Medina, with no architectural refinements. Early mosques built by the Muslims as their empire was expanding were simple. From these buildings developed the congregational or Friday mosque (*jami'*), essential features of which remain today unchanged for nearly 1400 years. The general plan consists of a large courtyard surrounded by arched porticoes, with more aisles or arcades on the side facing Mecca (*qibla*) than the other sides. The Great Umayyad Mosque in Damascus, which followed the plan of the Prophet's Mosque, became the prototype for many mosques built in various parts of the Islamic world.

Umayyad Mosque of Damascus, Syria.

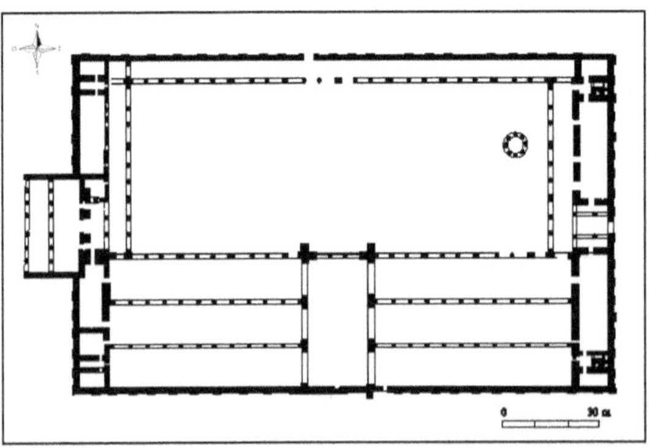

Two other types of mosques developed in Anatolia and afterwards in the Ottoman domains: the basilical and the dome types. The first type is a simple pillared hall or basilica that follows late Roman and Byzantine Syrian traditions, introduced with some modifications in the 5th/11th century. The second type, which developed during the Ottoman period, has its organisation of interior space under a single dome. The Ottoman architects in great imperial mosques created a new style of domed construction by merging the Islamic mosque tradition with that of dome building in Anatolia. The main dome rests on a hexagonal support system, while lateral bays are covered by smaller domes. This emphasis on an interior space dominated by a single dome became the starting point of a style that was to be introduced in the 10th/16th century. During this period, mosques became multipurpose social complexes consisting of a *zawiya*, a *madrasa*, a public kitchen, a bath, a *caravanserai* and a mausoleum of the founder. The supreme monument of this style is the Sülaymeniye Mosque in Istanbul built in 965/1557 by the great architect Sinan.

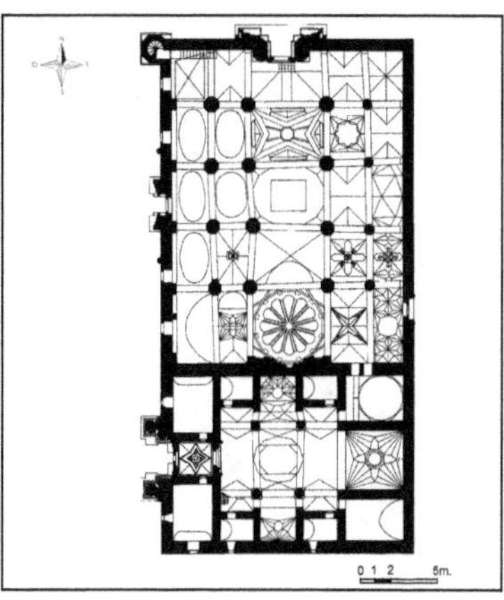

Great Mosque, Divriği, Turkey.

The minaret from the top of which the *muezzin* calls Muslims to prayer, is the most prominent marker of the mosque. In Syria the traditional minaret consists of a square-plan tower built of stone. In Mamluk Egypt minarets are each divided into three distinct zones: a square section at the bottom, an octagonal middle section and a circular section with a small dome on the top. Its shaft is richly decorated and the transition between each section is covered with a band of *muqarnas* decoration. Minarets in North Africa and Spain, that share the square-tower form with Syria, are decorated with panels of motifs around paired sets of windows. During the Ottoman period the octagonal or cylindrical minarets replaced the square tower. Often these are tall pointed minarets and although mosques generally have only one minaret, in major cities there are two, four or even six minarets.

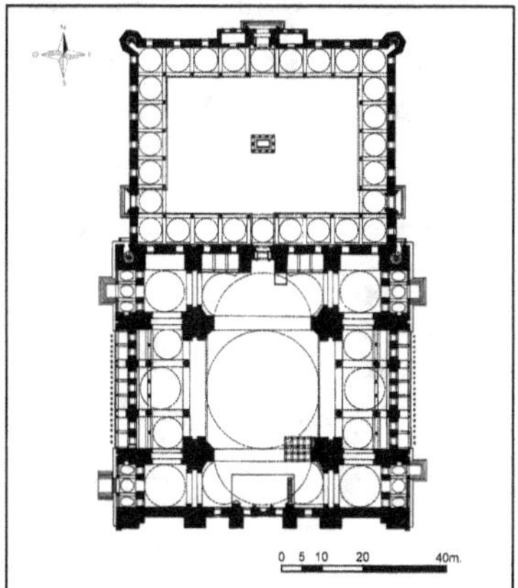

Sülaymeniye Mosque, Istanbul, Turkey.

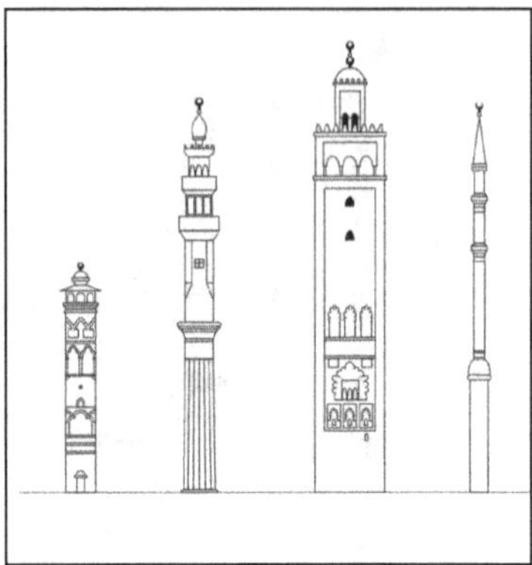
Typology of minarets.

Madrasas

It seems likely that the Seljuqs built the first *madrasas* in Persia in the early $5^{th}/11^{th}$ century when they were small structures with a domed courtyard and two lateral *iwans*. A later type developed that has an open courtyard with a central *iwan* and which is surrounded by arcades. During the $6^{th}/12^{th}$ century in Anatolia, the *madrasa* became multifunctional and was intended to serve as a medical school, mental hospital, a hospice with a public kitchen (*imaret*) and a mausoleum. The promotion of *Sunni* (Orthodox) Islam reached a new zenith in Syria and Egypt under the Zengids and the Ayyubids ($6^{th}/12^{th}$–early $7^{th}/13^{th}$ centuries). This era witnessed the introduction of the *madrasa* established by a civic or political leader for the advancement of Islamic jurisprudence. The foundation was funded by an endowment in perpetuity (*waqf*), usually the revenues of land or property in the form of an orchard, shops in a market (*suq*), or a bathhouse (*hammam*). The *madrasa* traditionally followed a cruciform plan with a central court surrounded by four *iwans*. Soon the *madrasa* became a dominant architectural form with mosques adopting a four-*iwan* plan. The *madrasa* gradually lost its sole religious and political function as a propaganda tool and tended to have a broader civic function, serving as a congregational mosque and a mausoleum for the benefactor.

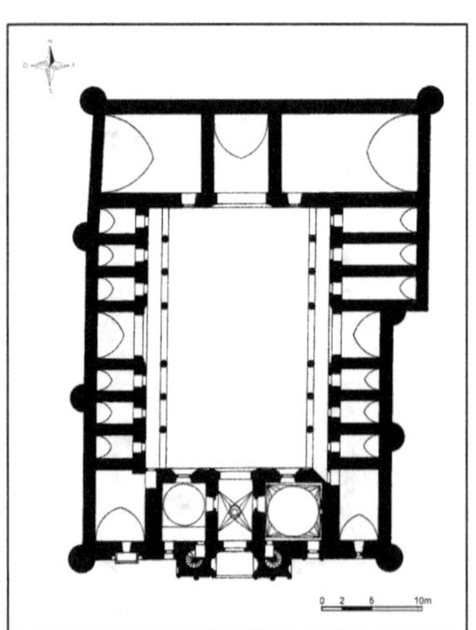

Sivas Gök Madrasa, Turkey.

The construction of m*adrasas* in Egypt, and particularly in Cairo, gathered new momentum with the arrival of the Mamluks. The typical

Cairene *madrasa* of this era was a multifunctional gigantic four-*iwan* structure with a stalactite (*muqarnas*) portal and splendid façades. With the advent of the Ottomans in the 10th/16th century, the joint foundation, typically a mosque-*madrasa*, became a widespread, large complex that enjoyed imperial patronage. The *iwan* disappeared gradually and was replaced by a dominant dome chamber. A substantial increase in the number of domed cells used by students is a characteristic of Ottoman *madrasas*.

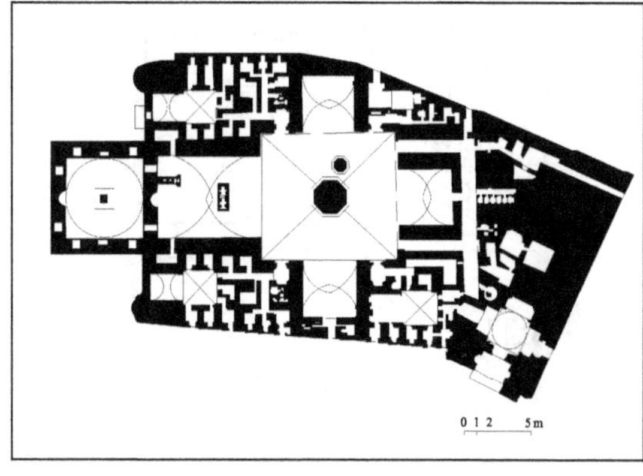

Mosque and Madrasa Sultan Hassan, Cairo, Egypt.

One of the various building types that by virtue of their function and of their form can be related to the *madrasa* is the *khanqa*. The term indicates an institution, rather than a particular kind of building, that houses members of a Muslim mystical (*sufi*) order. Several other words used by Muslim historians as synonyms for *khanqa* include: in the Maghrib, *zawiya*; in Ottoman domain, *tekke*; and in general, *ribat*. *Sufism* permanently dominated the *khanqa*, which originated in eastern Persia during the 4th/10th century. In its simplest form the *khanqa* was a house where a group of pupils gathered around a master (*shaykh*), and it had the facilities for assembly, prayer and communal living. The establishment of *khanqas* flourished under the Seljuqs during the 5th/11th and the 6th/12th centuries and benefited from the close association between *Sufism* and the *Shafi'i madhhab* (doctrine) favoured by the ruling elite.

Mausoleums

The terminology of the building type of the mausoleum used in Islamic sources is varied. The standard descriptive term *turbe* refers to the function of the building as for burial. Another term is *qubba* that refers to the most identifiable, the dome, and often marks a structure commemorating Biblical prophets, companions of the Prophet Muhammad and religious or military notables. The function of mausoleums is not limited simply to a place of burial

Qasr al-Khayr al-Sharqi, Syria.

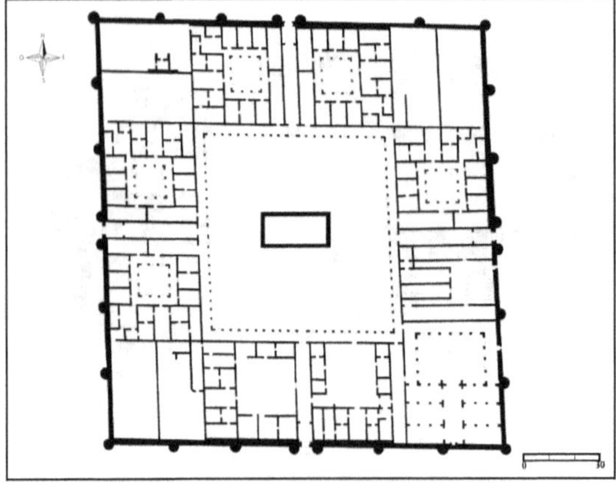

and commemoration, but also plays an important role in "popular" religion. They are venerated as tombs of local saints and became places of pilgrimage. Often the structure of a mausoleum is embellished with Qur'anic quotations and contains a *mihrab* within it to render it a place of prayer. In some cases the mausoleum became part of a joint foundation. Forms of medieval Islamic mausoleums are varied, but the traditional one has a domed square plan.

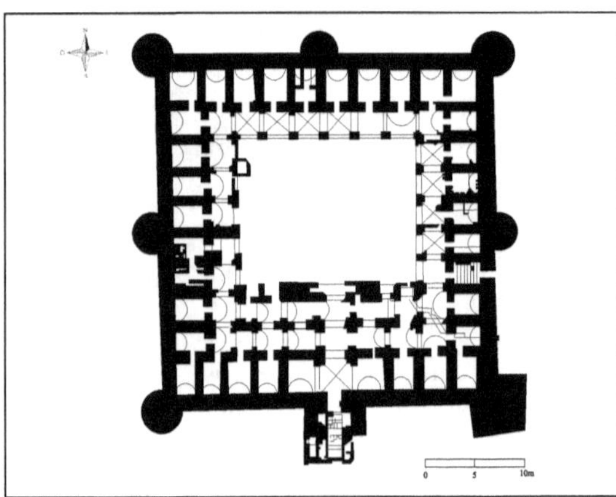

Ribat of Sousse, Tunisia.

Secular Architecture

Palaces

The Umayyad period is characterised by sumptuous palaces and bathhouses in remote desert regions. Their basic plan is largely derived from Roman military models. Although the decoration of these structures is eclectic, they constitute the best examples of the budding Islamic decorative style. Mosaics, mural paintings, stone or stucco sculpture were used for a remarkable variety of decorations and themes. Abbasid palaces in Iraq, such as those at Samarra and Ukhaidir, follow the same plan as their Umayyad forerunners, but are marked by an increase in size, the use of the great *iwan*, dome and courtyard, and the extensive use of stucco decorations. Palaces in the later Islamic period developed a distinctive style that was more decorative and less monumental. The most remarkable example of royal or princely palaces is the Alhambra. The vast area of the palace is broken up into a series of separate units: gardens, pavilions and courts. The most striking feature of Alhambra, however, is the decoration that provides an extraordinary effect in the interior of the building.

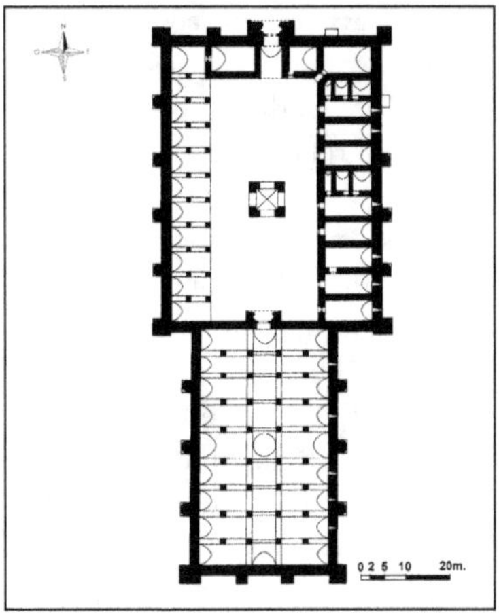

Aksaray Sultan Khan, Turkey.

Caravanserais

A *caravanserai* generally refers to a large structure that provides a lodging place for travellers and merchants. Normally, it has a square or rectangular floor plan, with a single projecting monumental entrance and towers in the exterior walls. A central courtyard is surrounded by porticoes and rooms for lodging travellers, storing merchandise and for the stabling of animals.

The characteristic type of building has a wide range of functions since it has been described as *khan*, *han*, *funduq*, *ribat*. These terms may imply no more than differences in regional vocabularies rather than being distinctive functions or types. The architectural sources of the various types of *caravanserai*s are difficult to identify. Some are perhaps derived from the Roman *castrum* or military camp to which the Umayyad desert palaces are related. Other types, in Mesopotamia and Persia, are associated with domestic architecture.

Urban Organisation

From about the 3rd / 10th century every town of any significance acquired fortified walls and towers, elaborate gates and a mighty citadel (*qal'a* or *qasba*) as the seat of power. These are massive constructions built in materials characteristic of the region in which they are found; stone in Syria, Palestine and Egypt, or brick, stone and rammed earth in the Iberian Peninsula and North Africa. A unique example of military architecture is the *ribat*. Technically, this is a fortified palace designated for the temporary or permanent warriors of Islam who committed themselves to the defence of frontiers. The *ribat* of Sousse in

Tunisia bears a resemblance to early Islamic palaces, but with a different interior arrangement of large halls, mosque and a minaret.

The division of the majority of Islamic cities into neighbourhoods is based on ethnic and religious affinity and it is also a system of urban organisation that facilitates the administration of the population. In the neighbourhood there is always a mosque. A bathhouse, a fountain, an oven and a group of stores are located either within or nearby. Its structure is formed by a network of streets, alleys and a collection of houses. Depending on the region and era, the home takes on diverse features governed by the historical and cultural traditions, climate and construction materials available.

The market (*suq*), which functions as the nerve-centre for local businesses, would be the most relevant characteristic of Islamic cities. Its distance from the mosque determines the spatial organisation of the markets by specialised guilds. For instance, the professions considered clean and honourable (bookmakers, perfume makers, tailors) are located in the mosque's immediate environs, and the noisy and foul-smelling crafts (blacksmiths, tanning, cloth dying) are situated progressively further from it. This geographic distribution responds to imperatives that rank on strictly technical grounds.

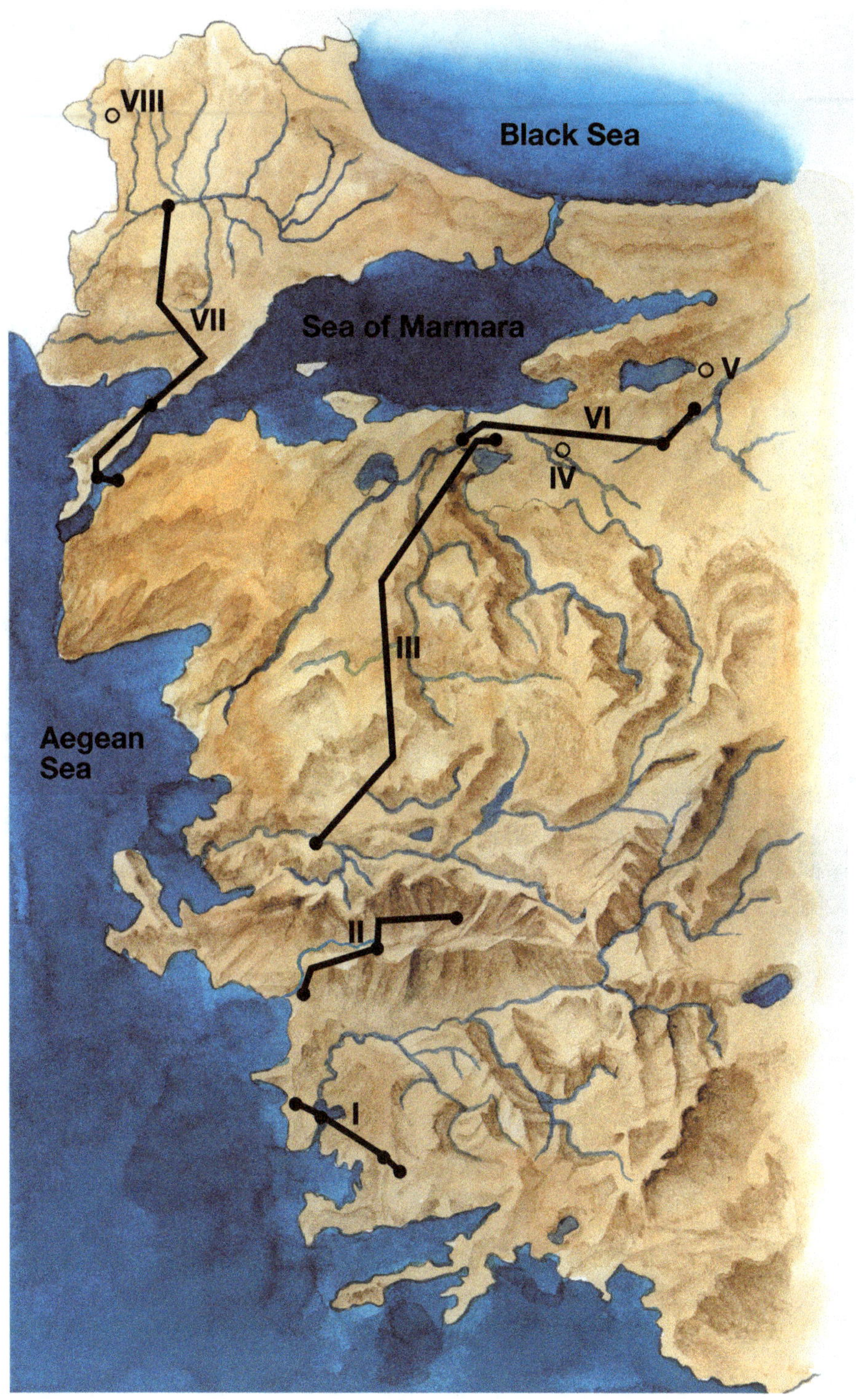
Black Sea
VIII
VII
Sea of Marmara
V
VI
IV
III
Aegean
Sea
II
I

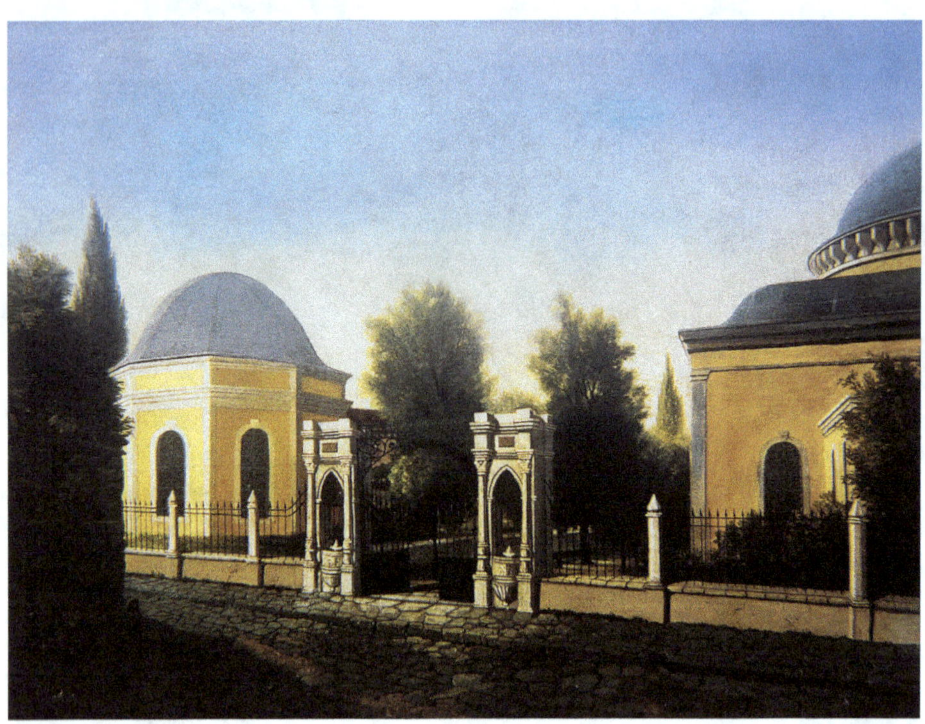

Türbes of Osman Gazi and Orhan Gazi, oil painting by Mineli Muhip, 19th century, İş Bank Collection, Istanbul.

EARLY OTTOMAN ART: THE LEGACY OF THE EMIRATES

Gönül Öney

The 14th and 15th centuries in West Anatolia marked the beginning of a new era with respect to the art and culture of Turkish communities. It was at this time, approximately 200 years after the conquest of Central Anatolia that the shores of the Aegean and Marmara Seas came under Turkish control. With the many ruins of ancient cities and the presence of Venetian and Genoese merchants in the region, many new horizons opened up to Turkish culture and architecture. The art that developed in West Anatolia under the administration of the ruling emirates, including the Ottomans, was heavily influenced by the present local art. Turkish art of the14th-15th century had its roots in the Central Asian, Great Seljuq, and Anatolian Seljuq periods and reached its zenith during the 16th century.

The buildings and works recommended for viewing on the eight itineraries suggested in this Museum With No Frontiers Exhibition are ones that are believed will contribute to the perception of Turkish culture in the Ottoman period. These routes, which run from southern to northern West Anatolia, were not brought together coincidentally, but were chosen with this aim in mind.

In almost every period of Anatolia's rich history that stretches back 9000 years, cultures that were essentially different from one another developed alongside each other. As a result of Anatolia's unique geographical location between Europe and Asia, the peninsula acted as a bridge between East and West. Various communities that immigrated to Anatolia preserved the cultural bonds with their original homelands.

Classical period West Anatolia civilisation (1050-323 BC) lasted until the foundation of the Ionian city-states. In the Hellenistic period (323-30 BC) the cities of Miletus (today Milet or Balat), Ephesus (today Efes and Selçuk), and Pergamum (today Bergama) were adorned with monumental buildings and statues. The Romans who took over this rich culture and art raised it to the highest level, especially in the West Anatolian cities of Aphrodisias, Tralles, Ephesus, and Pergamum. The remains of colonnaded roads, market areas, gymnasiums, theatres, palaces, baths, stadiums, aqueducts, and

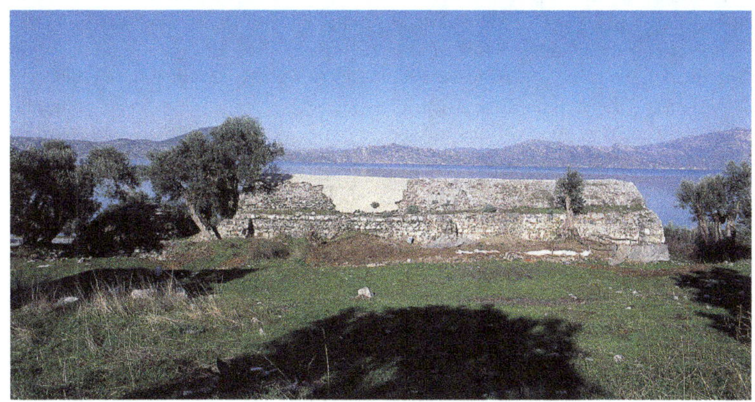

Bafa Han, view from the west, Bafa (Çamiçi).

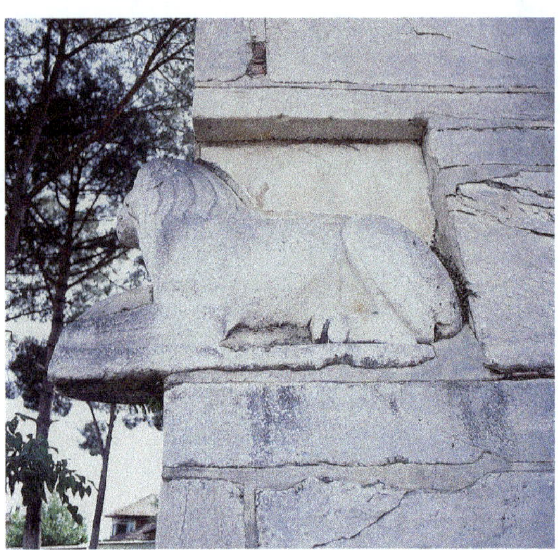

Great Mosque, re-used lion statue on the southeast corner, 1312-13, Aydınoğlu Mehmed Bey, Birgi.

statues that we see in the Hellenistic and Roman cities are among the period's most dazzling works. After the fall of the Roman Empire, especially during the Early Christian and Early Byzantine periods between the 4th and 6th centuries AD, West Anatolia in particular reached a new cultural peak. Ancient cities like Pergamum, Sardis, Ephesus, Priene, Miletus, and Hierapolis maintained their importance during the period of the Byzantine Empire whose architectural legacy and road system in West Anatolia assisted the rapid development of cultural and commercial life in the 14th and 15th centuries.

Turkish art was first produced in Anatolia during the Seljuq era (1077-1318). During the high times of the Anatolian Seljuq State, the influences of Persia, Syria, and Iraq, through which the Turks had passed during their migration from Central Asia to Anatolia, were kneaded together with Anatolia's own cultural and artistic accumulation of many centuries. While the heterogeneity of seeds from Byzantium, Central Asia, Persia, Arabian and the Antique world are clearly recognisable here and there; approaches and modes of research unique to the Seljuqs are especially evident. The Emirates period that followed the Seljuq rule did not merely absorb the evident Seljuq legacy, but was inclined towards new experiments and modes of inquiry. The Menteşe Emirate ruled over Halicarnassus (today Bodrum), the famous city of Classical civilisation, Miletus along with Milas, Muğla, and Beçin; the Aydın Emirate contained the cities of ancient Tralles (Aydın), Ephesus (Efes, Selçuk), and Teos (Seferihisar), along with Tire, Birgi, and İzmir; the Saruhan Emirate comprised a region stretching from ancient Magnesia ad Spilum (Manisa) to Pergamum (Bergama); the Karasi Emirate was situated in the Balıkesir region; and as for the Ottoman Emirate, it first occupied the region between the famous Byzantine city of Nicea (İznik) and Bursa, and later ruled over a broad area that stretched as far as Edirne. The re-used materials, like columns, column capitals and bases, of the Antique or Byzantine periods that one often comes across in monumental portals, and walls of the edifices of this period serve as reminders of the region's centuries-long heritage.

During the Ottoman period, whereas *Sufi* beliefs and old Turkish traditions such as *Ahi* organisations and Islamic traditions gained strength, a simultaneous movement began towards a cosmopolitan culture and social life, under the influence of the Islamic countries surrounding the Mediterranean, the Balkans, Byzantium and especially Constantinople. The presence of poets, itinerant shaykhs, *dervishes*, and artisans made the Ottoman Palace more colourful. The Turkish language was the uniting factor for the Anatolian mosaic. Strong Islamic traditions could not stop many Byzantine structures from being assigned new functions. For example, Orhan Gazi converted the famous Hagia Sophia (Ayasofya) Church in İznik into a mosque and had an adjoining *madrasa* added to it. Osman Gazi, Orhan Gazi, Murad I, and Bayezid I adorned the important Ottoman cities of İznik, Bursa, Yenisehir, and Edirne in particular with mosques, *madrasas*, *imarets*, *tabhanes*, *zawiyas*, *hammams*, *bedestens*, *hans*, *türbes*, bridges, and fortresses. Despite the rich architectural heritage that they passed down from the 14th-15th centuries to the present, no traces of their palaces and houses have survived. These buildings, which were probably constructed with non-durable materials like wood and sun-dried bricks, became one with the earth and disappeared as a result of fires and the harsh natural environment.

We believe people who are inquisitive, and interested in learning about the 14th- and 15th-century works of West Anatolia, will be inspired by this exhibition and catalogue to become more familiar with Classical Ottoman Art, as well as Turkish Art in a more general sense.

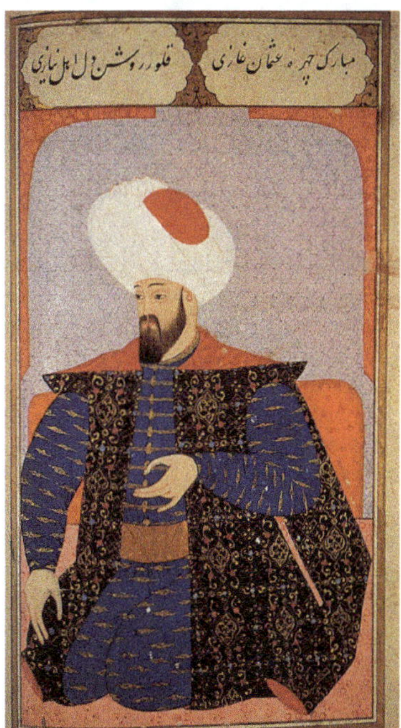

Osman Gazi, Illumination from Kıyafetü'l-İnsâniyye fî Şemâili'l'-Osmâniyye by Seyyid Lokman Çelebi, 1579, H.1563, 24b, Library of Topkapı Palace, Istanbul.

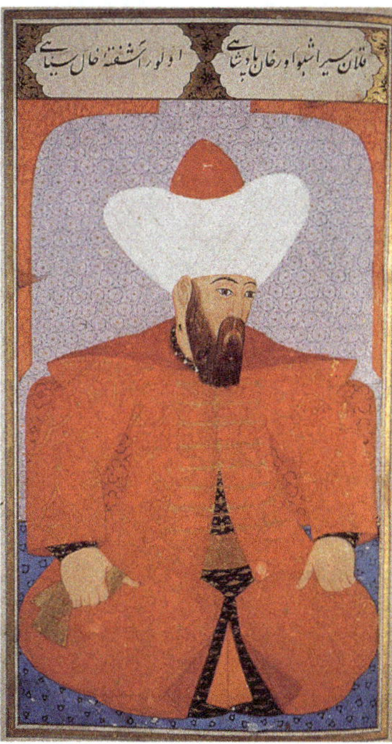

Orhan Gazi, Illumination from Kıyafetü'l-İnsâniyye fî Şemâili'l'-Osmâniyye by Seyyid Lokman Çelebi, 1579, H.1563, 29a, Library of Topkapı Palace, Istanbul.

14th- and 15th-CENTURY WEST ANATOLIAN HISTORY

Aydoğan Demir

Anatolia, a land to which many ethnic groups have migrated and which was destroyed by various invasions, met with the Turks as a group in ancient times. The Turks began to play an especially important military role during the Middle Ages in the time of the Abbasid Caliphate (750-1258) centred in Baghdad. In order to protect their boundaries against the Byzantine Empire (395-1453) and to raid Byzantine-controlled Anatolia, the Abbasids set up military bases in the cities of Tarsus, Adana, Misis, Maraş and Malatya in eastern and southern Anatolia. There were many Turks among the soldiers the Abbasids settled at these bases and an extremely large part of the Abbasid Caliph al-Mu'tasim's (833-842) army, which advanced as far as the shores of the Sakarya River in Anatolia, was also made up of Turks.

During the second half of the 11th century, the Great Seljuq Empire (1040-1157) directed the waves of immigrants flooding into Khorasan (a historical region located within the boundaries of today's Iran and the Republic of Turkmenistan) to the West, and to Anatolia in particular. As a result, Anatolia, except for the coasts, came under the administration of the Turks.

At the end of the 11th century (1096-1097), members of the First Crusaders who were trying to get to Jerusalem via Anatolia, spoke of places called "Romania" that were under Turkish sovereignty. One century later, the Third Crusaders, who were trying to cross Anatolia under the command of Friedrich I Barbarossa (r. 1152-1190), called the same places "Turcia/ Turchia/ Türkiye". Anatolia, with its unchanging ethnic structure consisting of Turks, Kurds, Rums, Armenians, Jews, and Christian Syrians, was witnessing the formation of Turkish-Islamic culture, a new culture formed under the inspiration of the monumental architecture constructed by the Seljuqs, Danishmendids, Mengücekids, Saltukids and Artukids.

Anatolian Seljuq Sultan Alaeddin Keykubad I (1220-1237), who ruled over the cities of Alanya and Antalya on the Mediterranean coast, the cities of Sinop and Samsun on the Black Sea coast, and a large part of Anatolia, took a series of measures to promote the development of trade in his country. In order to ensure safe travel on the Silk and Spice Routes that passed through Anatolia, Alaeddin Keykubad I encouraged the construction of fortress-like *caravanserais* begun by his forefathers. *Caravanserais* were buildings offering shelter, food, and sanitation provisions to merchants and other travellers, and care and food for their pack animals as well.

The other way in which trade was developed and made safe during this period was by special agreements entered into with interested states. In 1213 a commercial agreement was signed between the Anatolian Seljuqs and the Cypriots. Legal works that started before Alaeddin Keykubad I were examined in the finest detail during the reign of this sultan; on 8 March 1220, a pact was signed with the Venetians in order to insure protection of the lives and goods of Venetian merchants trading in Turkey. The ease with which Venetians and their allies could trade paved the way for the formation of Latin colonies in Turkey's most important cities.

The Italian communes, led by the Venetians, organised the Fourth Crusade in

1204; the Fourth-Crusader Army occupied Istanbul instead of going to Jerusalem, opening the way for the division of the Byzantine Empire, that was never again able to reach its previous strength. The Nicean Emperor Michael VIII Palaeologus (1259-1282) captured Istanbul back from the Latins in the year 1261 and he and his successors had to struggle with the Latins and the problems in the Balkans. Michael VIII Palaeologus could not, however, afford to take the necessary interest in West Anatolia; when he could not pay the guardsmen (*akritoi*) their wages, they left their posts along the borders. The borderland *Beys*, who had been waiting for such an opportunity, began occupying West Anatolia along the routes leading to the seas. Consequently, by the end of the 13th century, the Menteşe, Aydın, Saruhan, Karasi, and Ottoman Emirates were founded in West Anatolia.

It is necessary to treat in careful detail the subject of the relationship between the Turkish community, the Rums, and the other ethnic groups that came together in the areas governed by the West Anatolian Emirates, where truly important civilisations began to develop. The heterodox Islamic beliefs by which a large part of the Turks that settled in West Anatolia, especially those living in rural areas, led their lives, must have played an important role in relationships amongst these peoples. These beliefs, which we can call "People's Islam", contain traces of Shamanism, nature cults, Buddhism, Manichaeanism, Zoroastrianism, Christianity and Judaism. Approaching people with tolerance, participating in religious ceremonies with no segregation between the sexes, and imbibing alcoholic drinks at ceremonies were common to their way of life. Different ethnic groups mingled at the markets, the bazaar, and even in the administration of the emirates, which occasionally led to love affairs and even marriages. The following lines taken from a Turkish folk song are proof of how these people, who, far from ethnical discrimination, also approached each other lovingly:

How you wait on the rooftop,
beaming like the moon,
Your cheeks like an apple,
like a pomegranate.
Come, let us embrace, both of us
entwined into one being
I have only learned, you are Armenian, what if you are Armenian
You are my heart's desire,
my succour, my succour.

More important than the date and origin of this folk song is its inspiration from centuries-old, deeply held sentiments.

When in the mid-13th century, tradesmen from all lines of work gave up hope on the Anatolian Seljuq Sultanate, which was at this time under intense pressure from the Mongols, they began to organise themselves and founded a union that called its members by the name *Ahi*. It is generally accepted that this word is derived from the Turkish word "akı" meaning "munificent, generous young man" or the Arabic word "Akhi" meaning "my brother." The *Ahi* organisation founded on the concepts of "bravery" (chivalry), "morality" and "art," determined its own rules by which the unions had to abide, and permission to do work would not be granted to those who did

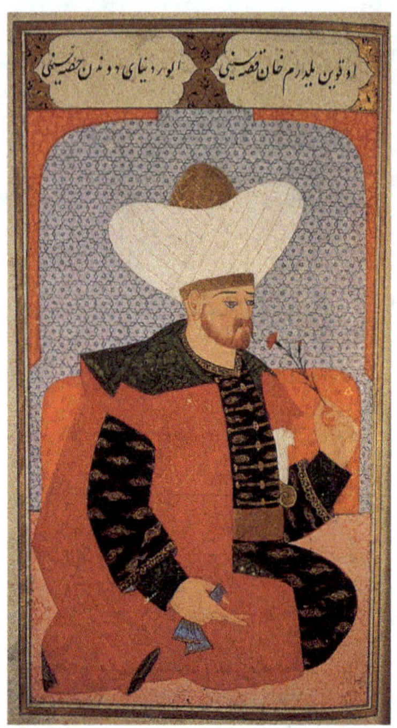

Bayezid I, Illumination from Kıyafetü'l-İnsâniyye fî Şemâili'l'-Osmâniyye by Seyyid Lokman Çelebi, 1579, H.1563, 36a, Library of Topkapı Palace, İstanbul.

not abide by their rules. In times of political chaos, the *Ahi*s defended the city they lived in and even administered it. *Ahi* leaders were experts in law, science, literature, and art.

According to the traveller Ibn Battuta (1304-1369), the *Ahi*s organised themselves by founding small *zawiya*s in cities, towns, and villages. Besides masters, assistant masters, and apprentices, *müderris*es, *kadı*s, poets, calligraphers, and regional administrators also attended the meetings held at the small *zawiya*s. High-level administrators, governors, commanders, teachers, judges, and doctors were educated among the *Ahi*s. Together with the people they educated, the *Ahis* took on important roles in institutions of the emirates, especially in the Ottoman Emirate. They did not interfere in the rights of the Armenian and Rum masters working in Anatolia but instead allowed them to freely continue working in their various occupations.

Religious men, *Ahi*s, and travellers wandering from one city to the next also stayed in the *Ahi's zawiya*s, which were sometimes built in a mosque structure and sometimes as independent units. The *zawiya*s fulfilled a social need by offering free food and lodging to their overnight guests in cities, towns, and even in the villages during times when travelling by road was not safe.

The Menteşe and Aydın Emirates also tried to assume control over the islands in the Aegean. The Papacy even organised a crusade and took back the coastal city of İzmir (1344) when Gazi Umur Bey (1334-1348) of Aydın Emirate became too powerful in the Aegean.

Not only wars but great alliances, too, took place in the Aegean. After boundaries became definite, trade relations were set up between the West Anatolian Emirates and the Latins and commercial agreements were signed. The cities of Balat (Miletus), Selçuk (Ayasuluğ, Ephesus) and Foça (Phocea) were important trade centres during this period. The capital of the Ottoman State, at the time, Bursa, was also among the cities that placed an emphasis on trade.

Although internal peace was eventually achieved among the people, the emirates were not slow to war with one another. One of Anatolia's strongest emirates, the Karamanids (1256-1483), maintained that it was the heir to the Anatolian Seljuq State. For this reason, the Karamanids and the other Anatolian Emirates, with the Ottomans leading, experienced heavy wars that caused great suffering. In order to prevent these wars full of resentment and hate, the Ottomans took as their ultimate goal the achievement of Anatolian unity and, by taking advantage of their opportunities, they took the other emirates under their sovereignty. But even if the West Anatolian Emirates had been re-established after Ottoman Sultan Bayezid I was defeated by Tamerlane in the Battle of Ankara (1402), in reality, all of the emirates were erased from the stage of history in the time of Sultans Mehmed I (r. 1413-1421) and Murad II (r. 1421-1451). The Anatolian *Beys* considered the development of the regions under their rule extremely important: scientific work was supported; they opened up their palaces to men of learning from various places; many works were translated from what may be considered that era's language of science: Arabic, into Turkish. In addition, original works written in the fields of medicine, astronomy, history, *fiqh*, Sufism, etc., were presented to the *Beys*.

Though the Ottoman Emirate founded by Osman Gazi in 1299 in the Marmara region was the smallest of the Anatolian Emirates, by intelligently using the advantages of their location, in a short time they became one of the most powerful. The Byzantine Empire (395-

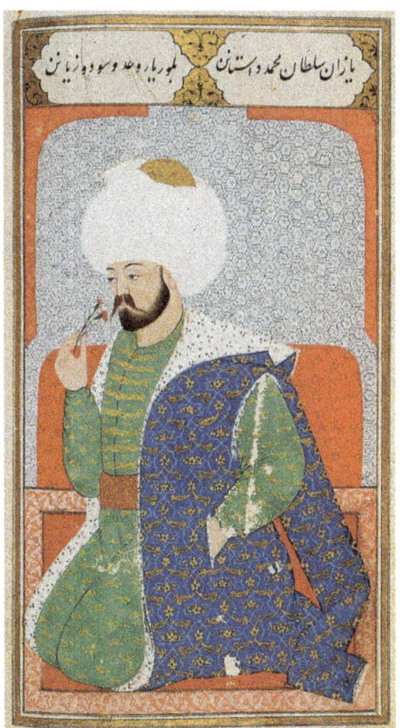

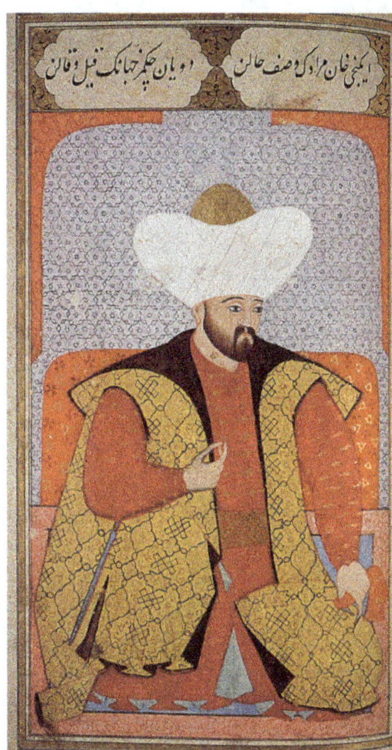

Mehmed I, Illumination from Kıyafetü'l-İnsâniyye fî Şemâili'l'-Osmâniyye by Seyyid Lokman Çelebi, 1579, H.1563, 40b, Library of Topkapı Palace, İstanbul.

Murad II, Illumination from Kıyafetü'l-İnsâniyye fî Şemâili'l'-Osmâniyye by Seyyid Lokman Çelebi, 1579, H.1563, 44a, Library of Topkapı Palace, İstanbul.

Portrait of Süleyman the Magnificent by Nigari, 1560-65, Topkapı Palace, H.2134, fol.16.

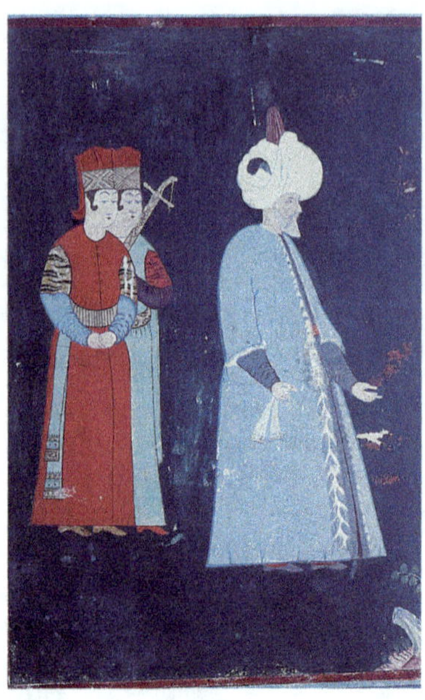

1453), which had acquired a feudal structure in the Marmara region, could not protect their land against the Ottoman State. As a result of disputes over the throne and the matter of protecting the Balkans against the Serbs, they were left with no choice but to ask Orhan Gazi (r. 1324-1362) for help. The Ottoman soldiers brought about Cantacuzenus' ascent to the position of emperor and achieved the withdrawal of the Serbs, and thus got acquainted with Rumelia.

In return for their help, the Byzantines gave the Çimpe (Tzympe) Fortress in Gelibolu (Gallipoli) to the Ottoman military units for use as a military base. From this point on, in 1354, the Ottomans began their conquests in Thrace. After the taking of Edirne during the reign of Sultan Murad I (1362-1389), the Ottoman troops looked for areas to rule over in Bulgaria, Macedonia, and Serbia. During the time of Sultan Bayezid I (r. 1389-1402), the boundaries of the Ottoman State reached the Danube and the Walachia Principality was brought under vassalage. When Sultan Bayezid I lost the Battle of Ankara in 1402, disputes over the throne broke out among his sons and the Interregnum was concluded finally in 1413 with the victory of Sultan Mehmed I.

Sultan Murad II caused the Crusaders, gathered with the aim of breaking the Ottoman State's superiority in the Balkans, to suffer a harsh defeat in Varna (1444) and Kosovo (1448).

Sultan Mehmed II (r. 1451-1481), who twice served as sultan while his father was still alive, had great ideals when he ascended the throne aged 19. Bringing history's longest rooted empire to an end by conquering Istanbul at the age of 21, he was saluted as the Roman Emperor by the Rum advisers who gathered around him. Sultan of an empire that stretched from the Danube to the Euphrates, Sultan Mehmed II, also known as Mehmed the Conqueror, in addition to the country's political developments, also considered public and scientific works to be a top priority. It is known that he personally oversaw the *madrasas*, that he listened to lectures by the *müderrises*, and that the ones he commended were awarded. Sultan Mehmed II knew Latin and Greek in addition to Turkish, Arabic, and Persian; of the books from his library that have survived to the present, 50 of them are about Western culture. He decorated the palace walls with Renaissance-style frescos, and in the year 1479, the Venetian painter Gentile Bellini painted a portrait of Sultan Mehmed II.

Some historians have raised doubts about Sultan Mehmed II falling off his horse during a campaign on 3 May 1481, and his consequent death at the age of 49. Sultan Mehmed II had reduced the living area of the Venetians on the Aegean and Black Seas and had led a campaign to southern Italy in 1480; therefore, in order to do away with Sultan Mehmed II, the Venetians arranged 12 assassination plots, as the well-known historian F. Babinger suggests.

Until the year 1495, Cem Sultan was a dangerous nuisance to his brother, Sultan Bayezid II, who ascended the throne in 1481. After losing two wars in an attempt to overtake the throne, Cem Sultan took refuge with the Knights of St. John who first took him to France, and then to Italy. Until the death of his brother in 1495, Sultan Bayezid II lived in fear that the release of Cem Sultan would cause another dispute for the throne and, for this reason, followed a passive political policy towards the West.

Sultan Bayezid II (r. 1481-1512), the last sultan of the 15th century, was succeeded by Sultans Selim I (r. 1512-1520) and Süleyman I, also known as Süleyman the Magnificent or the Lawgiver (r. 1520-1566), who brought the Ottoman State up to the status of World Empire and dominated the Mediterranean, Black Sea, and Indian Ocean.

The boundlessly tolerant Ottoman Sultans improved the land and protected scholars; the peaceful life they provided for their people has been named Pax Ottomana (Ottoman Peace) by some scholars.

ART AND SOCIAL LIFE IN THE EMIRATES AND EARLY OTTOMAN PERIODS

Gönül Öney

The Emirates and Early Ottoman periods are striking from an art historical point of view because of their extreme colourfulness, and their new experiments and influences. The Emirates, which declared their independence in various regions of Anatolia and whose strength increased as time went on, began intense public improvements as if they wanted to leave their mark on the regions they ruled. New works produced in various areas of Anatolia reflected traces of the vicinity's former architectural, cultural, and artistic traditions.

Plan of the İlyas Bey Mosque, 1404, İlyas Bey, Balat (from A. Durukan).

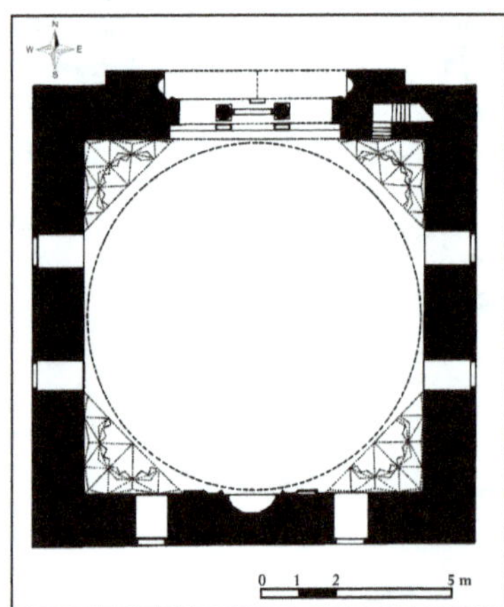

İlyas Bey Complex, north facade of the mosque, 1404, İlyas Bey, Balat.

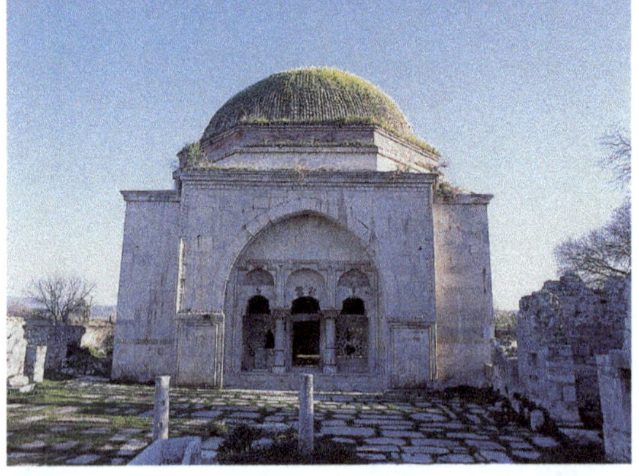

Our itineraries are located in West Anatolia where new modes of search and experimentation in architecture and art are more obvious since it was the first time this region had encountered Turkish-Islamic culture. The buildings and art works that first appeared during the Emirates and Early Ottoman periods deeply influenced Classical Ottoman art. After the 14th and 15th centuries – a period characterised by its constant search for and exploration of new and different artistic, cultural, and social modes – a settled, mature period was finally reached. Parallel to the growth in political strength during the 16th century, the mature style and design in every area of art left its mark on Anatolia and in all the Empire's activities.

Despite new experiments in Emirates and Early Ottoman Art, differences between the regions are not very clear-cut. An innovation tried in one area could also be seen in the neighbouring emirates. Like seeds thrown before the blowing wind, new experiments took root and blossomed in various regions.

We are going to try to introduce the art works briefly by separating them into various typological groups; works similar to those introduced here are found in Anatolia's other emirates as well. The Architecture, Architectural Ornamental, and Handicrafts are presented under separate headings and with general features in the belief that this is the easiest approach. The visitor/reader will find various examples from each group in the Itineraries.

Architecture

The presentation of a brief overview of Emirates and Early Ottoman architecture, in which each of the building types is dealt with separately, will make the comprehension of architectural development considerably easier.

Mosques and Masjids

Mosques (*Cami* in Turkish) and *masjids* (*mescit* in Turkish) are the most important buildings of the 14th and 15th centuries. The differences and innovations that appear in mosques and *masjids* over time are easier to comprehend if they are categorised according to their plan types.

Single-Domed Cubical Mosques and Masjids

Represented by plain examples, mosques and *masjids* from this group are often encountered in the Emirates and Early Ottoman period and the roots of this plan type extend back to the mosques and *masjids* of the Great Seljuq and Anatolian Seljuq periods. In addition to simple, plain examples without a minaret and a portico, there are also more magnificent examples of monumental dimensions with multi-bayed porticoes. There are both simple and complex examples of cubic single-domed mosques and *masjids* on our Itineraries.

The Beçin Yelli Mosque (beginning of the 15th century), İznik Yeşil Mosque (1392) and Balat İlyas Bey Mosque (1404) are a few examples in this group. As in Tire Yavukluoğlu Mosque Complex (15th century) and Edirne Bayezid II Mosque Complex (1488), a monumental courtyard surrounded with porticoes was added to the front of some single-domed cubical mosques and in the Tire example, the mosque and *madrasa* share the same courtyard. In these buildings of symmetrical design and monumental character, ornamentation is seen especially on the main facade.

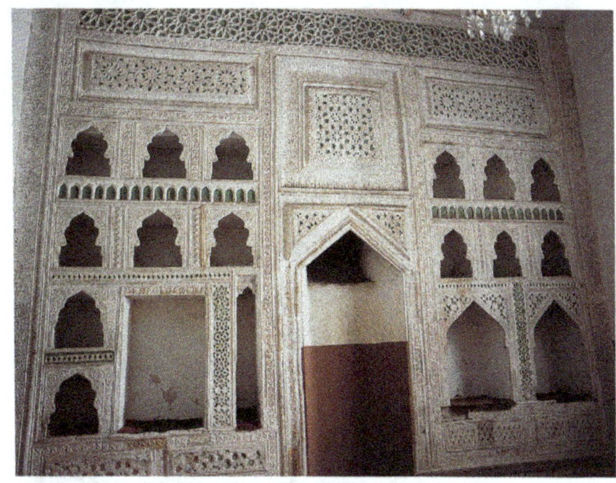

Yıldırım Mosque, fireplace and shelves in the tabhane, 1389-99, Bayezid I, Bursa.

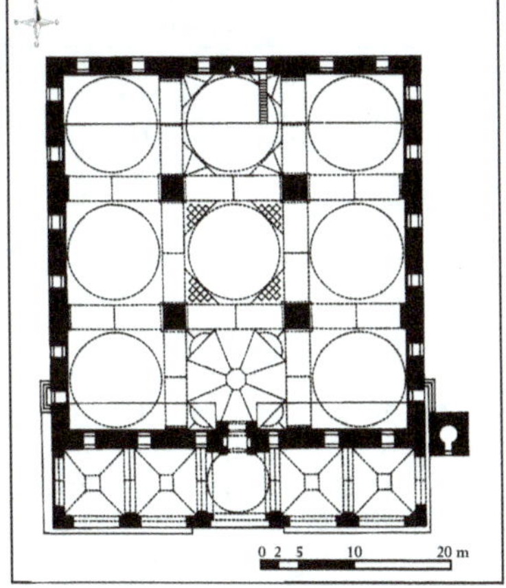

Plan of Eski Mosque, 1414, Mehmed I, Edirne (from Z. Sönmez).

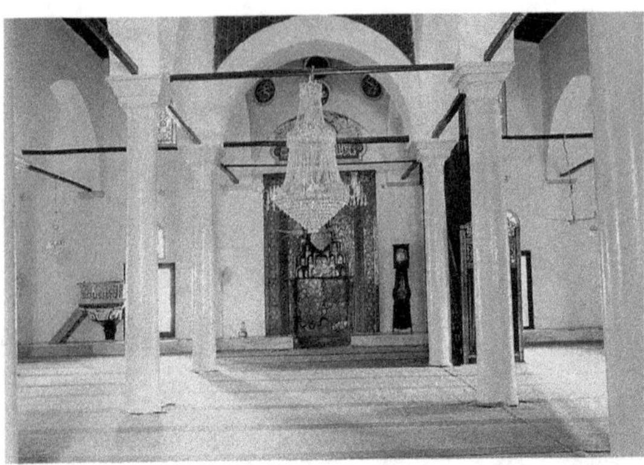

Great Mosque, prayer hall, 1312-13, Aydınoğlu Mehmed Bey, Birgi.

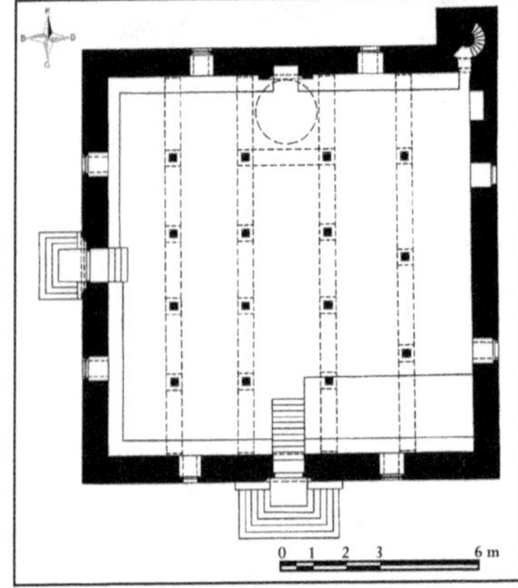

Plan of Great Mosque, 1312-13, Aydınoğlu Mehmed Bey, Birgi.

Mosques of Equal-Size Multiple Bays

These mosques, an altered application of the Seljuq mosques in the Kufa type with pillars at equal intervals, appeared during the Early Ottoman period. As we see in the examples of both the Bursa Great Mosque (1400) and Edirne Eski Mosque (1414), in this plan, the prayer hall is divided into bays of equal size each of which is covered by a dome. These mosques without courtyards are usually a square or a lateral rectangle in shape.

Basilical Mosques

The Basilical plan inspired by the many examples of Armenian and Byzantine basilicas in Anatolia, was also applied to mosques with a new synthesis. The prayer hall of basilical mosques is divided into three or five aisles, set off from one another with rows of pillars or columns extending perpendicularly to the *qibla* wall. Many examples have domes, especially over the central aisle, which is broader and higher. The Basilical plan, frequently seen in Anatolian mosques during the Seljuq period, is also encountered during the Emirates period, although less often: for example, Birgi Great Mosque (1312/13) and Milas Great Mosque (1378).

Mosques with Transept Aisles

In such a building the aisle parallel to the *qibla* wall is intersected by a perpendicular one; this intersection is centrally located in front of the *mihrab* and usually covered by a dome.
Continuing the influence of Syrian Umayyad-period mosques (e.g. Great [Umayyad] Mosque in Damascus), mosques with transept aisles were common in the Southeast Anatolian region during the Artukid period. However, this design was also applied to the Aydın Emirate's İsa Bey Mosque (1375) in Selçuk as a result of the Umayyad-,

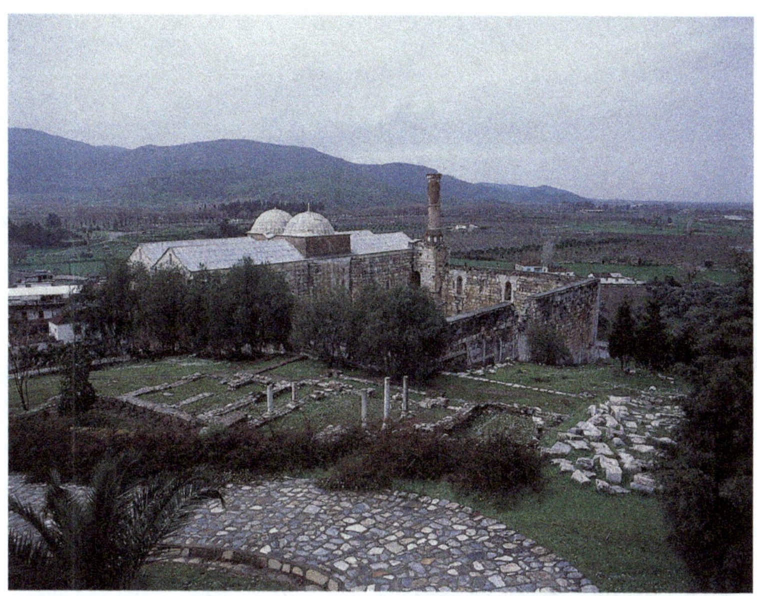

İsa Bey Mosque, view from the northeast, 1375, İsa Bey, Selçuk.

Fatimid-, Ayyubid-, and Mamluk-periods' particular architectural and ornamental characteristics reaching West Anatolia from Syria via the Mediterranean and the Aegean. The obvious Syrian characteristics in the buildings' plan and ornamentation must be related to the architect's Damascan origins; work similar to the colourful marble workmanship in the portal and facades are frequently encountered in medieval Syrian architecture.

The domes that crown the transept aisle of İsa Bey Mosque assume the status of a more developed central dome in Saruhan Emirate's Great Mosque in Manisa (1367). The re-used Byzantine columns in the courtyard reflect the region's synthesis of artistic periods and styles.

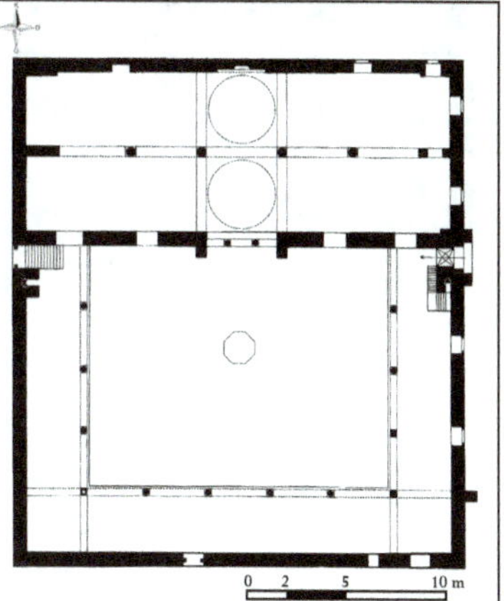

Plan of İsa Bey Mosque, 1375, İsa Bey, Selçuk (from Z. Sönmez).

Mosques with Tabhanes (Zawiyas)

These buildings are examples of a new mosque plan developed in the Emirates

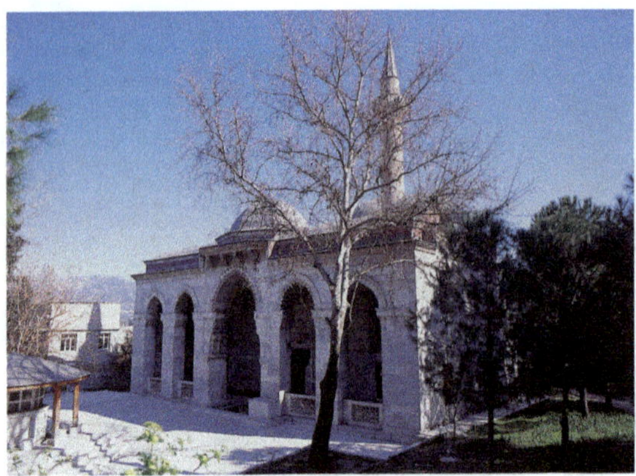

Firuz Bey Mosque, view from the northwest, 1396, Hoca Firuz, Milas.

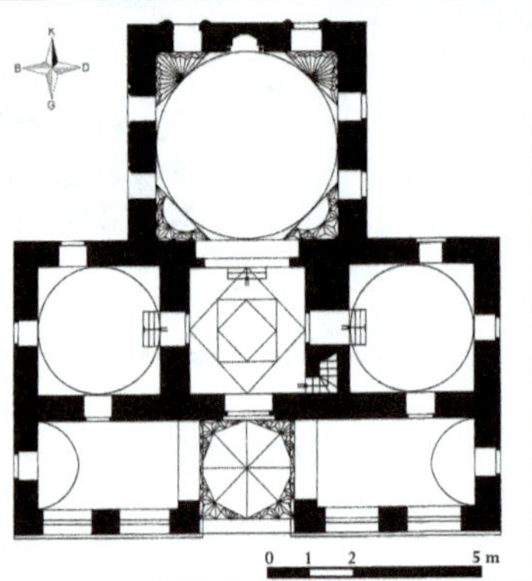

Plan of Firuz Bey Mosque, 1396, Hoca Firuz, Milas (from Z. Sönmez).

and Early Ottoman periods. The plan layout, which was applied at Bursa Orhan Gazi Mosque (1339/40) and Milas Firuz Bey Mosque (1396), reminds one of an upside down letter "T". Facing the direction of the *qibla* is a domed or vaulted *iwan* in which the prayer ritual is performed. In front of the prayer hall is a central area generally covered with a dome and flanked with *tabhanes* and in some examples *iwans* on both sides. These side rooms called *tabhanes* were used in order to shelter the itinerant dervishes.

There is a fireplace in each *tabhane* of the İznik Nilüfer Hatun İmaret (1388), which was commissioned by Sultan Murad I. We are familiar with examples of *tekkes* and *hanikahs*, in which itinerant *dervishes* and *shaykhs* were hosted from the Seljuq period, but we do not have much knowledge about them in the Emirates period. In the 14th and 15th centuries, the *Ahi* organisation's activities were conducted in the mosques with *tabhanes*. The Ottoman sultans, considered members of the organisation, owned a private loge. Itinerant *Ahi dervishes* were also sheltered in these *tabhanes*. In addition to religious authority, these people also influenced the social and cultural arenas. We know that various mosques with *tabhanes* were commissioned for itinerant *dervishes* during the time of the first Ottoman Sultan Osman Gazi (r. 1281–1324).

Complexes with Tabhane (Zawiya)

Most mosques with *Tabhane (zawiya)* or, by its other name, mosques with T-plans or multi-functional mosques, are the centres of large complexes, the construction of which was accelerated during the Early Ottoman period. Within the scope of the Ottoman sultans' urbanisation efforts, monumental complexes, including structures such as a mosque, *madrasa*, *darüşşifa*, *hammam*, *imaret*, *han*, and *türbe* were constructed in the city centres. These structures symbolised the power of the palace elite and the high-ranking government officials who commissioned them. The well-organised social and religious *waqf* system provided for the maintenance and orderly administration of the complexes. In addition to being a place of worship, this group of buildings served as a place where education was given, where the poor were fed free of charge, and where *dervish*es were entertained. The widespread tradition of mosque-complex construction in Syria and Egypt certainly influenced the spread of this tradition in Anatolia.

A structure with two floors and three *iwans*, the Bursa Hüdavendigar Mosque (1385) is an interesting mosque complex with its *madrasa, imaret* and spas. The facade arrangement reflecting the influence of 13th-century Byzantine buildings can be considered as a trace of the syntheses of different cultures, visible in most of the 14th- and 15th-century structures. The Bursa Yıldırım Complex (1389-1399) also consists of buildings of monumental dimensions. The Bursa Yeşil Mosque (1419-1424) commissioned by Sultan Mehmed I and the Muradiye Mosques that Sultan Murad II had built in Bursa (1426) and Edirne (1426/27), are mosques with *tabhanes* (*zawiyas*) located in large mosque complexes of the period.

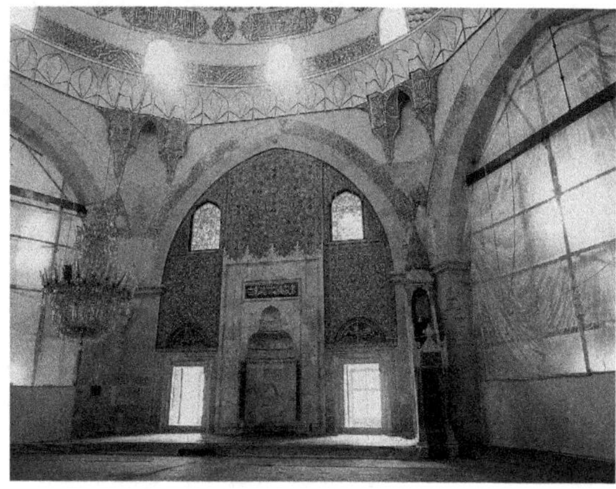

Üç Şerefeli Mosque, prayer hall, 1445, Murad II, Edirne.

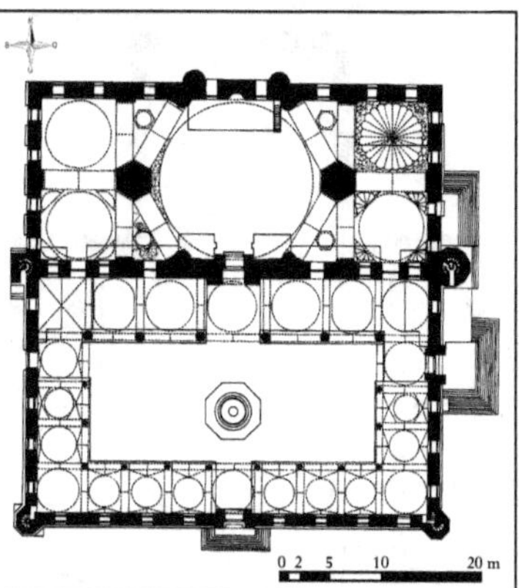

Plan of Üç Şerefeli Mosque, 1445, Murad II, Edirne (from Z. Sönmez).

Mosques with a Central Dome

Developed with the aim of gathering a congregation in one large unified space, structures with a central dome of an ever-increasing diameter underwent rapid development in the 14th and 15th centuries. The majority of these monumental mosques were the centres of large complexes.

As with the Edirne Üç Şerefeli Mosque (1445) commissioned by Sultan Murad II, the silhouettes of these mosques are arranged in a vertical line. It is possible to follow the development of the central-dome mosque type step by step in the Selçuk İsa Bey Mosque (1375), Manisa Great Mosque (1367), and Manisa Hatuniye Mosque (1491) respectively.

Madrasas and Darüşşifas

In the Islamic world, mosques were used outside of worshipping hours to

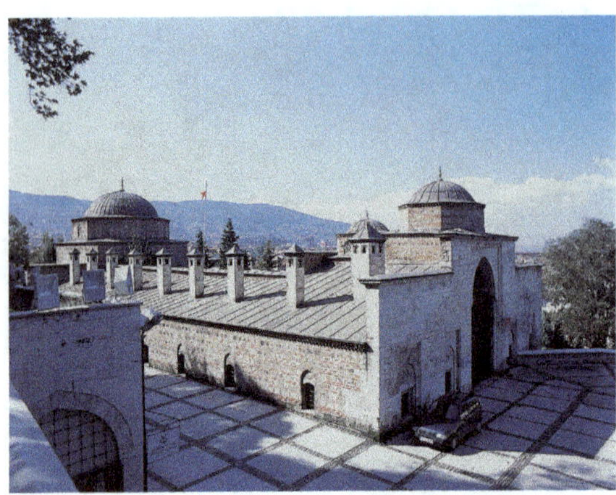

Yıldırım Madrasa, east and south fronts, 1389-99, Bayezid I, Bursa.

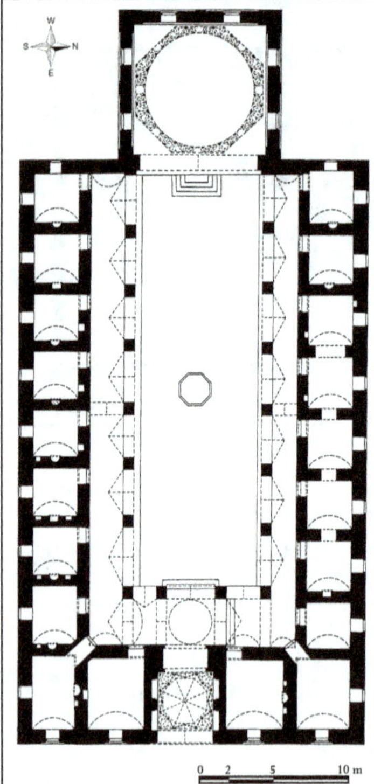

Plan of Yıldırım Madrasa, 1389-1399, Bayezid I, Bursa (from Y. Demiralp).

educate the religious community. Constructed very close to the mosque or adjoining it, *madrasas* were envisioned purely as educational institutions where advanced education would be given. The sultan, a high level administrator, or a wealthy person could commission a *madrasa*. The pious foundations called *waqfs* covered the maintenance and management expenses of the *madrasa* buildings as well as the costs of feeding the students, for the *madrasa* did not charge for education. In addition to Islamic sciences, lessons like philosophy, medicine, mathematics, and astronomy were also taught at the *madrasa,* the first examples of which were constructed in Persia during the time of the Great Seljuq *vizier* Nizam al-Mulk. The layout of the *madrasa* was applied in *şifahanes*, too, the institutions in which medical education was given. In the *madrasas* and *darüşşifas*, the chambers surrounded a large courtyard and a dome usually covered the main *iwan* located across from the entrance *iwan*. Although we do not know the exact function of the vaulted or domed rooms located on either side of the main *iwan,* it is thought that these areas, which are of greater dimensions than the student cells, were used as *dershanes* for the lectures and in most of the *madrasas* there are porticoes on at least two sides of the courtyard. This layout is the same in the Anatolian Seljuq *madrasas*.

Constructed in Beçin during the Menteşe Emirate period, Ahmet Gazi Madrasa (1375) is one of the earliest examples of a *madrasa* with two *iwans* and the tomb of its founder Ahmet Gazi is in the main *iwan* covered by a single dome. Bursa

Türbe of Şehzade Mustafa and Cem Sultan, mihrab and sarcophagi, 1479, Bursa.

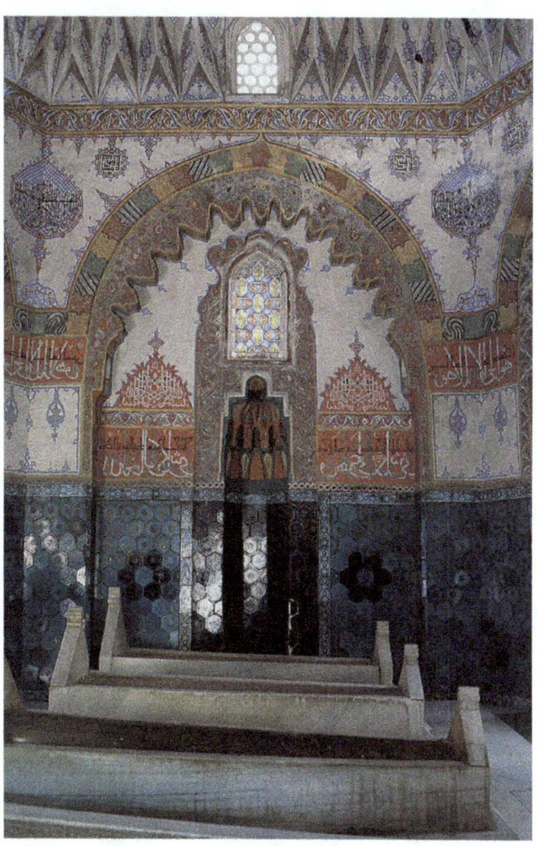

Yeşil Madrasa (1419-1424), Bursa Yıldırım Madrasa (1399), and İznik Süleyman Pasha Madrasa (mid-14th century) are monumental examples of Early Ottoman *madrasas* that we introduce on our Itineraries.

Türbes

Emirates- and Early Ottoman-period tombs exhibit great variety in appearance and design. With their polygonal or cylindrical shaped main body, *türbes* –the monumental tombs– are almost always covered with a dome. The conical or pyramidal spire of the Seljuq *türbes* is not encountered very often during the Emirates and Early Ottoman periods. The number of examples with crypts also decreased considerably during these periods. Osman Gazi, the first Ottoman Sultan, was buried in Bursa in an old Byzantine church. This is an indication of the Ottoman sultans' positive approach to architectural and cultural heritage.

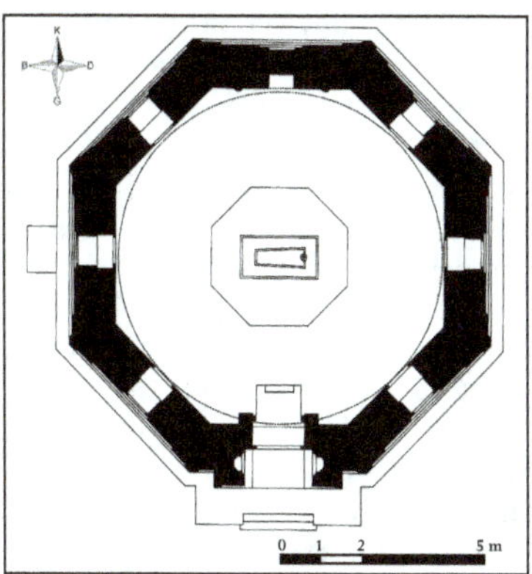

Plan of Yeşil Türbe, 1419-1424, Mehmed I, Bursa (from Z. Sönmez).

Although usually plain structures, some *türbes* are richly decorated. For example, the polygonal body of the Yeşil Türbe (1419-1424) in Bursa is decorated inside and out with tiles. Some Early Ottoman *türbes* such as the Bursa Hatuniye Türbe (1449) possess a monumental *iwan*-shaped portal that dominates the facade. There are also examples of *türbes* with square bodies covered by conical spires, such as the *türbes* of Bursa Gülşah Hatun

Saadet Hatun Hammam, Soyunmalık, 14th-15th century, Selçuk.

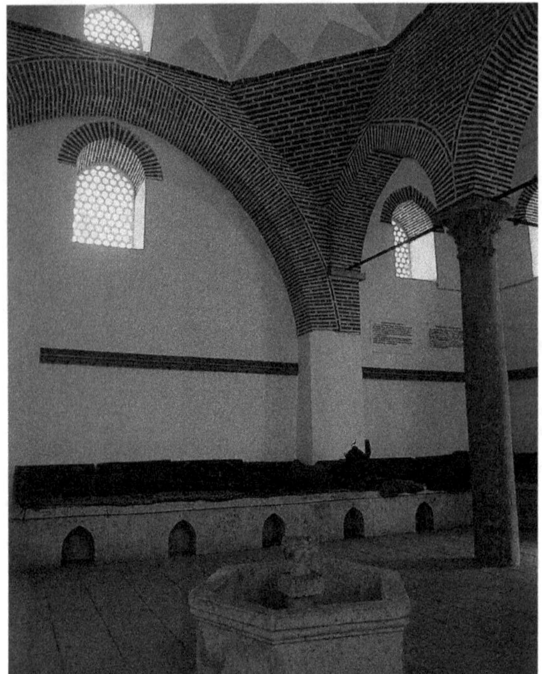

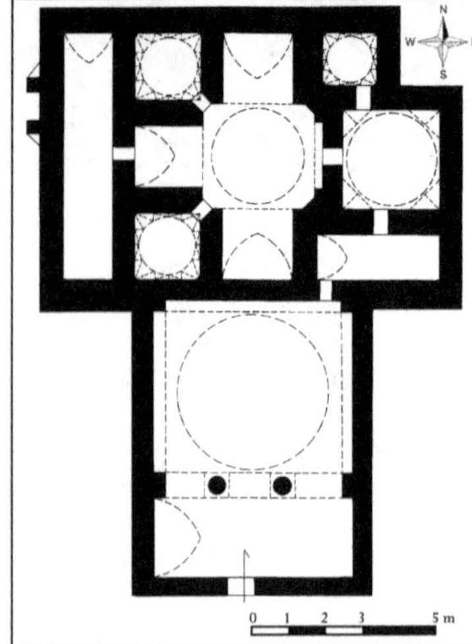

Plan of Saadet Hatun Hammam, 14th-15th Century, Selçuk (from E. Daş).

(1486) and Bursa Devlet Hatun (1413-1414). The roots of the 14th- and 15th-century *türbe* style stretch beyond the Anatolian Seljuqs and Great Seljuqs all the way to Central Asia. Interesting and dazzling examples like the Bursa Yeşil Türbe are rare amongst them, which generally do not differ much from one another in regard to exterior appearance and plan.

Hammams

Cleanliness is a matter of great importance in the Islamic religion. For example, every Muslim man or woman must wash their entire body with water after sexual intercourse. A Muslim must also wash his or her hands, face, and feet in a specific manner in order to be able to perform *namaz*, the ritual prayer. According to a Muslim expression, "cleanliness is the condition of religious faith". It is because of the importance of cleanliness that so many *hammams* were constructed in the Emirates- and Early Ottoman-period cities. In addition to small scale *hammams* like the İznik İsmail Bey Hammam (late 14th-early 15th century), there are also large, double *hammams* made up of separate areas for men and women. *Hammams* were usually built on spas or in near proximity to mosques and were an important source of income for the *waqfs*. The Turkish baths followed Roman baths as an example when it came to a heating system and units: *hammams* are heated with smoky hot air that circulates through the hypocaust under the floor and is released to the outside via ducts inside the walls; the

ılıklık (tepidarium) set aside for resting follows the domed *soyunmalık* (apoditerium) at the entrance for disrobing; and the actual bathing area called *sıcaklık* (calidarium) is the hottest section. In most *hammams*, the *sıcaklık* plan resembles a cross, such as in Selçuk Saadet Hatun Hammam with its three *iwans* or İznik Murad II Hammam with its four *iwans*. Bathers lie down for a massage and scrub with a *kese* on a hot platform in the centre of the sıcaklık. *Halvets* located in the corners of the hot-bath area are used as private bathing areas. Unlike the Roman baths, the Turkish baths do not have cold-bath areas with pools (*frigidarium*).
Ottoman *hammams* were an important part of social life and tradition that met the needs for entertainment, rest, and cleanliness and held a special place in the social life of women.

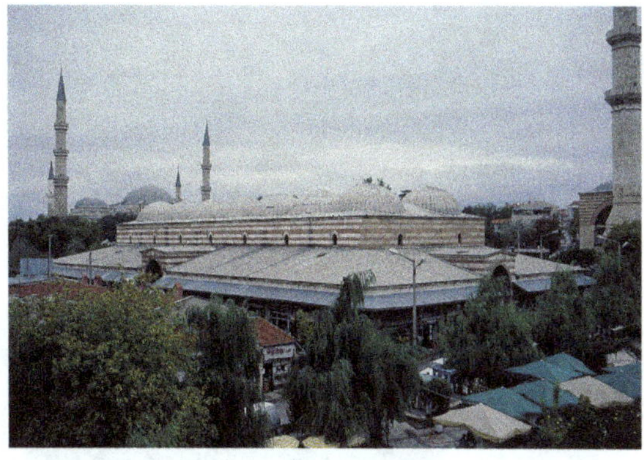

Bedesten, View from south, 1413-21, Mehmed I, Edirne.

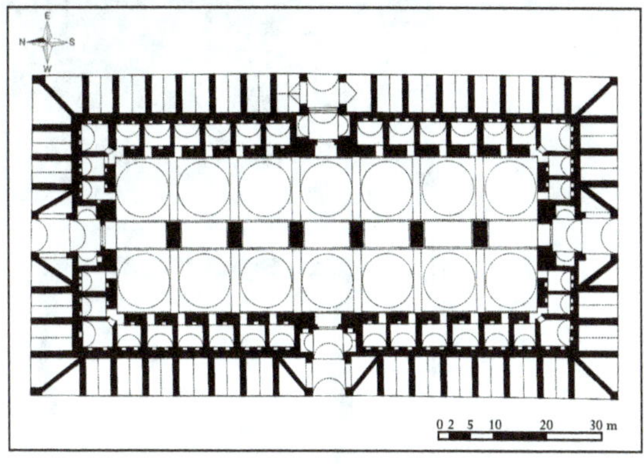

Plan of Edirne Bedesten (from E. H. Ayverdi).

Bedestens and Hans (Caravanserais)

Located on important trade routes, most of the *hans*, or by the other name – *caravanserais* –, that sheltered caravans and merchants were plain structures with a rectangular plan, a single entrance, and a fortress-like appearance. Travellers ate their meals and slept on benches in the courtyards and covered sections of these vaulted *hans*, in which *tandırs* were used for cooking and heating purposes. Typical structures of the Seljuq period, *menzil hans*, literally *hans* at a day's journey, on the roads between cities, were slowly overtaken by "city *hans*" during the Emirates and Early Ottoman periods. In the Ottoman *hans*, the stone benches usually adjoin the walls of the covered section; the fireplaces, used to cook food and provide heat when necessary, were constructed side by side on the walls and pack animals were tied to the edges of the stone benches and their fodder put in the feed trough that stretched along the stone bench. An Early Ottoman *han*, the Ulubat Issız Han (1394-95) on the edge of Apolyont (Ulubat) Lake, with its two fireplaces together with their chimneys resting upon short columns placed on

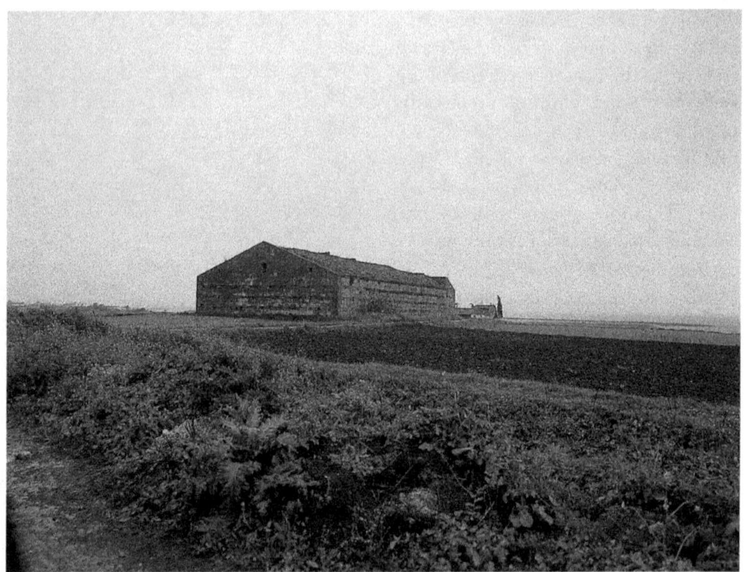

Issız Han, view from the north, 1394, İne (Eyne) Bey, Ulubat.

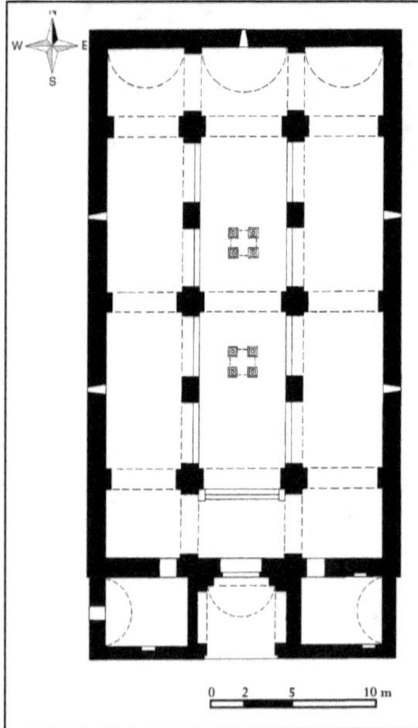

Plan of Issız Han, Ulubat (from E. H. Ayverdi).

the bench in the centre, is an example of the transition from Seljuq *han* to the Ottoman *han*.

Each city *han*, where caravans and merchants spent the night, was an important trade centre. Each city might have one or more *hans* depending upon the size of the city and the dimensions of trade therein. In the city *hans*, which were usually two-storied, there were rooms behind porticoes surrounding the open courtyard in the middle. For security reasons, a single door was used as both the entrance and the exit. There is a *masjid* and/or *şadırvan* in the centre of the courtyard of most of the *hans*, as in Bursa Koza Han (1492) for example. Shops were constructed adjoining the outer walls of some of the *hans*, and the *bedestens* as well. The Bursa Emir Han (14th century) is another typical example of a city *han*. Most of these *hans*, built

with wood and mud brick, have not survived to the present day.
Bedestens, *hans*, and bazaars are special structures that adorned the trade centres of large Ottoman cities. In the Early Ottoman period trade with the Mediterranean and the Balkan countries was quite healthy, and so the cities of Bursa and Edirne were famous for their *bedestens*, *hans*, and bazaars. The interior of the rectangular *bedestens* was divided by a row of stone piers into two distinct aisles the tops of whose bays were covered by domes of equal size. A door placed in the centre of each side provided access to the outside. There are also shops adjoining the outside walls in most of the *bedestens*. The Bursa Bedesten, which was commissioned by Bayezid I, as well as the Edirne Bedesten commissioned by Mehmed I, are still important trade centres today.
Bedestens are monumental buildings where merchants gathered and valuable goods were stored, protected, bought and sold. Valuable belongings like jewels and silk cloth, and the money deposited by the merchants for safekeeping would be kept in *bedestens*, which were secure, sound buildings. The *bedesten* merchants performed price and quality control and acted as experts in trade lawsuits; therefore, care was taken to ensure that the people who traded in the *bedestens* could be trusted. Employees working in the *bedestens* received their wages from the *waqf*. *Bedestens*, which were the centre of gravity for trade in the city, played an important role in the relationship between the state and guilds.
Bursa was an important textile- and silk-production centre of West Anatolia in the 15th century and the textiles for

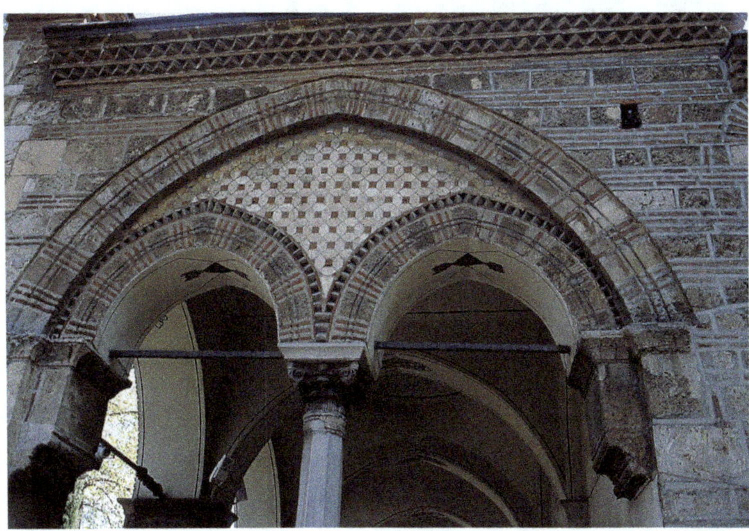

Orhan Mosque, west side of the portico, 1339-40, Orhan Gazi, Bursa.

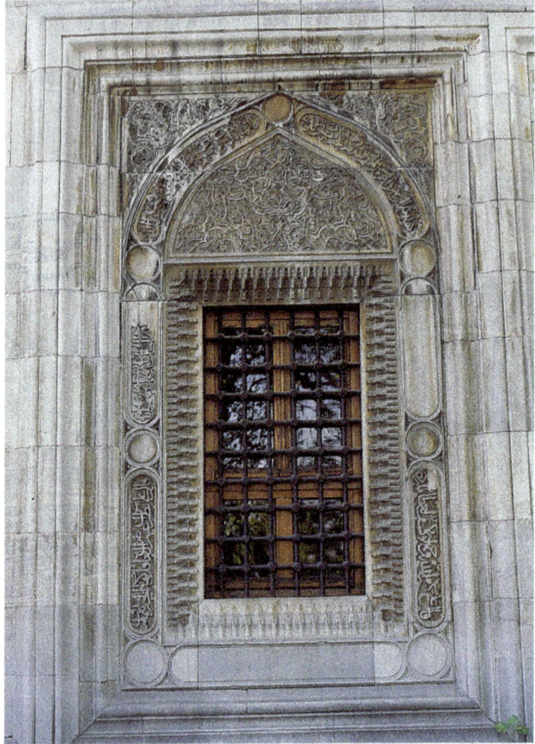

Yeşil Mosque, A window on the north facade, 1419-24, Mehmed I, Bursa.

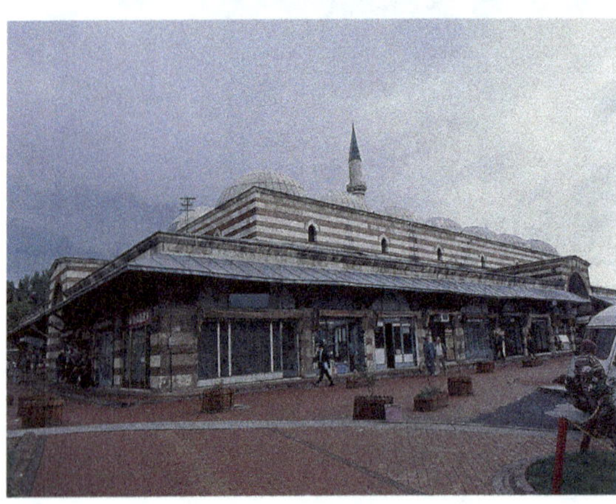

Bedesten, view from the southwest, 1413-21, Mehmed I, Edirne.

the palace were woven in Bursa, where at that time there were more than 10,000 weaving looms. Traditionally, the sultan's caftans and clothing would be bundled up, labelled and put in store after his death. Stored in the Istanbul Topkapı Palace, the materials in these bundles give extremely helpful information regarding the chronological development of Ottoman textile workmanship. According to the information we have obtained from these materials, the oldest cotton and silk cloths originating from Bursa belong to the time of Osman Gazi (r. 1281-1324), founder of the Ottoman State, and his nine caftans of white-cotton cloth were embellished with large yellow pomegranate motifs. In addition to Bursa, which was famous for its silk textiles with their stripes of cotton thread, Ödemiş, Bergama, Soma, and Edirne, too, were important cloth-weaving centres of this period. According to written sources, silk, velvet, taffeta, brocade, and cotton fabrics were exported from Bursa to Europe, Persia, and Russia. The valuable fabrics and caftans in various museums in America and Europe give an idea of the outstanding workmanship of these textiles. Because the textile workers from Bursa had difficulty meeting the demands for their products, people were concerned that the quality might decrease; therefore, an imperial edict binding fabric quality to standards was decreed in 1502. Ottoman fabrics contain seven colours red, blue, green, pink, yellow, black, and cream. Silver and gold thread was also used in the caftans of the sultans and the wealthy. Simple and plain fabrics were used for shirts and underwear.

Türbe of Murad II, woodwork under the eave, 1451, Murad II, Bursa.

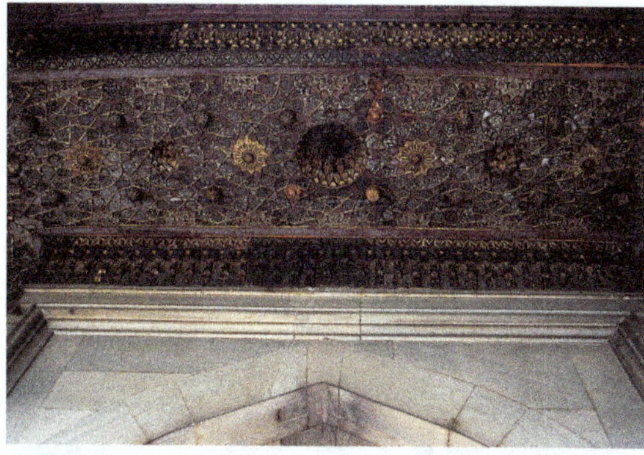

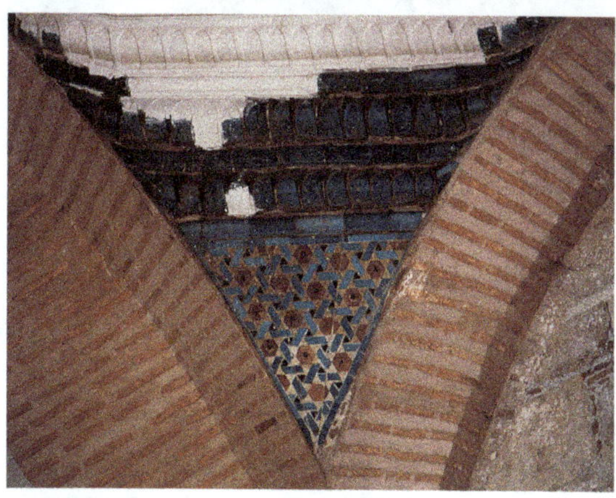

İsa Bey Mosque, detail of the transition to the dome, 1375, İsa Bey, Selçuk.

Architectural Ornamentation

Stonework

Stone was the main material used in architecture and architectural decoration of the Emirates and Early Ottoman periods. Stonemasons, who had become extremely skilful during the Seljuq period, continued their success in the 14th and 15th centuries. In the architecture of this period, wall facing was often made of alternating courses of stone and brick, numerous examples of which we see on 13th-century Byzantine structures too. Architectural ornamentation, usually quite plain, is seen much more often on front facades as opposed to the other sides of the building. Portals, casements, window tympana, arches, *mihrabs* and *minbars* made of stone or marble were ornamented with moulding, relief decorations, lattice work, and *muqarnas*. Rows of bi-chrome stone or marble; columns or piers, column capitals and, also sometimes, *mihrabs* are decorated with stone carvings; floral motifs of this period are much more realistic than they were in the Seljuq period.
Marble, widely used in Mediterranean architecture, was obtained from local quarries or old building remains. Columns and column capitals were commonly re-used materials.

Stucco and Painted Decoration

In the 14th and 15th centuries it was fashionable to have stucco shelves, niches, and fireplaces decorated with floral and geometric motifs moulded in bas-relief in the *tabhanes* of the mosques (as in the Bursa Yıldırım Mosque (1389-1399) for example). Another innovation brought about by this transition period are brown, black, blue, and red coloured *kalemişi* consisting of floral motifs and scripture on plaster, like the examples we see in buildings in Edirne and Bursa. The paintings applied on plaster to internal surfaces such as arches, domes and vaults are called *kalemişi*, just as the painted decoration executed on plaster on wooden structures. In many mosques, the internal surfaces of domes of porticoes surrounding

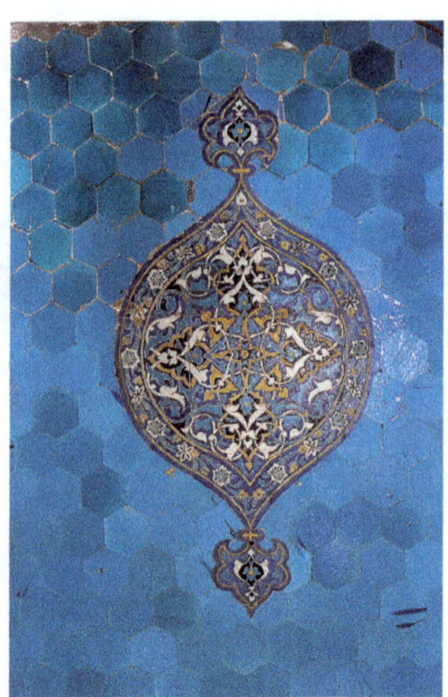

Yeşil Türbe, tilework şemse, 1419-24, Mehmed I, Bursa.

the courtyard are decorated with *kalemişi* paintings as well.

In some of the Early Ottoman-period structures in Bursa and Edirne, the wooden ceilings, cornices, window and door wings, *minbars*, bookstands, and drawers are decorated with lacquered floral and geometric designs in red, dark blue, yellow, green, and white. The designs and compositions on these decorations are the same as those seen on contemporary tiles, ceramics, textiles, and rugs. In later centuries, many wooden items with lacquer ornamentation were produced in Edirne; therefore, lacquer decorations are called "Edirne kari" (Edirne style). The most beautiful examples of this type of decoration are in the Bursa Muradiye Mosque (1426) and on the wooden lean-to roof of the Türbe of Murad II (1451).

Tiles

It is striking that less tile work was used in the Emirates and Early Ottoman-period architectural decoration in comparison with the Seljuq period (with the exception of a few examples in Edirne and Bursa). Apart from these few examples, glazed brick was preferred on the facade decorations of religious structures. The glazed-brick decorations on the minarets of the Birgi Great Mosque (1312/13), Manisa Great Mosque (1367), İznik Yeşil Mosque (1392), and Tire Yeşil İmaret Mosque (1441) are rare examples retaining the Seljuq style. In examples of later dates, the colours yellow, green, and white were added to the turquoise, purple, and dark blue of the Seljuq-period glazed bricks. Tile mosaic decoration, which reached its zenith during the Seljuq period, declined in importance in the 14th and 15th centuries when only a few examples continuing the old tradition successfully. In the tile-mosaic technique, those tiles glazed with turquoise, more uncommonly aubergine purple, cobalt blue, and black, are cut so as to form the desired motif and then put together. Tile mosaics of the Emirates and Early Ottoman periods are different from the Seljuq examples in that the designs are plainer and the pieces that form the designs are larger. In some examples white, green, and yellow were added to the turquoise, black, and cobalt blue of the Seljuq period.

The rare tile mosaic ornamentation of the Emirates period can be seen on the Birgi Great Mosque's *mihrab* (1312/13) and on the pendentives that support the dome in Selçuk İsa Bey Mosque (1375). In some

Early Ottoman buildings tile mosaics were used together with tiles in the *cuerda seca* (coloured glaze) technique, rare examples of which are found on the walls, arches, casements and *mihrabs* in the İznik Yeşil Mosque (1392), Bursa Yeşil Mosque, Yeşil Madrasa and Yeşil Türbe (1419-1424) as well as Bursa Muradiye (1426) and Edirne Muradiye (1426/27) Mosques.

The earliest examples in the *cuerda seca* technique appear in structures in Bursa and Edirne; the design is obtained by pressing a mould into a tile clay or carving out the design and then baking the plates in a kiln. A mixture of beeswax, vegetable oil, and manganese is spread between the colours so that they do not mix with one another during the firing. As soon as the beeswax melts, the mixture becomes transparent and the red colour of the clay underneath becomes visible. According to another method practised in Spain, thread is placed between the different coloured glazes; the thread burns during firing and the contours take the appearance of black lines. Thus, the term *cuerda seca* means "dry thread" in Spanish. This technique makes creation of intricate scriptural and floral designs easier and the colour scale consisting of turquoise, dark-blue, black, light purple, white, yellow, pistachio green, and gold gilding enabled the formation of rich complex designs. We do not have any definitive knowledge regarding the manufacturing centre of *cuerda seca* tiles but it is highly probable that masters who came with Tamerlane's army from Tabriz and Samarkand, where this technique was widely used, brought it to Anatolia. It is also believed that travelling master workmen manufactured the *cuerda seca* tiles in small workshops established close to buildings in Bursa, Edirne, and Istanbul.

In Early Ottoman-period structures, in addition to tile mosaics and *cuerda seca* tiles, designs were also made using monochrome glazed plates. Tile plates coloured turquoise, dark -and light- blue, green, and white were arranged geometrically leaving no gaps between the hexagonal, octagonal, rectangular, square, or triangular plates; sometimes gold leaf or impressed floral motifs also appear on the plates.

The Early Ottoman period's highest quality tiles, called the "blue-white" group, were used especially in buildings in İznik, Bursa, and Edirne. Ongoing excavations have proven that these tiles were produced in İznik in the first half of the 15th century. Successful examples of blue-white tiles

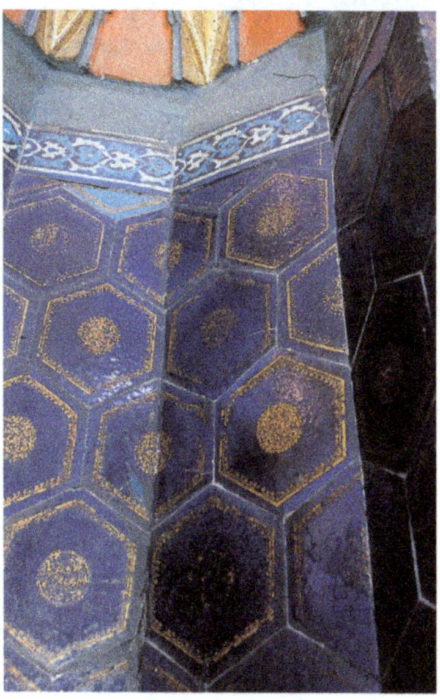

Türbe of Şehzade Mustafa and Cem Sultan, Detail from mihrab tiles, 1479, Bursa.

Great Mosque, minbar, 1377, Manisa.

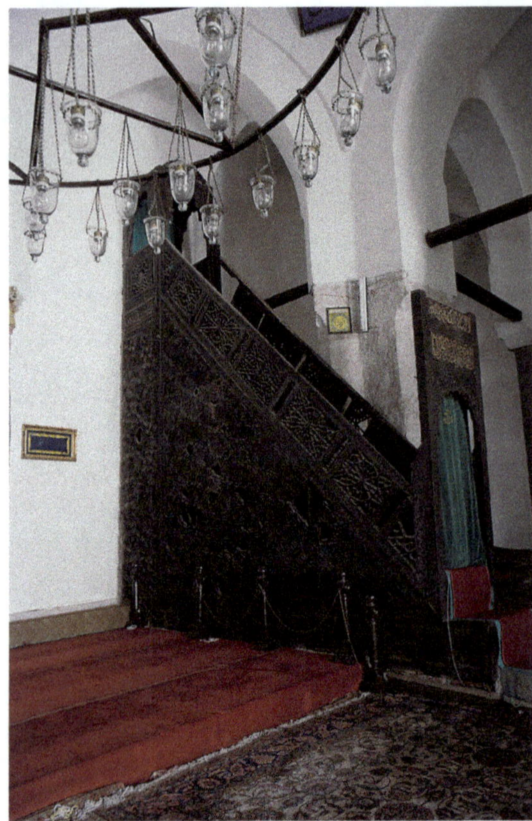

made with the under-glaze technique can be seen in the Türbe of Şehzade Mustafa and Cem Sultan in Bursa (1479), and Üç Şerefeli (1445) and Muradiye (1426/27) Mosques in Edirne.
The designs on these tiles have been worked with blue tones and turquoise beneath a transparent and colourless glaze. The clay of the hexagonal or rectangular shaped tile plates is hard and white like porcelain. Among the most striking motifs, are spring flowers, peonies, and cloud or dragon motifs of Far Eastern origin in a realistic style. These exhibit similarities with Ming-period Chinese Porcelain with regard to design and colour, and Far Eastern influence can be explained to a large degree by imported Chinese porcelain. A great number of blue-white ceramics influenced by Ming porcelain was found in the İznik excavations from which came most of the blue-white ceramics exhibited in the İznik and Bursa museums.

Woodwork

Wooden items made from a variety of materials like walnut, apple, pear, rose, and cedar are another important material that enriched 14th- and 15th-century architecture. Valuable bookrests, *minbars*, window shutters and door wings, banisters and lecterns that decorated Seljuq structures can also be seen in Emirates and Early Ottoman-period structures, although fewer in number. Noteworthy works manufactured using different techniques are on display in Manisa, Bursa, and Edirne Museums.
Some of the most intricate and masterly examples in the art of woodcarving are on the *minbars* located to the right of the *mihrabs*. The wood working technique called *kündekari* used on the side surfaces of the Manisa Great Mosque's (1367), Birgi Great Mosque's (1312/13) and Bursa Great Mosque's (1400) *minbars* is the legacy of the Seljuq period. Appearing in Egypt and Syria in the 12th century, *kündekari* is a type of basting: wooden pieces in octagonal, diamond, and star shapes and decorated with carved *rumis* were attached to

one another without using nails or glue but by means of rods with mortise. Because the pieces are held together with mortise and tenon (or tongue-and-groove), once the wood dries, they do not separate or split. A wooden framework that reinforces the *minbar* also supports the surface of the interlocking *kündekari*. This technique was used especially on the side surfaces of the *minbar*, and sometimes also on door and window wings. A technique that resembles *kündekari*, but uses glue or nails to hold the small wooden pieces together, is called fake *kündekari*.

The most widespread decorations of 14th- and 15th-century wood craftsmanship are floral or geometric motifs and scripture with flat or rounded surfaces. Birgi Great Mosque's wooden window wings and *minbar* (1322) are some of the most beautiful examples of the period's woodwork. The surfaces of 15th-century wooden works were also inlaid with mother-of-pearl, bone, ivory and even jade. Woodwork examples with inlaid and engraved ornamentation are exhibited at Edirne, Bursa, and İznik museums. The wood inlay technique was developed in the 13th century in Damascus and applied to a great number of works during the 14th-century Mamluk period.

Rugs

In Islamic countries, carpets and prayer rugs, traditionally donated to mosques, lend mosques a warm atmosphere with their lively colours and designs and West Anatolia was an important carpet-weaving region in the 14th century. Ibn Batuta, the famous traveller who visited Anatolia in the 14th century, says that Anatolian carpets were praised and exported to various countries. These rugs using a special knot, called "Turkish Double Knot" or "Gördes Knot", which were pure wool carpets. The main colours are tones of red and blue together with yellow, cream, purple, and brown, with green also used to a

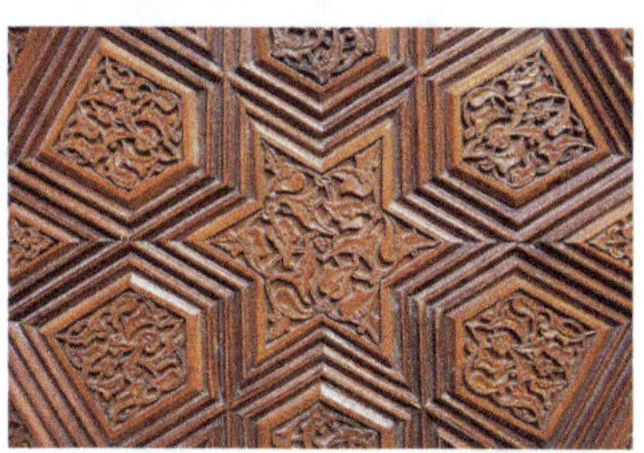

Great Mosque, detail of wooden door wings, 1400, Bayezid I, Bursa.

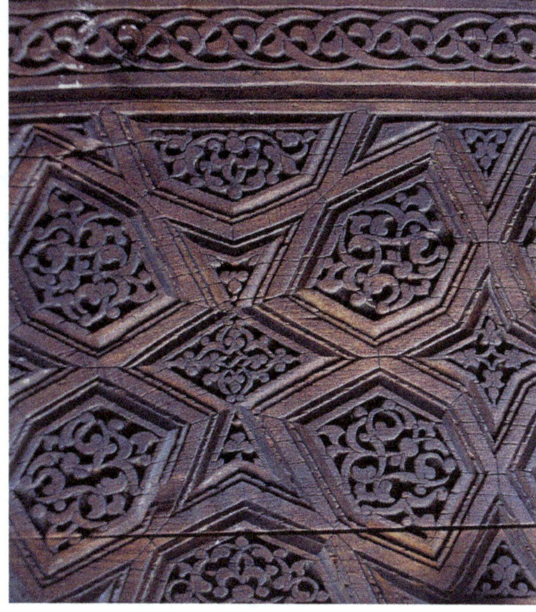

Great Mosque, detail of wooden window shutters, 1312-13, Aydınoğlu Mehmed Bey, Birgi.

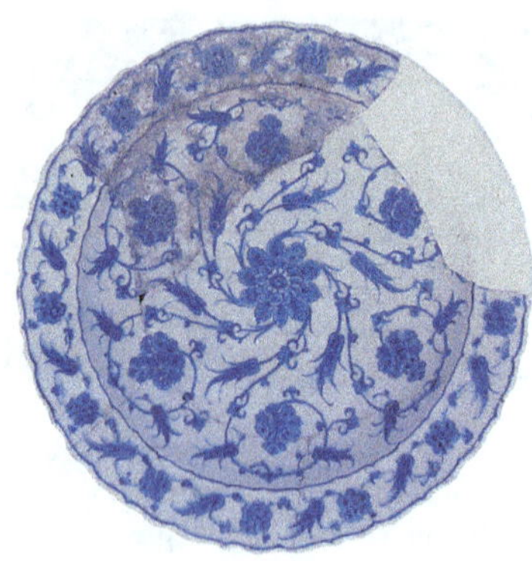

Ceramic Plate (Inv. No. 4377), 15th century, İznik Museum.

lesser degree. The fame of carpets and prayer rugs woven in Milas, İzmir, Uşak, Kula, Gördes, Bergama, Balıkesir, Çanakkale, Ezine, and Bandırma still continues today. Milas Great Mosque still has some authentic rugs of later dates on the floor and the invaluable pieces from Edirne Muradiye Mosque are on display at Turkish-Islamic Arts Museum in İstanbul. It is a great pity that nowadays monochrome, machine-made carpets are found in most of the West Anatolian mosques.

The Seljuqs brought the carpet-weaving tradition with them. It is highly probable that the first rugs woven in Konya and its environs date back to the 13th century. The carpet-weaving tradition increased in variety as it continued in the 14th- and 15th- century Emirates and Early Ottoman period.

In 1935-36, the Swedish researcher C. J. Lamm found up to 100 carpet fragments large and small in old Cairo (Fustat). Today these fragments are in the Stockholm National Museum, Gothenburg Röhs Museum, and Athens Benaki Museum. Of the examples published by C. J. Lamm, seven are Seljuq, while the others are 14th- and 15th-century Anatolian rugs. Most of these are decorated with abstract animal figures, and some of them with geometric designs; similar fragments are also found in Istanbul and Konya museums.

Today our greatest source of information about carpets with animal figures are paintings by 14th- and 15th-century Italian, Flemish, Dutch, and Spanish painters. Turkish rugs imported from Anatolia are often depicted in paintings of this period beneath the figures' feet or spread out on tables. The rugs, which are painted in great detail, have large hexagonal and octagonal rosettes decorated with abstract geometric tree-of-life patterns, birds, double-headed eagles, stags, and scenes of animals fighting. The borders of carpets with animal figures have geometric motifs or a decoration reminiscent of Kufic script. It is striking that the paintings depict the carpets down to the finest details while remaining true to the originals.

By the 15th century animal figures on rugs were replaced by large rugs with mostly geometric designs and plain prayer rugs, as seen in some paintings of the15th century. There are paintings by Hans Holbein, Lorenzo Lotto, Gentile Bellini, and Giovanni Bellini, which it is believed were produced in the vicinity of Uşak in West Anatolia. Often seen on Hans Holbein's paintings, these have been termed the "Holbein Carpets".

Unfortunately, it is impossible to find examples of these historic carpets in West Anatolian museums today. The same designs, however, are still used in the rather high-quality carpets woven in various cities in West Anatolia. This tradition is also kept alive by quality-carpets manufactured in villages and carpet-weaving centres. Fabrics and carpets were exported for centuries from İzmir and its environs to Europe and above all to Italy.

Handicrafts Exhibited in the Museums of West Anatolian

The examples of handicrafts from the Emirates and Early Ottoman periods that have survived up until today are simple and unadorned. Usually archaeological finds pre-dating the Turkish period, and ethnographic works belonging to the late Ottoman period, are exhibited in the museums that are detailed in our itineraries. The limited number of ceramic, metal, carpet, and wooden works dating from the 14th and 15th centuries makes one think that Turkish museums need to attach more importance to building collections of the Turkish era. A look at the examples displayed in the museums of West Anatolian will suffice to give us an idea about handicrafts produced in the Emirates and Early Ottoman periods.

Ceramic Arts

Pottery from the Miletus, Beçin, Selçuk-Ephesus, İznik, and Edirne excavations, as well as chance finds, show that ceramics of the Emirates and Early Ottoman periods are different from those of the Seljuq period. The most widespread examples are ceramics called "Miletus ware" because they were first unearthed and published in the Miletus excavations. Later finds, however, from the excavations and research on İznik in particular, suggested that these ceramics were produced in İznik. Various examples of "Miletus-ware" ceramics are displayed in Bursa and İznik museums. These red-clay ceramics produced for daily use were decorated with cobalt blue, black, turquoise, green floral designs, rosettes, geometric shapes and radial lines beneath a transparent, achromatic, or sometimes turquoise coloured glaze.

In addition to Miletus ware, examples in the "sgraffito" technique in which abstract shapes are worked with incised lines or examples of designs painted beneath glaze on a paste-like material called "slip" have also been recovered at excavations carried out in West Anatolia. Abstract floral and geometric motifs were used on these ceramics too. In the slip technique, the colours used under the transparent colourless glaze are beige, blue, green, brown or yellow and the motifs are slightly raised.

The colours and designs used in the ceramic group classified as "blue-white" because of its colours were also used on ceramic plates, as we stated earlier. İznik and Kütahya were the manufacturing centres of the blue-white ceramics, which were produced in large quantities in the 15th and 16th centuries. The clay of quality blue-white ceramics is white and hard like porcelain. Once again the designs, worked under a transparent and colourless glaze, are reminiscent of 15th-century Ming-period Chinese porcelain. The design is drawn with blue tones on a white background beneath a hard and high-quality transparent glaze. Various examples of blue-white ceramics and of

"Haliç ware" (Golden Horn ware) ceramics such as bowls, plates and mugs are exhibited in the İznik and Bursa Museums.

Blue-white fragments found on excavations in İznik present an idea of the variety available in this type of ceramic ware. Examples of vases, goblets, cups, sugar bowls, lamps, and so on, together with many tile kiln remains prove that İznik was the main manufacturing centre. According to inscriptions, *fermans*, and recovered fragments, blue-white ceramics were also manufactured in Kütahya, where most of today's ceramics are produced. Blue-white ceramics continued to be manufactured in the classic Ottoman style with more realistic motifs in the 16th century as well.

Metal Art

Our knowledge of metal art during the Emirates and Early Ottomans period is extremely limited but fragments preserved in various collections and museums show that the Seljuq metal arts tradition continued in this period. In the 13th century, Iranian and Seljuq master craftsmen escaping from the Mongol invasion continued the Great Seljuq metal art tradition while settling in Iraq and Syria. We know from inscriptions that Syrian master craftsmen took orders from Anatolian Emirates in the 13th century, right through to the 15th century and it is thought that some Syrian masters migrating to Anatolia also brought the tradition with them to their new homeland. The 14th-15th-century examples of metalwork that have survived are made of brass, iron, and bronze; works made of gold and silver are extremely rare. The craftsmanship of metalwork in Anatolia exhibits a wide-ranging variety and exemplifies the extreme care craftsmen took with their work. For example, washtubs, bowls, trays, long-spouted ewers, vases, candelabra, pen cases, oil lamps, incense burners, pestle and mortars, mirrors, belt buckles, and door knockers.

Of the limited quantity of metalwork on display in West Anatolian Museums, it is thought that the gold and silver inlaid-bronze candelabra dating from the end of the 13th or beginning of the 14th century in the Bursa Turkish and Islamic Arts Museum, were manufactured at Siirt in Southeast Anatolia. The bronze brazier found in the same museum is a beautiful example of 14th-century metal art. Some of the valuable metal objects belonging to the Early Ottoman period are exhibited in museums in Istanbul and abroad. According to its inscription a bronze candelabrum from the year 1329, currently in the Louvre Museum in Paris, was made for Orhan Gazi. Exhibited in the same museum, a bronze decanter belonging to Sultan Mehmed II is among the period's finest examples of metalwork. The workmanship on some of the inscribed candelabra stored in the Istanbul Topkapı Palace and Turkish and Islamic Arts Museums is striking. A pair of inscribed bronze candelabrum ordered for the mosque of the Bayezid II's Mosque Complex in Edirne is also displayed in the Turkish Islamic Arts Museum. Although few in number, these examples show that 14th- and 15th-century metal workmanship in Anatolia, while not inventing a new style, nevertheless formed a foundation for metalwork of the Ottoman period.

Book Art

In the 14th and 15th centuries, the rulers of the Western Anatolian Emirates took up patronage for books and the art of manuscript illumination. Valuable manuscripts illuminated with gilding and colourful ornamentation can be found in the Tire Necip Pasha Library.

Bursa was famous for the artists, known as *müzehhip*, who decorated manuscripts and did the bookbinding and who were taken under the patronage of the Ottoman sultans. Valuable calligraphy and manuscripts dating to the 14th and 15th centuries is found in the Bursa Turkish and Islamic Arts Museum as well as the Istanbul Topkapı Palace Museum.

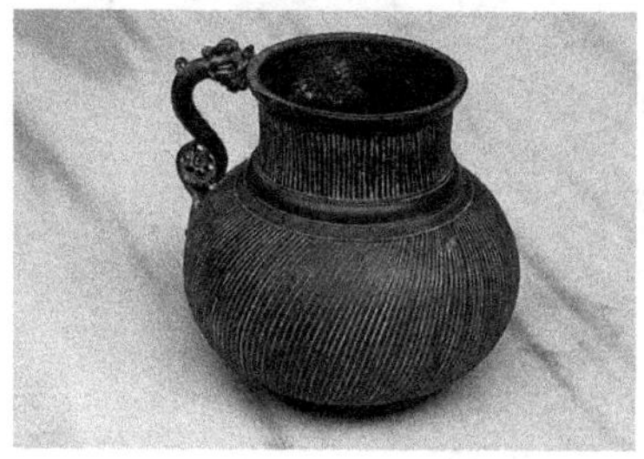

Cast bronze jug (Inv. No. 764), 15th century, Bursa Turkish and Islamic Arts Museum.

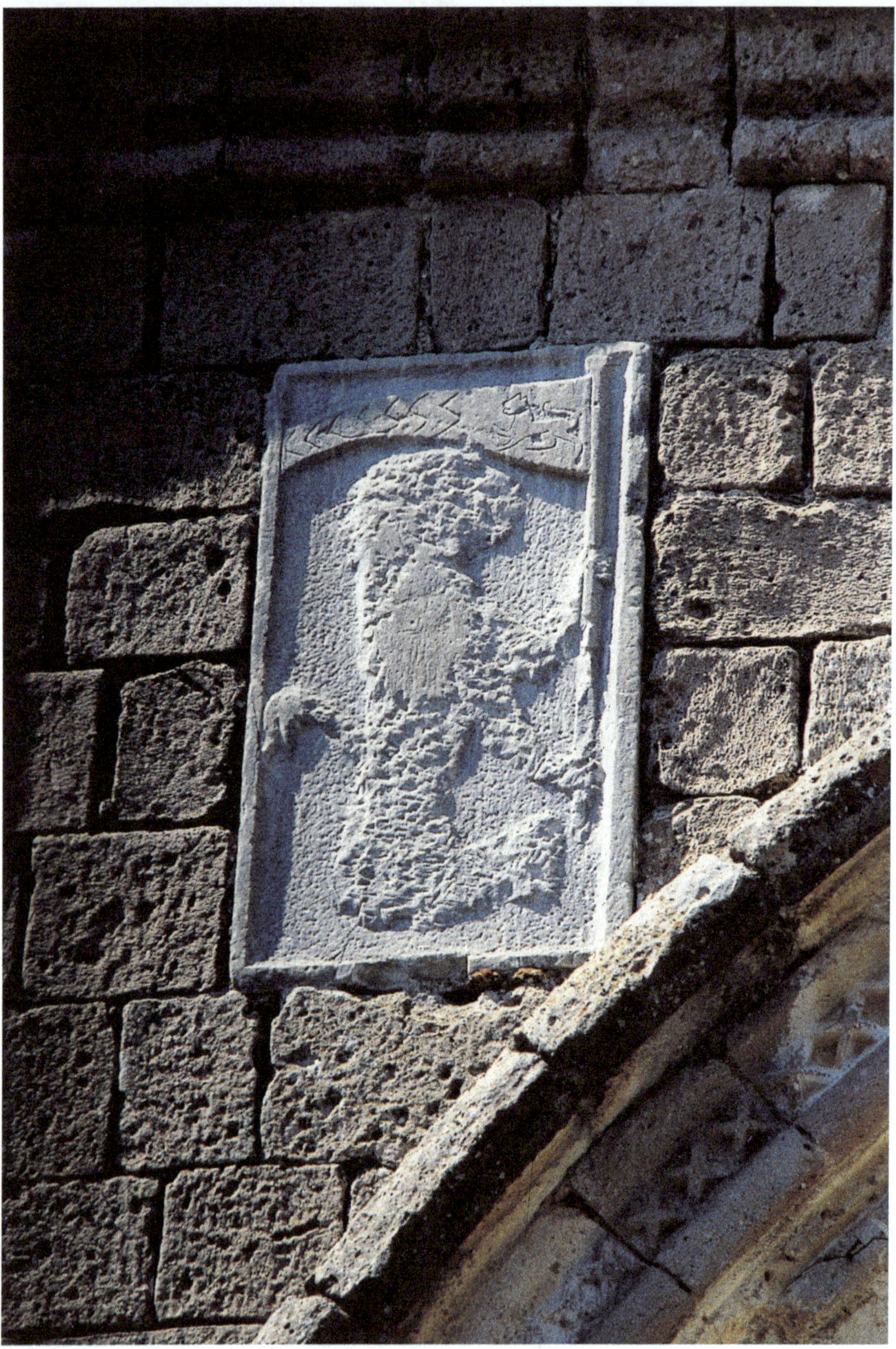

Sultan of the Coasts

Aydoğan Demir, Yekta Demiralp, Rahmi H. Ünal

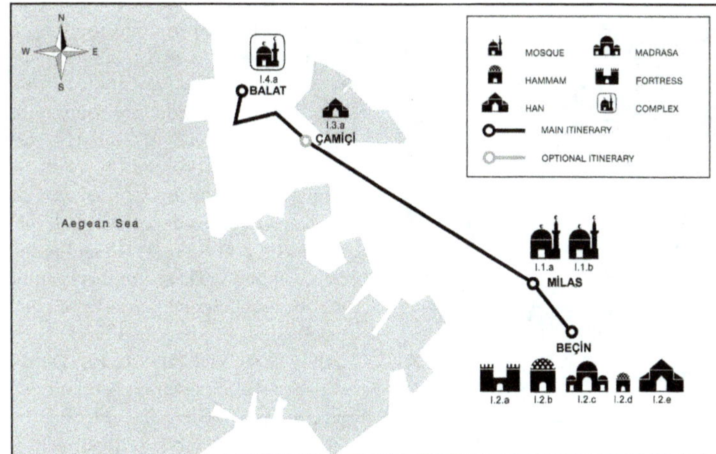

Ahmet Gazi Madrasa, Lion relief on the left spandrel of the main iwan, 1375, Ahmet Gazi, Beçin.

The Byzantine Empire, an important power in the Balkans and in West and North Anatolia at the end of the 11th century, found itself unable to overcome the devastating effects of the Fourth Crusade (1204). The Anatolian Seljuq Sultans, who ruled over much of Anatolia, also fell in defeat against Mongolian attacks (1243). Distressed by Mongolian oppression, hundreds of thousands of people under the command of Turcoman *Beys* and some Seljuq administrators broke the resistance of the Byzantines, already greatly weakened in West Anatolia, and settled in the region.

Menteşe Bey and his successors occupied the area that was antique Caria and founded the Menteşe Emirate there (1280). They proceeded to co-operate with the local seamen, that is, the Rums, in order to develop themselves further by opening up to the seas. They controlled a part of Rhodes for a short time until the arrival of the Knights of St. John (1310). That Ahmet Gazi, who had a beautiful *madrasa* constructed in Beçin (1375), saw himself deserving of the title "Sultan of the Coasts" must be an expression of his aspiration to establish sovereignty over the seas. Having in hand the important trading port of Balat (Miletus), the Menteşe Emirate guaranteed peaceful trade by entering into six agreements with the Venetians between the years 1331-1414. According to these agreements, Venetian merchants would be free to trade on Menteşe land, allowed to settle in Balat, and able to worship at a church that would be named Saint Nicholas. The Venetian Consulate residing in Balat would act as the special trial authority on cases of interest to the Venetians; another Venetian would not be held responsible and arrested in place of a Venetian merchant who was in debt because of business. In order to increase the volume of trade, the Menteşe Beys minted silver currency of illustrated Neapolitan type with Latin script, called "Gigliati". The Menteşe Emirate's economy, based upon bountiful plains and safe trade, created an important source for the country's development as it aspired to a rich and prosperous condition. Thanks to this healthy economy, monumental works were constructed in Beçin, Milas, and Balat.

Crossing the Çanakkale Straits (Dardanelles), Ottoman forces conquered Thrace and progressed as far as Kosovo in the 1350s. Then, once they had locked

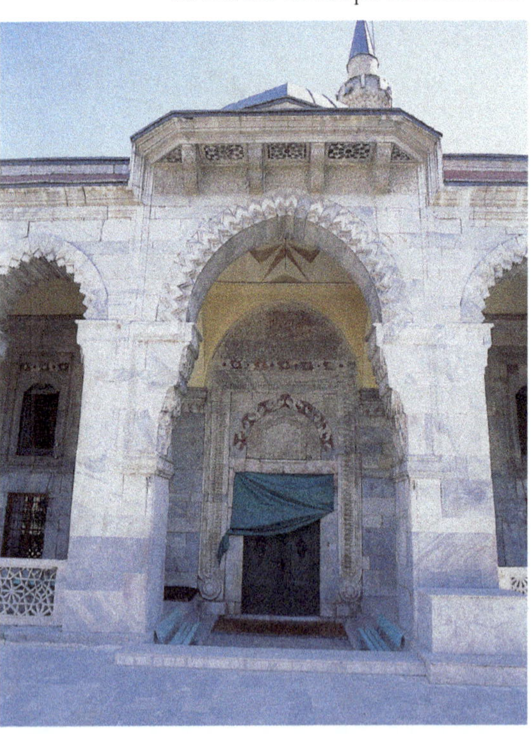

Great Mosque, Entrance facade, 1378, Ahmet Gazi, Milas.

the Byzantines into Istanbul and its surroundings, they proceeded to annex the emirates in West Anatolia to Ottoman land. It has not yet been definitely determined in which year the Aydın and Menteşe Emirates were conquered. However, it is believed that Balat was captured in the years 1389-90. When Ahmet Gazi passed away in 1391, he was buried in the *madrasa* he had built in Beçin. The governor of Menteşe –the region is still named after him– under the Ottoman Sultan Beyazid I, Hoca Firuz commissioned the construction of the Firuz Bey Mosque in Milas, the construction of which was completed on 29 November 1396.
In 1424 the Ottoman State eradicated the Menteşe Emirate that had been re-established after the Battle of Ankara in 1402. After this date, towns like Beçin and Balat in Menteşe –an Ottoman *sanjak* (province) then– became less important and were eventually abandoned.

A. D.

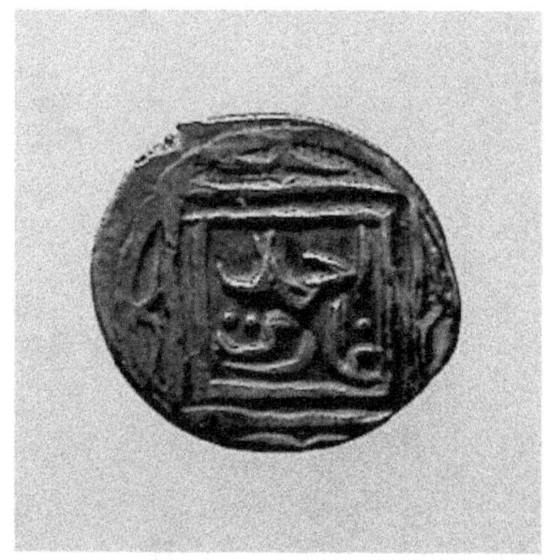

Silver coin minted in the name of Ahmet Gazi (1359-91), Üstün Erek Collection.

This itinerary begins in the town centre of Milas in the ancient region of Caria and continues straight to the north until you reach your destination in the ancient region of Ionia. Having looked around Milas town centre and at the works in Beçin Fortress, continue down the main road heading north on D. 525. After passing the rugged territory on the southern shore of Lake Bafa, you reach Söke Plain, which was created by centuries of alluvium accumulation from the Büyük Menderes River (ancient Meandre River). Once you reach Söke, you need to decide where to spend the night: If you like, you can spend the night at the starting point of the next route, Selçuk, or, if you prefer, you can spend the night at the more lively coastal town of Kuşadaşı. Those visitors who decide to continue in the direction of Selçuk, can stop for a rest at the town of Ortaklar on the way and drop by one of its many restaurants for a taste of the region's famous çöp şiş (a kebab made by grilling very small cubes of meat that have been strung on a small skewer over charcoal) and ayran (a drink made of yoghurt and water) or grilled sucuk (a very spicy sausage).
If you are using public transport, you may not be able to complete your visits in a single day. However, a good transport network exists between cities in Turkey. You can reach Beçin from Milas by taking one of the dolmush *minibuses (shared cabs or vans) that leave from the front of the Great Mosque, opposite the Museum. To get to Balat by bus, you must first go to Söke and board a Balat or Didim dolmush at the bus station. Bafa* Han *is located on the Milas-Söke main road; however, it is difficult to visit this building unless you have your own transport. Be especially careful driving on the road that stretches along the Söke Plain, there are tractors on the road loaded with cotton bales many of which are poorly lit and marked, especially during harvest season (September-October).*

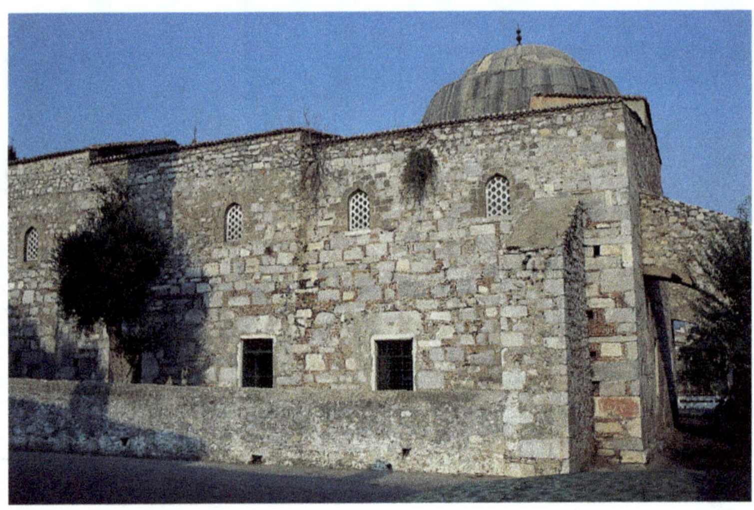

Great Mosque, west facade, 1378, Ahmet Gazi, Milas.

I.1 MİLAS

Known as Mylasa during Antiquity, Milas was the Carian capital in ancient times; however, Halicarnassus (present day Bodrum) assumed this title during the reign of Caria's Persian Satrap Mausolus (4th century BC). Due to the good relations he established with the Persians, Mausolus was able to rule without hindrance. Upon his death, his wife had a monumental grave (mausoleum) constructed for his burial: one of the Seven Wonders of the World, only traces of whose foundations are visible today. Mylasa continued to be important during the Hellenistic period due to the proximity of the religious centre Labranda (13 km. to the east), and later, during the Roman period, it served as an administrative centre. Not very much is known about Milas during the Byzantine period. We do know, however, that the city regained its importance with the founding of the Menteşe Emirate.

I.1.a **Great Mosque (Ulu Cami)**

Hoca Bedrettin District (Mahallesi), İnönü Avenue, Milas. Across the street from the Museum.

Ruling between the years 1359-1391, the famous Menteşe Emir Ahmet Gazi administered a section of the land that had been divided up amongst his siblings after his father's death. Not only did Ahmet Bey remain in power longer than any other Menteşe Bey, his period of reign was also the Emirate's most brilliant. A few of the buildings that Ahmet Gazi had constructed in Beçin, Milas, Balat, Fethiye, and Çine, are still standing today. Of these, the Milas Great Mosque has

been completely restored in the last few years and is still open for worship.
The walls of the mosque, which is located in a beautiful garden full of shrubs and trees, were built with bricks, and stones gathered from ancient buildings; the blocks with inscriptions and the decorative brickwork here and there are especially noteworthy. Besides the main entrance in the centre of the north facade, there is also an entrance on both the east and west fronts. The stairs located to the right of the portal on the north facade were constructed to provide access to the roof for the chanting of the call to prayer. According to the Arabic inscription above the entrance, the mosque's construction was completed in October 1378. Another inscription, written in Ottoman on the top part of the entrance on the west facade, is a *waqf* charter dating from 1904. The variety seen in the building's supports and roof shows that it underwent important renovations at various times in history: the rather massive buttresses on all of the facades must be later additions.
Both the plan and roof design of Milas Great Mosque continues the Seljuq tradition. Like the Seljuq mosques with basilical plans, this mosque also has aisles that are perpendicular to the *qibla* wall; while the aisles are covered with various types of vaults, the bay in front of the *mihrab* is distinctly differentiated from the rest with a dome. The marble *minbar* decorated with several rosettes was renovated in 1879; however, the inscription of the former *minbar*, dated January 1380, was copied onto the new one.

R. H. Ü.

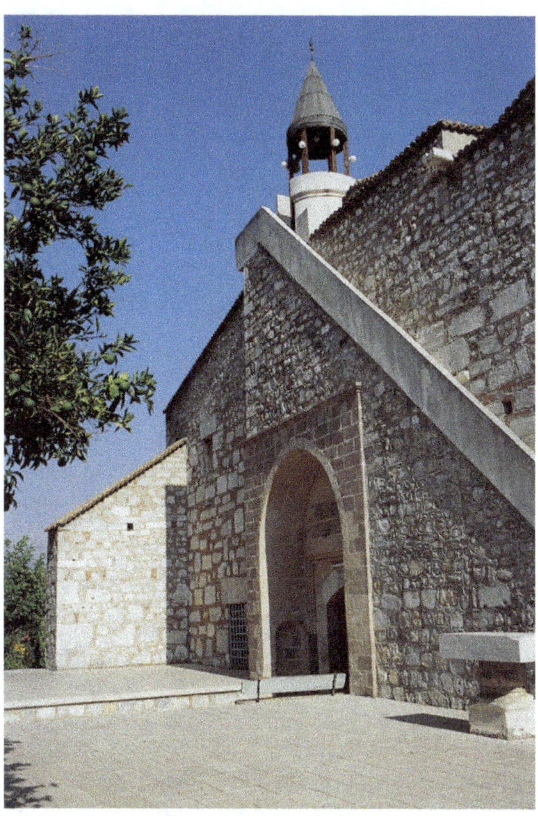

Firuz Bey Mosque, view from the northwest, 1396, Hoca Firuz, Milas.

I.1.b **Firuz Bey Mosque**

Firuz Pasha District (Mahallesi), Kışla Avenue, Milas. Continue north along the main street in front of Great Mosque and turn left at Kışla Caddesi.

This mosque is located in the middle of a spacious courtyard in the town centre. The *madrasa* cells lined up along the courtyard's western edge lost their special features as a result of renovation and the graves in the mosque courtyard were transferred to another cemetery in the 1930s. The build-

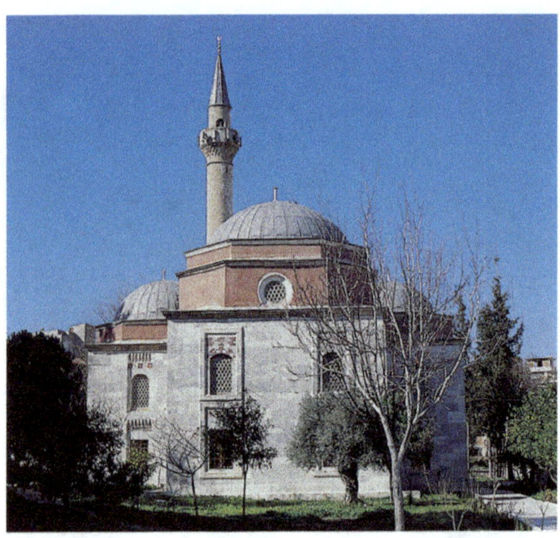

Firuz Bey Mosque, south facade, 1396, Hoca Firuz, Milas.

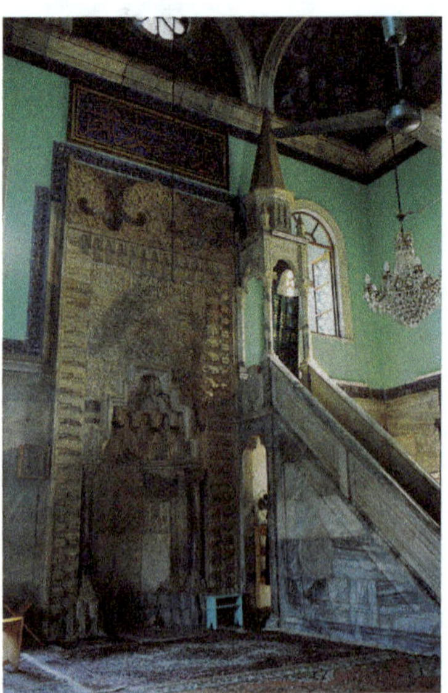

Firuz Bey Mosque, mihrab, 1396, Hoca Firuz, Milas.

ing, completed in 1396, recently underwent a complete renovation and is still open for worship. All the external facades are faced with blue-veined marble plates. The Turkish traveller Evliya Çelebi wrote that, "because of the blue-coloured marble, the Turks named the building the 'Gök Camii' (Sky Blue Mosque)". The two rows of windows are very attractive: each window has a unique decorative composition. The minaret usually located on one of the side walls, on the end closest to the entrance side and rising from a special base, is here, however, placed on top of the wall of the prayer hall. The portico in front, striking with its elaborate arches, lattice marble balustrades with geometric decoration and an elegant portal, is five arched but three bayed, the central one of which is topped with a dome, while the side bays are covered with cradle vaults. The floral ornamentation seen around the inscription panel above the entrance and below the portico's central bay are indications of a break with the Seljuq tradition. A variant of multifunctional mosques that served as a place of worship as well as a guesthouse, the Firuz Bey Mosque has *tabhane*s at both its east and west ends, and the inner court between the tabhanes and the prayer hall are much smaller than normal. The elegant domes are covered with paintings of a later date; yet the *mihrab* catches the eye immediately with its carvings, and the plain marble *minbar* has a simple *Solomon's-knot* (David's-star) motif as decoration. An architect named Hassan Ibn Abdullah constructed the building, while a master craftsman named Musa Ibn Adil executed the ornamentation.

R. H. Ü.

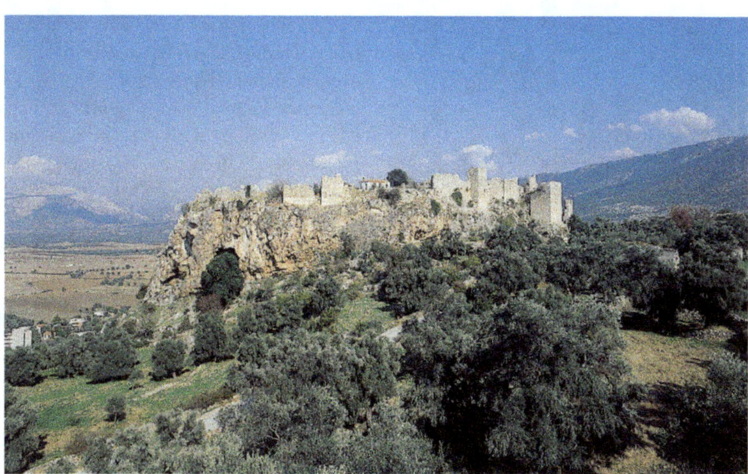

Beçin Fortress, general view from the west, 4th-14th century, Beçin.

Milas is a lovely, lively town with a variety of things to offer the visitor: the Museum located in the old town has a small but good collection of works from antiquity; the old town full of Ottoman houses with charming local-style chimneys; the Gümüşkesen Tomb from Roman times; the local market on Tuesdays...
The remains of the Mausoleum, one of the Seven Wonders of the World, is located in Bodrum (ancient Halicarnassus), 50 km. from Milas. The St. Peter's Fortress, constructed by the Knights of St. John using stones from the mausoleum, is a worldwide famous Underwater Archaeology Museum today. Bodrum is a charming coastal town that attracts both native and foreign tourists during the summer months.

Beçin is situated to the south of Milas, just 4 km. from the city centre. You can reach Beçin by taking one of the Beçin dolmush *minibuses that leave from the front of the Great Mosque.*

I.2 BEÇİN

Built on top of a flat plateau on the edge of the Milas Plain, and 200 m. above, the fortress rises majestically on a weird looking rocky outcrop, like a crown over the head of the modern town. The remains on the top and outskirts of the steep slope to the north have given rise to speculation that this area was used as a necropolis during antiquity. The remains of foundations dating to the Hellenistic period to the east, along with the temple (4th century BC) at the southeast corner of the city walls, are evidence that the fortress existed before the Turkish period.
The town of Beçin was probably a small settlement when it passed into the hands of the Menteşe Beys towards the end of the 13th century. The small dimensions of the Byzantine chapel situated in the ruins of the town supports this thesis. The famous Arab traveller Ibn Battuta, who visited the city in the 1330s, lends further credence

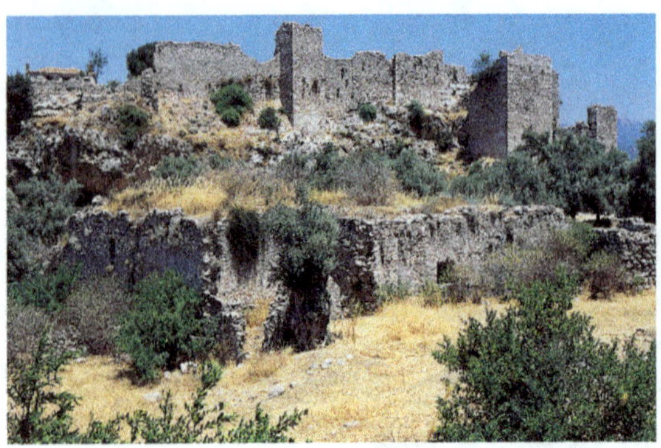

Büyük hammam, general view from the southwest, 14th century, Beçin.

to this theory when he writes that it was "a newly founded city with new buildings and *masjids*". That the majority of what remains of the ruined city dates back to the Turkish period, is proof that the city developed rapidly during the period. Due to a rapid increase in population and development, the majority of the town's buildings originate in the 14th century.

R. H. Ü.

I.2.a **Fortress**

The road turns right in front of the stairs going up to the fortress. Just in front is a fountain, probably dating to the Menteşe period, and a few steps up on the right is a cistern that provided the water for the fortress. In spite of the large number of water sources and wells in the ruined city of Beçin itself, it was impossible for water to be brought to the fortress because it rises on a steep mass of stone 50 m. higher than the plateau upon which the city lies.

A section of the circular city walls, currently in need of restoration, rest in the south upon the foundations of an ancient temple which is thought to be dedicated to Zeus though it still has not been examined in detail. The dilapidated houses inside the fortress, though today deserted, were used up until the 1980s and the oldest of them dates back 100 years at the most. The presence of a deteriorated 14th-century *hammam* makes one think that the settlement inside the fortress should be much older.

R. H. Ü.

I.2.b **Büyük Hammam**

The famous Turkish traveller Evliya Çelebi, who visited Beçin in the middle of the 17th century, reports that there was no *hammam* in Beçin. However, because the ruins of five *hammams* are visible in the city today, it must be concluded that the baths were either in ruins or no longer operating at the time of Evliya Çelebi's visit.

The Büyük Hammam, literally the Large Hammam, located in the olive grove to the right of the road from the fortress to the Ahmet Gazi Madrasa, is one of the city's most magnificent structures. Although much of its roof has caved in, great portions of the wall are still standing. The vaulted rectangular room to the north is the water depot and on the outside can be seen the stokehole arch through which the fire was fed. The large hall to the east is the *soyunmalık*. Excavations have revealed two fountains, one in the *soyunmalık*, the other in the *ılıklık*. A particularly interesting characteristic of this *hammam* is the existence of two doors that provide access to the outside in the disrobing area, as almost all baths have only one entrance to the disrobing area so as to prevent heat loss.

Some Turkish baths were constructed as two separate, adjoining baths designated for men and women. In these baths, the entrance to the section set aside for women opens onto a generally not too busy side street so that women could comfortably enter and exit the baths. There are no *hammams* designated for women only, other than these double *hammams*. In case of a single *hammam* only women would be allowed into the baths on one or two days of the week. Of the two entrances seen at the Büyük Hammam, the one on the east side opens onto the street, while on the west is a secondary entrance of small dimensions not visible from the street. On the days that the *hammam* was set aside for women, the main entrance looking onto the street would probably have been closed so that women customers could enter and exit through this door at the rear of the building.

Passing through the small chamber to the west is the *ılıklık*; to its north it adjoins the *sıcaklık* with three *iwans* forming a T-shape and in the corners are the *halvets*. The whole floor is covered with large, re-used marble blocks and the walls bear traces of plaster.

R. H. Ü.

I.2.c **Ahmet Gazi Madrasa**

This *madrasa*, commissioned by the famous Menteşe *Bey* Ahmet Gazi, is the best preserved of all the buildings of the Menteşe Emirate to have survived until the present day. Restoration work, begun in recent years, still continues. According to the Arabic inscription above the entrance, "the Great Ruler, the Sultan of the Coasts Ahmet Gazi" had this *madrasa* built in the year 1375. Ahmet Gazi's use of the title "Sultan of the Coasts" proves that efforts to establish sovereignty over the Aegean, which were increased during the time of the Menteşe rulers Mesut Bey and Orhan Bey, came to a successful conclusion. The commercial activities and human traffic revived with the Aegean islands, Italy and southern France during this period, resulted in the first appearance of some foreign elements in Turkish architecture. Although it has all the components of the traditional Seljuq portal, there are important differences in detail on the *madrasa*'s entrance. From up close, the numerous mouldings that frame the main niche of the entrance recall portals of the Gothic Order.

The *iwan* of the main entrance is located opposite the main *iwan* of the structure. The *madrasa*'s eight chambers and two *iwans* open onto a courtyard of lateral rectangular shape. The porticoes that we are used to seeing in most of the *madrasa* courtyards are

Büyük hammam, soyunmalık after excavation and conservation, 14th century, Beçin.

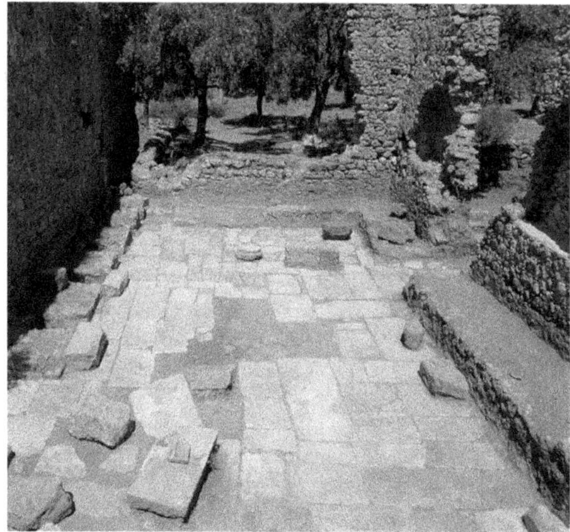

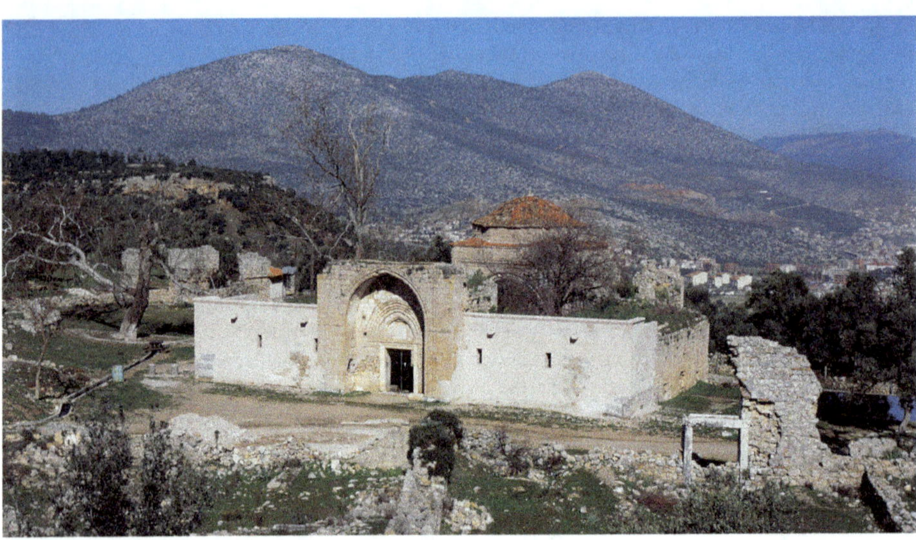

Ahmet Gazi madrasa, Entrance facade, 1375, Ahmet Gazi, Beçin.

not present here. The two large chambers on either side of the main *iwan* are classrooms. There is a fireplace in each of the cells as well as in the classrooms. On the spandrels of the *iwan*'s main arch are two lion figures which are very simply engraved and each holding a banner in its hands; the lion on the left holds a banner that reads "Ahmed Gazi" in Arabic script. We know that some animal figures like the "eagle" and the "lion" were used as symbols of the sultan during the Seljuq period, too; however, none of these were depicted carrying banners in their hands as they do here. Of the two graves in the main *iwan*, the one closer to the courtyard belongs to Ahmet Gazi. It has been suggested that the grave adjoining might belong to another Menteşe ruler, Şücaeddin Bey. The locals, who believe that these are the graves of great religious people, make offerings and pray when they visit the graves.

R. H. Ü.

I.2.d **Bey Hammam** (option)

The Bey Hammam is located 25 m.north of a large two-storey mansion located 50 m. to the west of the *madrasa*; the mansion probably belonged to one of the city's prominent people, perhaps even to Menteşe Bey.

Likely to have been constructed at the beginning of the 15th century, Bey Hammam lies approximately 100 m. away from the Büyük Hammam, which is dated to the second half of the 14th century. The close proximity of these two functionally identical structures leads one to believe that Bey Hammam may have been a private bathhouse belonging to the nearby mansion. The ornamental remains, traces of which can still be seen on the plaster inside the structure, shows that the building's workmanship was very fine. Although the superstructure has completely collapsed, a considerable portion of the walls is still standing. Excavations have revealed the foundations of the ruined disrobing area.

R. H. Ü.

I.2.e **Kızıl Han**

Directly across from Ahmet Gazi Madrasa in the town centre stands Orhan Mosque (1330-31), the largest one in Beçin. The road continues left round Orhan Mosque, past another fountain on the right, and then arrives at the Kızıl Han.
One of the most important Silk routes stretching from Europe to China traversed Anatolia; since the end of the 12th century, the Turks who ruled over Anatolia realised the material benefits brought about by transit trade and took measures in order to develop it. *Caravanserais*, constructed with this aim of development in mind, ensured traders a safe place to spend the night, while the market places established nearby made trading possible. Trade activities suddenly came alive once the emirates in West Anatolia, which had been in dispute with one another in the 14th century, came under Ottoman rule in the early 15th century and the region was made safe. Thus, the first *hans* constructed in West Anatolian towns like Bergama, Menemen and Tire, date to the 15th century.
The *hans* in West Anatolia are not magnificent and imposing like *caravanserais* of the Seljuq period. The two *hans* in Beçin, partly in good condition, are also plain, unimposing structures. Kızıl Han is a two-storey structure; its walls are still standing today, although its superstructure has almost entirely collapsed. Its general layout resembles the Döger *Caravanserai* near Afyon. Made up of a single lateral rectangular area, the ground floor is the stable where the pack animals were tethered and where some of the travellers would have spent the night. Traces of a staircase that would have led to two rooms on the upper floor are still visible to the left of the entrance door; travellers spent the night in these upper rooms, too.

R. H. Ü.

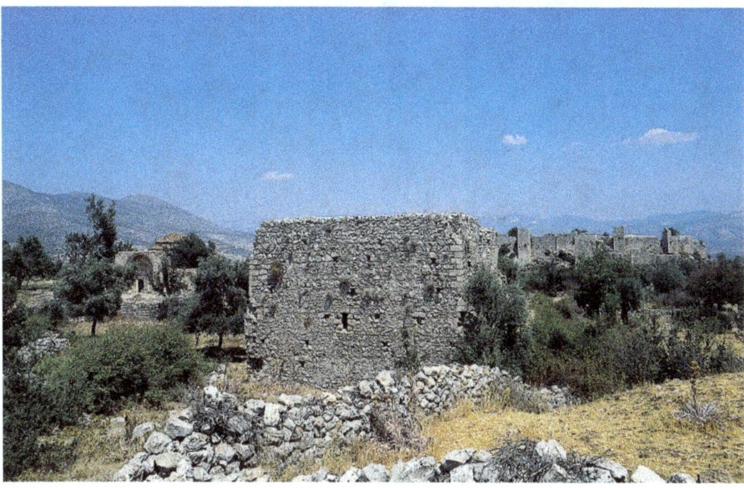

Kızıl Han, south facade, 15th century, Beçin.

Bafa Han is on the way to Söke from Milas (D.525) and right on the border between Aydın - Muğla provinces, and about 40 km. away from Milas.

I.3 ÇAMİÇİ

I.3.a **Bafa Han** (option)

The caravan traffic between the Menteşe Emirate's important city port of Balat (Miletus) and the capital Beçin was quite heavy. Though this traffic slowly began to decrease after the Emirate ceased to exist, it nevertheless continued for a very long time. Thus the Turkish traveller Evliya Çelebi, who visited Balat in the 1670's, recounts that active maritime trade was taking place in the town. The Bafa Han is located on the caravan route that stretches from Balat to Milas and Beçin. The *han* is made of a single rectangular area, and its entrance looks onto the road that passes in front of it.

The cistern adjoining the *han*, believed to have been built in the 14th century, attracts more attention than the *han*'s simple plan. A great number of cisterns exist in the rather rugged territory of Muğla province's rural area. Although not rich in natural water resources, the region receives the second highest rainfall in Turkey. These cisterns were constructed to collect rainwater in the autumn, winter, and spring months, to be used during the summer months, when almost no rain falls. Furthermore, water was always needed by travellers and pack animals spending the night at the *han*.

In order to collect water for the cistern, small channels were constructed on the long sides of the *han* at the level of the eaves. Rainwater that fell on the roof of the *han* was directed to the cylindrical

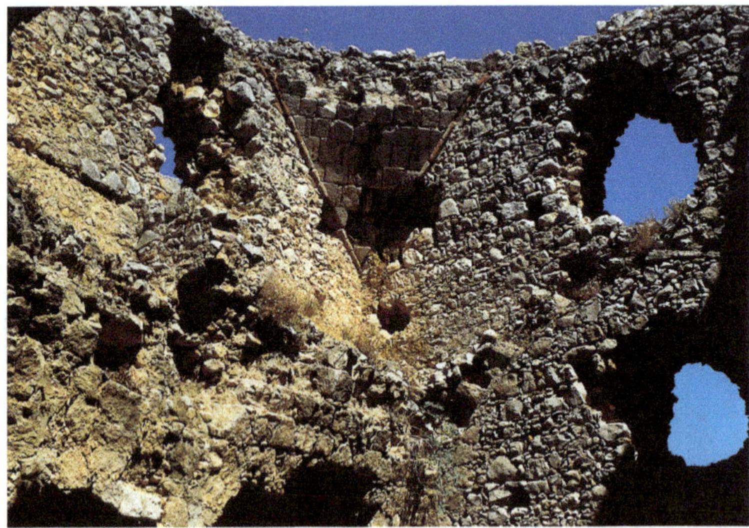

Kızıl Han, a pendentive in the northern upper-storey room, 15th century, Beçin.

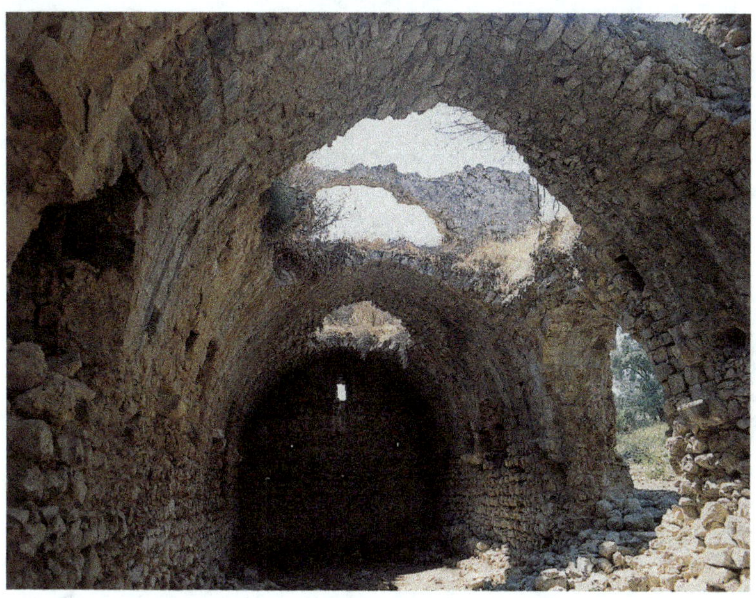

Kızıl Han, covered section, 15th century, Beçin.

cistern by means of these channels. The cistern is in good enough condition to be used even today, with the help of some simple renovation.

R. H. Ü.

The Milas-Söke main road (D.525) runs along the southern shore of Lake Bafa, a National Nature Park today. The steep stone-covered mountains (Beş Parmak Mountains) that descend sharply on the lake's northern shore offer an attractive view. If before reaching the lake you turn north from the village of Çamiçi and follow the shore of the lake, you will arrive at the remains of the ancient city of Heraclea-under-Latmus (today's Kapıkırı).

Balat is the Turkish name of the ancient city of Miletus. To get from Milas to Miletus you must take the main road D.525 in the direction of Akköy for approximately 55 km. If you are using public transport, go to Söke first and board a dolmush minibus to Balat. İlyas Bey Mosque Complex stands among the magnificent remains of buildings from the ancient world.

I.4 BALAT

The ancient city of Miletus, upon which Balat was founded, was one of the most important cities of the Ionian region. In those days, the city was located on a peninsula in the area where Büyük Menderes River (ancient Meandre) poured into the sea; however, today the city is nine km. from the sea because alluvium carried by the river has filled in the region. Laid out according to the famous city planner Hippodamus' grid plan, the

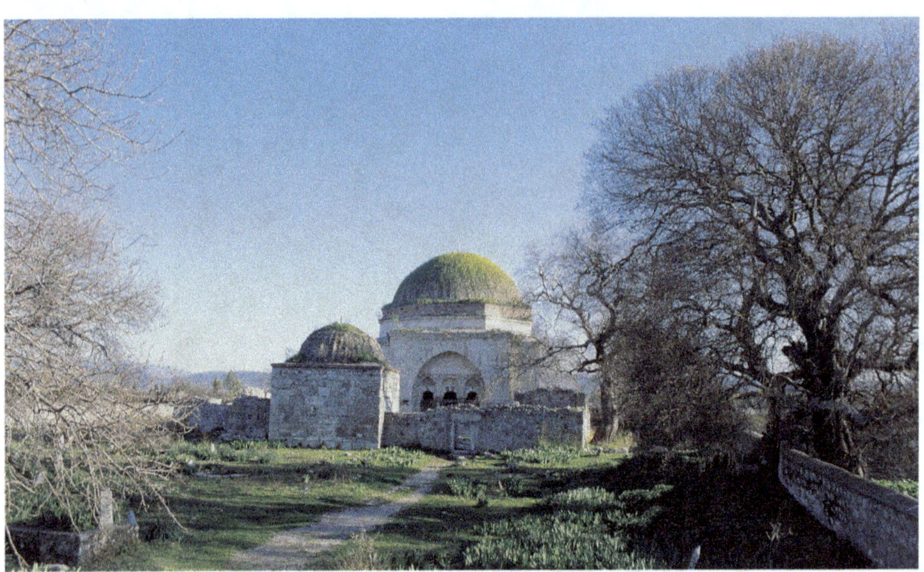

İlyas Bey Complex, view of mosque and madrasa from the north, 1404, İlyas Bey, Balat.

city became rich with the colonies it founded on the coasts of the Mediterranean and Black Seas and thereby became a chief site in the Ionian world. Although the city had once been home to the famous philosophers Thales, Anaximenes, and Anaximander (7th-5th century BC), and architects like Hippodamus (5th century BC) and Isidorus (who built Ayasofya in Istanbul in the 6th century AD), it only managed to preserve its importance up to the Roman period. After that it began to lose its popularity, once trade came to a halt as its harbours filled up with alluvium and became swamps. From this point on, it searched in vain for its magnificent days of the past. During the Byzantine period, a fortress was constructed on the hilltop where the theatre was located. In fact, the name Balat comes from the Turkish interpretation of the Greek name "Palatia" meaning palace.

At the beginning of the 1390s, the Menteşe Emirate was annexed to Ottoman territory. However, in the war that ensued between Sultan Beyazid I and Tamerlane around Ankara in 1402, İlyas Bey from the Menteşe dynastic house participated as an ally of Tamerlane. Once Sultan Beyazid I was defeated and taken prisoner, Tamerlane reinstated İlyas Bey to the Menteşe throne, as he did with the other rulers who assisted him. The capital of the re-established Menteşe Emirate was transferred from Beçin to Balat. The new capital became a market site where goods like saffron, sesame, honey, beeswax, and rugs were sold, especially during the time of the Menteşe Emirate. Wheat was also exported from here to Cyprus and Rhodes during this period. By the 19th century, however, the city was in a state of complete abandonment.

The structure can be reached either by proceeding along the ruins of the ancient city of Miletus (by passing through Faustina Baths), or by taking the main road leading from the ticket office to Balat village, and then following the road that turns left approximately 200 m. later. It is necessary for visitors travelling by car to park at the car park next to the ticket office.

I.4.a İlyas Bey Complex

The two separate paths that lead from the main road and Faustina Baths join up by the cemetery to the west of the *hammam*. Going through an opening in the modern walls one reaches the outer courtyard. Past the graves is the entrance to the inner courtyard shared by the mosque and the *madrasa*. The main entrance of the complex seems to be the gate structure on the east, which is connected via a path to another gate in the northeast corner of the inner courtyard. A tower-like structure to the west of the outer courtyard is hidden under the large tree behind the wall. Approaching the entrance to the inner courtyard, the section seen on the left, without a window, topped with a dome is the *dershane* of the *madrasa*; the large dome in the distance belongs to the mosque.

İlyas Bey Mosque

Although not of any special importance architecturally, the fine marble workmanship and rich ornamentation of the İlyas Bey Mosque is especially attractive. The walls are faced on the outside with marble from the ruins of Miletus; the marble work on the facade is similar to that seen in Milas Firuz Bey Mosque or the Selçuk İsa Bey Mosque, as well as in contemporary structures in neighbouring towns. Although this use of marble was

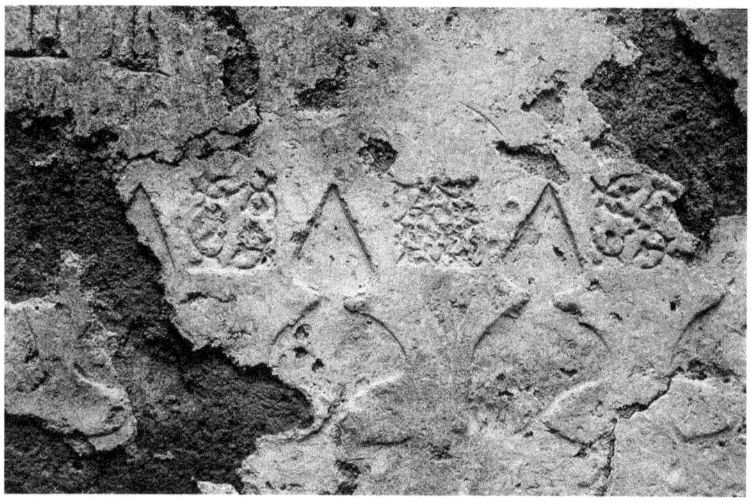

İlyas Bey Hammam, detail from the plaster decoration in the halvet, early 15th century, İlyas Bey, Balat.

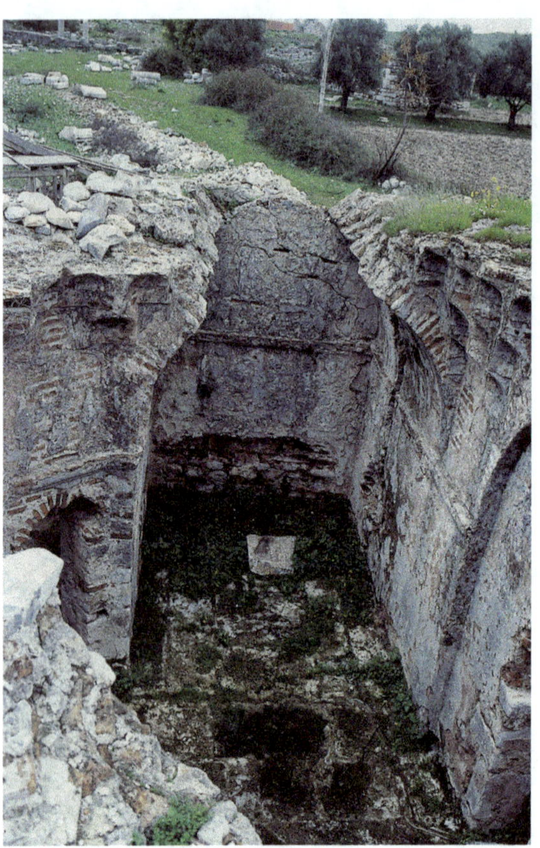

İlyas Bey Hammam, sıcaklık, early 15th century, İlyas Bey, Balat.

almost certainly due to the abundance of available marble from ancient ruins in the vicinity it may also be seen as a response to the architectural fashion of the period, a style we see in Italy, as well. On the eastern, western and southern fronts are four windows arranged in two rows; among the rich decorations on these window frames, the colourful stone inlay work is especially worth noting.

The design of the monumental entrance on the northern facade is different from the traditional designs of the Seljuq period that continued partially during the Emirates period. Two arches of the three-arched doorway are closed with latticed marble banisters. The arches have elaborate marble work. According to the Arabic inscription located on the central arch, İlyas Ibn Mehmed of the Menteşeoğulları Emirate commissioned the building, which was completed around the middle of the year 1404.

Walls over two 2 m. thick hold up the large, 14 m. diameter dome that covers a square prayer hall. The ornamentation seen here on the ceilings of the lower row of windows, consisting bands of calligraphy along with colourful inlaid stones, is present in very few structures. The marble *mihrab* (with a height of over 7 m. and a width of over 5 m.) also has superb stonework. The minaret, which would have been located above the northeast corner and reached via stairs set inside the wall, no longer exists.

İlyas Bey Madrasa

The *madrasa* cells surrounding the mosque courtyard on the east, west, and north sides are of various dimensions. The chambers' lack of orderly planning is in contradiction to the extremely careful workmanship of the mosque; therefore, the *madrasa* must have been constructed after the mosque. The small domed area across from the mosque is the *dershane*. Excavations conducted over the past several years have revealed the foundations of another *madrasa* adjoining the chambers at the west wing of the courtyard. This second *madrasa* is of an even later date.

Hammam

It is generally believed that İlyas Bey also commissioned the two *hammams* north of the mosque. It is not known for certain why two separate *hammams* with a 2 m. wide passageway in between were built right next to each other. In written sources, there are entries relating to the construction of *hammams*, which indicate that they would be built first to allow workers involved in the construction of the mosque to bathe when necessary. According to Islamic tradition, Muslims are required to wash their bodies completely and perform ablutions after sexual intercourse because a Muslim who goes onto the streets without having washed after sexual intercourse is believed to have committed a sin. Thus, it is thought that the smaller of the two baths here was constructed for the use of the workers. However, once it was realised that this bath of very small dimensions was going to be insufficient, a second, larger bath must have been constructed right next to it. After the construction of the mosque was complete, the newly built Büyük Hammam was supposedly set aside for men and the small one for women. In the Büyük Hammam, the rectangular vaulted chamber on the west is the water tank. The entrance is to the northeast into the *soyunmalık,* which is now in ruins. Going through a small room in the northeast corner, one reaches a small chamber –*ılıklık*– connected to another small chamber to the south –maybe the *traşlık*– and a very small one to the north adjoining the passageway. The large hall to the west is the *sıcaklık* with a T-shaped main section and two *halvets* in the corners. There are traces of beautiful plaster decoration on the walls formed by pressing moulds onto the wet plaster.

R. H. Ü.

EDUCATION IN THE *MADRASA*

Yekta Demiralp

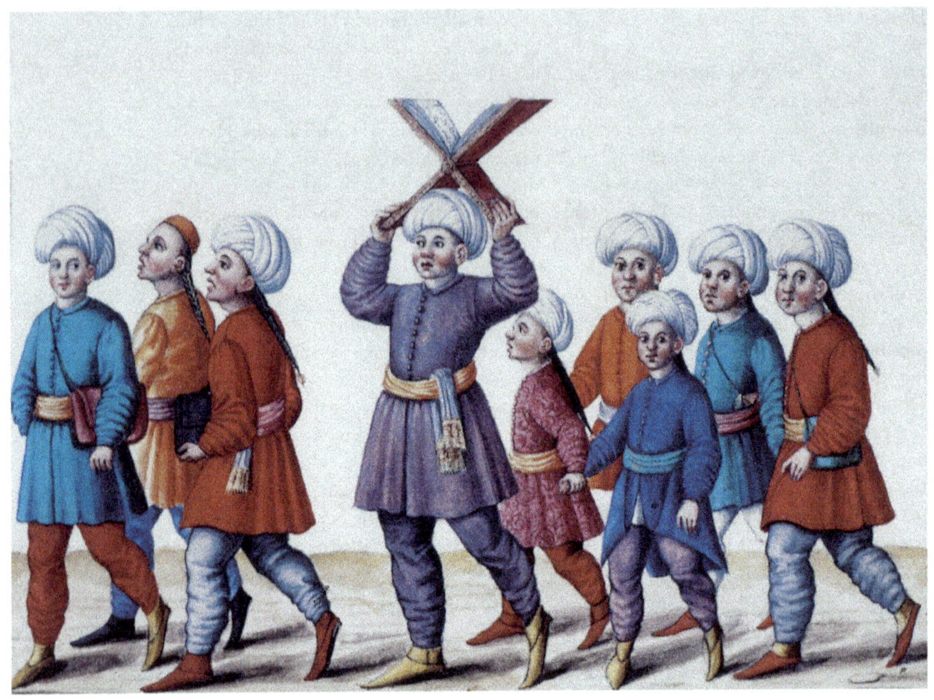

Madrasa students, Codex Vindobonensis, 8626, Österreichische Nationalbibliothek, Vienna.

Madrasas were educational institutions that first appeared in Islamic countries. Before *madrasas*, mosques were used as schools only outside the hours of worship and the education consisted solely of making students memorise the Koran and giving them religious information. In later times, it was considered inappropriate for mosques, which were used as places of worship, to be simultaneously used as schools, and so *hodjas* began giving lessons in their homes.

The earliest traces of buildings known as *madrasas* Date to the 10th century and are found in the Khorasan and Transoxiana. These buildings consisted of rooms lined up around an internal courtyard: an *iwan* in the middle of each side and student cells located in between. This layout also influenced the plans of *madrasas* constructed in Anatolia: a courtyard, *iwan*, winter *dershane* and student cells are found in all of the *madrasas* constructed in this period that have survived up to the present day. In addition to these architectural elements, some *madrasas* also have elements like *masjids*, *türbes*, fountains, and minarets. Not all of the *madrasas* constructed during the Anatolian Emirates and especially the Ottoman periods have the same plan layout.

Madrasas built by wealthy people and high state officials were not bound to the state; therefore, the state did not meet the expenses for feeding students or other expenses such as employee salaries and the structure's maintenance and repair work. For this reason, those who had the *madrasas* built would devote to their *madrasas* a part of their properties that regularly brought in income so that the *madrasa*'s expenses could be met after their death as well. As a result, each *madrasa* was a *waqf* institution.

The lessons taught, the periods when school was in session, the hours of daily lessons, and holidays differed from one *madrasa* to another. A *madrasa* was named according to the particular type of education given there: for example, *madrasas* in which the sayings of the prophet were taught were called *Darülhadis*; those in which people were made to memorise the Koran were called *Darülhuffaz*; and those where medicine was taught were called *Darüttıb*. Lessons were taught by teachers called *müderris* and in every *madrasa*, there was one or more *muid* that helped the students and made them repeat the lessons given by the *müderris*. Every *madrasa* had a doorman, a cleaning person, a librarian, and a "pointillist" who checked the attendance of the *madrasa* staff and students and reported absentees to the *waqf* board of trustees. Education in various fields was given in the *madrasas*, which were rated according to the wage of the *müderris*.

Between 20 to 40 students were educated in a single *madrasa*. However, *madrasas* constructed by the Ottoman sultans would accept as many students as there were student cells. In addition to meeting all their expenses, students were also given a small allowance.

Y. D.

Located 20 km. to the south of Balat, the Didyma Apollo Temple (Didim) still preserves its magnificence in spite of being largely in ruins today. The Altınkum beach is just 5 km. from the temple.

16 km. north of Balat, on the Balat-Söke main road, the ancient city of Priene charms its visitors with its magnificent location.

Another corner of the region worth visiting is the Dilek Peninsula National Park which functions as a plant and animal reserve and is located 30 km. south of Kuşadası. However, the Büyük Menderes River Delta, part of the National Park, can be visited by turning north at the village of Tuzburgazı; also the old village of Doğanbey will give a taste of Aegean and Mediterranean cultures.

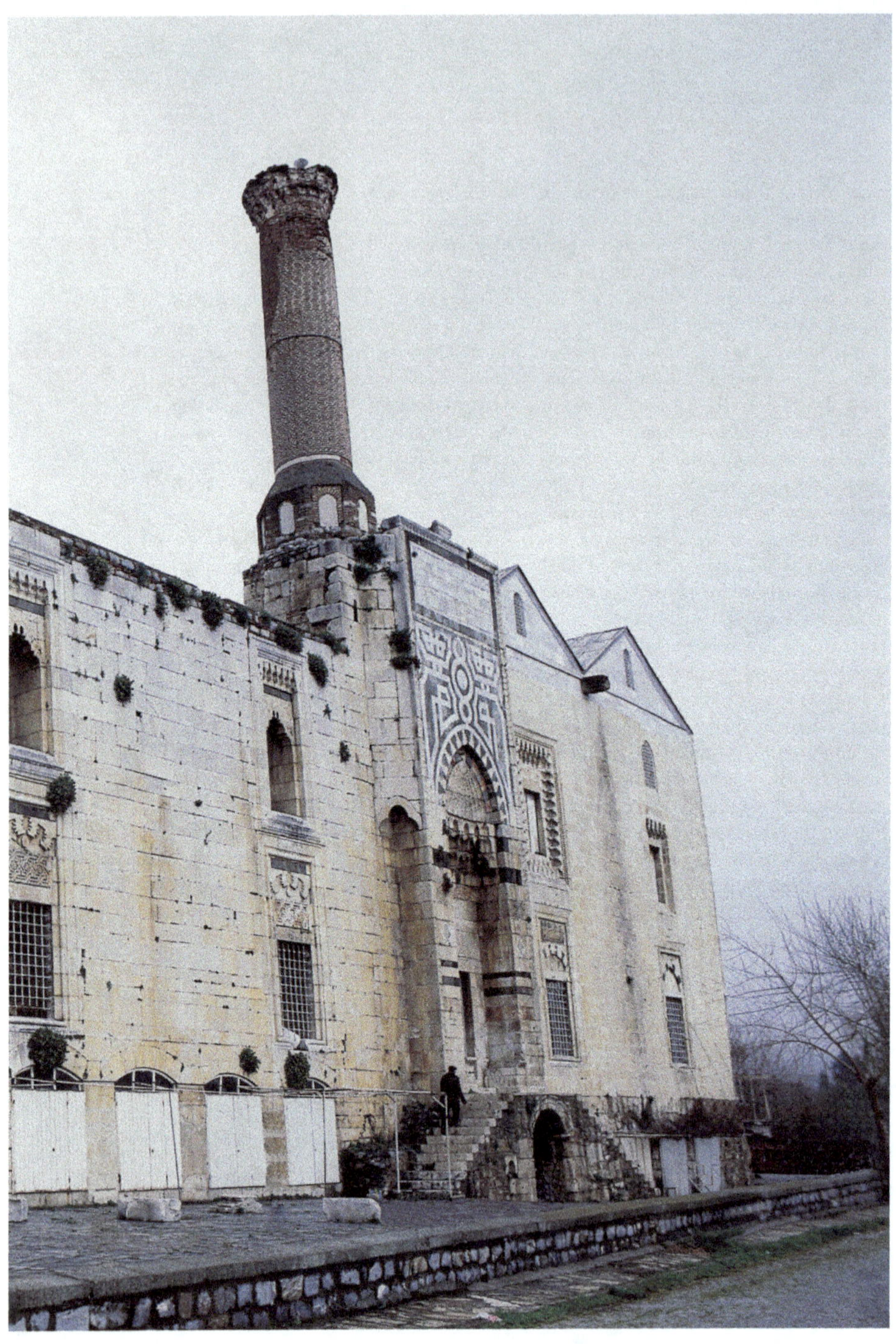

Protectors of the Arts and Artists

Lale Bulut, Ertan Daş, Aydoğan Demir, İnci Kuyulu

II.1 SELÇUK

II.1.a Saadet Hatun Hammam
II.1.b İsa Bey Hammam
II.1.c İsa Bey Mosque
II.1.d Citadel

II.2 TİRE

II.2.a Kutu Han
II.2.b Yahşi Bey (Yeşil İmaret) Mosque
II.2.c Yavukluoğlu (Yoğurtluoğlu) Complex

II.3 BİRGİ

II.3.a Great Mosque (Ulu Cami)
II.3.b Türbe of Aydınoğlu Mehmed Bey
II.3.c Türbe of Şah Sultan (option)

Burial Traditions Among the Turks

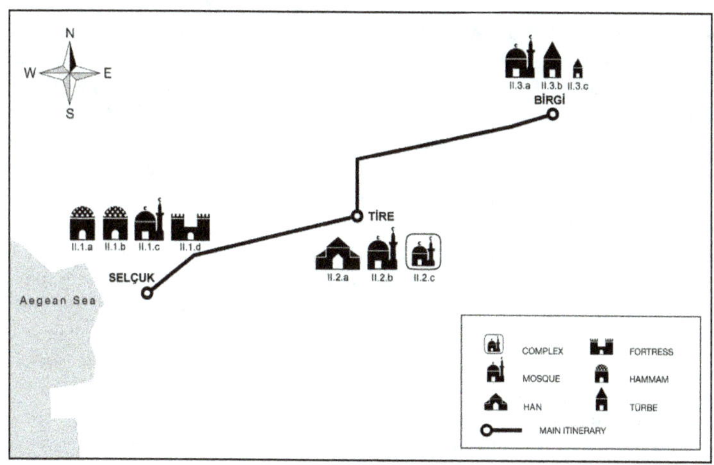

İsa Bey Mosque, west facade, 1375, İsa Bey, Selçuk.

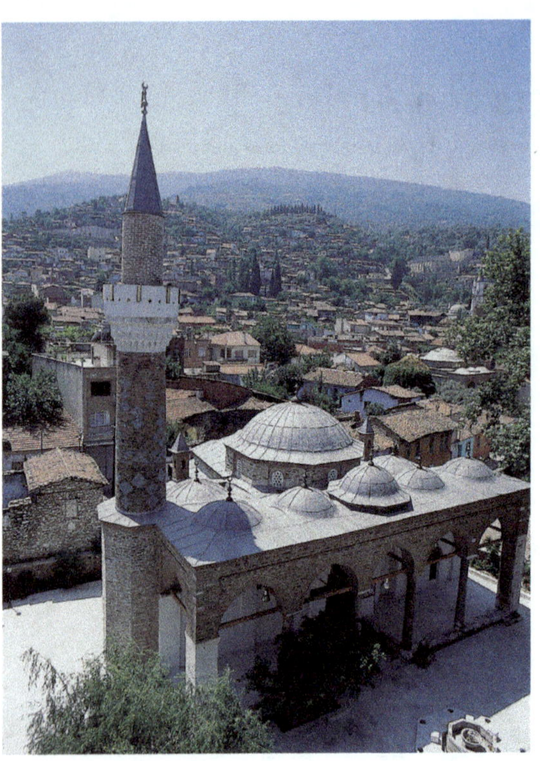

Yahşi Bey Mosque, general view from the northeast, 1441, Halil Yahşi Bey, Tire.

Mehmed Bey, son of Aydın, founded an Emirate at the beginning of the 14th century (1308) conquering Ayasuluğ (Selçuk-Ephesus), Tire, and Birgi in West Anatolia and later annexing the city of İzmir in 1317.

The Aydın Beys wasted no time in opening up to the seas; they launched campaigns to Evvoia Island, Peloponnesos Peninsula, Gelibolu, and Thrace, in particular, with their naval forces stationed in Ayasuluğ and İzmir. Venice and Genoa were the states most disturbed by these developments. Thanks to the Holy Union that it established against the danger of Aydın Emirate, Venice was able to carry on its existence in the Aegean. Because the rulers saw the destruction taking place on both sides of the war, they did not hesitate to make peace and sign trade treaties from time to time: cease-fires, peace, and trade treaties were signed between Aydın Emirate and Venice four times between the years 1337-1371.

A large part of the income from booty brought by these war-filled years, products provided by the bountiful land, and the tariffs, which increased thanks to the treaties with Venice, were spent on the construction of monumental works or religious and social functions. Mehmed Bey's (r. 1308-1334) Great Mosque in Birgi and İsa Bey's (r. 1360-1390) mosque and hammam in Selçuk are beautiful examples that are still with us today. Because Tire continued to be a lively commercial centre for many long centuries, a great number of *hans* were constructed in addition to mosques, *madrasas*, and *hammams*.

Scholars were held in high esteem in the Aydın Emirate. When the famous traveller Ibn Batuta came to Birgi in 1333, he was received by Mehmed Bey and treated with great respect. Michael Ducas, grandfather of the Byzantine historian Ducas (1400-1470), and a scholar himself, took refuge under İsa Bey after he managed to escape with his life from the disputes over the throne between the Cantecuzenus and the Palaeologus dynasties in Istanbul. İsa Bey provided Michael Ducas with everything necessary for his well-being and treated him like an important guest. In his book (1381) that he dedicated to İsa Bey, Hacı Pasha, a famous physician, introduced him both as a scholar and a sultan that supported scholars.

Although he insisted for a long time on defending his Emirate against the

Ottomans, in the end, Cüneyd (r. 1405-1426), the last Aydın Emir, had to surrender in 1426. After this date, land belonging to the Emirate was administered by the Ottomans as the Aydın Sanjak.

A. D.

II.1 SELÇUK

We know that throughout history some cities have changed their locations for socio-economic or natural reasons. Ephesus too changed its location at least three times for various reasons. There are different views as to where the exact location of the ancient city of Ephesus, an important trading port beginning in ancient times, was first settled. Not directly connected to the process of relocation, it is also known that the city changed its name frequently too. The ancient settlement of Ephesus, known as Hagios Theologos in the Middle Ages, took the name Ayasuluğ in the Turkish period and the name Selçuk in 1914. The city, which was re-established towards the end of the 4th century BC, in a narrow valley between Panayır Mountain and Bülbül Mountain, lived in prosperity during the Hellenistic and Roman periods. However, as a result of its harbour filling up with alluvium carried by the Küçük Menderes River, its connection to the sea was cut off and therefore, it lost the special feature of being a city port. In addition to being an important religious and commercial centre (the Temple of Artemis, one of the Seven Wonders of the World, was in Ephesus), it is clear that it was an important cultural and artistic centre as well. The large-scale 25,000-person capacity theatre still stands as proof of this. Ephesus is one of the seven churches of Christianity in the Book of Revelation. The spread of Christianity during Saint Paul's lengthy stay here, the presence of the tomb of Saint John, and the claim that the Virgin Mary lived in Ephesus for a while and died there means that the city holds great importance for Christians. Moreover, the Third Ecumenical Council was held in Ephesus in AD 431 debating the divine and human nature of Christ and concluded with the victory of Monophysitism and Nestorianism's conviction as heresy. In 449 a synod also gathered here to enforce Monophysitism. Intense building activity took place in Selçuk, one of Aydın Emirate's important cities that served as the capital of the Emirate between the years 1348-1390. The great majority of the buildings in the city that have survived up to the present day, stem from this period. Mehmed Bey's son İsa Bey commissioned Selçuk's most magnificent edifice, İsa Bey Mosque; some western travellers have thought that the building was converted into a mosque from the church of St. John.

The second itinerary begins at Selçuk and continues along the Küçük Menderes Plain. Since Ephesus, one of antiquity's most important cities, is also close to Selçuk, you can easily spend a large part of the first half of the day here. If you do not have a private car, you can reach Selçuk, Tire, Ödemiş, and Birgi by means of public transport that you pick up at the towns' bus stations. İzmir, the region's largest city, is a convenient place to spend the night and has accommodation offering various degrees of comfort.

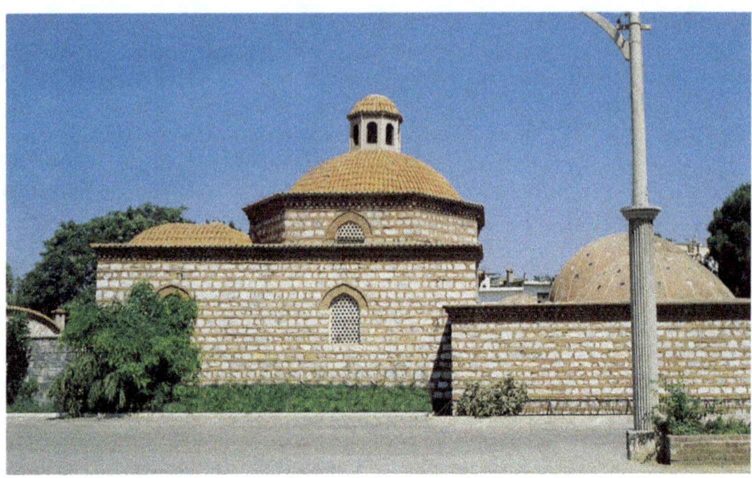

Saadet Hatun Hammam, east facade, 14th-15th century, Selçuk.

II.1.a **Saadet Hatun Hammam**

The Saadet Hatun Hammam is being used today as the Selçuk-Efes Museum's exhibition hall and is part of the museum's Ethnography Section. The Selçuk-Efes Museum is in the town centre on Ugur Mumcu Sevgi Road, behind the park at the junction. The museum is open between the hours of 08:00-12:00 and 13:00-17:30 in the winter months and 08:30-12:00 and 13:00-18:00 in the summer months. It is open every day of the week. There is an entrance fee. At the entrance, please inquire whether the hammam section is open.

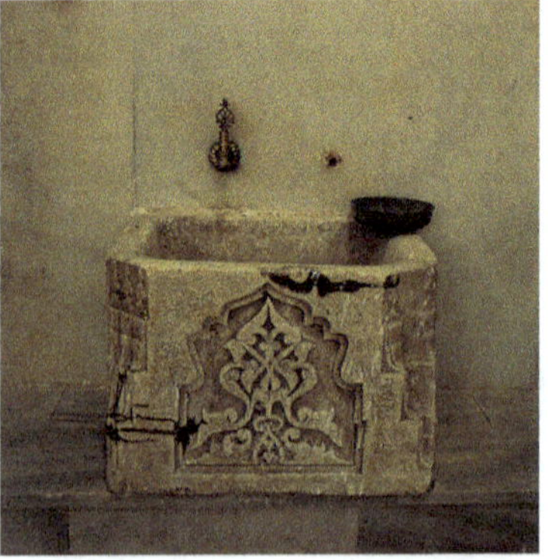

Saadet Hatun Hammam, marble basin in the sıcaklık, 14th-15th century, Selçuk.

Past the courtyard of the museum, first the *külhan* under the water tank is seen on the left. The broken inscription above the south entrance is partially readable and provides no date and a misreading caused this *hammam* to be known with the name Saadet Hatun (Lady Saadet) but this name is not found in archival documents. However, there is mention of a *hammam* that İsa Bey's wife Azize Hatun had built; therefore, the "Hatun Hammam" mentioned in the sources might be this one.
The entrance opens into the *soyunmalık,* enlarged into a rectangle with an additional area by the entrance. The building was restored between the years 1969-1972 and the *soyunmalık* is today used for displaying objects used in the Turkish *hammam* tradition. During the day *hammams* are generally lit by means of light wells in the superstructure, but during

the hours when the light is not sufficient oil lamps and candles were also lit. But here, aside from the windows on the walls, a polygonal lantern with a cupola was placed in the centre of the dome, the *sıcaklık*, however, is lit by light wells in the dome, every single one of which is fitted with a glass jar. Past the *ılıklık* and the *traşlık* is the *sıcaklık* consisting of three *iwans* and two *halvets*; forming the centre of this fan-like arrangement is a platform, normally very hot, on which people used to lie and sweat and be massaged and scrubbed. The re-used marble basins in the *iwans* and the *halvets* are attractive with their extremely fine decorations consisting of oil lamps, water birds, and floral motifs. A window opens from the central *iwan* onto the water tank stretching along the *sıcaklık* for purposes of cleaning and maintenance.

İ. K.

After leaving Selçuk-Efes Museum, turn from the parking area in the direction of Kuşadası and then turn right onto Kalinger street 30 m. later. Then 300 m. ahead, past the lonely column of the Artemision on the left, you will see İsa Bey Hammam enclosed by a chain-link fence.

II.1.b **İsa Bey Hammam**

Kalinger Street, Selçuk.

It is not known for certain whether or not this building, to the southwest of İsa Bey's Mosque, belonged to İsa Bey. Today there is no building inscription, but it is thought that an inscribed slab found in the garden of a nearby house and moved to Selçuk-Efes Museum might belong to this building. The inscription describes a *hammam* commissioned by Hoca Ali during the rule of İsa Bey in October-November 1364. Because of this, some researchers suggest that this *hammam* was not commissioned by İsa Bey. We do not have much information about the name Hoca Ali that is mentioned in the inscription; probably an important person of İsa Bey's period, Hoca Ali's gravestone dated 1378 is located in the courtyard of İsa Bey Mosque.

Its environs and interior have been cleaned with the excavation work in the recent years. The building has a plan layout common to the 14th and 15th centuries. Adjoining the *hammam* on the east are the remains of a row of chambers, which are supposedly shops with no organic connection to the *hammam*, although examples of shops adjoining the sides of some Turkish *hammams* are known. On the south is a low arch opening into the *külhan* under the water depot.

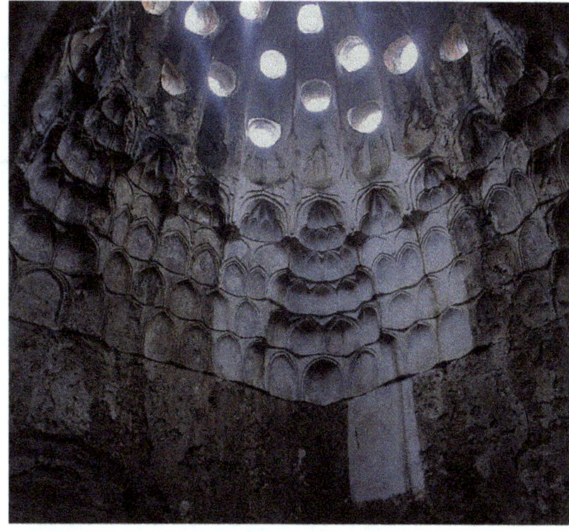

İsa Bey Hammam, transitional to the ılıklık dome, 14th–15th century, Selçuk.

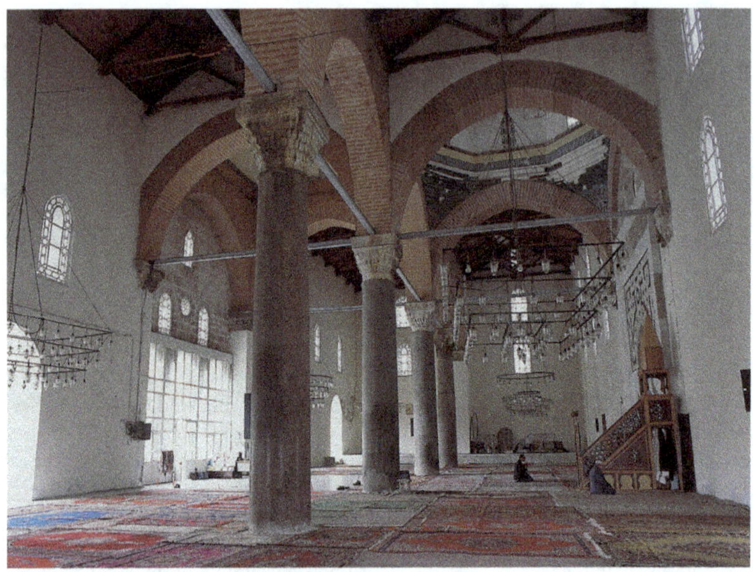

İsa Bey Mosque, prayer hall, 1375, İsa Bey, Selçuk.

The chambers adjoining the western facade, however, must be later additions. In some Turkish *hammams* there are special sections called "keçelik" that were constructed for the manufacture of felt. It is thought that of the sections added later, the one on the north might be a "keçelik".

The walls of the *soyunmalık* on the northern side are preserved only at ground level. With two of the four columns still standing, the *soyunmalık* has traces of a star-shaped fountain in the centre of the marble floor. Apart from the *soyunmalık*, the rest of the *hammam* is quite well preserved. The visitor passes from the *soyunmalık* to the corridor, *ılıklık*, and *sıcaklık* respectively. The *sıcaklık* consists of four *iwans* forming a cross with a dome in the centre and four *halvets* in the corners, each covered by a dome. Light coming through the wells in the domes, now without the glass jars, though, creates an exotic play of light and shadow inside. The water depot adjoins the southern wall of the *sıcaklık*. As seen in most *hammams*, there is a small window on the wall between the *sıcaklık* and the water tank for the purpose of cleaning and maintenance.

İ. K.

II.1.c **İsa Bey Mosque**

The building is at the northern end of Kalinger Street. It is open all day April-October, but only at prayer times during the winter months.

Kalinger Street ends at a tall wall –the qibla wall of İsa Bey Mosque– with a blocked archway in the middle, which is said to be the entrance when the structure was in use as a *caravanserai* in the 19th

century. This plain south facade forms a contrast to the main facade on the west. Located at the foot of Ayasuluğ Hill, the road on the right continues up hill to the Church of St. John and the citadel.
On the west is a superb facade with two rows of windows, a monumental portal, and a row of shops at ground level. The windows have elaborate frames with *muqarnas* and stone-inlay work. Two flights of steps crown a fountain beneath and reach the slender portal, which is especially attractive with its restored coloured marble work and fine craftsmanship. The inscription band reads the name of the founder as İsa Bey, son of Mehmed son of Aydın and the date of construction as 13 March 1375 by the architect Ali ibn al Dmashki (Ali, son of the Damascene). İsa Bey, who had this mosque built, was the youngest son of Aydın Emirate's founder Mehmed Bey, who divided the administration of the cities he conquered amongst his sons, but because İsa Bey was very young, he worked alongside his father. İsa Bey became the head of Aydın Emirate after his father and his older brothers Gazi Umur Bey and Hızır Bey, and ruled for approximately 30 years. When the Ottoman Sultan Bayezid I captured Alaşehir (ancient Philadelphia, one of the seven churches), İsa Bey showed devotion and obedience to the Sultan. Once Aydın Emirate became part of the Ottoman territory, its centre too moved from Ayasuluğ to Tire. The Ottoman dynasty increased their strength and power by establishing familial relations with the rulers of the Anatolian Emirates. In fact, once he had captured the lands belonging to Aydın Emirate, Sultan Bayezid I married Hafsa Hatun, İsa Bey's daughter.
The portal still bears the broken minaret; the second of which used to stand on the eastern portal of the courtyard. Selçuk İsa Bey Mosque has two minarets, something rarely seen in mosques of the Emirates period. On entering the courtyard notice the prayer hall to the right, and the eastern portal straight opposite the western and the northern portal, in the middle of the north wall of the courtyard. The northern and eastern portals are at a higher level than the courtyard thanks to the sloping terrain; the passageways of the eastern and the western portals have beautiful stone ornamentation on their ceilings, under the minarets. As understood from the remaining traces, the courtyard was originally enclosed on three sides with porticoes, therefore, it is one of the earliest examples of this kind of layout encountered before the Ottoman period.
The transept aisle that runs perpendicular to the *qibla* is covered with two domes; the lateral aisles parallel to the *qibla* wall have a pitched wooden roof; this layout is reminiscent of the famous Grand Mosque in Damascus. Both its plan and the colourful stone decorations on its portals and windows exhibit Syrian influence, which is explained by the architect's Damascan origins. There are tile decorations on the rim and pendentives of the dome above the transept aisle before the *mihrab*.
The original *mihrab* and *minbar* of this structure were destroyed in the 19th century. Although it is maintained by some that a section of the *mihrab* is being used again in İzmir Kestanepazarı Mosque, this is not correct, and the fragmented *mihrab* inscription is in the Agora Open Air Museum in İzmir.

İ. K.

The gravestones described below are displayed in the courtyard of İsa Bey Mosque. The Selçuk-Efes Museum is responsible for them, but they do not have inventory numbers.

Gravestone of Hoca Ali Ibn Salih

This is the gravestone of Hoca Ali Ibn Salih, who passed away in the year 1378. The stone is composed of three sections on top of one another, being the cylindrical base, polygonal body, and a polygonal finial. All the surfaces of the stone are ornamented with bands of scripture, which contain information about the "identity of the deceased" as well as terse sayings about death and life. In addition, it is also written that a master stonemason named Halil carved the stone. In Anatolia, the name of the stonemason was usually not written on the gravestones, which makes this one particularly noteworthy.

L. B.

Gravestone of Hacı Umur Ibn Menteşe

This magnificent gravestone belongs to Hacı Umur Ibn Menteşe, a member of the Menteşe dynasty, who passed away in the year 1400. The stone was carved out of an ancient column. On each face of the body, arranged with four faces and in two levels, there are pointed arched inscription panels. On these inscriptions is written "The identity of the deceased" and that "every living creature on earth is mortal". Inside the curvature of the arches are rosettes with flowers filling the spaces between them. The sharp corner lines have been softened with spiral columns. The base

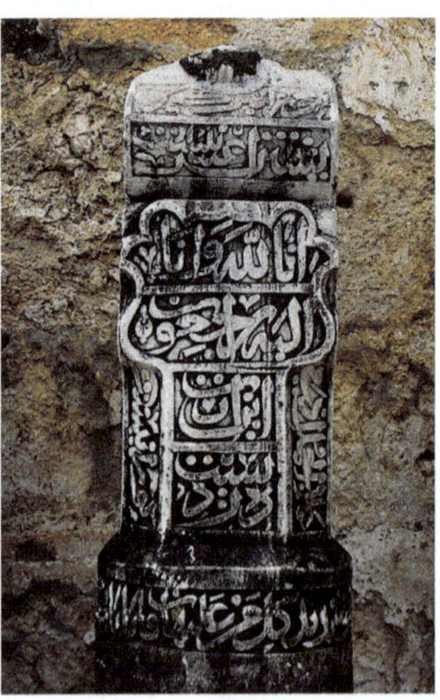

Gravestone of Hoca Ali Ibn Salih, 1378, Selçuk.

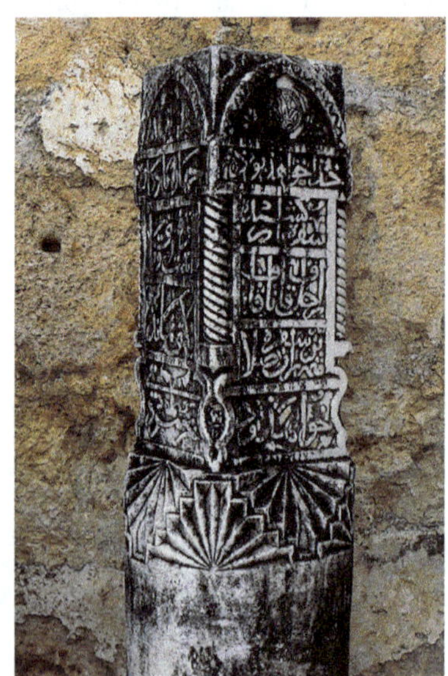

Gravestone of Hacı Umur Ibn Menteşe, 1400, Selçuk.

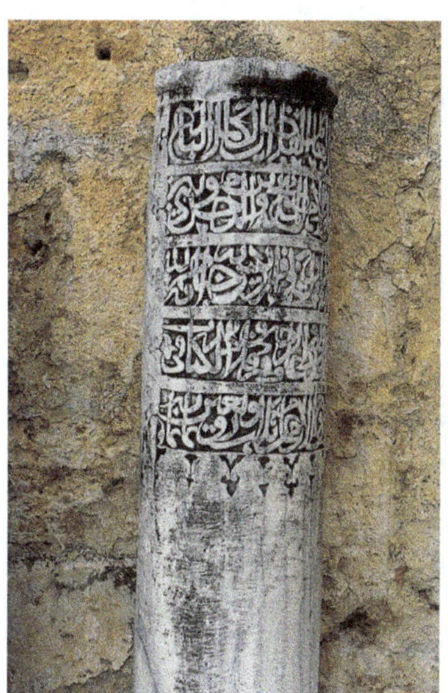

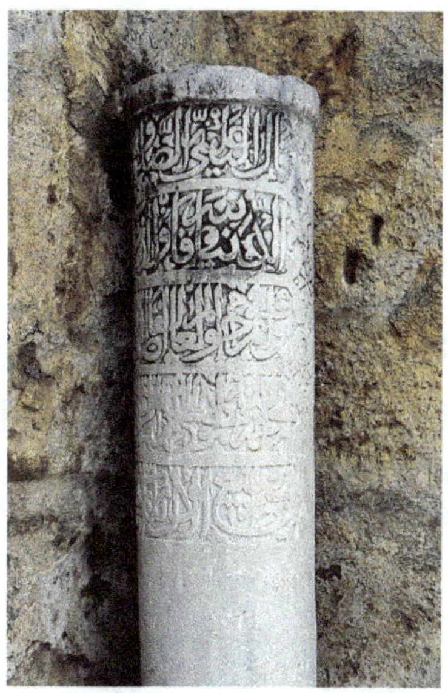

Gravestone of Muhlisüddin Hasan, 1439, Selçuk.

Gravestone of Hasan Ibn Kadı Baba Yulug, 1439, Selçuk.

upon which the body sits is ornamented with oyster-shell motifs.

L. B.

Gravestone of Muhlisüddin Hassan

This is the gravestone of a person named Hassan, who passed away on 30 August 1439. On the cylindrical marble gravestone, the inscriptions have been placed in cartouches. The palmette-like motifs below and on the edges of the inscriptions are particularly attractive. The owner of the gravestone, whose name is recorded as Muhlisüddin Hassan on the inscription, asks that passers-by will pray for him.

L. B.

Gravestone of Hassan Ibn Kadı Baba Yulug

This is the gravestone of Hassan Ibn Kadı Baba Yulug, who passed away in 1439. The cylindrical gravestone is very plain. The identity of the deceased and date of death are stated in the inscriptions written inside cartouches.

L. B.

II.1.d **Citadel**

The citadel is reached through St. John's Church on Ayasuluğ hill. However, it is not open to visitors.

The history of the Ayasuluğ Citadel stretches back as far as the 4th century AD. During the time of Byzantine Emperor Justinian (AD 527-565), a large church was constructed in the name of St. John next to the fortress and later surrounded by walls. St. John's Church was enclosed within the walls when the fortifications were extended because of the threat of Arab raids. The

Selçuk

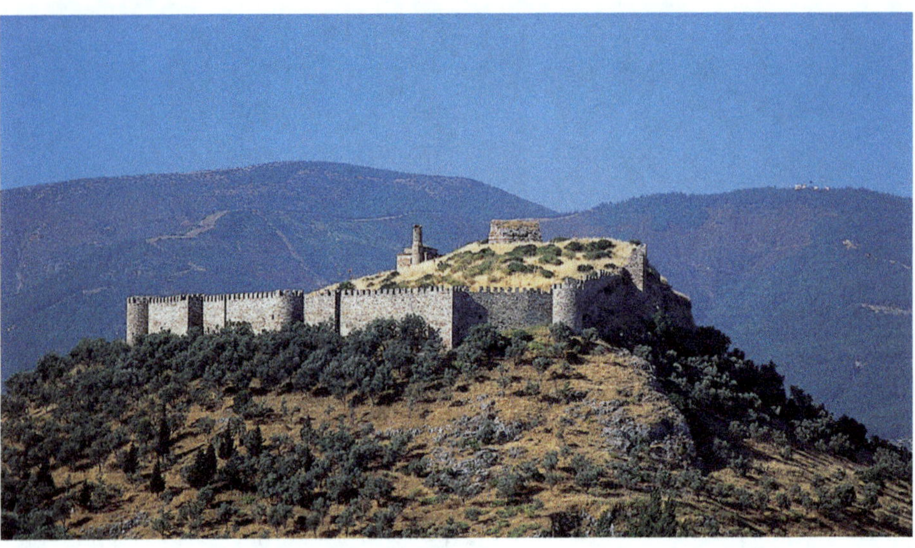

Selçuk Citadel, general view from the north, 15th century, Selçuk.

fortress was reinforced through periodic repairs after the city's fall to the hands of Mehmed Bey, son of Aydın, in 1304. During the Turkish period Ayasuluğ ranked high as one of the East Mediterranean's most lively trading centres and important harbours. Merchants from, for instance, Venice, Genoa and Pisa dealt in international trade here. Evidence of the importance of this town is several-fold: the Venetian Consulate became intensely active in the city beginning in 1337; the Genoese Consulate was founded here in 1351; the number of westerners living in the city increased and trade agreements were made between the Aydın Emirate and westerners.

As its importance continued throughout the Ottoman period, up to 60 military guards charged with protecting the citadel were present in the time of Sultan Mehmed II. At the end of the 16th century, various tax exemptions were granted to those working on the renovation of the citadel. Evliya Çelebi, who visited Ayasuluğ in 1671, states that the citadel, founded on a steep stone outcrop, had a circumference of 300 footsteps (approximately 200 meters) and that about 40 people were on duty.

The walls constructed of re-used materials are still in good condition today; the main entrance preserves its original shape; an old Byzantine chapel, several cisterns, and a small mosque are located within the walls.

İ. K.

The village of Şirince, founded by Rums who left after the Turks took the city, is a long way from the main road and has a calm atmosphere and a beautiful view. Most of the houses, with their regionally specific architecture, date from the 19th century. There are two churches, one of which was recently restored. Drinking a cup of well-steeped tea at the village café in the public square will make you forget all about the tiredness of the day. In order to get to Şirince, after leaving Selçuk, heading in the direction of İzmir, turn right (east) immediately after the city exit.

II.2 TİRE

Mehmed Bey, who divided his Emirate up among his sons, left the administration of Tire, one of the most important towns, to his fourth son Süleyman Şah. In 1390, Sultan Bayezid I, who annexed the Aydın Emirate onto the Ottoman State, forced İsa Bey of the Aydın dynasty to reside in Tire. From this point on, the Aydın dynasty, re-based in Tire, played an important role in the town's development. The Battle of Ankara that took place between Sultan Bayezid I and Tamerlane in 1402 resulted in the re-establishment of the Anatolian Emirates, which had supposedly been wiped off the stage of history. The battle's victor, Tamerlane, reinstated the administration of the emirates that Bayezid had added to Ottoman lands to the former owners; Musa Bey and his brother of the Aydın dynasty hosted Tamerlane in Tire during the winter of 1402-1403.

II.2.a **Kutu Han**

It is located at Tahtakale Square in Yeni Mahalle. Every day of the week except Tuesday, on the second floor of the building, two master workmen make rope from hemp using extremely simple methods and tools.

We begin to see city *hans* for the first time during the Emirates period. The number

Kutu Han, chambers on the second storey of the west wing, 15th century, Tire.

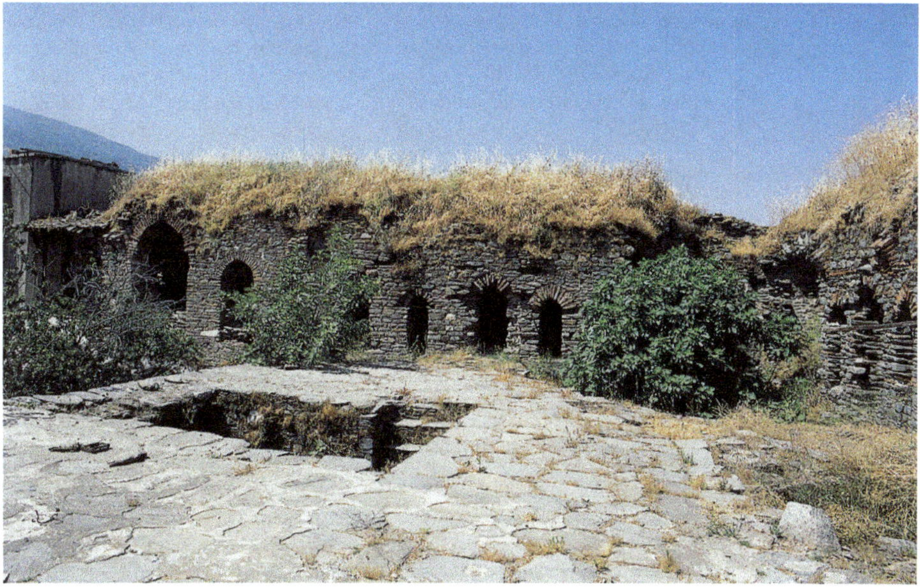

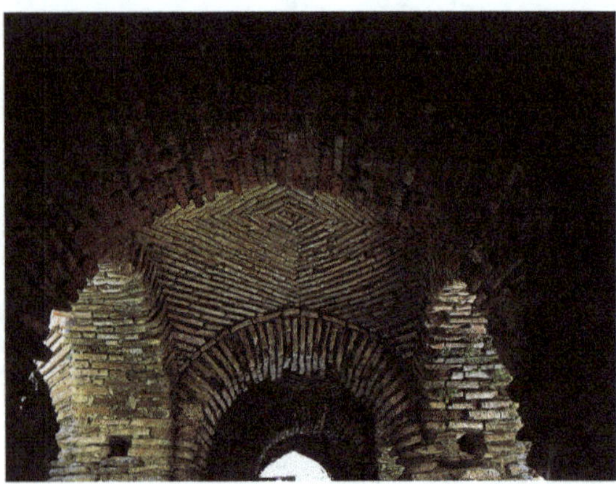

Kutu Han, vault from the stables, 15th century, Tire.

of *hans* constructed in a city was proportionate to that particular town's size and volume of trade activity. City *hans* are generally two-storied buildings consisting a square or rectangular courtyard surrounded with porticoes behind which rooms were located. Warehouses and stables were located on the lower floors and the upper floors were most likely to have been used as shops or boarding rooms.

Evliya Çelebi, one of the travellers who visited Tire in the 17th century, writes that 144 mosques and *masjids*, 30 *madrasas*, 60 *mekteps*, 13 *hammams*, 270 fountains, and 27 *hans* were present in Tire. These numbers indicate that Tire was a developed town. Today, the number of *hans* present in Tire is much lower than the figure given by Evliya Çelebi. However, the city's five *hans*, although only partially standing today, are proof of its once lively commercial life.

One of Sultan Murad II's high-ranking officers, Halil Yahşi Bey acted as governor of Aydın Province and made important contributions to Tire's development during the Early Ottoman period. All the structures devoted in the *waqf* charter to Yahşi Bey's İmaret Mosque, like Çöplü Han, *Arasta*, Toma Han, and Tahtakale Hammam are in the neighbourhood of Tahtakale (Yenipazar Market), which continues to be Tire's commercial centre, just as it was in the 15th century. Halil Yahşi Bey must have had Kutu Han built some time between his appointment as governor of Aydın Province in 1425-26 and 1441 when its *waqf* charter was prepared.

Kutu Han is a two-storied city *han* surrounded on the outside by 9 shops on the south, 11 shops on the west, and 10 shops on the north, which are all shaped like *iwans* closed off from the street with glass panes. Adjoining the eastern facade is an *arasta* –somewhat altered due to restorations– consisting a long, narrow covered corridor flanked with a total of 26 shops on both sides.

A broad doorway on the west side opens into the square courtyard. Additional shop areas were formed by closing off the porticoes on the courtyard's eastern, western, and southern sides. To the north of the courtyard are the stables with attractive cross-vaulted roofs built with bricks. In the middle of the northern side of the courtyard is a set of stairs leading to the terrace over the stables and the top floor. The porticoes located in front of the cells on the top floor and surrounding the courtyard have almost entirely collapsed. Cells of approximately equal sizes are lined up behind the porticoes.

İ. K.

II.2.b **Yahşi Bey (Yeşil İmaret) Mosque**

Cumhuriyet District (Mahallesi) 52, Aydınoğlu Street, Tire.

Yahşi Bey Mosque, used for a while as the Archaeology Museum, is one of the city's most important edifices. The mosque was definitely commissioned by Halil Yahşi Bey, one of Sultan Murad II's high-ranking officers, after Tire was taken under Ottoman rule; however, we do not know much about Halil Yahşi Bey. It is understood from the *waqf* charter dating to 1441 that he turned his vineyards and orchards in Ayasuluğ (Selçuk) together with buildings in Tire that provided income like *hans*, *hammams*, shops, etc. over to a *waqf*, in order to have this mosque survive through the centuries. The building must have been complete by the date of the *waqf* charter or a few years before.

Of the Tire mosques, the traveller Evliya Çelebi, who visited Tire in 1671, was most interested in the Yahşi Bey Mosque. He states that the building was constructed as a centre for the Mevlevi (whirling) *dervishes* and later converted into a mosque; its congregation was large due to the large number of *Mevlevis* residing in the vicinity.

Approaching from the street on the east, one faces the minaret unusually located on the northeast. The building was also given the name Yeşil İmaret thanks to the minaret decorated with reddish-brown, turquoise and green glazed bricks arranged in diamond shapes. According to a story, after the master workman had completed construction of the building, he prostrated himself and begged Allah, "Forgive me O Lord if I wasted any materials I used in the construction of this mosque and minaret or if I knowingly used too little mortar or plaster". The building was constructed with stone and brick; in the north of the mosque is a portico with five domed bays. Passing through the plain portal with a canopy of *muqarnas* one enters the central court surmounted with a dome and flanked with a *tabhane* on the east and the west each of which has a single fireplace and niche. The *tabhanes*' wooden door and window wings are ornamented with delicate workmanship as are the door wings of the portal. According to the inscription on the entrance wings, the name of the master woodworker was İlyas Ibn Mahmud. To the south is the prayer hall, very attractive with its unusual pentagonal shape surmounted with a semi-dome designed as an oyster shell. The wall paintings exposed during the restorations are visible today, along with paintings of a later date; and the *mihrab* is designed as a deep niche projecting out and decorated with paintings as well.

İ. K.

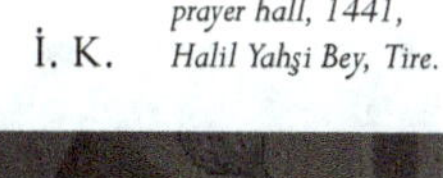

Yahşi Bey Mosque, prayer hall, 1441, Halil Yahşi Bey, Tire.

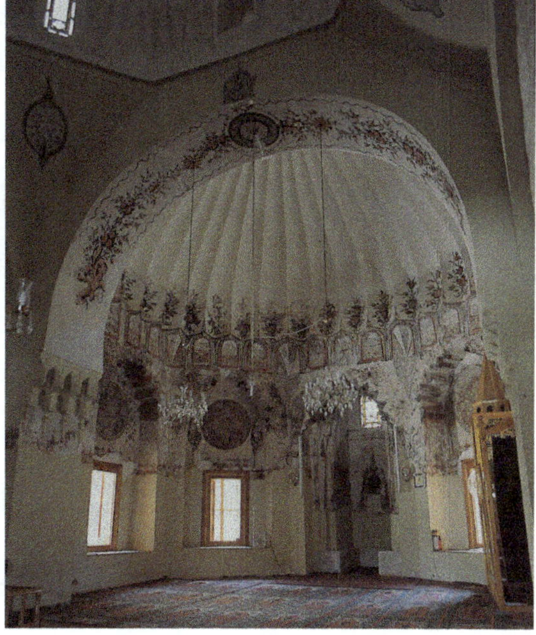

II.2.c Yavukluoğlu (Yoğurtluoğlu) Complex

Turan District (Mahallesi) 7, Kaplan Road, Tire. Work has begun in order to convert the mosque complex, which was restored several years ago, into a school for the handicapped. If you request the Belediye *or* Zabıta, *an official will accompany you and open the complex for you.*
Following the signpost for Kaplan, Yavukluoğlu Mosque Complex will be on your left, hidden among the olive trees, a little later.

Yahşi Bey Mosque, detail of the wooden door of the tabhane on the west, 1441, Halil Yahşi Bey, Tire.

Another important building in Tire constructed during the Ottoman period is the Yavukluoğlu Mosque Complex. Although it is not known for certain who had the 15th-century mosque built, it is said to be a person by the name of Yavukluoğlu or Yoğurtluoğlu Mehmed Bey. The story goes that Yavukluoğlu Mehmed Bey ruled over the western section of Tire, while the ruler of the eastern section of the town was Kazanoğlu Mehmed Bey, who commissioned the Kazanoğlu Mosque. In the 15th century these two local potentates became enemies and the attempts of the people of Tire to make peace between them failed. As time went on, their animosity increased and in the end Yavukluoğlu Mehmed Bey had Kazanoğlu Mehmed Bey killed. However, Yavukluoğlu Mehmed Bey deeply regretted his actions and he went to the holy man Buğday Dede's tomb and wept. Putting his regret into words, he wished for this local Saint to show him the way. Buğday Dede appeared before Yoğurtluoğlu Mehmed Bey and told him that if he held Kazanoğlu Mehmed Bey's funeral, he would be cleansed of his ill will. According to another version of the legend, the people of Tire successfully made peace between the two local potentates: they said that Kazanoğlu was going to visit the older Yavukluoğlu in person in order to make peace. Then as soon as Yavukluoğlu accepted the request, they went to Kazanoğlu and told him that Yavukluoğlu had invited him personally. When Kazanoğlu too accepted this offer, they brought the two enemies together and their animosity came to an end.
Consisting a mosque, *madrasa*, *muvakkithane*, a soup kitachen or a *mektep* and a *hammam*, which has since fallen into ruins, the complex rises on a slight slope, from the north upwards to the south and has recently undergone restoration, which

Yavukluoğlu Complex, General view from the southeast, 15th century, Yavukluoğlu Mehmed Bey, Tire.

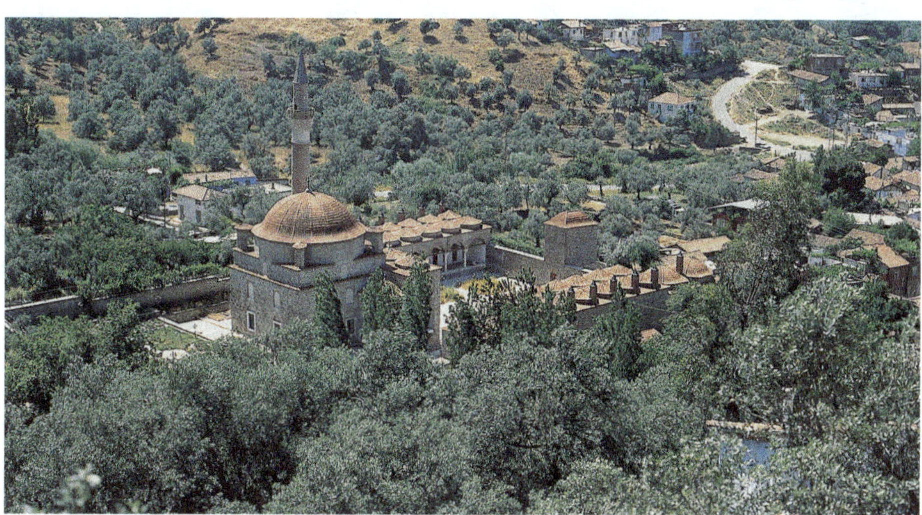

was completed in 1997 after seven years. Of the structures that make up the mosque complex, the mosque and *madrasa* share the same courtyard; the mosque placed on the southern side of the courtyard is a simple square structure surmounted by a dome. In the front is a five-bayed portico, with lovely arches, ending at the minaret on the west; to the east adjoins a room with a *mihrab*, whose function is not clear but it is suggested that it may be the library. By the eastern entrance to the courtyard is a room, which functions as a place to take the ritual ablution. Each *madrasa* cell on the eastern and western sides has a fireplace and is covered by a dome; in the front are domed porticoes, a bit shorter in length though. The courtyard is bounded by a blind wall to the north, pierced with a doorway in the middle, which is topped with a room, presumably the *muvakkithane* –the observatory or the clock room. Such rooms are known from ancient times and were built near mosques and equipped with necessary instruments in order to work out the times of sunrise and sunset for the calls to prayer; the person in charge, a combination of an astronomer and an astrologer, would also give astrological service. In the adjoining area to the north, on the east side, is a two-section building which might have been a soup kitchen or a *mektep*.

İ. K.

Yavukluoğlu Complex, showing the chambers on the west wing and the portico in front, 15th century, Yavukluoğlu Mehmed Bey, Tire.

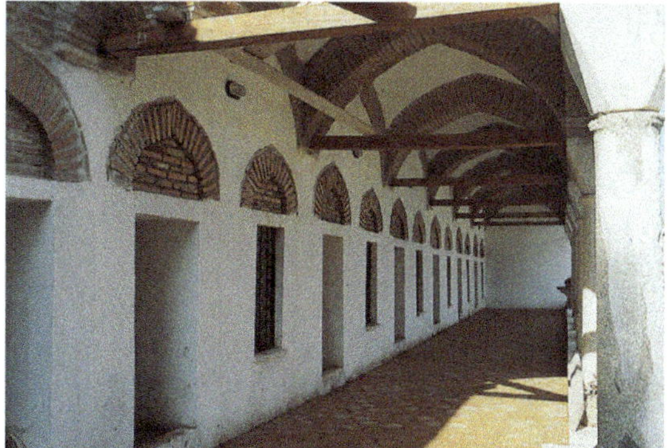

Yavukluoğlu Complex, south facade of the mosque, 15th century, Yavukluoğlu Mehmed Bey, Tire.

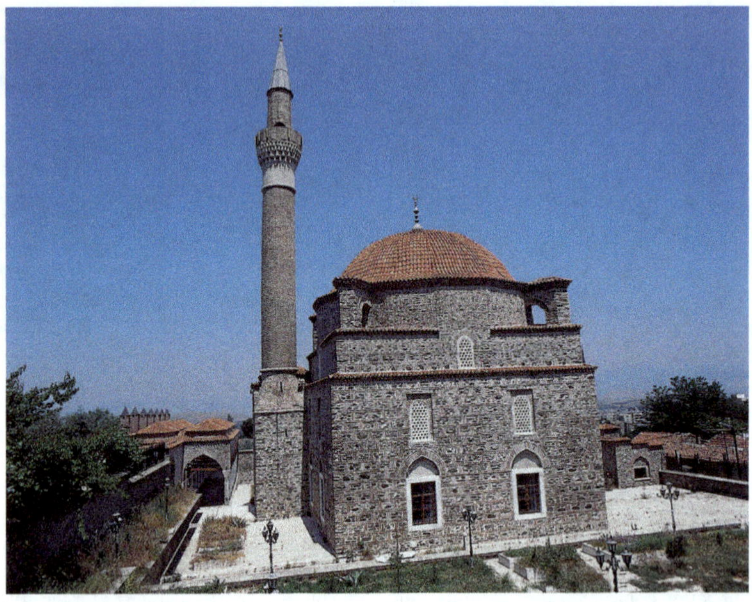

If you continue along the road up hill instead of turning back from Yavukluoğlu Mosque Complex, you will reach the Kaplan area overlooking the Küçük Menderes Plain. There are several restaurants here.
There is a market twice a week in Tire: at the Tuesday market all kinds of goods are sold; at the Friday market, though, the villagers sell fruits and vegetables they have grown. Tire is famous for its köfte *(a kind of meatball). Strolling in the old parts of the town with labyrinthine-like streets, you will find many more mosques,* hammams, *old houses –some of which are very dilapidated. The small Archaeological Museum has an interesting collection of artefacts from Antiquity and the Middle Ages; the Ottoman tombstones in the backyard and the 19th-century Çanakkale pottery are noteworthy.*

There are regular dolmush *minibuses from Tire bus station to Ödemiş and from Ödemiş bus station to Birgi.*

II.3 BİRGİ

Mehmed Bey, one of the commanders of the Germiyan Emirate's army, founded an Emirate named after his father Aydın, in the regions of ancient Lydia and Ionia in West Anatolia and made Birgi his centre. Also known by his nickname "Mübarizüddin", "the Warrior for the Religion", Mehmed Bey divided up the regions he had conquered among his sons. Mehmed Bey carried out various raids on the Aegean and Rumelian shores with the naval forces he had established in Ayasu-

luğ and İzmir. When Mehmed Bey passed away in 1334, his son Umur Bey took his place.
Ibn Batuta, who in the year 1333 visited Birgi, stayed for 14 days at the palace of Mehmed Bey, the founder of the Emirate. According to information the traveller gives about the palace, Mehmed Bey's quarters were located in a high section. At the corners of the pool in the middle of the apartment were bronze statues of lions with water flowing out of their mouths and the inner courtyard was surrounded with rooms side by side. The traveller speaks with praise of 20 young Rum men with long blonde hair wearing satin dresses that welcomed them on arrival at the palace, and of the golden spoons and ceramic bowls he saw there.

II.3.a **Great Mosque**

One of the first works constructed in Birgi during the Aydın Emirate period is the Great Mosque, rising on top of a steep creek bank. Entering the courtyard the visitor is faced with a rather rectangular appearance at first, broken by a triangular pediment above the portal with a lean-to roof. This plain and somewhat unattractive northern facade, built with unhewn stones, is accentuated by the marble frames of the lower windows and the marble portal ornamented with carved rosettes, a tree-of-life motif and an inscription giving the name of the founder as Mehmed Bey, son of Aydın and the date of construction as 1312-13. Going through the portal one enters the central aisle of the prayer hall designed as a basilica with five aisles separated from

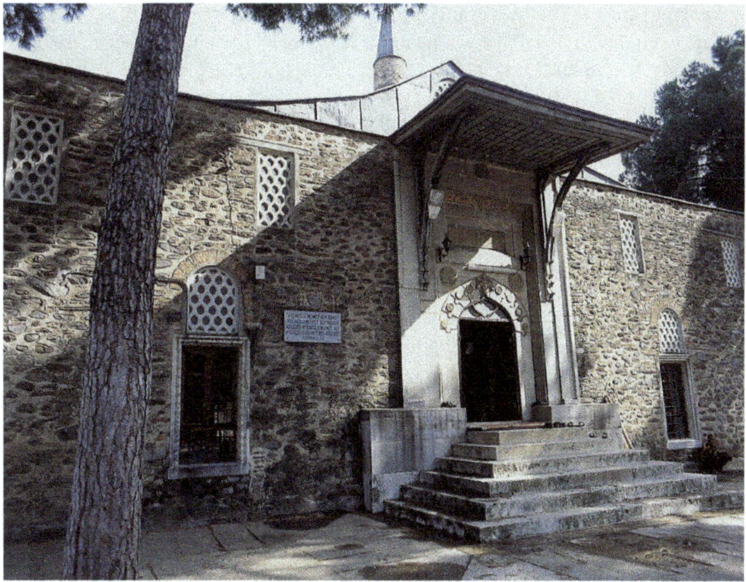

Great Mosque, north facade, 1312-13, Aydınoğlu Mehmed Bey, Birgi.

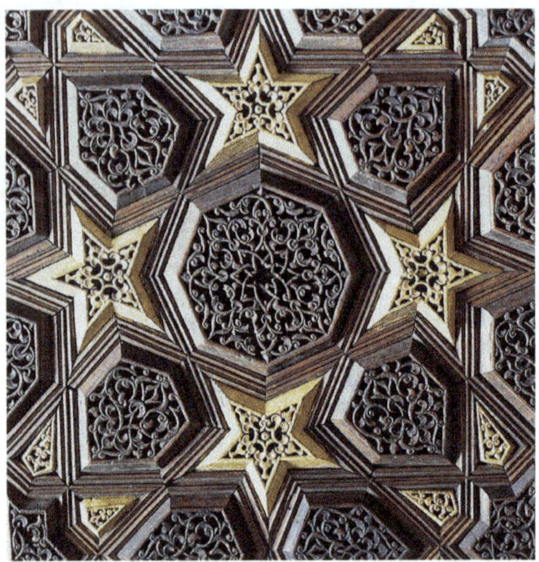

Great Mosque, detail of wooden minbar, 1322, Aydınoğlu Mehmed Bey, Birgi.

one another by rows of re-used columns supporting arches. The ceiling and roof, today covered with metal plates, is made of wood; the square area before the *mihrab* is covered with a dome.

The structure has dazzling examples of tile art and woodwork: the *mihrab* in tile-mosaic technique with turquoise and aubergine-purple tiles following the Seljuq tradition; the northern arch of this square area before the *mihrab* is also decorated in tile mosaic.

The building's *minbar* and window wings are exquisite examples of 14th-century wood workmanship. There are different decorations on every single one of the wooden wings attached to the inner side of the lower row of windows; all bear religious inscriptions. The *minbar* made of walnut wood is ornamented in the *kündekari* technique without any nails or glue. There are numerous Arabic inscriptions on the *minbar*, mainly religious; according to the ones on the right side, the *minbar* was made in 1322 by a master craftsman named Muzaffereddin Ibn Abdülvahid. The door wings of the *minbar*, stolen in 1995, were recovered as they were being sold at an auction in London.

On leaving the prayer hall, one should observe the mosque from the outside starting with the east facade. The windows are arranged in two rows; the lower ones on the east have different ornamentation. There is another portal in the middle of the eastern facade, which is quite plain like the northern one. The marble blocks on the eastern and southern facades of the building facing the street are re-used material from earlier structures, as is the statue of a lion placed in the southeast corner. The base of the minaret is built of marble blocks and it adjoins the western end of the southern facade which is entirely faced with marble; its body rising directly from the base is decorated in zigzags and chevrons with glazed bricks and tile mosaics. The western facade is very plain and the building just 1.30 m. to the west is the Türbe of Mehmed Bey.

İ. K.

II.3.b Türbe of Aydınoğlu Mehmed Bey

Mehmed Bey, son of Aydın, became ill after falling off his horse during a hunt, and passed away in 1334. The *türbe* in which he is buried is located just to the west of Great Mosque, the mosque he had built. It was most likely to have been constructed while Mehmed Bey was still healthy. The inscription on the *türbe* door reads 9 January 1334; this must be either the date of Mehmed Bey's death, or the date he was buried in the *türbe*.

The modest grave to the right of the entrance door is known among the people as the King's Daughter's Grave. According to one legend, the daughter of Birgi's Byzantine Christian ruler saw Mehmed Bey at war as he besieged the city and she fell in love with him. She wrote a letter to Mehmed Bey informing him that she accepted Islam and she was secretly going to open the city gate. The people, who learned that the Christian ruler's daughter had helped Mehmed Bey capture the city in this way, killed her at the place where the grave is today. As soon as Mehmed Bey conquered the city, he had the young woman buried at the place she had been killed. Similar stories relating to the conquering of various Byzantine fortresses are common.

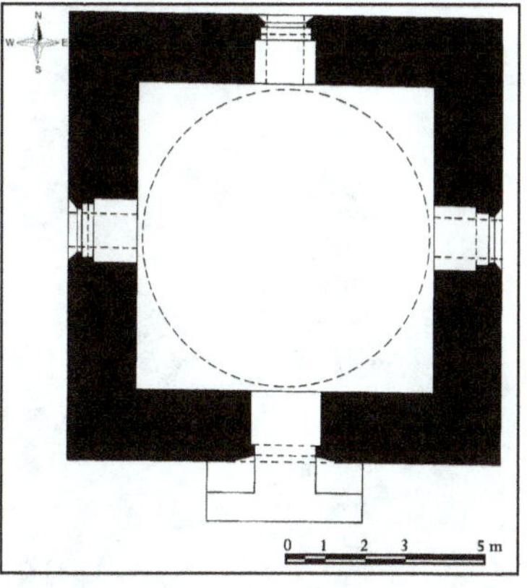

Plan of Aydınoğlu Mehmed Bey Turbe, Birgi (from R. H. Ünal).

This plain, square building is faced with marble blocks and topped with a dome. There are rectangular windows on the eastern, western, and northern fronts; the entrance door, which has a marble frame like the windows, is in the middle of the southern facade. The wooden

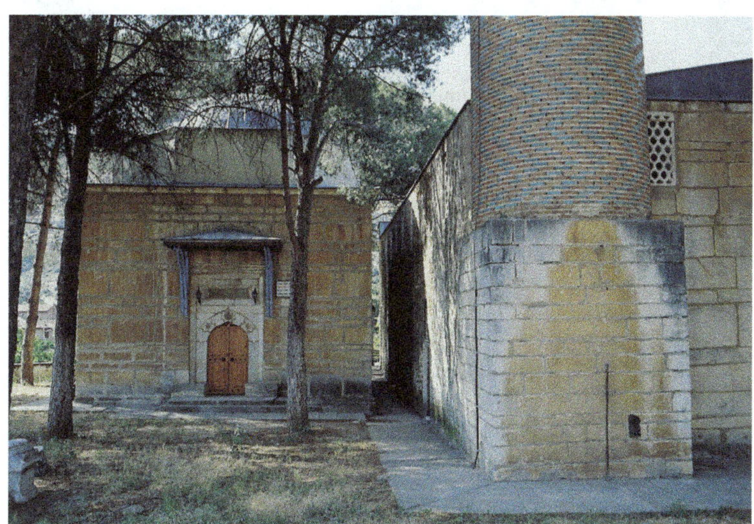

Türbe of Aydınoğlu Mehmed Bey, south facade, 1334, Aydınoğlu Mehmed Bey, Birgi.

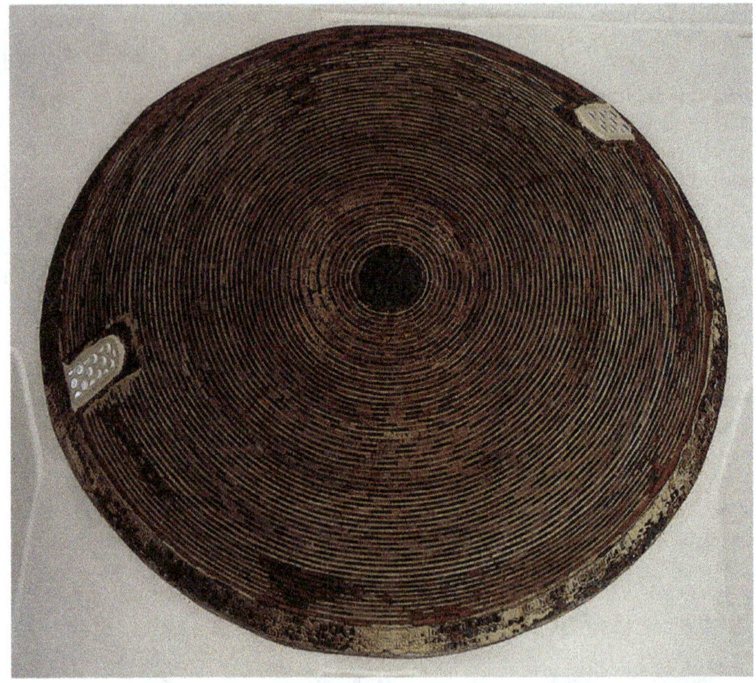

Türbe of Aydınoğlu Mehmed Bey, dome, 1334, Aydınoğlu Mehmed Bey, Birgi.

lean-to roof above the entrance is a recent addition and the ornamented marble blocks above are re-used Byzantine material. On entering, raise your eyes to the inner side of the dome, which is decorated with concentric rows of glazed bricks, and the band along the edge and medallion in the centre are of tile mosaic.

The graves of four members of the Aydın dynasty are found in the *türbe*. There is no date on the head- or footstones; only the names of those buried are given. Once through the entrance, the first grave belongs to one of Mehmed Bey's sons, İsa Bey, who is thought to have died before 1402. The second grave belongs to Bahadır Bey, sometimes referred to in sources as İbrahim Bey, who is thought to have passed away sometime before 1347. The third grave belongs to Mehmed Bey, son of Aydın; and the fourth is that of Umur Bey, Mehmed Bey's second son also known by the name Bahaeddin Bey, who died in battle in 1348.

İ. K.

The Türbe of Şah Sultan is opposite the Great Mosque on the south, outside the courtyard. When you exit the mosque's courtyard and turn right, you reach the türbe *100 m. ahead. Today it stands in the middle of the road.*

II.3.c **Türbe of Şah Sultan** (option)

This hexagonal building, also known as Türbe of Ümmü Sultan, is built with unhewn stones and brick; re-used materials were also used here and there. In the last renovation, a concrete eve was added to the structure and the dome's external surface was coated with concrete. A portal slightly protrudes from the hexagonal body on the south, which is flanked with windows on both sides. The building is entered through an archway with a low ceiling, directly above which is a two-line Arabic inscription on a marble plaque telling that Mehmed Bey had this *türbe* built for his sister, Sultan Şah Hatun and it was completed in June 1310. The interior is also a regular hexagon in plan, surmounted by a brick dome; there are shallow niches covered by pointed arches made of bricks on each face of the hexagon; some of the arches were damaged during restoration. There is a grave without any special characteristics with broken foot- and headstones inside the *türbe*. There is no sign that might indicate the existence of a crypt.

İ. K.

BURIAL TRADITIONS AMONG THE TURKS

Ertan Daş

Shamanism, a religion widespread among the Turks before they accepted Islam, was a kind of belief that fundamentally worshipped nature and supernatural spirits. The religious leader –shaman– would establish a relationship with the supernatural spirits, perform magic, and heal the sick. As in all religions, the shaman religion also believed in the revival of the dead. Thus wealthy followers of shamanism made sheltered graves for themselves so that the bodies present in the grave would not be damaged until the day of resurrection. We also observe that, just as boats were placed in the graves of Egyptian pharaohs so that they would be able to travel on the Nile once they were resurrected, nomadic Turks were buried with their horses.

The Turks continued to be influenced by the beliefs dealing with the burial cult that they acquired in Central Asia even after they converted to Islam. According to Islamic belief, when a person, who is made of earth, dies, he or she is buried in the earth and will return to earth. According to Islamic tradition, the body is buried so that the head is in the direction of the west, his face turned towards the *qibla*, and the body rests on the right arm. Mummifying the body goes against Islamic belief. Nevertheless, mummified bodies are encountered in some of the *türbe*s in the Anatolian towns of Amasya, Kemah, Harput, etc. In spite of poor conditions of preservation, these mummies have survived until the present day.

Ever since the Karahanid period (842-1212), Turkish architecture has produced extremely interesting burial memorials. Especially during the Seljuq period (12th-13th century) in various examples of *kümbet*s –another name for monumental tombs– the dead were buried in a basement crypt. Closed to visitors, this section is generally covered with earth up to half its height; there is a small opening on one of the facades providing access to the crypt for maintenance and cleaning; however, beginning in the Emirates period (14th century), the crypt floor slowly disappeared. The body of the *kümbet* rising over the crypt can have a cubic, polygonal or cylindrical shape; a *mihrab* and a symbolic sarcophagus made of wood, plaster, or stone is also found on this floor; the structure is usually covered by a dome. During the Anatolian Seljuq period, the dome was concealed from the outside by a pyramidal or conical spire, which slowly began to disappear during the Ottoman period.

During the Seljuq, Emirates, and Ottoman periods in Anatolia, cemeteries were not very far from the town centre. Usually religious men or high-ranking government officials were buried in the small graveyards formed in mosque courtyards.

In Anatolia and most other Islamic countries, a stone is erected at the head and foot ends of graves that are independent or inside *türbe*s. These stones are important documents that give us information detailing the beliefs, aesthetic taste, understanding of art, and even health of the period in which they were made. The ornamentation of gravestones with writing and decorations is a tradition that has been continuous in Anatolia since Seljuq times. In the vicinities of Erzurum and Diyarbakır in the East and Southeast Anatolia respectively there are gravestones of the Akkoyunids and Karakoyunids that are shaped like sheep and rams and embellished with decorative figures.

The nomadic tribes of Turcomans carried this tradition into Central Anatolia as far as Afyon and Aydın. In Ahlat, the Seljuq-period city famous for its gravestones, and in some other Anatolian cities, gravestones bear decorations of figures showing traces of shamanist traditions as well as floral and geometric decorations. Bird figures symbolising the spirits' rise to the sky in shaman belief, figure predominantly on the stones along with other figures, like lions symbolising strength and power, dragons, and eagles. In the vicinities of Konya and Akşehir there are examples of gravestones with human figures on them showing some of the work the deceased did in his or her lifetime (a man training a falcon, a woman embroidering with a tambour, etc.). Figurative decorations on gravestones disappeared at the beginning in the Emirates period. During this period, a form of gravestone that closely resembled a *mihrab* became widespread and was in fashion throughout the 14th and 15th centuries, especially in the West Anatolian Emirates.

Traditional Turkish decorating could not rescue itself from the western influence seen in various branches of art in Anatolia beginning in the 17th century; especially in West Anatolia, although gravestone forms did not undergo any major changes, the decorating program was heavily influenced by trends like Baroque, Empire, and Rococo. The few examples we see of gravestones carved in humanoid shapes may have been influenced by European sculpture, but they might also be connected to the Central Asian *balbal* tradition. While the triangular pediment on women's gravestones (quite common in this period) contains abundant and various decorations, men's gravestones are much plainer.

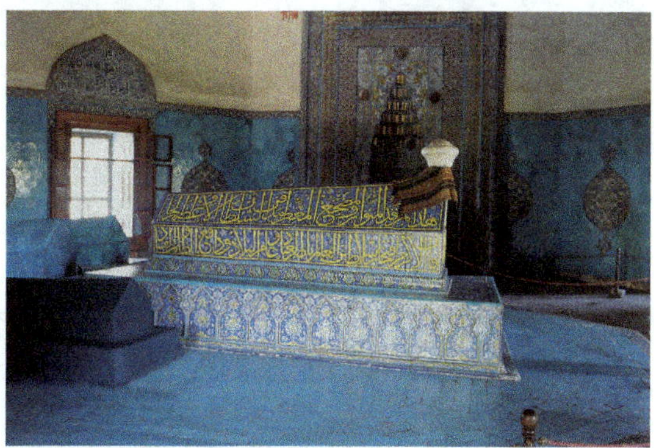

Yeşil Türbe, tile sarcophagus of Sultan Mehmed I, 1419-24, Mehmed I, Bursa.

Women's gravestones usually get slightly broader from the bottom to the top and end in a triangular pediment. In earlier periods, men's gravestones were shaped like rectangular prisms. During the Ottoman period, a turban-like capital symbolising the occupation of the deceased was added. Men's gravestones in the shape of columns are also encountered.

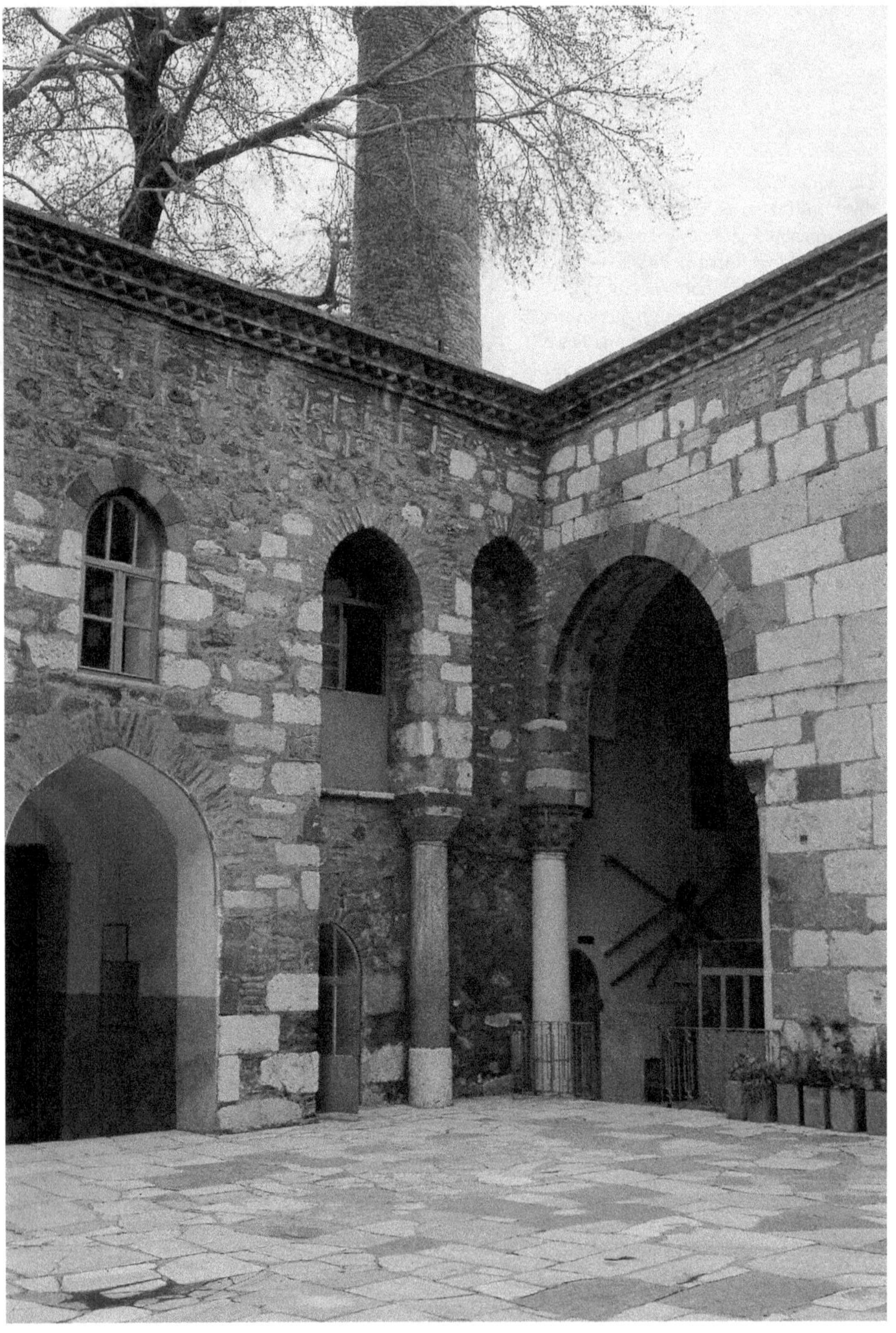

Manisa: City of Princes

Lale Bulut, Şakir Çakmak, Aydoğan Demir, Rahmi H. Ünal

III.1 MANISA

III.1.a Manisa Archaeological Museum
III.1.b Hatuniye Complex
III.1.c Great Mosque (Ulu Cami) Complex
III.1.d Karaköy (Sinan Bey) Madrasa (option)

III.2 ULUBAT

III.2.a Issız Han

Trade in Anatolia

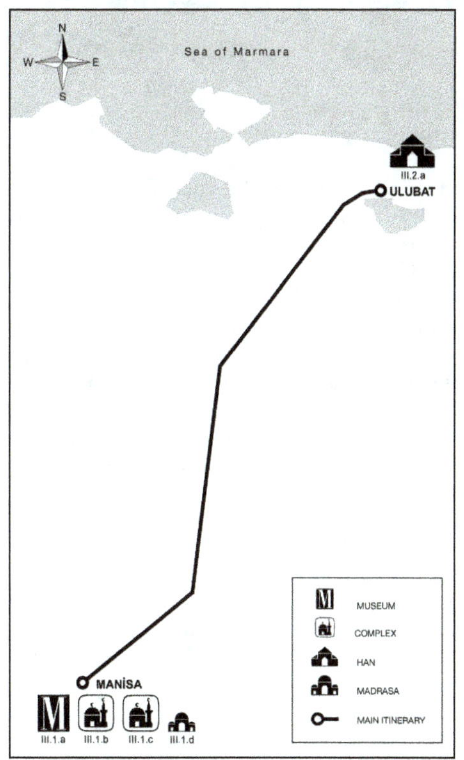

Great Mosque (Ulu Cami) Complex, madrasa, courtyard, 1378, İshak Çelebi, Manisa.

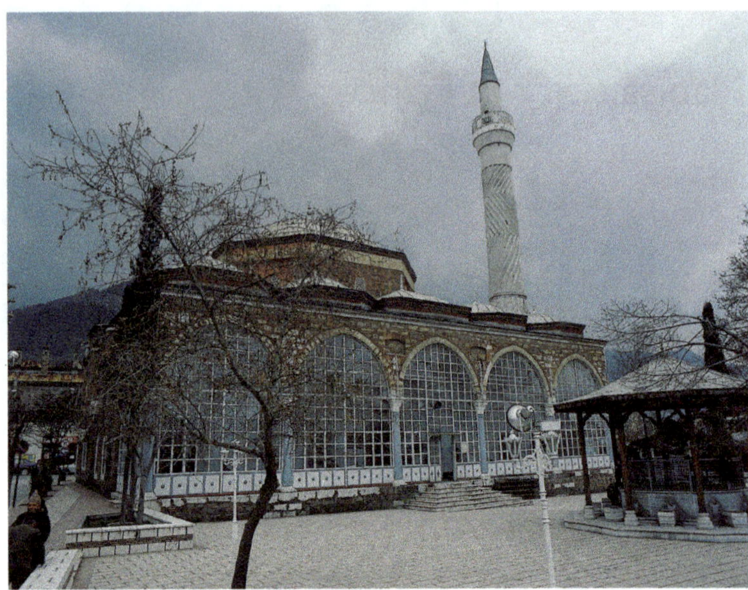

Hatuniye Complex, General view of the mosque from the northeast, 1491, Hüsnüşah Hatun, Manisa.

Saruhan Bey (r. 1305-1345) founded an Emirate in the region of ancient Lydia in the year 1305. In 1313 the city of Manisa, which had been an important trading centre connecting the Aegean Region to Central Anatolia or the Marmara Region since ancient times, became the centre of this Emirate that ruled over the bountiful plains of the Gediz River (ancient Hermus). The presence of large *hans* in the city that have survived until the present day support this view. However, the Saruhan Emirate was unable to establish sovereignty over the seas like the Menteşe and Aydın Emirates did. Since Foça (ancient Phocea), a very busy and sheltered harbour, was under the domination of the Genoese in the 14th century, the Saruhanids had to make do with their harbours of secondary importance. The Genoese, who controlled Foça, paid taxes though, to the Saruhan Beys in order to continue their presence in the area.

The Saruhan Beys used the income from the fertile Gediz Plain, taxes, and trade to have, among other things, mosques, *madrasas*, *hammams*, *hans*, *zawiyas* and *türbes*, built in various cities, beginning with Manisa. Two of the most famous of these structures, Manisa Great Mosque and Madrasa along with the *Mevlevihane*, were commissioned by İshak Bey (r. 1362-1388).

In the Ottoman era Manisa was one of the most famous cities of the crown princes. In the 14th and 15th centuries, quite a few princes became sultans after first acting as a governor in Manisa. The Sehzadeler Palace, literally Princes, Palace, not a trace of which is left today, would have been built after the royal palaces in İstanbul and Edirne. The Sultan Meadow on Spil Mountain was a place to which the princes migrated in order to rest in the summer heat and enjoy themselves. The princes would stay together with their mothers, both of whom embellished Manisa with monumental works: one of the most beautiful of which is Hatuniye Mosque Complex (1491), constructed in the name of Hüsnüsah Hatun, the wife of Sultan Bayezid II (r. 1481-1512) and the mother of Şehinşah.

After Sultan Bayezid I (r. 1389-1402) lost the Battle of Ankara to Tamurlane (r. 1369-1405), the ruler of Transoxiana and Persia, the Ottoman State experienced a period of internal disorder and social despair. The disciples of Shaykh Bedreddin (d.1419), a *Kadıasker* in the Ottoman Government, were trying to spread a doctrine of religious communism maintaining that food, clothing, sown fields –everything other than women– must be used communally by the people. In Manisa, Torlak Kemal, a Jew who converted to Islam and who was a disciple of Shaykh Bedreddin, worked hard to spread these ideas and caused an uprising that had a considerable effect upon the region. The Ottoman State only managed to suppress the Torlak Kemal Uprising with difficulty.

The city of Manisa was administered as part of the Saruhan Sanjak during the time of the Ottomans. Manisa, once important because of its location on busy trade routes, has preserved its place up to the present day.

A. D.

You must use your time carefully if you want to visit all the suggested works in this itinerary because you cover close to 300 km. in order to reach Bursa, the starting point of the next itinerary. Furthermore, one of the interesting buildings you should see is Issiz Han, close to Ulubat on D. 565, which is the highway you will be taking. If you are spending the night in Izmir, you can reach Manisa easily with the intercity buses. Although the distances between the buildings to be visited are not great, those who want to save time may want to rent a car or take a taxi or the dolmush *minibuses. Our recommendation is to pass the first half of the day in Manisa and then head straight for Ulubat stopping on the way for Manisa Kebab for lunch. The highway takes you through West Anatolia's most fertile lands. Those who take a night journey, between Manisa and Akhisar in the months of July-August will be amazed at the sight of the burning lights that resemble fireflies in all the fields; these are the lamps of farmers gathering tobacco in the coolness of the evening.*

Great Mosque (Ulu Cami) Complex, Madrasa, re-used capitals in the courtyard, 1378, İshak Çelebi, Manisa.

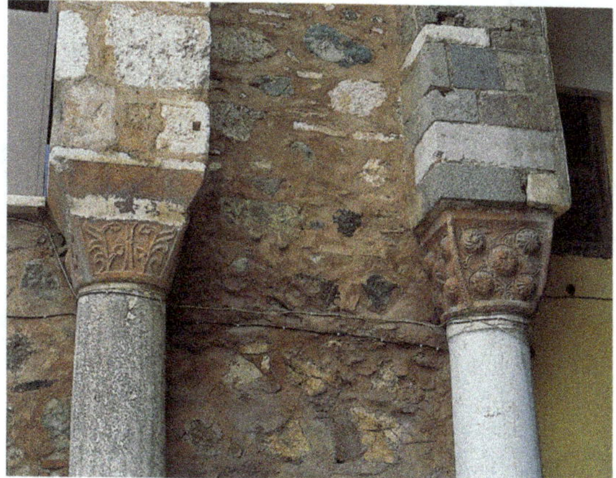

Pair of armlets, 15th century, Archaeology Museum, Manisa.

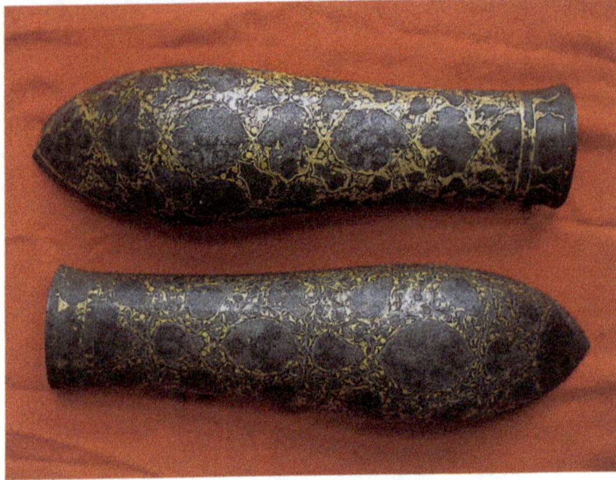

III.1 MANISA

Manisa –Magnesia ad Sipylum of ancient times– was founded by Thessalians towards the end of the 2nd millennium BC on their return from the Trojan War. It exhibits a history parallel to that of West Anatolia. The area passed into the hands of Lydian King Croesus in the 6th century BC but was soon taken over by the Persians in 546 BC. Persian rule came to an end with Alexander the Great's victory at Granicus in 334 BC. In the Hellenistic era the city came under the control of the Pergamene Kingdom. The city and its inhabitants prospered during the time of the Roman Empire and the city preserved its importance during the Byzantine period until the 13th century. Emperor John III Ducas Vatatzes had a fortress built here at the beginning of the 13th century during the Latin occupation of İstanbul and he was buried here, too, when he died. Following the recapture of İstanbul by the Byzantines, the city began to lose its importance until it eventually passed into the hands of the Turks in 1313.

III.1.a **Archaeological Museum**

Saruhan District, 107 Murad Avenue. The madrasa and imaret sections of the Muradiye Complex (16th-century Ottoman) are used today as the Archaeological and Ethnographical Museum. The finds from Sardis and nearby areas are displayed in the imaret *and the Turkish-Islamic artefacts in the* madrasa.
The museum is open 08:00-12:00 and 13:00-16:30 during the winter months and 08:30-12:30 and 13:30-17:00 during the summer months. There is an entrance fee.

Pair of Iron Armlets

During the Ottoman era, soldiers used equipment like armour, armlets, and shields during war to protect their bodies

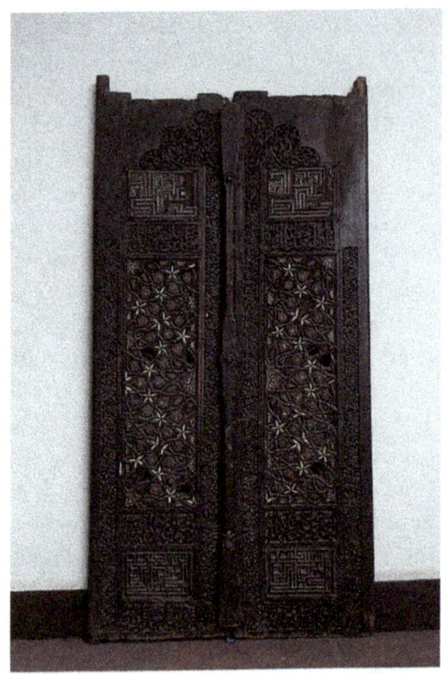

Wooden door wings from Great Mosque minbar, 1377, Hacı Mahmud Ibn Abdülaziz, Manisa.

from sword and arrow blows. The armlet worn by the warriors was a kind of armour designed to protect the part of the arm between the wrist and the elbow. Basically, it is made up of two side wings tied with chain hoops to the main body that goes over the arm. Because most of the extant examples are products of fine-quality workmanship and are richly decorated, it leads one to believe that armlets were tools used by high-ranking soldiers. The examples displayed in the Manisa Museum consist only of the main parts, as the wings are missing. The surfaces of both armlets are decorated with engraving and gold gilding. Although they look a lot alike, the armlets exhibit differences regarding decoration. For this reason, it is thought that the two pieces belong to different pairs of armlets. The armlets are decorated with engraved large sunbursts (*şemse*), cartouches, and tulip designs, while the area between the motifs is filled with a gilded plant composition exhibiting even finer workmanship. These two armlets are dated to the 15th century. There are contemporary examples of armlets similar to these at the Military Museum in İstanbul.

L. B.

Manisa Great Mosque's Minbar Door Wings

The Manisa Great Mosque's *minbar* was made by a master named Hacı Mehmed Ibn Abdülaziz from Antep in 1377 at the order of İshak Çelebi, one of the Saruhan Beys; today it is being restored and its doors are protected in the Manisa Museum. The *minbar* door wings, made of ebony wood, exhibit quite careful workmanship. Ornamental panels and panels with inscriptions are symmetrically arranged on the door. The large rectangular panels surrounded by ornamental and inscribed strips are the most interesting components of the composition. Star and polygonal shapes formed with long and narrow strips of wood are decorated with mother-of-pearl, ivory, and wood components of various types and colours. We learn from the inscriptions on the door wings that the decorative composition was prepared by a master craftsman named Fakih Ibn Yusuf.

L. B.

III.1.b **Hatuniye Complex**

On Borsa Avenue in Anafartalar District. Leaving the Museum, follow the Murad Avenue to the right (east), the complex is a further one street to the north.

Manisa, the capital of the Saruhan Emirate, continued to be an important city after it came under Ottoman rule in 1410. It is one of several Anatolian cities in which crown princes learned about state administration. Şehinşah, one of Sultan Beyazid II's sons, was one of the *şehzades* educated in Manisa. While he was performing his duties here, his mother Hüsnüşah Hatun, who was staying with him, had a large mosque complex consisting of a mosque, a *han*, a *hammam*, an *imaret*, and a *mektep* built. In order to meet maintenance and repair expenses, as well as pay the wages of the people working at the complex she had built, she had a *waqf* charter prepared in 1497 and devoted various real-estate that would provide the *waqf* with an income. Of the

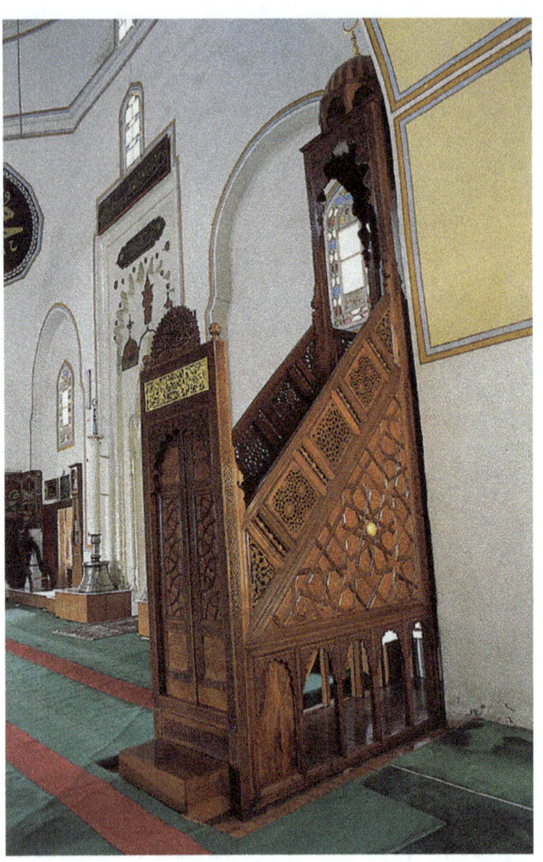

Hatuniye Mosque, minbar, 1491, Hüsnüşah Hatun, Manisa.

buildings that formed the mosque complex, only the mosque, *han*, and *mektep* have survived up to the present day.

Hatuniye Mosque

Facing a beautiful park in the market area of the town, the Hatuniye Mosque stands attractively in solitude. At first sight, the walls built with cut-stone (andesite and marble) and brick courses, are breathtaking. On the northwest corner of the structure's main body rises the minaret with a cylindrical body decorated with zigzag mouldings, its socle decorated with attractive brickwork. The facade is somewhat altered with the addition of glass panes but closing your eyes to such infelicities, you notice the five-bayed portico supported with beautiful re-used Byzantine columns and capitals. Four of the five bays are surmounted with domes, and the central one by a higher flat-topped cross vault. Behind them the high dome of the prayer hall rises. Entering the portico, one notices that it is plain without decoration. The inscription over the doorway tells us that the mosque was completed in 1491. The prayer hall was originally designed as a square room flanked with two *tabhanes* on either side surmounted by domes, but later the separating walls were removed and the *tabhanes* were adjoined. The wooden *minbar*, dated to 1495 according to its inscription, is of exclusive craftsmanship and is decorated with rich geometric and floral compositions. The mosque was renovated in 1643, 1672 and 1831, and is still open for worship.

Mektep

Immediately to the west of the mosque is a smaller structure with two domes. This is the *mektep*, believed to have been commissioned by Hüsnüşah Hatun. However, no mention is made of it in the *waqf* charter of the mosque complex; therefore, it is generally believed that this primary school was built shortly after the establishment of the *waqf* charter in 1497. It is a small building composed of two units, each covered by a dome; today, one unit is used as a shop and the other as an office.

Kurşunlu Han

Across the street to the south of the mosque stands the Hatuniye Han, the last of the complex's buildings that is still standing. It is commonly known as "Kurşunlu Han" or "Lead Han" because its domes are covered with lead sheets. The main entrance is in the middle of the west side. Built with stone and brick, the building –a typical city *han*– is two storied and has a courtyard. Both floors have porticoes opening onto the courtyard but are closed off with glass panes today. There are 36 rooms on the ground floor and 38 on the upper floor; all the rooms on the ground floor are covered with vaults, while the rooms on the top floor are covered with vaults or domes. In all the rooms there is a fireplace and niches in which to place belongings. The *han*, built to provide income for the mosque complex, is described in detail in the 1497 *waqf* charter, which also states that there were a stable and 21 shops. However, the stables, known to have adjoined the eastern facade, have not survived to the present day. Of the shops constructed adjoining the *han*'s north and west fronts, the ones in the north were torn down in order to widen a road passing through here. It is known that the building underwent various renovations in 1643 and 1677; it was also thoroughly renovated between the years 1966-1970. Today it is used as a student dormitory and can shortly be visited when accompanied by one of the directors in charge.

S. Ç.

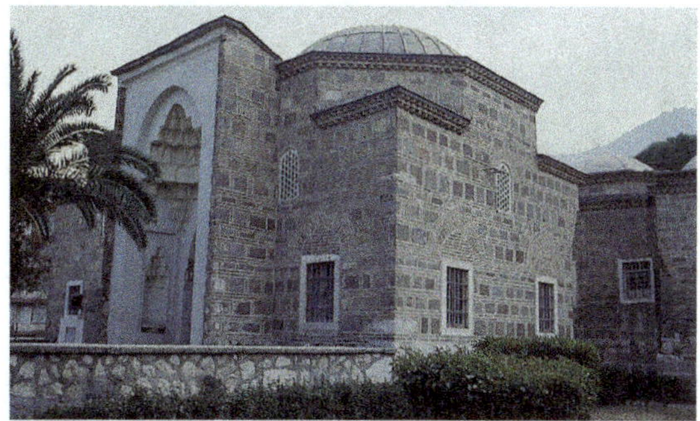

Hatuniye Complex Mektep, general view 1491, Hüsnüşah Hatun, Manisa.

III.1.c Great Mosque (Ulu Cami) Complex

Located on Ulutepe Avenue in İshak Çelebi District. From Hatuniye Complex, continue up hill to the south and reaching Ulutepe Street, turn right. The Complex is located up the hill from the Museum and can also be reached via the staircase-streets behind the Muradiye Mosque.

Among the many works that were constructed in Manisa during the Saruhan Emirate period, Great Mosque, which forms a complex together with a *madrasa*

Hatuniye Complex Kurşunlu Han, general view, 1491, Hüsnüşah Hatun, Manisa.

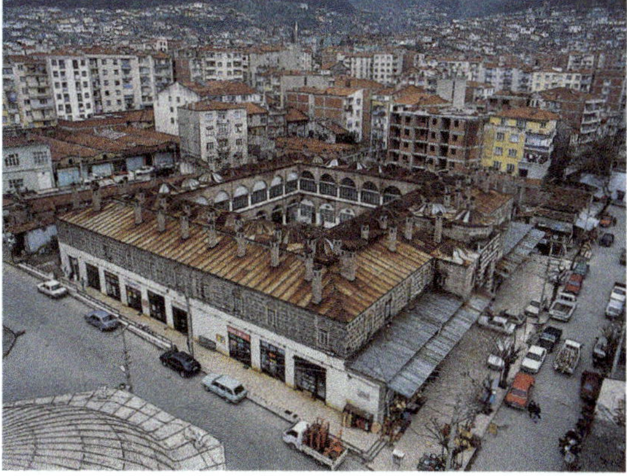

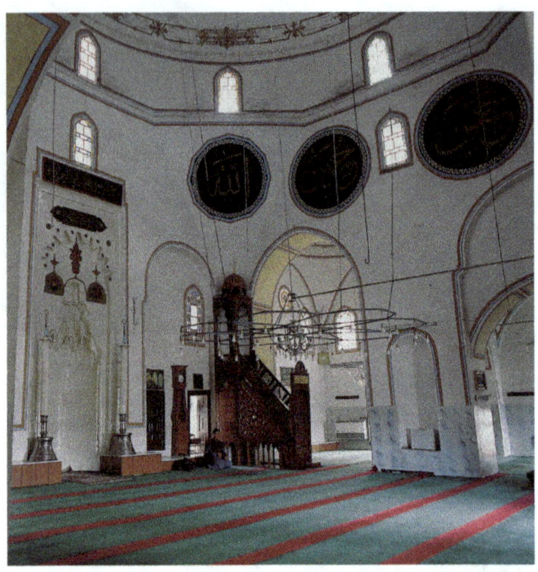

Hatuniye Mosque, interior, 1491, Hüsnüşah Hatun, Manisa.

and a *hammam*, is one of the most important. Approaching from below, past the *hammam* in ruins now, the mosque comes into sight first, rising majestically —somewhat obstructed by the ex-fire-watch tower in front— and the *madrasa* to the right is hidden behind plane trees. The complex was constructed by architect Emet Ibn Osman for Muzaffereddin İshak Çelebi (1366-1388), the Saruhan Bey.

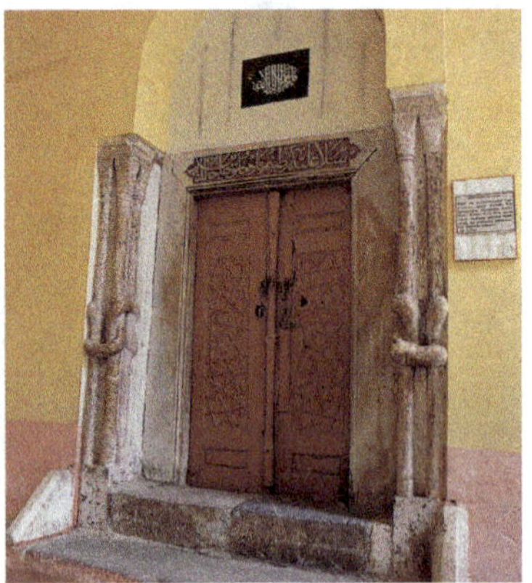

Great Mosque (Ulu Cami) Complex, Madrasa, türbe door, 1378, İshak Çelebi, Manisa.

Great Mosque

The mosque and the adjoining *madrasa* stand on a steep slope; therefore, the northeast section stands taller than the rest of the complex. Built of re-used marble blocks, some of which have Byzantine decoration on them, and roughly cut-stones, the mosque has three portals, one in the middle of the north side, and one on the east side, and the other on the west opening into the *madrasa*. The eastern portal is much plainer and has a few re-used Byzantine pieces as decoration. Today the only entrance in use is the northern portal, which has some very beautiful ornamentation. Most noteworthy are the low arch of the doorway, the underlying brickwork of *muqarnas* in the canopy now exposed, the rosettes on the side walls and the inscription itself which records the date of construction for the mosque as 1367. Past the portal is the courtyard, one of the earliest examples of a courtyard with a portico; however, there is no portico in front of the prayer hall. The re-used Byzantine columns and capitals are elaborate, and the doorway to the west gives access to the *madrasa*. The prayer hall itself is surmounted with a large dome supported by eight pillars and the remaining bays are covered with cross- vaults —though they look different due to thick layers of plaster— as are the bays in the courtyard. The *minbar*, made in 1377 by an artist named Hacı Mehmed Ibn Abdülaziz from Antep, and under restoration at the moment, is one of the masterpieces of Turkish art in

Manisa

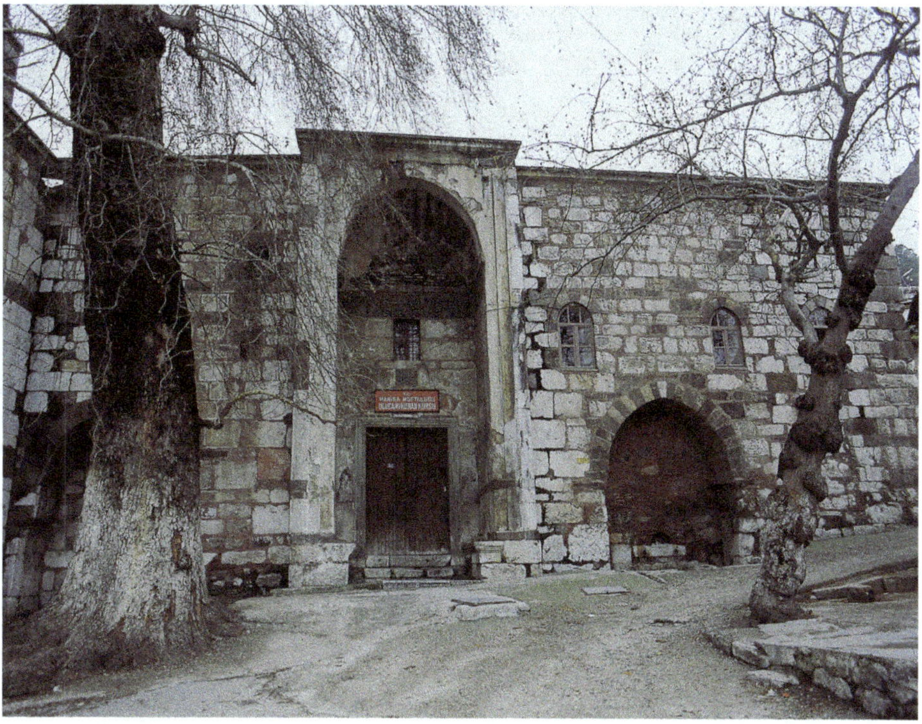

Great Mosque (Ulu Cami) Complex, madrasa, north facade, 1378, İshak Çelebi, Manisa.

wood; Bursa Great Mosque's *minbar* is also the work of the same artist. The minaret, decorated here and there with glazed bricks, is a later addition and can be entered today from the roof. Manisa Great Mosque –like İsa Bey Mosque in Selçuk– with its monumental central dome and courtyard with porticoes, represents an important step in the development of Turkish architecture.

Madrasa

The *madrasa*, adjoining the Great Mosque on the west and also known as Fethiye Madrasa, can be entered either through the

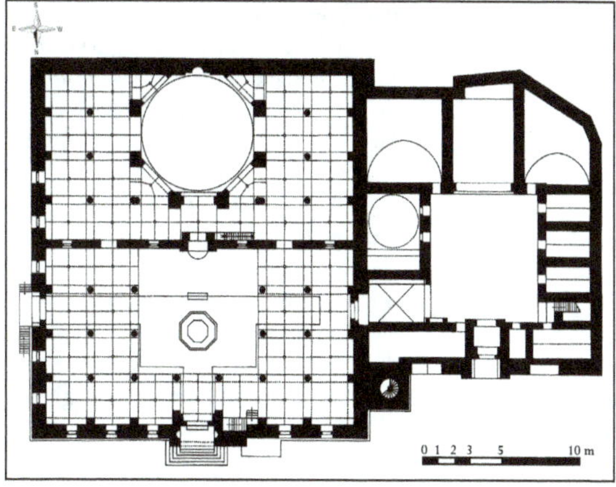

Plan of the Great Mosque and madrasa, Manisa (from Z. Sönmez).

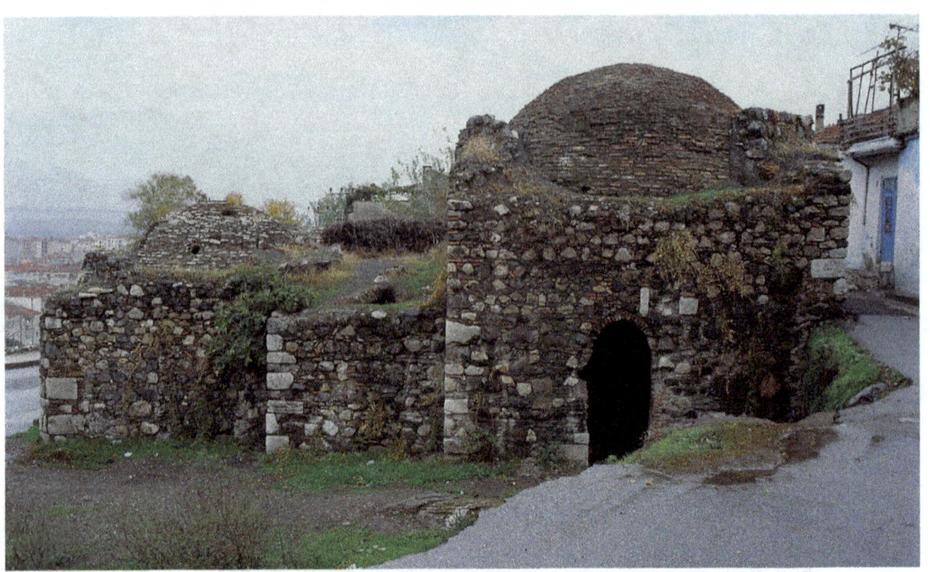

Great Mosque hammam, west front, second half of the 14th century, İshak Çelebi, Manisa.

mosque's courtyard, or through the portal on the north side, which resembles the northern portal of the mosque; and the niches on either side of it are fountains. The inscription dates it to 1378 that is later than the mosque. Once inside, the open courtyard without porticoes is surrounded by a two-storey structure; evidently the students' only choice was to concentrate on their studies. In the south is the *dershane* –an *iwan* with a vault; the flaws seen in the plan of the *madrasa* and in its location according to the mosque can be attributed to the sloping terrain of the land.

In the passageway to the mosque is the *türbe* of İshak Çelebi, the founder of the complex; the elegant doorjambs of re-used knotted columns from a Byzantine structure are noteworthy. In the *türbe* there are four symbolic sarcophagi –one belongs to İshak Çelebi, it is not known to whom the other three once belonged.

Hammam

To the northeast of the mosque is the deteriorated Çukur Hammam, another building that belongs to the complex. The *hammam*, today partially standing, is quite a magnificent building that has a *sıcaklık* with four *iwans*. Sources recount an event that occurred in this *hammam*: Ottoman Sultan Mehmed I, son of Bayezid I, conquered Manisa in 1410 and had Hızırşah, the Emirate's last administrator, caught and executed in this *hammam*: the Saruhan Emirate disappeared together with this event.

Ş. Ç.

This is an excellent place to have a break: sipping a glass of sage tea at the coffee house nearby, enjoy the scenery before you.

III.1.d **Karaköy (Sinan Bey) Madrasa** (option)

Tunca District, 39 Temiz Street. From the Museum continue to the west; at the lights and the sign for "Niobe" turn left; it is in the first street on the left. From Great Mosque, continue to Ulutepe Avenue to the west and then to the north; it is in the last street on the right before the lights.

It is known that a great number of *madrasas* were constructed in Manisa during the Saruhan and Ottoman periods. Only four of these *madrasas* (Great Mosque [14th c.], Sinan Bey [15th c.], Hafsa Sultan [16th c.], and Muradiye [16th c.] Madrasas) have survived up to the present day. Of these buildings, the only example dating to the early Ottoman period is Sinan Bey Madrasa. This building, also known as the Karaköy Madrasa, does not have an inscription. According to its *waqf* charter dated 1549, the *madrasa* together with a *mektep* –which has not survived– were commissioned by a person named Sinan Bey, who according to some researchers, was one of the treasurers during Sultan Mehmed II's reign (1451-1481). According to some other scholars, though, he was one of the same Sultan's *müderris*. Although the *waqf* charter dates to 1549, the *madrasa*'s architectural characteristics indicate that it was constructed in the middle of the 15th century, which is the accepted view.

Constructed out of stone and brick, the building is entered through the monumental entrance in the middle of the north facade. The courtyard is surrounded with porticoes on all four sides. On the east and west wings of the courtyard, there is a total of 10 student cells, in all of which there is one fireplace and various numbers of niches. The cells and porticoes are covered with cross-vaults, which is striking because this type of vault, uncommon in Turkish architecture, was quite fashionable and used in 14th- and 15th-century buildings in West Anatolian cities like Manisa, Tire and Menemen. To the south of the courtyard is the *dershane* reached via a set of stairs. In most of the Anatolian *madrasas*, the *dershane* area was also used as a *masjid*. Here, the *dershane*, together with the portico in front of it, were raised above the rest of the structure, providing the area with an independent masjid quality. The *dershane / masjid* is covered with a dome supported by squinches filled with *muqarnas*. The Sinan Bey Madrasa was thoroughly renovated in 1985 and is used today as a Handcrafts Centre in which silver-working ateliers are found.

Ş. Ç.

Spil Mountain, located just behind the city of Manisa, offers a rare opportunity for those who want to rest and be alone with nature. For those who would like to spend more time in Manisa, a visit to the Muradiye Mosque Complex and Sultaniye Mosque Complex (16th century) are recommended. Manisa also offers the "Mesir Festival", organized every year during the last week of April. "Mesir macunu" (a gum-like confection) was first made in the 16th century by Muslihüddin Merkez Efendi, the manager of Sultaniye Mosque Complex at the time. He devised the mixture for use in the medical treatment of Hafsa Sultan, the wife of Yavuz Sultan Selim I. It has become a tradition to distribute "mesir macunu" to the people every year from the Sultaniye Mosque, across the street from the Museum. This is done with great festivity. It is also believed that "mesir macunu", which contains 41 ingredients including clover, ginger, coriander, cumin, cinnamon, vanilla, orange rind and sugar, has, in addition to its characteristics as an energiser and appetiser that eases digestion and eliminates tiredness, an aphrodisiac quality.

It is not difficult to reach Ulubat with the intercity buses but Issız Han is on the edge of the lake some way from the main road.

III.2 ULUBAT

III.2.a **Issız Han**

The building is used as a warehouse today. The han'*s main entrance, which looks onto the lake (to the south), is usually locked. The key is at the farm about 100 m. away.*

The caravan route that connected the Ottoman State's second capital, Bursa, to the west and south reaches Karacabey by following the north shore of Lake Ulubat (Apolyont). In 1394, İne (Eyne) Bey, one of the commanding officers during the eras of the Ottoman Sultans Murad I (1362-1389) and Bayezid I (1389-1402), commissioned the construction of a *han* on this road. This *han*, located on the shore of Lake Ulubat close to Seyran Village which is part of the Karacabey township, is also known among the people as the Susuz Han. İne Bey devoted the income of a village and a mill to this *han* in order to meet the building's maintenance and renovation expenses and pay the workers' wages. According to the articles of the *waqf* charter, services were provided to travellers staying at the *han* free of charge. It is known that in addition to Issız Han, İne Bey also commissioned the construction of various structures in Bergama, Balıkesir, and Bursa. İne Bey, who played an active role during the Interregnum following the Battle of Ankara (1402), was killed in 1405 during throne disputes amongst the sons of Sultan Bayezid I.

Located in the middle of fields, Issız Han is an interesting building from an archi-

Issız Han, view from the north, 1394, İne (Eyne) Bey, Ulubat.

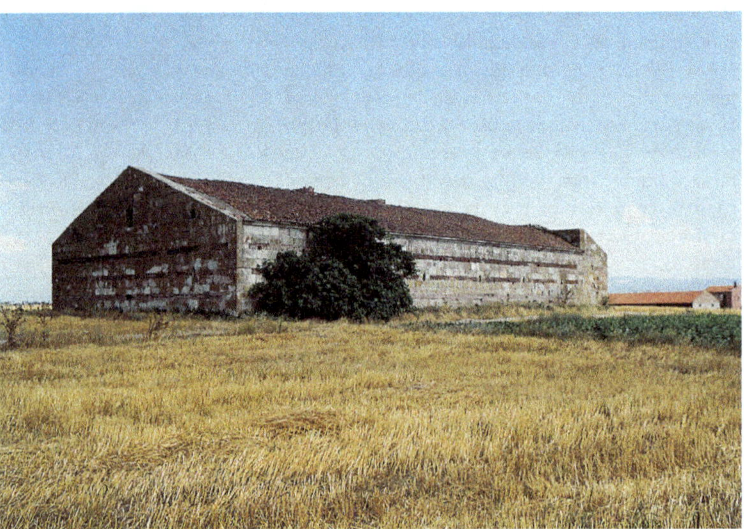

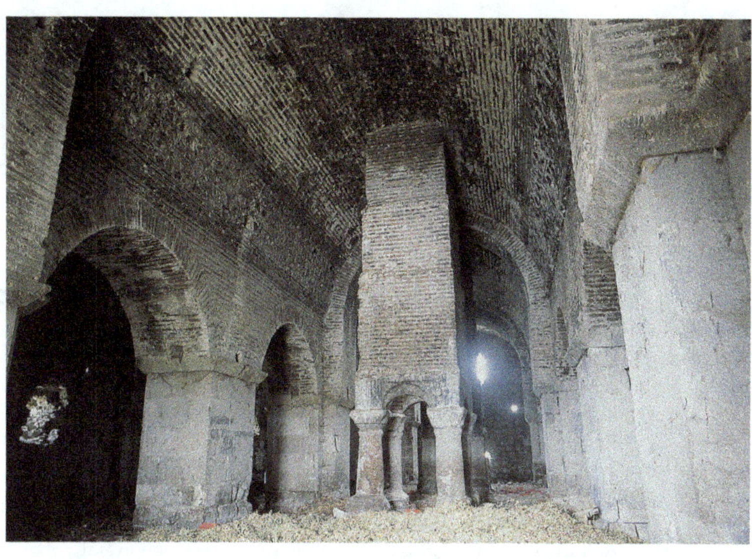

Issız Han, interior, 1394, İne (Eyne) Bey, Ulubat.

tectural perspective. Its plan, which lacks a courtyard but has three aisles, is frequently encountered in the Emirates-period (14th-15th century) buildings. On either side of the entrance there are two rooms for special travellers and the others would spend the night on the bench inside. In the middle of the bench are two fireplaces, the chimneys of which rest upon four short columns; this is the only *han* in Anatolia known to have this type of fireplace. There is no fireplace by the classic definition in any of the *hans* constructed during the Seljuq period when *tandırs*, consisting of a clay-lined pit or earthen jar buried in the ground, were utilised to cook food and for heating. Furthermore, The fireplaces in Issız Han are not on the wall, but are located on the bench in the centre of the building. In this respect, it can be said that Issız Han is a building that symbolizes the transition from the Anatolian Seljuq *han* with its *tandirs* in the benches to Ottoman *hans* with normal fireplaces located on the wall.

Ş. Ç.

TRADE IN ANATOLIA

Rahmi H. Ünal

Anatolia, forming a crossroads due to its geographic location, has been the stage of lively trade ever since the oldest periods of history. The most important of the various Silk Roads between the East and the West passed through Anatolia. Turkish tribes, raiding Central Anatolia since the 11th century, made great efforts to establish permanent dominance over the region up until the second half of the 12th century. It is only after this point in history, during the period of Seljuq Sultan Kılıç Arslan II, that Anatolia's new rulers could take measures to develop trade in the country. Because the development of trade is impossible in a country where it is not safe to travel, the sultans made the security of travellers' lives and goods a priority. They applied what may be the first insurance in history to the goods of the tradesmen. The Anatolian Seljuqs signed an agreement with the Cypriots in 1213 and with the Venetians in 1220, according to which both parties were mutually committed to indemnify damage or loss encountered on their own lands by travelling tradesmen from the other country.

Construction of *caravanserais* –or, by their other name, *hans*– began in the time of Seljuq Sultan Kılıç Arslan II and continued apace in the time of Alâaddin Keykubad I and Gıyaseddin Keyhusrev II. The Mongols, who took the Seljuqs under their hegemony in 1243, also considered trade and the construction of *hans* important. On the caravan routes of Silk and Spice Roads, sultans or important government officials built *caravanserais*, which were protective buildings that offered travellers minimal comforts. The architecture of *hans* of this period reminds one of small fortresses: the majority of them consisting a covered section and a courtyard; the only entrance through a monumental portal opened directly into the courtyard and from the courtyard only one portal provided access to the covered

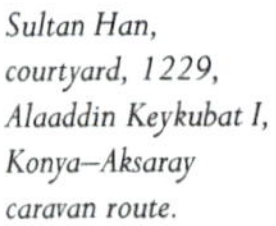

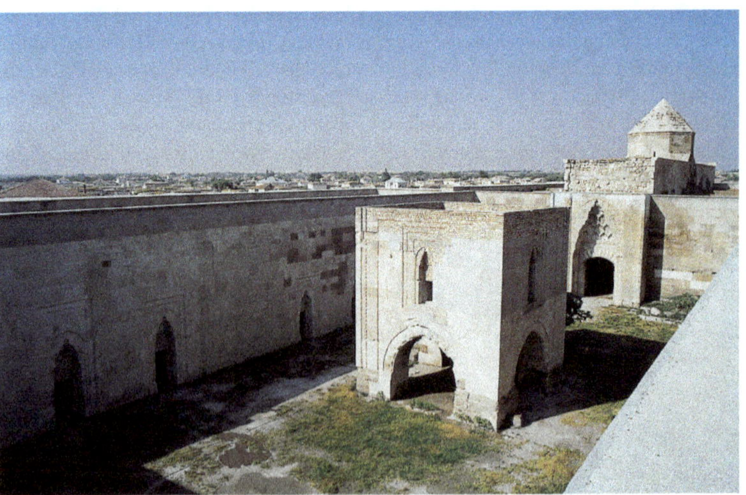

Sultan Han, courtyard, 1229, Alaaddin Keykubat I, Konya–Aksaray caravan route.

section. Caravans that wished to spend the night in a safe place after dark would stay in these buildings, which were constructed at certain intervals along the trade routes. The distance between *hans* outside settlement centres was never more than 40 km; in fact, this distance is sometimes as little as 5-10 km., on rugged terrain. Hence, such *hans* are called *menzil han*, literally a *han* at a day's journey. Small villages arose in the surroundings of some *hans* that were constructed in previously uninhabited areas. However, once the Seljuqs' central authority began to vanish towards the end of the 13th century, local potentates headed towards West Anatolia began to found emirates. As a result of the appearance of a great number of small emirates in Anatolian territory, safety could no longer be established on the caravan routes and transit trade began to lose its importance. *Caravanserais* constructed during this politically unstable period were smaller and without courtyards, and could not match the magnificence of the Seljuq *caravanserais*. Also in this period the city *hans* began appearing in ever increasing numbers.

After the Portuguese sailor Bartolemeu Dias' discovery of the Cape of Good Hope in 1488, European tradesmen usually preferred the sea route when doing trade with the East. As the routes that tied the East to the West began to lose their importance, the routes that connected the city centres in the central regions of Anatolia to the port cities began to gain importance and *hans* of small dimensions were constructed along these routes. In connection to these developments *hans*, intended to meet the needs of storing tradesmen's goods, selling, and even providing places to spend the night, began to be built in the city centres. The magnificent and large-size *hans* of the 16th and 17th century that have survived to our day reveal that the caravan routes once again reached their previous level of liveliness once political stability had been re-established during the period of the Ottoman Empire. However, the plan layouts of these *hans* did not resemble the *menzil hans* lined up all along the caravan routes because they were constructed for a different purpose. City *hans* are usually two storied with rooms lined up around a courtyard in the centre. In these *hans*, the rooms on the lower floor were generally used as depots; the rooms on the upper floor, though, were designated as offices or boarding rooms.

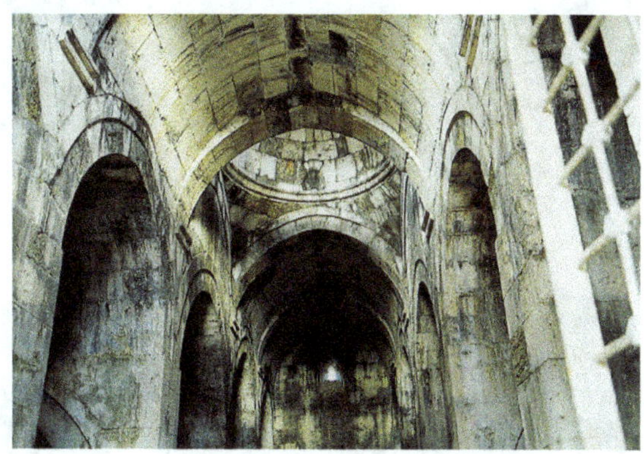

Susuz Han, interior, first half of 13th century, Burdur–Antalya caravan route.

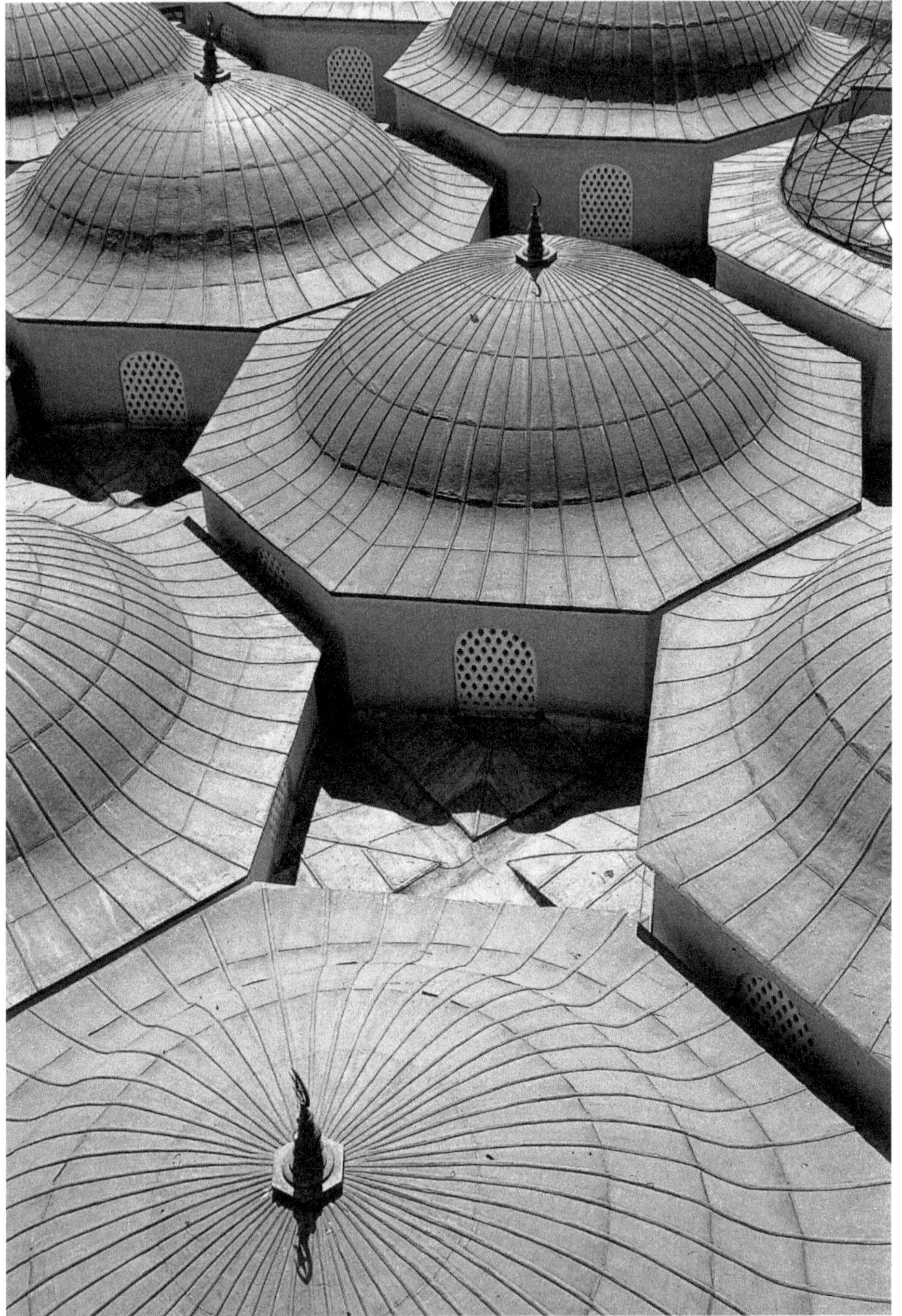

Bursa: City of Sultans

Lale Bulut, Aydoğan Demir, Yekta Demiralp

IV.1 BURSA

First Day

IV.1.a Yeşil Complex
IV.1.b Yıldırım Complex
IV.1.c Orhan Mosque
IV.1.d Koza Han
IV.1.e Great Mosque (Great Cami)
IV.1.f Emir Han (option)

Second Day

IV.1.g Türbe of Osman Gazi
IV.1.h Türbe of Orhan Gazi
IV.1.i Muradiye Complex
IV.1.j Ahmet Pasha Madrasa (option)
IV.1.k Sulphur Spas (Kükürtlü Kaplıca)
IV.1.l Old Spas (Eski Kaplıca)
IV.1.m Hüdavendigar Mosque

The Hammam *Tradition*
The Battle of Ankara

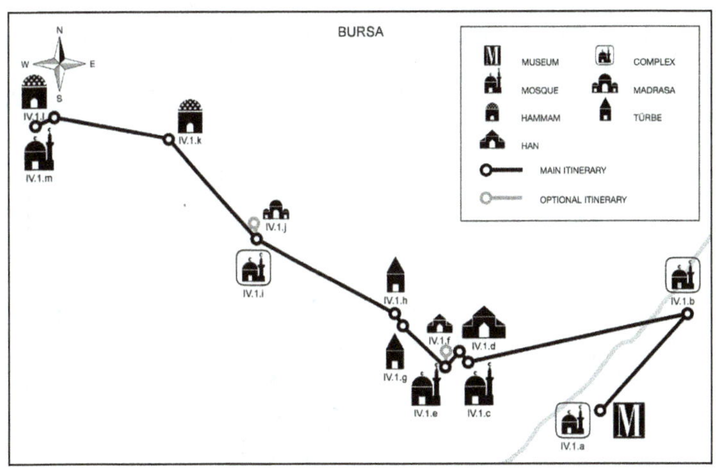

Great Mosque, Domes, 1400, Bayezid I, Bursa.

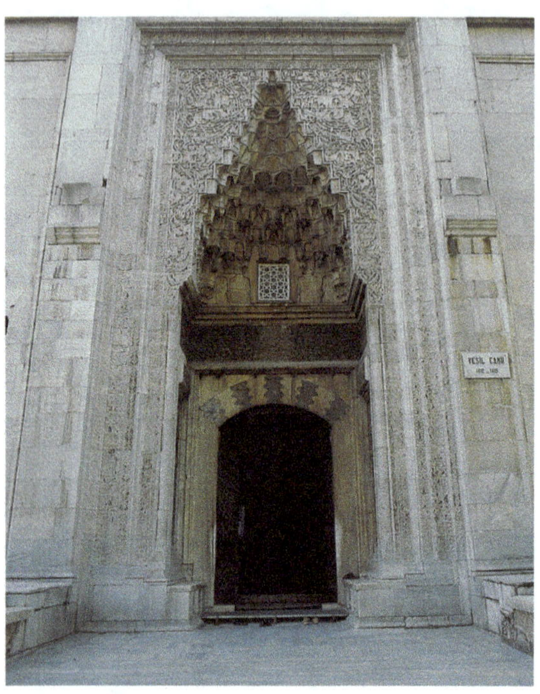

Yeşil Complex, main door, 1419-1424, Mehmed I, Bursa.

Bursa, situated on the slopes of Uludağ (Mysian Olympus), with its abundant water supply and fertile plains, has attracted settlers throughout history. An important city of the ancient kingdom of Bithynia, Prusa (today's Bursa) contains evidence of all of the Anatolian civilisations starting from the middle of the first millennium BC. The Anatolian Seljuq State, which was founded in 1075 and had its first centre at İznik (ancient Nicea), established sovereignty over Bursa during its foundation period, even if only for a short time. Once the Seljuqs moved their centre to Konya, having been defeated by the armies of the First Crusade in 1097, they were unable to maintain constant possession of the Marmara region. In 1113 the Seljuq troops once again took the shores of the Marmara including Bursa but, as before, they were unable to secure their hold on the region.

While various emirates were being established in West Anatolia towards the end of the 13th and the beginning of the 14th century, a Turcoman Bey named Ertuğrul (d.1281) and his son Osman (r. 1281-1324) were attempting to settle the region of ancient Bithynia. Osman's heroes, reminiscent of European knights of the Middle Ages, engaged in battles with small Byzantine landowners; these battles were full of honour and romanticism for both sides. Nevertheless, after the establishment of Ottoman dominance over the region, both communities lived in peace for hundreds of years.

Founded by Osman Gazi in 1299, the Emirate captured Prusa, one of the most important towns of the Byzantine Empire, in the year 1326 during the reign of Orhan Gazi (1324-1362). This city, whose name among the people was transformed into Bursa, became the centre of the newly founded Ottoman State.

In a short time many *hans* were constructed in Bursa, a developed commercial and industrial centre. The city became famous as a weaving- and silk-production centre in particular.

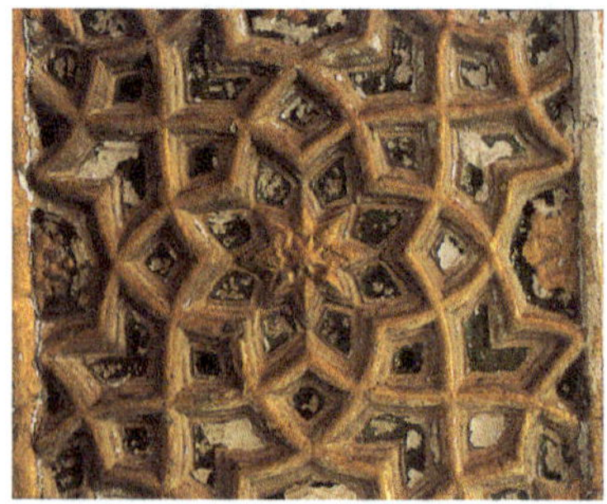

Orhan Mosque, detail from mihrab, 1339-40, Orhan Gazi, Bursa.

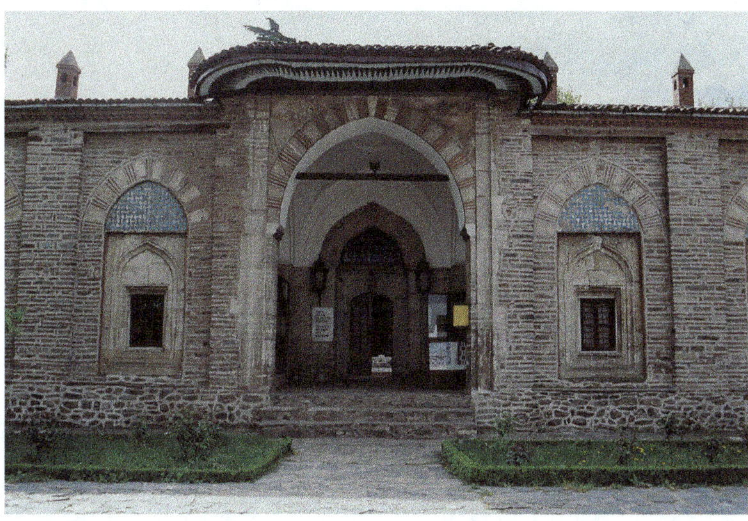

Yeşil Madrasa, entrance iwan, 1419-24, Mehmed I, Bursa.

The Ottoman sultans who ruled from the beginning of the14th century until the middle of the 15th century were Orhan Gazi (1324-1362; also known as Orhan Bey), Murad I (1362-1389; also known as Hüdavendigar), Bayezid I (1389-1402; also known as Yıldırım), Mehmed I (1413-1421; also known as Çelebi), and Murad II (1421-1451), all of whom improved the city by having various religious and public buildings constructed.

At the time of the founding of the state, the Ottoman sultans were broadminded men who lived in a simple manner. After he took Bursa, Orhan Gazi sent a gift of alcoholic drink to Geyikli Baba, a heterodox religious figure who had joined the conquest of Bursa. Sultan Bayezid I was also a sultan who used alcohol; according to legend, when he asked Emir Sultan, a religious leader, whether or not he liked the newly built Great Mosque, Emir Sultan replied: "The mosque has one deficiency: there should be taverns on all four sides so that there's a pretext for you to come".

Bursa is also a city of *türbes*: the first six Ottoman Sultans are buried in *türbes* here. Of these, the *türbe* of Sultan Mehmed I is a dazzling architectural work with its tiles and architecture.

Bursa is famous for its *hammams*, spas, and fountains. The Ottomans tried to make its social services available to all the citizens, regardless of differences in religion and language. For example, after Orhan Gazi captured Bursa, he had pipes installed to bring water to the Jewish quarter of the city.

A. D.

IV.1 BURSA

IV.1.a **Yeşil Complex**

Çelebi Sultan District (Mahallesi), on Yeşil Street. An entrance fee is charged for the

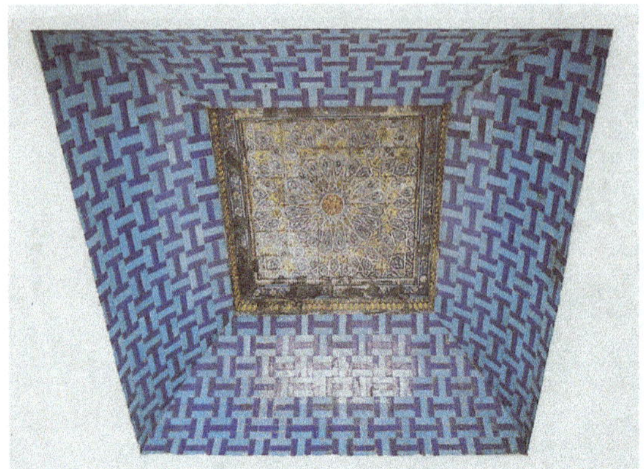

Yeşil Madrasa, tile vault of western iwan, 1419-24, Mehmed I, Bursa.

madrasa, which is also the Museum of Turkish and Islamic Arts, and the visitor is asked to make a donation at the türbe. The museum is open between 08.00-12.00 and 13.00-16.30 in the winter and 08:30 -12:30 and 13.30-17.00 in the summer. It is closed on Mondays. The complex is very close to the heart of the town and is a popular place among the locals.

Today Yeşil Complex is composed of a mosque, a *madrasa*, an *imaret* and a *türbe*. It takes its name, which means "Green", from the turquoise tiles that decorate the mosque, *madrasa*, and especially its *türbe*. After his victory over the power struggle during the Interregnum following the Battle of Ankara (28 July 1402), Mehmed I, also known as Çelebi Mehmed, ascended the Ottoman throne in 1413. He began building the Yeşil Complex a short time later as a potent display of the magnificence of the state, which had just regained its power. However, in 1421, Mehmed fell ill while hunting in Edirne, became paralysed, and passed away shortly thereafter. As a result of the sultan's sudden death, the construction of the complex could not be completed. Because of his fear of the opposition, Mehmed's son, Murad II, concealed his father's death until he ascended the throne. Later, Mehmed's body was placed in the *türbe* of his complex, which was completed after his death. The *imaret* to the southeast of the mosque was recently restored and is closed to visitors. The *hammam,* still in use, to the west of the *türbe*, is not mentioned in the *waqf* charter.

Yeşil Madrasa (Museum of Turkish and Islamic Arts)

The *madrasa*, about 100 m. to the west of the mosque, is situated in the middle of a yard and is today used as the Museum of Turkish and Islamic Arts. Approaching from the street one reaches the back first; walking past the eastern side observing the remains of the basic geometric tile decorations the window tympana, the entrance opening to the outside like an *iwan* is in the middle of the northern side. The columns and capitals that support the portico were gathered from various Byzantine buildings. Most of portico's bays, which surround the courtyard on three sides, are covered with a single dome each, while the cells are covered with vaults and the vault of the western *iwan* is decorated with lovely turquoise and dark-blue tiles. Today, a staircase built to provide access to the upper storey, is found on the side wings: the *madrasa* was planned as a two storey structure, but because of the sudden death of Mehmed I, the upper storey was never completed. The domed *dershane* directly opposite the entrance protrudes outside and it is understood from the *mihrab* on the *qibla* wall that it also served as a prayer room.
The first *müderris* appointed to the *madrasa* was the son of Molla Şemseddin Fenari,

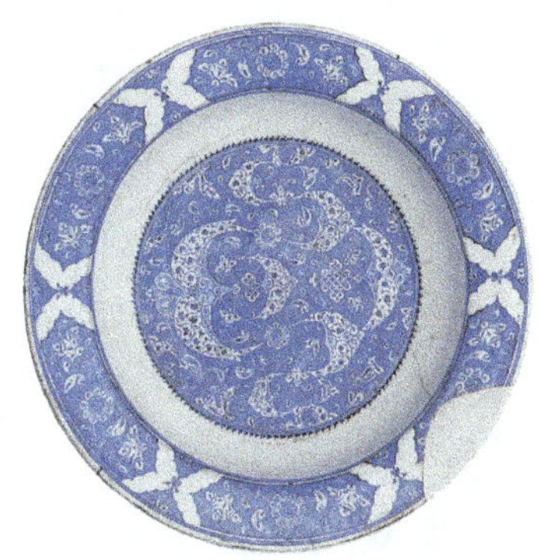

Ceramic plata, 15th century, Turkish and Islamic Arts Museum (Inv. Num. 814), Bursa.

the renowned Ottoman intellectual. It must have seemed strange for an 18-year-old to reach a position that required so much responsibility. Thus, at the first lecture he gave at the *madrasa*, both students and learned men from Bursa and environs directed questions at him in a kind of examination. After this it became a custom for all *müderrises* of this *madrasa* to be examined in this way.

The museum has a very nice, well displayed collection with, among other things, examples of woodwork, ceramic work, metalwork, manuscripts, *fermans* and embroidery work. The ceramic examples described below are displayed in the showcases in the western *iwan* and the others are in the cells on the east.

Y. D.

Ceramic Plate

(Inv. Num. 814, 15th century)

Researchers agree that İznik white-clay ceramics first appeared in the 15th century. These ceramics made of hard, white clay and thin, smooth transparent glaze were the result of changes made by tile experts in the preparation of the clay. Some innovations and changes in the decoration of these ceramics are especially noteworthy. It is believed that the introduction of Chinese ceramics into the Ottoman court played an important role in these developments. Deep bowls, large-footed vessels, wide shallow plates with decorated borders, plates with wavy edges, pitchers, and jars were the favourite types of ceramics used in daily life in this period.

This plate of white clay produced in İznik is of the group of ceramics known as "blue-white". The centre is indented and the edges are turned out. The decoration is done with the under-glaze technique. The white ornamentation consists of foliage, large *rumis* and Chinese clouds in the centre indentation and the edge, painted on a cobalt-blue background.

L. B.

Bronze Brazier

(Inv. Num. 107, 15th century)

People have developed various methods for heating the places they live in. In the Middle Ages, heating was provided by fireplaces, clay-lined pit stoves called

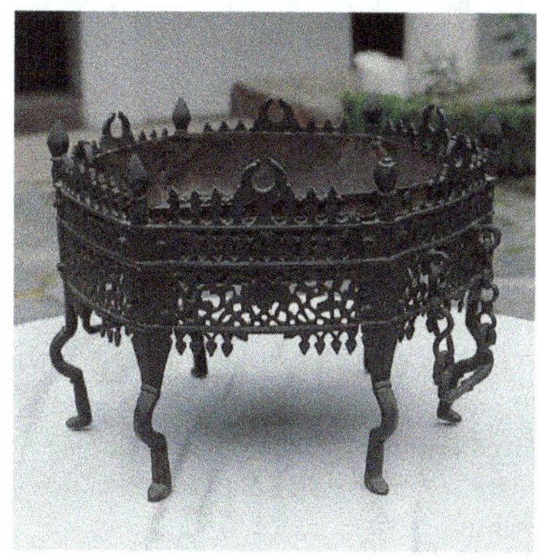

Bronze brazier, 15th century, Turkish and Islamic Arts Museum (Inv. Num. 107), Bursa.

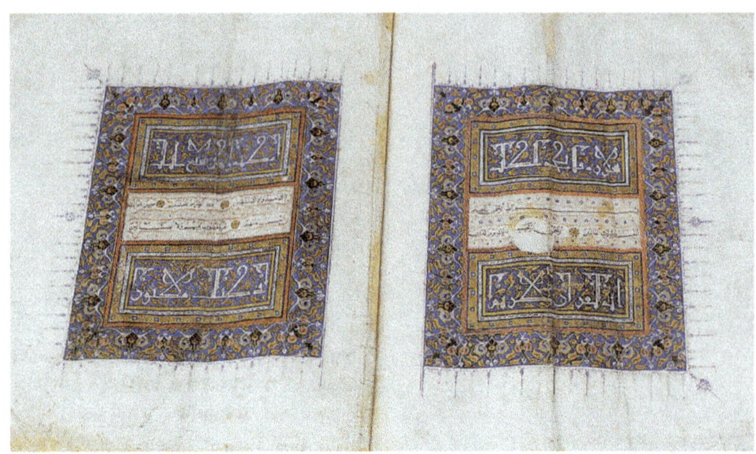

The Koran, 1435, Turkish and Islamic Arts Museum (Inv. Num. 207), Bursa.

tandırs and braziers. Fireplaces were most often used to heat large spaces such as the covered areas in *caravanserais*; because of the loss of heat and the large amount of fuel consumed, this method of heating was used in the residences of the wealthy. The people of lower economic means preferred to heat their living spaces with braziers or *tandırs*.

Braziers are vessels made of baked clay or metal, into which hot coals are placed. The body of the container, in which the fire is set, is placed on a footed stand. To prevent damage that could be caused by red-hot ashes and coals that fall to the ground, large pieces of "brazier board" or a "brazier tray" are placed under the stand. Brazier board was usually made of wood that does not easily catch fire, like hornbeam or oak.

This brazier is cast iron. The hexagonal body rests on six curled feet and has two handles. The six sides are each decorated with symmetrically placed lattice floral motifs.

The Koran

(Inv. Num. 207, 1435, Sultan Murad II)

Muslims believe that the *Qur'an* (or Koran), the holy book of Islam, is the word of God delivered to Muhammad by the angel Gabriel. The first sura of the *Qur'an* was delivered in 610 and this transaction continued over the next 23 years until the Prophet's death. As the revelations came, they were memorised by Mohammed and other Muslims and, at the same time, scribes wrote the verses on various materials like rocks, scapulae, date leaves, and animal hides. However, in the Prophet's lifetime it was never thought to bring these various texts together into one book but after his death, in the time of *Caliph* Abu Bakr, all existing texts were examined and placed in one volume.

The *Qur'an* is divided into 114 chapters, each of which is called a *sura*; each of the verses that make up the *sura* is called an *ayet* in Turkish. Because of disagreement about where the verses begin and end,

there is no unanimous opinion on the exact number of the more than 6000 verses in the *Qur'an*.
This *Koran* is hand written in the *naskhi* style of Arabic lettering; the titles and beginnings of the *suras* are decorated with gold; a great amount of gold gilding has been used in the ornamentation. The floral motifs on the exterior surface of the brown-leather binding with a folded cover were applied with a mould. On the inner-side surfaces of the covers and the folded cover are decorations in the *katı'* technique, the background of which is affixed with cloth. Floral motifs within rosettes were applied with paint and gold gilding.

L. B.

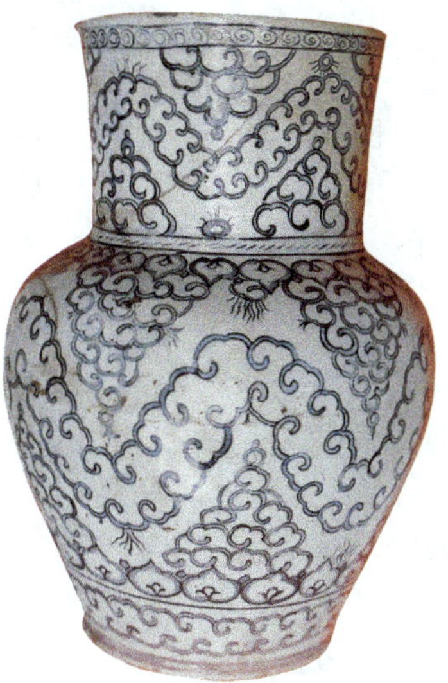

Ceramic vase, 15th century, Turkish and Islamic Arts Museum (Inv. Num. 3374), Bursa.

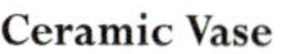

Ceramic Vase

(Inv. Num. 3374, 15th century)

This is an example of İznik "blue-white" ceramic ware. Its pear-shaped body narrows at the bottom and it has a cylindrical neck. The designs drawn in the underglaze technique, are repeated on the body and the neck, and consist of stylised cloud motifs and curled leaves applied in blue, on a white background.

L. B.

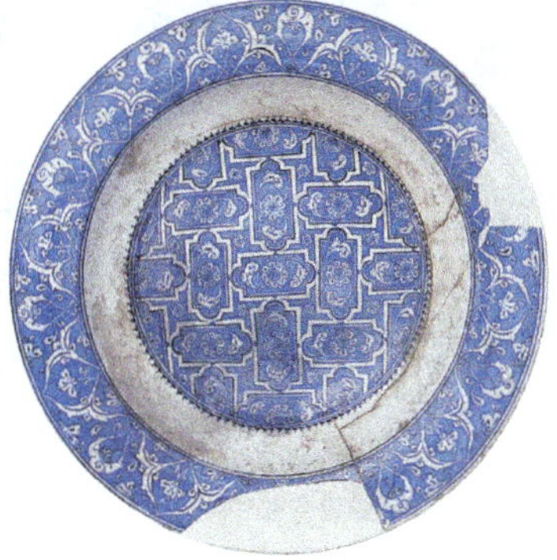

Ceramic plate, 15th century, Turkish and Islamic Arts Museum (Inv. No. 813), Bursa.

Ceramic Plate

(Inv. Num. 813, 15th century)

This is an example of İznik "blue-white" ceramic ware. Though the clay of these ceramics is white and hard like porcelain, it is not translucent in the same way. The glaze is very thin, colourless, transparent and shiny. Because of these qualities, the glaze does not crack during the firing process. In "blue-white" ceramic ware, the colour contrast between the background and the motifs is what catches the eye.
This plate with a depressed centre and a projecting rim is decorated in the underglaze technique. On the border strip, white *rumis* and *palmettes* have been painted on a cobalt-blue background. The circular area in the centre of the plate is

Ferman, 1458, Turkish and Islamic Arts Museum (Inv. Num. 4320), Bursa.

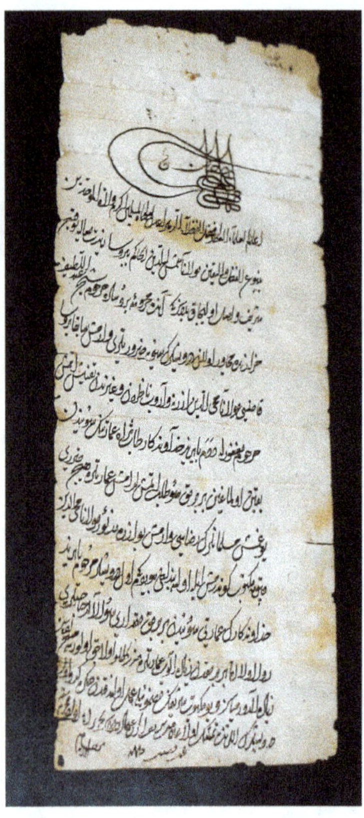

decorated with a geometric composition, the empty spaces of which are filled with small-flower and leaf motifs.

L. B.

Ferman (Inv. Num. 4320, dated 1458)

Fermans are the written orders of the sultans. *Fermans* kept in Ottoman archives, various museums, and private collections supply important information about the administration and the socio-economic condition of the state. At the same time, these documents are rare examples of the art of decorative writing. These documents bore the *tuğra* or elaborately inscribed signature of the sultan and their contents were ordered according to a certain pattern. For example, a *ferman* consisted of the salutation, *tuğra*, titles, prayer, narrative, command, the repeating of the command, and date, in that order. In certain *fermans*, there are also "threat" sentences stating the punishment to be carried out if the order is not obeyed or the duty is not performed. Furthermore, it is interesting that curses in the form of "May earth and heaven reject those who disobey this command" are also found on some *fermans*.

The example here is a decree sent from Edirne by Sultan Mehmed II to the Bursa Kadı Şemseddin in 1458. Written in gilded black ink, the *ferman* makes mention of dervishes living around the *imaret* built by the sultan's great grandfather Murad I, also known as Hüdavendigar. It is understood from the *ferman* that the *dervish*es requested some of the water brought to the Hüdavendigar İmaret for their own use and that the sultan assented to their request.

L. B.

Ceramic Plate (Inv. Num. 2659, end 14th century, beginning 15th century)

This is an example of the "Miletus type" of İznik ceramic ware. This group of ceramics is distinguishable by the use of cobalt-blue designs on a white *engobe* background. Although free leaf designs, star motifs in the centre, and radial lines are frequently seen on these plates, there is no known example where a composition has been repeated a second time. In this

Ceramic plate, end of 14th century-beginning of 15th century, Turkish and Islamic Arts Museum (Inv. Num. 2659), Bursa.

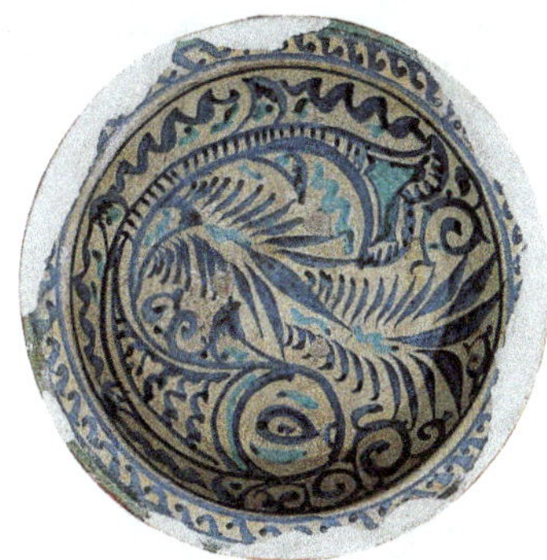

example, a large fish with its body conforming to the circular shape of the bowl is seen among curled branches.

L. B.

Yeşil Mosque

Approaching from the back, the pale gold of the cut-stone walls gives way to full marble on the northern facade, which is decorated with exquisite stone craftsmanship especially around the windows –though unfinished– and on the portal. On the lower level are four windows and two outdoor *mihrabs* and above them are four loggias. One of the most interesting features of the facade is the absence of a portico: corbels still visible on the front indicate that a portico was planned but, for some reason, never completed. The inscription above the low arch of the portal gives the name of the architect as Hacı İvaz. On entering, there are two corridors on both sides leading to a room in the northern corner and to the steps leading upstairs, which is not open to visitors. There is then is a small and dark *iwan*-like chamber, covered with dark-green tiles which are set with medallions decorated in the *cuerda seca* technique. Reaching the inner court it is impossible not to be carried away with the decoration –like heaven, as Evliya Çelebi says– so different from other mosques in Bursa of this period. This example of Ottoman tiling to adorn a mosque breaks away from preceding Seljuq examples, setting a style that was to be developed in the following century when the İznik kilns were producing their highest quality, though in a way very different from that seen here.
A soaring dome with a lantern covers the central court. The fountain has a nicely carved marble water jet in the centre. To the east and the west, the two large *iwans*, whose walls are covered with tiles, are again surmounted with soaring fluted domes. The two recesses flanking the entrance to the north of the central court were for the *müezzins*; the loggia above the entrance is the royal loge upstairs. All the walls and flat ceilings of these three small recesses are completely covered with tiles; the ones in the royal loge upstairs are particularly richly decorated. Gold floral decorations on the hexagonal tiles on the *iwans* on the east and west sides are noteworthy, as are those on the

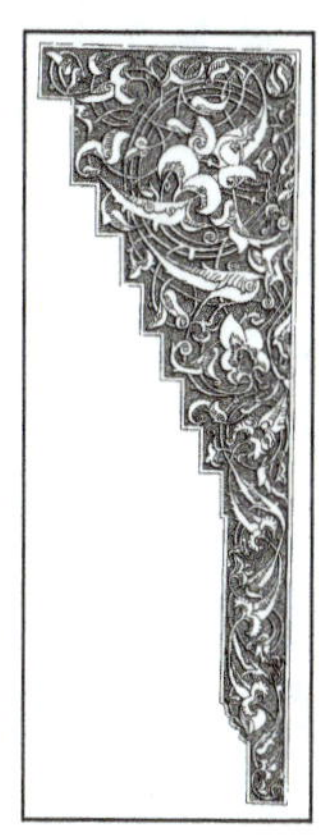

Decoration on the portal of Yeşil Mosque, Bursa (from Ş. Çakmak).

Yeşil Mosque, View from the south, 1419-24, Mehmed I, Bursa.

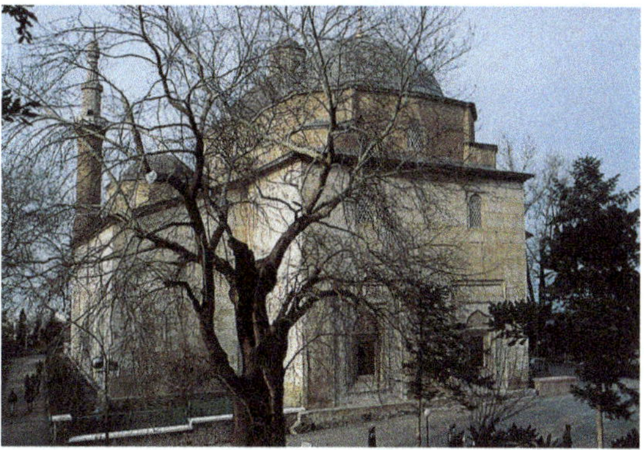

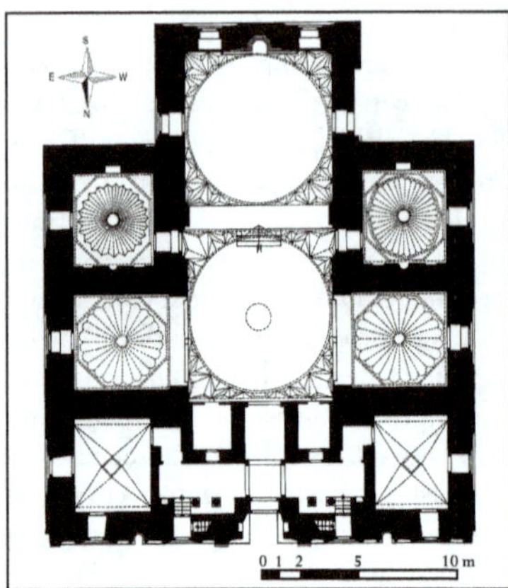

Plan of Yeşil Mosque, Bursa (from Z. Sönmez).

walls of two recesses located on the ground floor.

This mosque was designed to provide lodging and a meeting area for the wandering *dervishes* who played an important role in the social and religious life of the time –though today the whole structure is used as a mosque. The *tabhanes* located between the *iwans* and the prayer hall, provided with fireplaces and shelving, were used as lodging for the *dervishes*. The niches and fireplaces in the *tabhanes* in the southeast and southwest are superbly decorated with geometric and floral motifs in stucco. On the inner surfaces of their domes, traces of wall painting can be seen, as in the domes over the *iwans*. The prayer hall to the south, separated from the central court with a "Bursa arch", is again covered with superb tiles and the *mihrab* is especially outstanding; as Evliya Çelebi says, he is incapable of describing it. According to an inscription on the upper part of one of the two columns flanking the *mihrab* niche, the tiles were manufactured by artisans from Tabriz (Iran). The Persian influences can also be seen on the tiles on the *mihrab* as well as the upper floor chambers. The mosque was open for worship in 1419, but the decoration was not completed until1424. According to the inscriptions in the royal loge, Nakkash Ali carried out the painting of the decorations and supervised the ornamentation while the tile master was Muhammed al-Majnun.

Y. D.

Yeşil Türbe

To the south of Yeşil Mosque

Located on a small hillock, Yeşil Türbe rises at a considerably higher level than Yeşil Mosque. Almost the entire body of this octagonal *türbe* is covered with turquoise tiles; the tympana of the lower row of the paired windows on each face

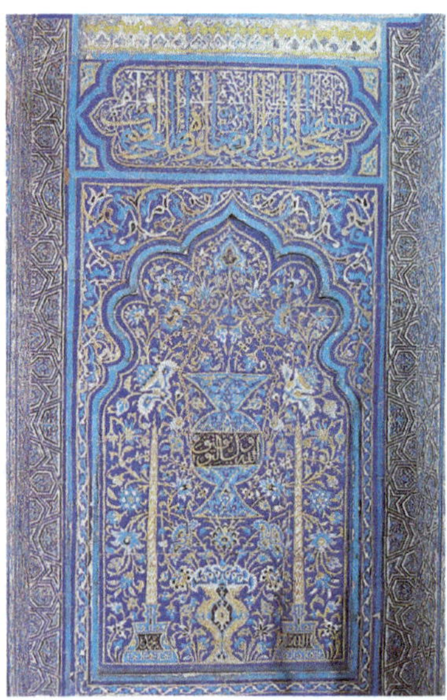

Yeşil Türbe, Detail from the mihrab, 1419-24, Mehmed I, Bursa.

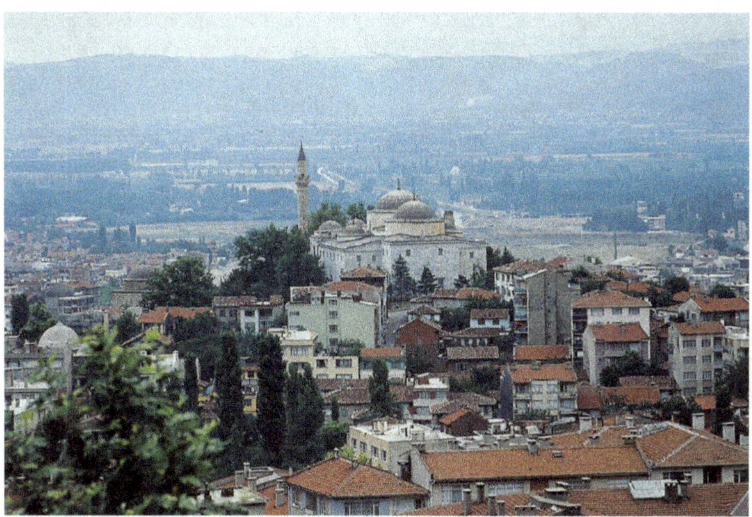

Yıldırım Complex, General view from the south, 1389-99, Bayezid I, Bursa.

of the *türbe* are also decorated with tiles. The tiles, which once covered the facade of the portal, have completely disappeared; yet, the oyster-shell conch resting on Turkish triangles and the niches on the sides are still very attractive. *Kündekari* technique is used on both wings of the magnificent wooden door. There are six panels in all: two large and four small; extending around these panels is an inscription that includes the names of Sultan Mehmed I; the architect Hacı İvaz, son of Ahi Bayezid; and the tile master craftsman, Hacı Ali, son of Ahmet, who was originally from Tabriz.

Inside, the lower section of the walls is covered with hexagonal tiles. Between the windows, there is also one large multicoloured *şemse* sunburst in *cuerda seca* technique. The *mihrab* is also decorated with tiles and its rich ornamentation is every bit as glorious as the *mihrab* of Yeşil Mosque. Unique decorative elements are found in the tile-mosaic that adorns the ceilings of the lower row of casements. The dome rises on a lovely cornice of Turkish triangles. Four of the sarcophagi present in the *türbe* are decorated with tiles; the tile sarcophagus of Sultan Mehmed I located in the centre is especially beautiful, and of the highest standard of workmanship. The other graves belong to his sons Mustafa, Mahmud, and Yusuf, along with the women sultans, including the nanny of the sultan. Currently closed to visitors, the crypt floor has an interesting plan consisting of five areas, three small, and two large; no other example of such a crypt, consisting of several areas, is known.

Y. D.

IV.1.b **Yıldırım Complex**

Yıldırım District (Mahallesi), Bursa.

In this complex built by Sultan Bayezid I there is a mosque, a *madrasa*, a *darüşşifa*, an *imaret*, a *hammam*, and a *türbe*; all the

Yıldırım Madrasa, dome with muqarnas on the eastern portico, 1389-1399, Bayezid I, Bursa.

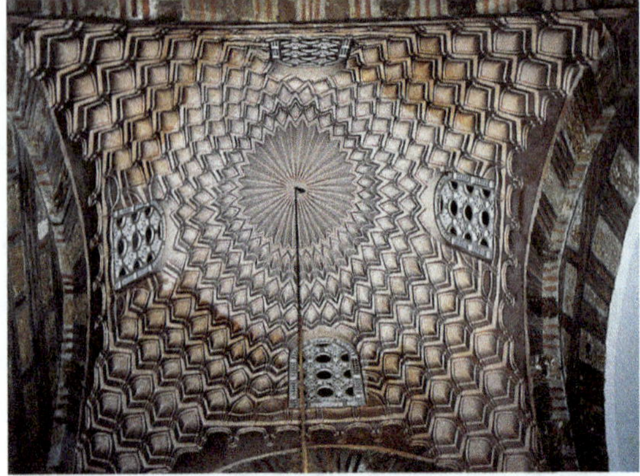

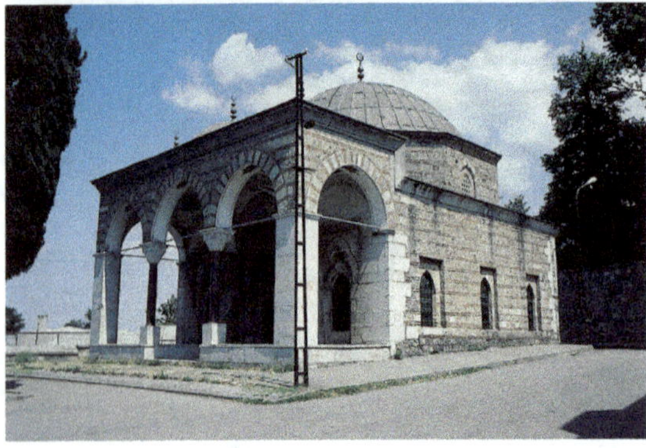

Türbe of Bayezid I, entrance facade, 1406, Emir Süleyman Çelebi, Bursa.

structures except the *imaret* have survived to the present day. The whole complex is called "Yıldırım" based on the epithet of Sultan Bayezid I who is also known as Sultan Yıldırım Bayezid. Yıldırım means lightning or thunderbolt in Turkish, suggesting that the sultan was able to move his armies "as quick as lightning" in order to crush his enemies. Hence the name and most of the edifices he had built are called Yıldırım Mosque, Yıldırım Complex, etc. This complex is located on a hill, some way away from the town centre and stands in a lovely park, set on terraces due to the slope. The *hammam* hidden among the houses is still in use.

Yıldırım Mosque

The mosque, the central building of the complex, is built with cut stone. The mosque's present minaret is a later addition; the original minarets in the northeast and northwest corners collapsed at an unknown time. The five-bayed portico in the front is also built with cut stone and surmounted with domes. The two loggias above the outdoor *mihrab*s located on either side of the portal were to provide light for the staircase to the original minarets. Passing through the plain portal *iwan* topped with a tiny dome, one emerges into the inner court covered by a soaring dome and flanked with *iwan*s on both sides. These *iwans* are also flanked on both sides with rooms covered with flat-topped cross-vaults but only the ones to the south, also flanking the prayer hall, have furnishings of spectacular stucco fireplace and shelving enhanced with embedded tile pieces. The mosque was designed to respond to the needs of the *Ahi dervish*es by providing them with meeting and boarding places; hence the rooms with the fireplace and shelving are the *tabhane*s. There is a monumental arch separating the inner court from the prayer hall; this is the first example of a "Bursa arch" with its top flat and recessed, another beautiful example of which can be seen in Yeşil Mosque. There is no record of construction, but it is believed that building must have taken place sometime between Bayezid I's ascension to the throne in 1389 and the preparation of the *waqf* charter in 1399.

Y. D.

Orhan Mosque, mihrab, 1339-40, Orhan Gazi, Bursa.

Yıldırım Madrasa

The *madrasa*, on a lower terrace to the northwest of the mosque, is today used as a health centre. The attractive walls built with alternating courses of stones and bricks are enhanced with the decoration in the tympana of the windows. The presence of a pair of small niches placed together on the side walls of the entrance to the *iwan*, rising higher than the rest of the structure, is a rarely seen characteristic and its dome is very attractive with its Turkish triangles. The dome covering the portico is very striking with its *muqarnas* decoration. There were latrines in the corner to the right of the entrance, but they were removed during recent repair work. Behind the vaulted porticos are student cells surrounding the courtyard on three sides, and the large *iwan* opposite the entrance fully protrudes and was used as a summer *dershane*. Strangely enough, there is not a winter *dershane* in this *madrasa* as there is in other *madrasas* of this period; in such *madrasas*, during the winter, either the front of the *iwan* was closed with wooden panes or classes were held in the complex's mosque.

Y. D.

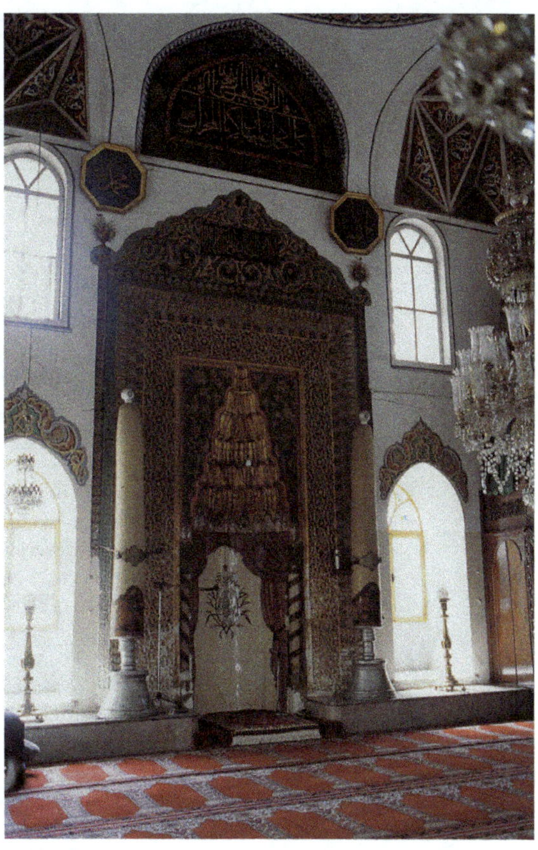

Darüşşifa

The *darüşşifa*, one of the most important buildings in the complex, has been restored in recent years. It is important for it is one of the few Ottoman *darüşşifas* that have survived up to the present day. Built on a steep slope to the east of the mosque, the cells and porticoes on the side wings are graded with steps and the brickwork is noteworthy.

Y. D.

Türbe

The *türbe* in this complex belongs to Bayezid I, who was defeated and taken prisoner by Tamerlane at the Battle of Ankara (1402). Some historians say he committed suicide; others maintain that he fell ill and died in Akşehir in central Anatolia. After his death, he was buried in Akşehir in the *türbe* of Seyyid Mahmud Hayran, but later his body was handed over to his son Musa Çelebi and sent to

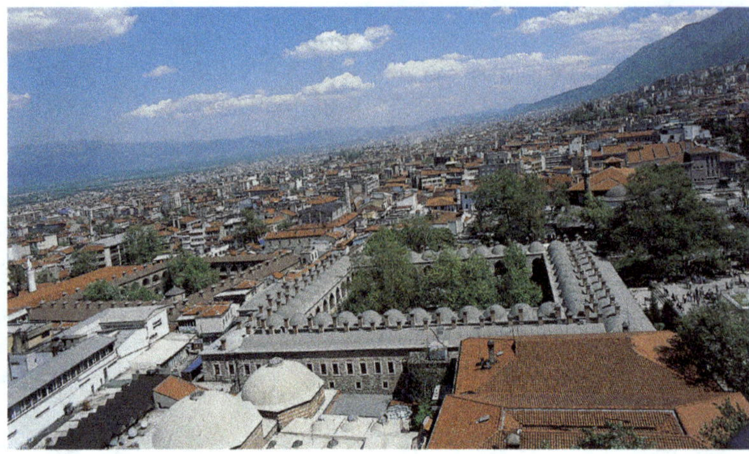

Koza Han, general view, 1492, Bayezid II, Bursa.

Bursa at the order of Tamerlane. Because it was his will to be buried near the mosque he had built, his body was buried near the mosque in 1403-1404; in 1406, his son Emir Süleyman Çelebi had the present *türbe* constructed over his grave. During his siege of Bursa in 1413, Karamanid Bey Mehmed II took vengeance on his father's murderer, Bayezid I, by removing his body from the grave and burning it.
The *türbe* of Bayezid I is a simple square building surmounted by a dome and the three-bayed portico in front served as a model for later Ottoman *türbe*s with porticoes.

Y. D.

The following monuments: c, d, e, and f are almost side by side; Orhan Mosque is to the east of the square, a small structure compared to the large Great Mosque at the western end of the square. From Orhan Mosque towards the west is Koza Han; then, past some shops hiding the Bey Hammam of Orhan's Complex, is the Emir Han and Great Mosque. This area, known as Heykel, is the heart of the town and always very lively. Adjoining them on the north are more hans *and the* bedesten *of the Early Ottoman period forming the central market area of Bursa. The* hans *are closed on Sundays and religious holidays.*

IV.1.c **Orhan Mosque**

Orhan, who ascended the throne in 1324, captured Bursa in 1326 and entered the city with a magnificent ceremony. In order to develop the city, which had not yet expanded beyond its city walls, Orhan had the "Lower Fortress" built towards the east as well as the mosque complex that bears his name. Of the buildings that made up the complex, the *madrasa*, *mektep*, and *imaret* have not survived to the present day.
In 1413, while Sultan Mehmed I was away in Rumelia on a military expedition, Karamanid Bey Mehmed II besieged Bursa. Hacı İvaz Pasha withdrew to the

citadel and tried to defend the old city. In the last days of the one-month-long siege Karamanid Bey Mehmed Bey II set fire to both Great Mosque and Orhan Mosque. The fire damaged the portico and the main facade. According to the inscription above the entrance Orhan had this mosque built in 1339-1340, and after the Karamanid Bey Mehmed II destroyed it during his occupation of Bursa, the *Vizier* Bayezid Pasha repaired it on the order of Sultan Mehmed I in 1417.

The five-bayed portico to the north of Orhan Mosque is very attractive with spandrels decorated in stone and brick. Orhan Mosque was planned to accommodate the needs of the wandering *Ahi dervish*es by providing them with a lodging and meeting area. The domed *iwans* that flank the domed central court were constructed with this aim in mind. A dome covers the main prayer hall and the *mihrab* is one of the most beautiful, coulourfully painted examples of an Anatolian stucco *mihrab*.

IV.1.d **Koza Han**

In Bursa, a great number of the *hans* that survive in good condition today date from the 14th and 15th centuries indicating that Bursa was an important commercial centre during these centuries. Some *hans* built in the commercial centres of Anatolia were given names such as Salt Han, Silk Han, Rice Han, and Copper Han, thus emphasising the particular commodity that each *han* traded. The presence of two separate *hans* called İpek (Silk) Han and Koza (Cocoon) Han provides evidence that Bursa was an important silk centre in the 14th and 15th centuries, as it was during the Byzantine era, when it was also known as an active silk centre. The story goes that a Chinese princess who was migrating to Bursa brought some silkworm eggs, then, when she was forbidden to take the eggs out of China, she hid them in her hair.

Silk is a natural fibre obtained from the cocoons of silkworms (*Bombyx mori*). Silk production begins with the incubation of silkworm eggs, two thousand of which weigh only one gram. Under favourable conditions, the silkworms hatch in 11-14 days and feed on mulberry leaves for 24-28 days. Next, they secrete the fibre and imprison themselves in the cocoons within 48-72 hours. The silkworm in the cocoon undergoes metamorphosis and comes out of the cocoon by cutting it as a winged moth. It is necessary to kill the worm before it comes out so that the cocoon fibres are not damaged: this process called “drowning” is done by either treating the cocoons with steam or hot air, or stretching them out to dry in the sun. In the final stage, the cocoons are softened using various methods, the cocoon fibres are caught by a small besom and wound onto spinning wheels and crude silk thread is spun. From each cocoon between 300 and 1400 m. of silk is obtained. As silk is obtained by killing the insect inside the cocoon, silk cloth is religiously unlawful according to Islamic sages.

This two-storey *han* has one entrance to the south opening to the upper floor and an attractive portal to the north opening on to the courtyard, which is surrounded by two-storied porticoes on four sides. The upper portico, made of wood up until recent times, has been renovated in order to resemble the lower one. The

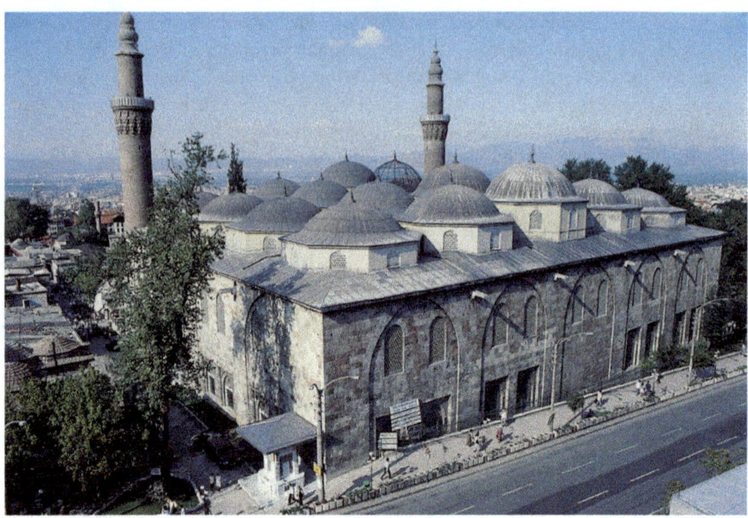

Great Mosque, general view from the southwest, 1400, Bayezid I, Bursa.

octagonal two-storey structure in the courtyard has the *masjid* upstairs and the ablution fountain below; an octagonal column in the middle and eight other piers in the corners support the vaulting and the *masjid*. Sultan Bayezid II built Koza Han between 1489-92 in order to provide income for the *imaret* of his mosque complex in İstanbul.

Y. D.

IV.1.e **Great Mosque (Ulu Cami)**

Bayezid I, who ascended the throne after his father Murad I was killed in battle in 1389, constructed the Bursa Great Mosque. Bayezid had his brother, Yakup Çelebi, killed in a struggle for the throne. The story goes that when Sultan Bayezid I defeated the Crusaders at Niğbolu (Nicopolis) on the Danube in 1396, he vowed that he would build 20 mosques with his newly won booty. However, he was in fact convinced to build one mosque with 20 domes instead and the structure was completed in 1400. It is reported that Tamerlane used the mosque for stabling and storing hay during his occupation of Bursa. And according to another legend, in 1413, during the final days of his 31-day occupation of the city, the Karamanid Bey Mehmed II tried to burn the mosque down by piling wood around it. As a result of the damage done –presumably by this attempt according to some researchers– to the stones in lower part of the walls and the portals, the mosque's exterior surface was plastered with mortar. In the 1950s the ashlars of the facades were completely renewed.

Atatürk Avenue extends along the south *qibla* wall, which is built with cut stones, punctuated by arches and windows, as are the other fronts. The rectangular structure has three entrances: the main portal in the middle of the north facade is more elaborate than the other portals on the east and the west fronts. Adjoining the northern corners are two minarets. Once inside, there is a very different atmosphere than in the typical Bursa mosques with *tabhanes*: this mosque's large prayer hall is arranged in 20 bays, separated from one another by 12 huge piers aligned in three rows of four, supporting 20 domes of equal size. These piers destroy the integrity of the space and give the mosque a dark and oppressive atmosphere. This example, which continues the Anatolian Seljuq tradition of mosques with equal size multiple bays, lacks the integrity seen in 16th-century Ottoman mosques; another Early Ottoman example with this layout is the Eski Mosque in Edirne. Like the minarets outside, the painted decoration inside is a 19th-century renovation. The real masterpiece here is the *minbar* of walnut wood made in the *kündekari* technique famous for its workmanship and decoration. The sides of the *minbar* are composed of small geometric pieces decorated with floral motifs; these interlocking pieces are held together without the use of glue or any other binding material. According to Evliya Çelebi, it is so beautifully decorated that even if all the artisans of the world come together, they could not have produced anything similar; except the *minbar* in Sinop on the Black Sea coast. Hacı Mehmed bin Abdülaziz of Antep, the artisan of this *minbar*, also made the *minbar* of Manisa Great Mosque.

IV.1.f **Emir Han** (option)

Emir Han, also known as Bey Han, is part of the first royal complex of Bursa, commissioned by Orhan Gazi, composing a mosque, *hammam*, *madrasa*, *mektep*, and *imaret*. When the site was chosen, great attention was paid to the development of the town, and the complex was constructed in an empty area to the east. The area was enlivened by the construction of this complex and even today forms Bursa's commercial centre.

Entering the *han* through the simple gate by the northeast minaret of Great Mosque, one arrives on the upper floor; there is another gate on the north opening into the street on the lower level. The *han* consists of rooms, located behind porticoes, and surrounding a courtyard and a small stable downstairs. There are no windows in the 36 lower rooms; in the upper 38 rooms there is a fireplace and a window opening outwards. There is no inscription, but it is believed that it was built in the second half of the 14th century. Emir Han is one of the earliest examples of the Ottoman city *hans*.

Second day

The Türbes *of Osman Gazi and Orhan Gazi are located in Tophane District (Mahallesi), on Osmangazi Avenue within the old citadel of Bursa. It is also a good area for a stroll, up the hill and past some of the old renovated houses. The view from the terrace, where the* türbes *are located, is quite magnificent.*

IV.1.g **Türbe of Osman Gazi**

Next to the Türbe *of Orhan Gazi.*

Osman Gazi, who founded the Ottoman State that bears his name, passed the throne to his son Orhan while he was still alive because of his age and ill health. It is

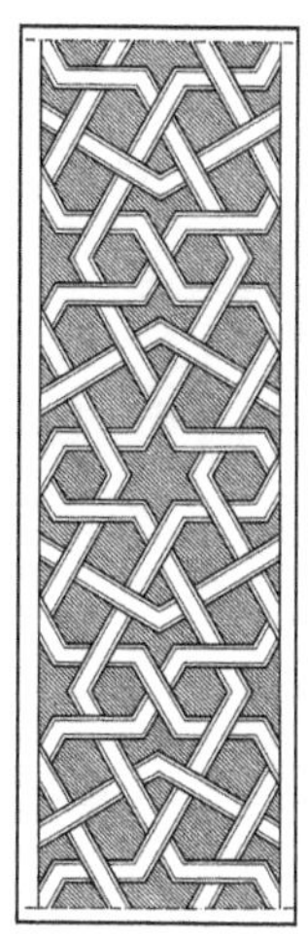

Decoration on the portal of Great Mosque, Bursa (from Ş. Çakmak).

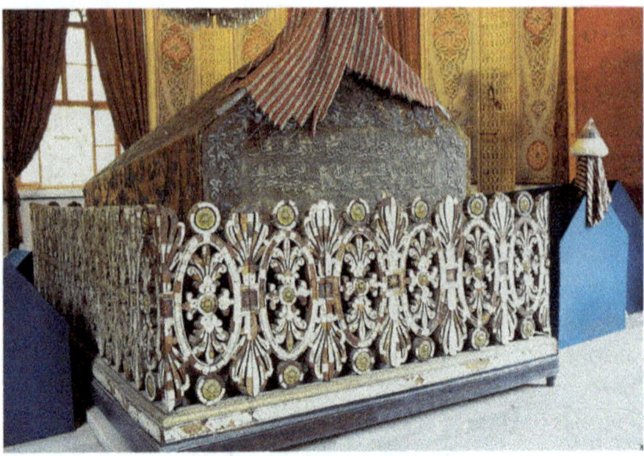

Osman Gazi Türbe, wooden sarcophagus, 1863, Sultan Abdülaziz, Bursa.

said that, before the conquest of Bursa, he told his son Orhan Gazi that when he died he wanted to be buried in Bursa beneath the "Silver Dome". It is not certain whether Bursa was conquered before or after Osman's death.

What Osman described as the "Silver Dome" was a Byzantine chapel occupying an elevated area of Bursa; from a distance the structure and its lead-covered dome gave the impression of being made of silver. Osman Gazi was buried here as he had requested but his *türbe* suffered major damage in a fire that destroyed more than half of Bursa in 1801 and it was completely ruined in the earthquake of 1855. It was impossible to repair, so at the order of Sultan Abdülaziz the present *türbe* was constructed on the old foundations in 1863.

The octagonal structure is covered with a dome. Its architectural style and decoration belongs to the "Westernisation Period" of Turkish architecture: from the 17th century onwards, Turkish architecture and decoration fell under the influence of European art; Baroque, Rococo and Empire styles deeply affected traditional Ottoman architecture and design. In this building there are examples of intricate wall paintings with floral motifs. Of the 17 sarcophagi placed on a marble floor, only five have been identified. Osman's sarcophagus, located in the centre, is surrounded with a latticed wooden screen inlaid with mother-of-pearl.

Y. D.

IV.1.h **Türbe of Orhan Gazi**

Next to the Türbe *of Osman Gazi.*

Orhan Gazi, who ascended the throne in 1324 as the second Ottoman Sultan, passed away in 1362. In his time, the first steps were taken to organise the army and to systemise such matters as the distribution of money, clothing, and land. Orhan extended Ottoman boundaries with his conquests; he seized Bursa in 1326 and entered the city with great celebration and then made it the capital of the young Ottoman Emirate. Immediately after the conquest, various buildings were constructed which began to improve and beautify the city and thus the first large Ottoman mosque complex consisting of a mosque, *madrasa*, *mektep*, *hammam*, *imaret*, and *han* was built in Orhan's time.

When Orhan died in 1362, he was interred in another Byzantine structure nearby the "Silver Dome" where his father was buried.

Orhan Gazi's *türbe*, like that of his father, was damaged in the fire of 1801 and completely collapsed in the earthquake of 1855; Sultan Abdülaziz had the present *türbe* built on the old foundations in 1863. The central section of this square structure is covered with a dome supported by four huge columns, while the corridors surrounding it are covered with vaults. It is understood from the beautiful *opus sectile* decoration on the floor that a Byzantine building originally occupied the place where Orhan Gazi Türbe now stands. There are 20 other sarcophagi in the *türbe* whereas Orhan's sarcophagus is surrounded with a screen of lattice brass.

Y. D.

Around the Muradiye Complex are other sites of interest like the 17th-century Muradiye Konak and Hüsnü Züber Evi.

IV.1.i **Muradiye Complex**

In Muradiye District (Mahallesi). Follow the signs for Muradiye.

Among the buildings constructed by Ottoman Sultans, mosques occupy an important place. Generally, structures with various functions, such as *madrasas*, *hammams*, *darüşşifas*, *imarets*, etc., were placed in the mosque's surroundings. Thus every sultan commissioned a group of buildings known as a "Complex", which bore the sultan's name and met various social needs. The complex built by Murad II in Bursa consists of a mosque, *madrasa*, *hammam* and *imaret* as well as *türbes* dating from various periods; this is the last imperial complex to be built in Bursa.

Y. D.

Muradiye Mosque

In the earthquake of 1855, many historical buildings in Bursa suffered great damage and minarets either wholly or partially collapsed. At that time, Ahmet

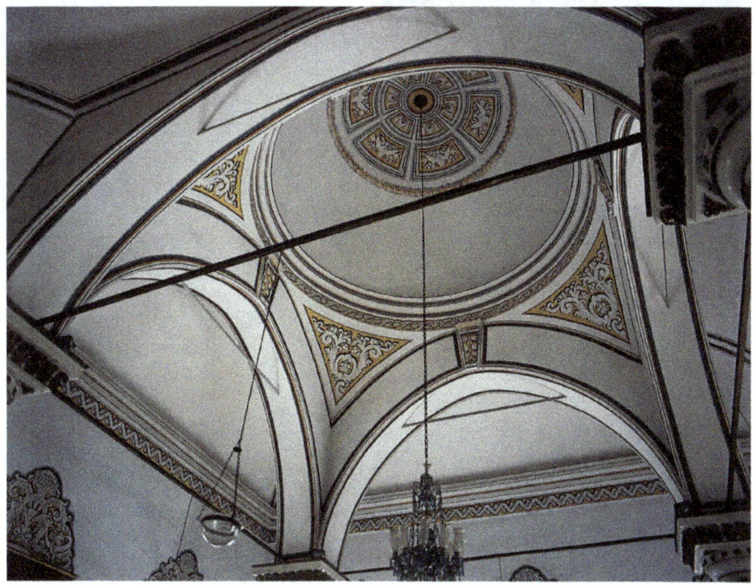

Orhan Gazi Türbe, dome, 1863, Sultan Abdülaziz, Bursa.

Muradiye Mosque, prayer hall, 1426, Murad II, Bursa.

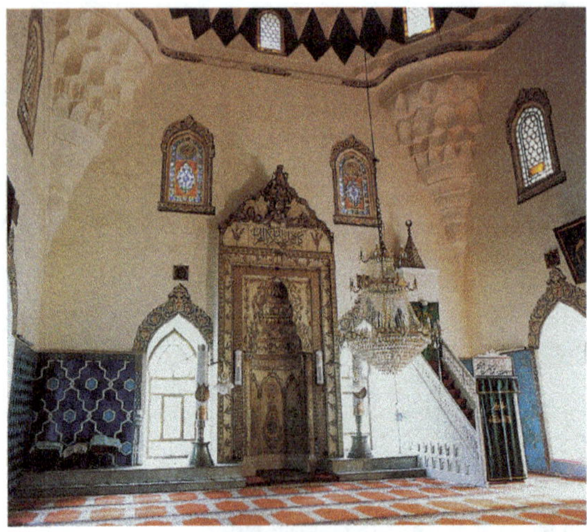

Muradiye Mosque, detail of wooden door wings, 1426, Murad II, Bursa.

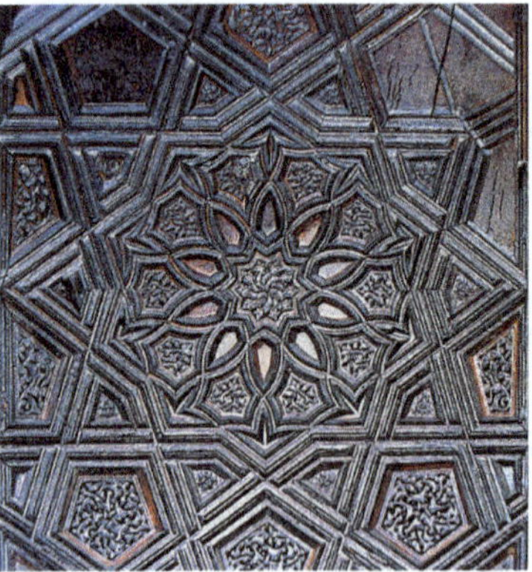

Vefik Pasha, the governor of Bursa, engaged a French architect by the name of Léon Parvillé to undertake the repairs. In many of the buildings, the repairs carried out by this architect were not in complete accordance with the original style of the buildings. For example, the minarets were rebuilt according to the taste and building traditions of the 19th century; the northwest minaret here was also restored by Parvillé, who removed the walls dividing the *tabhanes* on the east and west from the prayer hall transforming them into *iwans*. The spandrels of the five-bay portico are all decorated very attractively with geometric motifs implemented in stone, brick, and tiles reminiscent of brick ornamentation found on the facades of late Byzantine buildings. Use of yellow in the tiles, seen in the portico's window tympana, began in the early 15th century and is characteristic of that period. The entrance to the mosque is almost like a tiny room covered with a flat ceiling and decorated with tiles and *kalemişi*. According to the inscription above the entrance, the construction was begun in May 1425 and completed in 1426. The carved ornamentation on the wings of the wooden door to the prayer hall is a very fine example of the period. The Muradiye Mosque includes all the characteristics of mosques with *tabhanes*; an interesting feature here is the "U-shaped" corridor, originally the entrance to the *tabhanes*. The dome soaring above the central court is slightly larger than that of the prayer hall, which is supported by very striking conical squinches, and the *iwans* on the sides are also covered with domes. The walls of the prayer hall are covered with tiles to a certain height, and the painted decoration and exotic shape of the windows are from 19th-century renovations.

Y. D.

Muradiye Madrasa

It is used as a TB clinic today; therefore, visitors are allowed into the courtyard only when the clinic is open.

Muradiye Madrasa, main iwan, 1426, Murad II, Bursa.

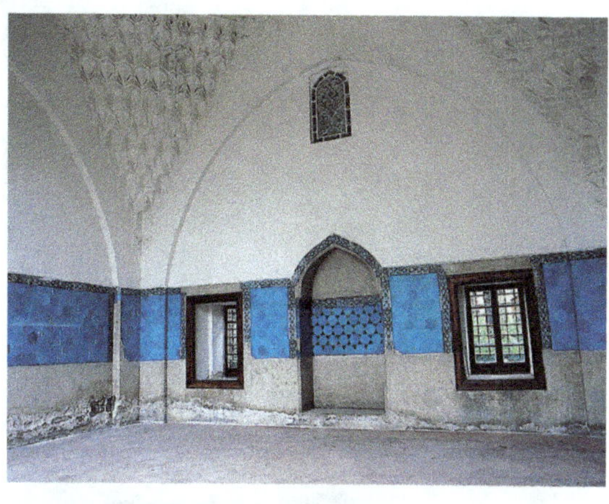

The *madrasa* to the west of the mosque is the second largest building in the complex. Further to the west of the *madrasa* is the third largest building, the *hammam,* now no longer in use. Immediately to the south of the mosque and *madrasa* is a lovely garden with venerable plane trees and cypresses where the *türbe* of Murad II together with other *türbes* dating from various periods are located.

The *madrasa*, recently extensively restored, was built with alternating courses of stone and brick. This technique of wall construction, which has been used in Turkish architecture since the 14th century, made its first appearance in Byzantine architecture.

The *iwan*-like portal to the north is topped with a dome resting upon a cornice of Turkish triangles. Again, the window tympana are decorated with brick and stonework. There is a domed *dershane iwan* on the south side of the square courtyard surrounded with porticoes on the other three sides, behind which lies the student cells. Stone and brick decoration similar to that on the portico spandrels of Muradiye Mosque is also found in the *madrasa*, especially on the *iwan* facade. The *dershane* has a rectangular *mihrab* niche with turquoise and dark-blue tiles on its south wall showing that this area was also used as a prayer hall.

Since the classroom would have been used in the winter as well as the summer, it is surprising that one side of it is completely exposed to the outside. In pre-Ottoman Anatolian *madrasas*, there was at least one winter *dershane* next to the large *iwan* where lessons were given in the summer. There are examples in Ottoman *madrasas* of only one *dershane* for winter or summer, while there are also examples of *madrasas* without a *dershane;* in the latter case, lessons were given in a nearby mosque or in the mosque of the same complex. In those *madrasas* with only a summer *dershane*, it is supposed that the exposed side was most likely closed with wooden panes during the winter months.

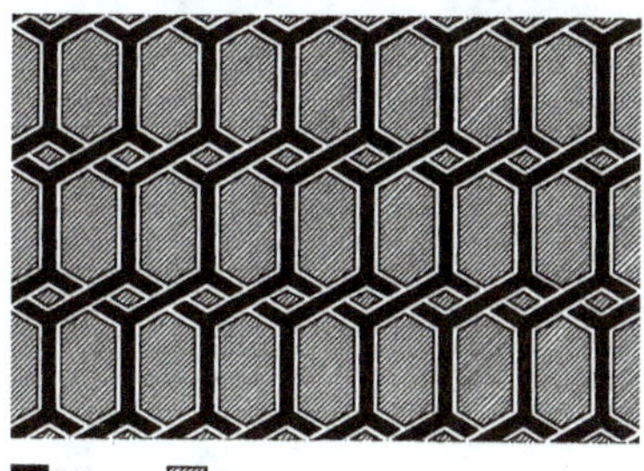

Decoration on the iwan facade, Muradiye Madrasa, Bursa (from Y. Demiralp).

Y. D.

Türbes

In the courtyard to the south of the mosque and madrasa, *there are* türbes *dating from various periods. The most attractive from the point of view of architectural plan and décor are*

Türbe of Murad II, entrance facade, 1451, Bursa.

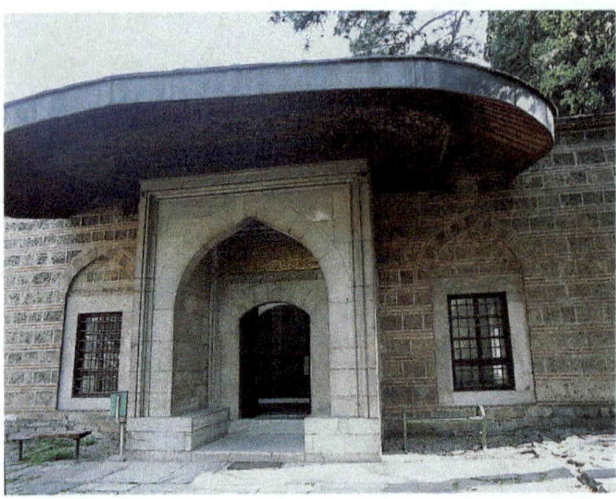

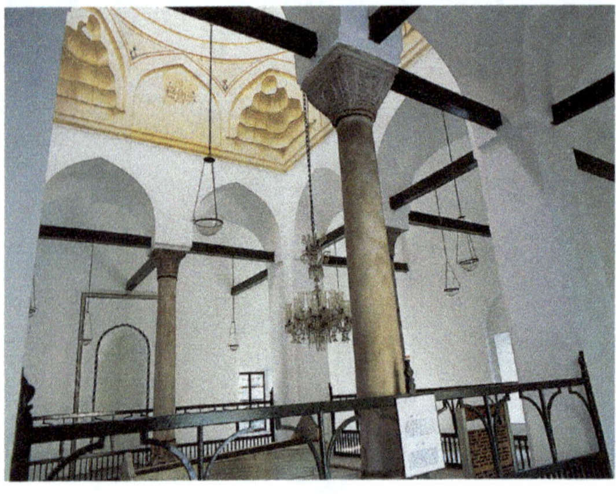

Türbe of Murad II, interior, 1451, Bursa.

those of Murad II, Hatuniye, Cem Sultan, and Şehzade Mustafa. If you find any of them closed, the guards at the entrance will open up for you. There is an entrance fee.

The Türbe of Murad II

Murad II, who had this mosque complex built, came to the throne in 1421 but in 1444 he left it to his twelve-year-old son Mehmed II and retired to Manisa to live in contemplation and mysticisim. When Sultan Mehmed II suffered a crisis because of the weight of administration, he invited his father to take the throne again. According to legend, Sultan Mehmed II said to his unwilling father, "If you are the Sultan, come and do your duty; if I am the Sultan, I command you to take the throne and rule the state". Murad thus returned to the throne, but in 1451, he fell ill and died in Edirne. According to his will, written in 1446 in Arabic and Turkish, he asked to be buried in the ground and near his son, Alaaddin Ali, in Bursa. In the same will it was stipulated that the *türbe* should have four corners; its roof should have an opening and its perimeter closed; no one should be buried beside him and if he should die away from Bursa, his body should be brought back and buried on a Thursday. Sultan Murad II is the last Ottoman Sultan buried in Bursa; his son Mehmed II and all his successors preferred the new capital of Istanbul.

The *türbe* is a square structure built with alternating rows of brick and stone and adjoins another *türbe* to the east. The underside of the wooden eaves, above a deep niche-shaped entrance projecting out from the north wall, is decorated delicately with *kalemişi* and thin lathes. The inside of the *türbe* is very well illuminated because of numerous windows on the walls. The simple grave of Sultan Murad II in the centre is surrounded on all four sides by one re-used Byzantine column between the pillars in the corners. The square area becomes a circle at the top and has been left open so that, according to the will of Murad II, "the Mercy of God might come unto him by the shining

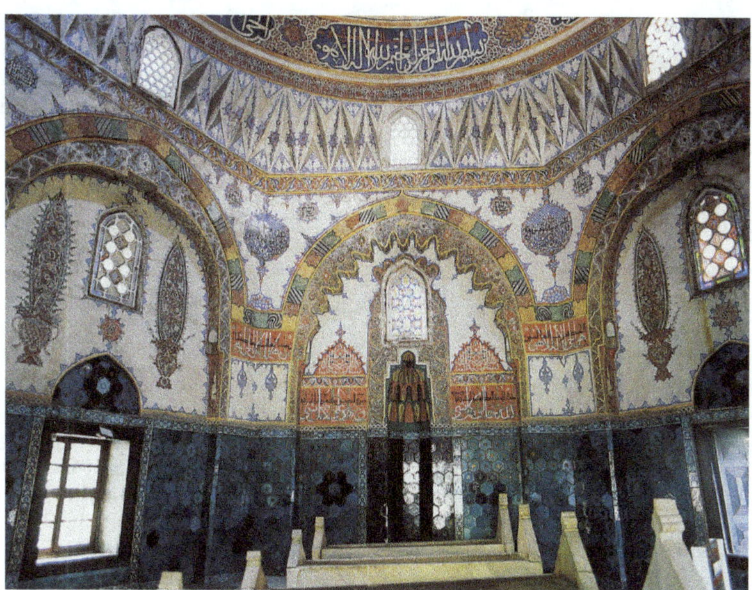

Türbe of Şehzade Mustafa and Cem Sultan, interior, 1479, Bursa.

of the Sun and Moon and falling of the rain and dew of Heaven upon his grave". There is a very plain *mihrab* niche in the south wall. A door, originally a window, leads to the adjoining *türbe* of his son Alaaddin Ali, which based on architectural evidence, is believed to have been built after that of Murad II.

Y. D.

The Türbe of Şehzade Mustafa and Cem Sultan

The *türbe* was built for Sultan Mustafa, son of Sultan Mehmed II. On his return from the Battle of Otlukbeli in 1473, Sultan Mustafa suffered kidney failure and subsequently passed away near Niğde in Central Anatolia. His body was taken first to Konya, and then later moved to Bursa, where it was interred in the *türbe* of his uncle Alaaddin Ali. His body was later placed in this *türbe*, constructed in 1479. In 1495 Cem Sultan died in Naples, and in 1499, his body was handed over to Ottoman officials and then buried next to his brother in this *türbe*. After the death of his father, Sultan Mehmed II, in 1481, Cem Sultan fought with his brother Bayezid II for the throne; he was defeated twice and, after the second defeat, sought refuge with the Knights of St. John in Rhodes. He was taken first to Nice and then turned over to the Papacy. When Charles VIII, the King of France, entered Rome in 1495, he gave Cem Sultan his freedom again. Cem Sultan went to Naples with the French king and died there the next day.

This hexagonal structure is built with alternating rows of stone and brick and has an entrance on the north side like a deep, broad niche projecting out. Inside the *türbe*, there is a *mihrab* opposite the entrance. The four plain sarcophagi lined up next to each other beginning at the entrance belong to Cem Sultan; Sultan Mustafa; Sultan Abdullah, a son of Bayezid II; closest to the *mihrab*, is the sarcophagus of Alem Shah, another son of Bayezid II respectively. The light coming through the windows on the central axis of each front, and the lantern in the centre of the dome rising on a cornice of Turkish triangles, causes a play of colour and light on the turquoise and dark-blue hexagonal tiles with gold gilding which cover the walls up to a height of 2.5 m. The upper walls and the dome are decorated with splendid paintings in bright and lively colours that were recently restored to their original condition; among the motifs the stylised cypresses, oil-lamps, rosettes, and religious inscriptions are noteworthy.

Y. D.

IV.1.j Ahmet Pasha Madrasa (option)

In Muradiye Mahallesi; just to the north of Muradiye Complex, on Beşikçiler Avenue.

This building is also known as "Geyikli Madrasa" or "Poet Ahmet Pasha Madrasa", and was built by Ahmet Pasha, who was a *kadı* and a *müderris* in various *madrasas*. Sultan Mehmed II employed Ahmet Pasha, first as *kadıasker*, and later as *vizier*.
The structure is located directly to the north of the Muradiye Complex and overlooks the plains of Bursa. Approaching from the Muradiye Complex one enters the outer courtyard and passes first the *türbe*, a hexagonal building covered with a dome. Its inscription explains that Ahmet Pasha died in 1496-97. Both the *türbe* and the *madrasa* are built with alternating rows of stone and brick. The entrance to the *madrasa* is through the middle of the eastern student cells. The courtyard is flanked with student cells, both east and west; on the south is the *dershane iwan* protruding out, whereas the north side looks over the plains of Bursa and has been left open as a terrace. Vaults resting upon columns cover the portico and student cells, each of which has a fireplace and a niche. The *madrasa* has no construction inscription; to judge from the date of Ahmet Pasha's death, it must have been built towards the end of the 15th century. It is especially interesting that the structure doesn't have a winter *dershane*. As of beginning 2001, the restoration work was about complete and there are plans to use the building as a handicrafts centre.

Y. D.

IV.1.k (Kükürtlü Kaplıca) Sulphur Spas

On Kükürtlü Avenue, Bursa. It is currently being used as rehabilitation centre by Uludağ University and it is not open to visitors but you may stroll around the peaceful gardens where it is located.

According to legend, the spring's name comes from the sulphur content of the water. It consists of two separate *hammams*, one for men and the other for women. The men's section was built by Sultan Murad I (1362-1389) while the women's *hammam,* as well as the men's *soyunmalık,* were built by Sultan Bayezid II (1481-1512). In Ottoman times, *waqfs* were established in order to meet repair and maintenance costs, as well as the cost of workers' wages for the building of structures like mosques and *türbes*. It was the income from structures dedicated to the *waqf*, like *hammams*, thermal springs, and *hans*, that allowed these expenses to be met. Murad I, who commissioned the construction of the men's section of Kükürtlü Kaplıca, did not donate the structure to any *waqf*, and he requested that no payment should be received from those who bathed in the spas. The *soyunmalık* is ample and bright; the central hot platform is in the middle of the *sıcaklık*. Also there are chambers lined with one-person bathtubs for therapy purposes.

Y. D.

IV.1.1 Old Spas (Eski Kaplıca)

In Çekirge Square, in the courtyard of Kervansaray Thermal Hotel. It is open to the public every day of the week between the hours of 07.30-22.30. Men and women use separate areas of the spa. There is a fee. Non-bathers are welcome to have a look inside.

Spas are bath complexes built close to therapeutic water flowing from the ground. The plan of these Spas, which were constructed to offer treatment for various discomforts, may be different from that of ordinary *hammams*. For example, in the *sıcaklık* there is no *halvet*; instead, many of them have a pool filled with therapeutic water.

Bursa was a city of spas in Byzantine times too. In the year 525, Empress Theodora, the wife of Byzantine Emperor Justinian I, came to Bursa with 4000 attendants and stayed for quite a while. According to legend, because the number of existing buildings was insufficient, a quantity of tents had to be pitched in the surrounding area to accommodate so many people. Also known as the "Pear Hammam", Eski Kaplıca was built in the time of Murad I (r. 1362-1389). The *soyunmalık* (apodyterium) built in 1511 by Sultan Bayezid II rises above a basement due to the sloping

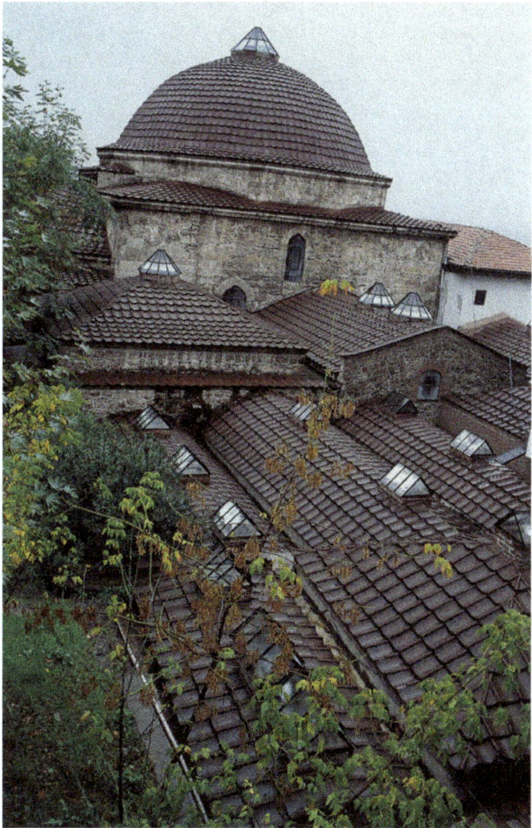

Kükürtlü Kaplıca, general view from the south, 1362-89, Murad I, Bursa.

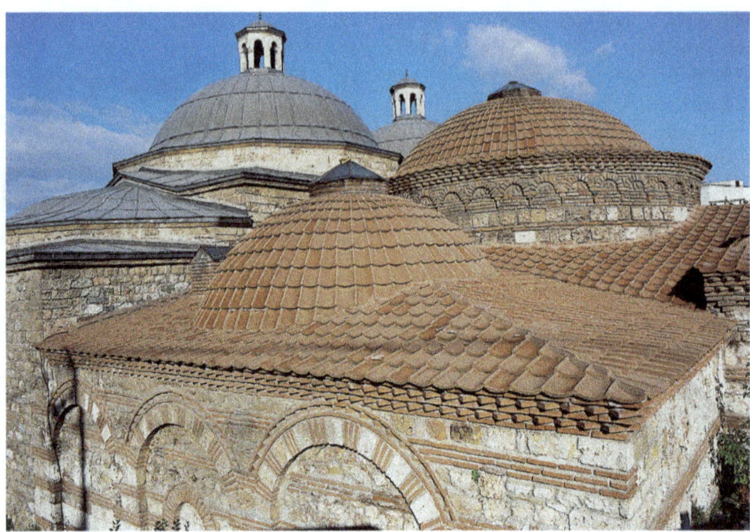

Eski Kaplıca, general view from the northwest, 1362-89, Murad I, Bursa.

terrain. It is not clear what this area was used for, but some researchers have suggested that it was a stable to house the animals of those who came to the *hammam*.

This structure has very attractive brickwork on the facade, and the larger domes covered with lead sheets are the additions by Sultan Bayezid II. The men's section of Eski Kaplıca is composed of a *soyunmalık* for disrobing, a *ılıklık* (tepidarium), and *sıcaklık* (caldarium). The *sıcaklık* is square on the outside and octagonal on the inside; opposite one another on four of the octagon's walls are semi-circular recesses; the circular pool in the centre is 7 m. in diameter. Many sections of the building, most of all the *sıcaklık*, were built re-using Byzantine architectural pieces; for this reason, some Western scholars have maintained that this was a Byzantine structure.

Y. D.

IV.1.m **Hüdavendigar Mosque**

In Çekirge Area, in Hüdavendigar Mahallesi. Just up the street to the west of Eski Kaplıca.

Upon the death of his father, Orhan Gazi in 1362, Sultan Murad I was called to Bursa and ascended the throne. His two brothers challenged him, but Murad had them captured in Eskişehir and then had them killed. In 1368, during his reign, the capital was moved from Bursa to Edirne. In 1386, while fighting at Rumelia, his son Savcı Bey, then governor of Bursa, declared himself sultan; when Sultan Murad I learned of this, he returned to Bursa where he had his son's eyes burned with a red-hot iron and later had him killed. "Hüdavendigar" is the epithet of Sultan Murad I and literally means Sultan. The complex is located on top of a steep slope with a beautiful view of the town below. On the approach is a small domed

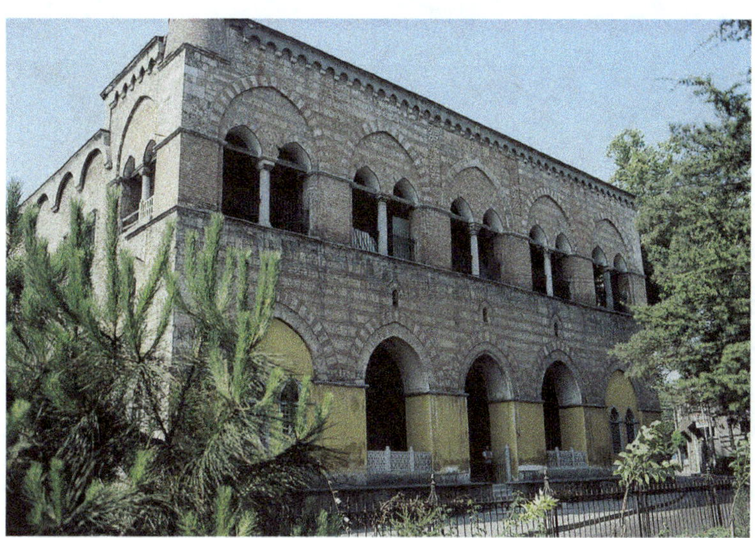

Hüdavendigar Mosque, view from the northeast, 1385, Murad I, Bursa.

structure on the left, which once housed the latrines; the visitor will then be amazed at the north facade, which has a two-storey and five-bayed portico; a two-storied portico on the facade is rarely found in Anatolian Turkish architecture. A very eye-catching cornice of arches under the eaves runs all around the structure. Columns, elegant capitals, and decorative elements taken from Byzantine buildings can be seen in the floors, while the brickwork panels are also very attractive. Because of the unusual arrangement of the main facade and the Byzantine architectural elements, some Western researchers have suggested that this building was originally a Byzantine palace. However, the structure is in the right direction for a *qibla* and its architectural layout does not leave this question in suspension.

Hüdavendigar Mosque is a rare example in Anatolian Turkish architecture also from the point of view that it combines a

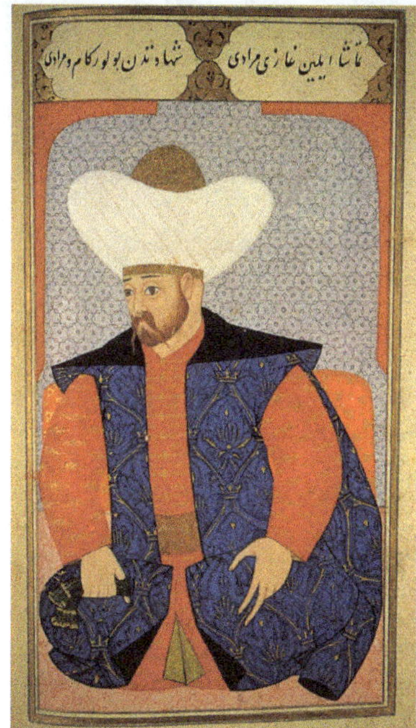

Murad I, Illumination from Kıyafetü'l-İnsâniyye fî Şemâili'l-Osmâniyye by Seyyid Lokman Çelebi, 1579, H.1563, 32b, Library of Topkapı Palace, İstanbul.

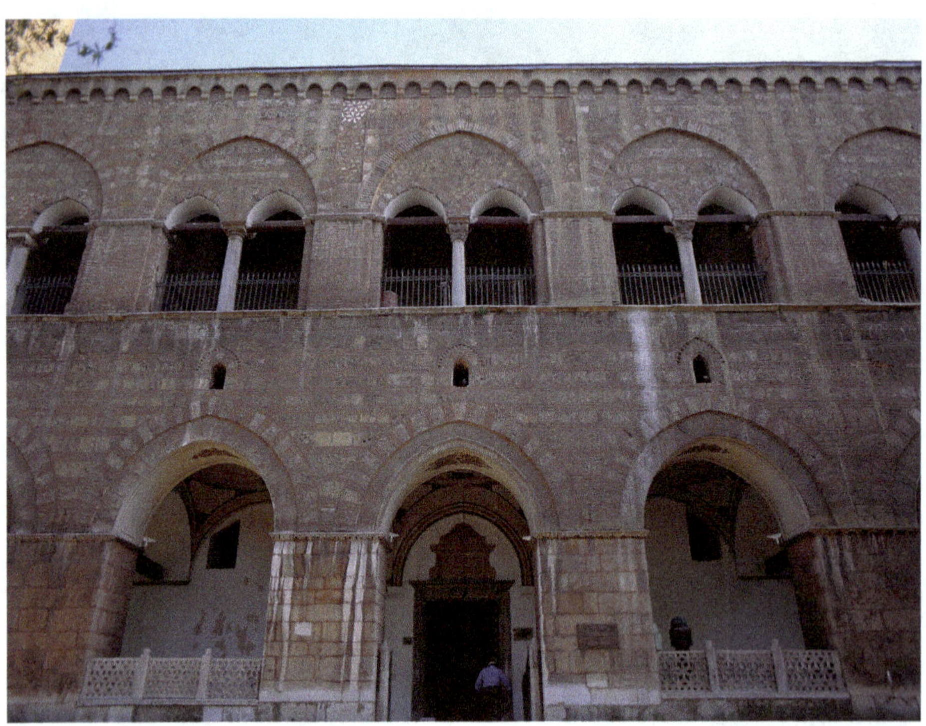

Hüdavendigar Mosque, north facade, 1385, Murad I, Bursa.

mosque and a *madrasa* under a single roof; a *madrasa* was built on the upper level of the structure; the portal on the north facade is used jointly by the mosque and the *madrasa*. According to the inscription above the entrance, the building was renovated in 1904 at the order of Sultan Abdülhamid II. The entrances on the east and west walls were opened later. The *madrasa* upstairs, normally not open to visitors, is reached via the staircase by the entrance foyer of the mosque. The *madrasa* has 16 barrel-vaulted cells aligned around the central court downstairs. As the prayer hall and the central court on the lower floor are two storeys high, the *madrasa* upstairs has no courtyard. The corridor that runs in front of the cells extends all around the perimeter of the central court and the prayer hall. The fireplaces in the corners of some cells are later additions.

The mosque downstairs was designed to provide accommodation for the itinerant *dervishes*. The entrance foyer opens to a smaller *iwan*-shaped lobby before the central court, which is surmounted with a high dome. To the east and west are a barrel-vaulted *iwan* flanked with barrel-vaulted *tabhanes* on both sides. Opposite the entrance is the prayer hall, another barrel-vaulted *iwan,* with an apse-like *mihrab*

niche protruding out. The painted decorations are from later renovations.
This mosque is part of a complex containing a *madrasa*, *imaret*, and a *türbe*. It is understood from the *waqf* charter that the founder was Sultan Murad I; there is no construction inscription; for this reason, it is generally accepted that the complex was completed in 1385, the year the *waqf* charter was prepared.
In the complex, the *imaret,* which is used as the Tourism Directorate today, to the west of the mosque, and the *türbe* to its north both underwent later restorations.

Y. D.

Uludag Mountain (2554 m.), which lies directly behind Bursa, is Turkey's most popular skiing centre. Although there are not many visitors during the summer months, the people of Bursa enjoy picnicking there during the holidays. There is a cable car (Teleferik in Turkish) that takes visitors from the city up to a point close to the summit. You can take a taxi or the dolmush *minibuses from the Heykel square by the Great Mosque to the cable car station; and* dolmushes *are also available from the landing station at Sarıalan to the hotel area, where there is a ski lift. There are "cook it yourself, eat it yourself" barbecue restaurants at Sarıalan. If you prefer the main road, you can take a taxi or the buses that leave from the city bus station and go up to the summit. The winding road up to the summit is 36 km. long.*
Uludağ is a National Park with a landscape covered by various types of trees like laurel, olive, chestnut, elm, oak, Oriental plane, pine, juniper, and poplar, as well as rich vegetation.
Bursa's peaches, chestnuts (especially chestnut purée), and Iskender Kebab, are as famous as its towels and silk fabrics. Those who eat the Iskender Kebab (a local form of Döner Kebab) should also have a taste of şıra (very slightly fermented grape juice) made from dried grapes.

Aydoğan Demir

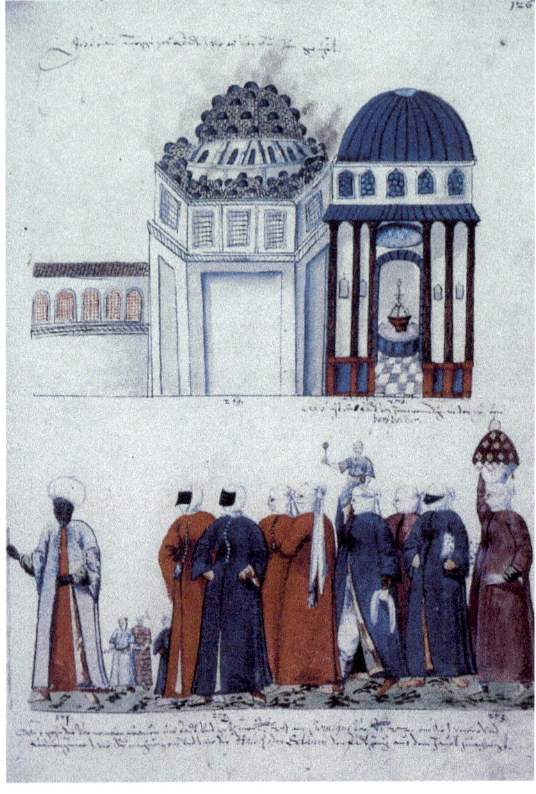

Women on the way to the hammam, Ain Turggische Hochzeit, J.2a, 1582, Sächsische Landesbibliothek, Dresden.

Bath culture, which goes back as far as the second millennium BC in Egypt, Mesopotamia, and Anatolia, experienced its golden age during the time of the Romans. In addition to bathing, sports, and entertainment, literary discussions were also held in Roman baths. The Umayyads (661-750), who conquered the Byzantine Empire's land in the Middle East, also adopted the bath culture. The Islamic religion's stipulation that one must wash his or her entire body after sexual intercourse assisted the spread of *hammam* culture in the Turkish-Islamic world.

During the Middle Ages, the network of water distribution was limited. For this reason, only very rich people could bathe in private baths in their mansions, while the majority of people bathed and enjoyed themselves at *hammams* open to the public. The beauty and spaciousness of the interior was of first order importance for the *hammams* built during the Emirates and Early Ottoman periods. The first building constructed in a mosque complex was always the *hammam*. Thus the hundreds of workers working on the construction of the complex could benefit from it. Many Western travellers have praised the spaciousness, beauty, and cleanliness of the Turkish *hammam* interiors.

The Turkish *hammams* had other functions as well as bathing: administrators and poets would come together in them to converse or for a few drinks. For example, during his Anatolian military campaign (1402), Tamerlane (r. 1370-1405) conversed with the famous poet Ahmeti at a *hammam;* Süleyman Çelebi, one of Bayezid I's (r. 1389-1402) sons, enjoyed arranging meetings at which alcohol was served at the Edirne *hammams*.

Hammams were a place of freedom for Turkish women, as their appearance in public was restricted according to Muslim law. Men had to give their spouses money to go to the *hammam* at least once a week; not giving money to women for the *hammam* counted as grounds for divorce. Wealthy women would take their maidservants with them, and with their embroidered towels, fine shirts, mother-of-pearl inlaid *hammam* clogs, silver bowls, and ivory combs, they would put on a veritable show. One would go to the *hammam* in the morning and return in the evening. Here sweetmeats and savoury foods would be eaten, *sherbet* drunk, musical instruments played and people would dance. Women with grown-up sons would choose potential daughters-in-law in the *hammam*.

There were regulations governing matters such as not re-using a razor after shaving the head of someone with scabies and not charging more than the official price. Cleanliness of the *hammams,* which were also an important source of income for *waqf* foundations, was of the utmost importance.

Architecturally, a *hammam* consists of different sections: although traditionally related to Roman baths, Turkish *hammams* are quite different from them in plan. Except for the "cold bath" (*frigidarium*) section, all the elements of Roman baths are also present in Turkish baths. The section of the *hammam* with direct access to the outside is called the *soyunmalık* (equivalent of *apoditerium*) where people disrobed or put their clothes back on. The *ılıklık* (equivalent of *tepidarium*) is the warm-bath area and acts as a small passage between the *hammam*'s disrobing area and the hot-bath units. In some *hammams*, there is another small area between the *ılıklık* and *soyunmalık* called the *aralık* in Turkish, which simply means the "passageway". The *sıcaklık* (the equivalent of *calidarium*) section usually consists of a central part, where there is generally a hot platform on which people lie down to sweat before getting scrubbed and massaged; and private bathing chambers called *halvets* are usually located in the corners. Designed as a separate unit, the water depot is where the water is heated from underneath as is the building itself.

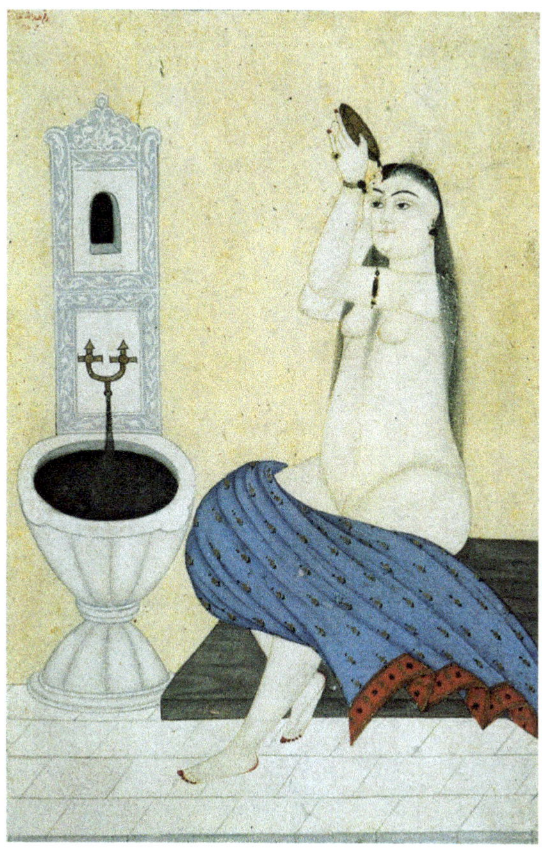

Woman in the hammam, Abdullah Buhari, 1741-42, Library of Topkapı Palace, YY.1043.

Some Turkish *hammams* were constructed as two separate, adjoining baths designated for men and women. In these double *hammams*, the entrance to the women's section opens onto a generally not-too-busy side street so that women could comfortably enter and exit the baths. There are no *hammams* designated for women only, other than these double *hammams*. In case of a single *hammam*, one or two days a week there would be a women-only session.

THE BATTLE OF ANKARA

Aydoğan Demir

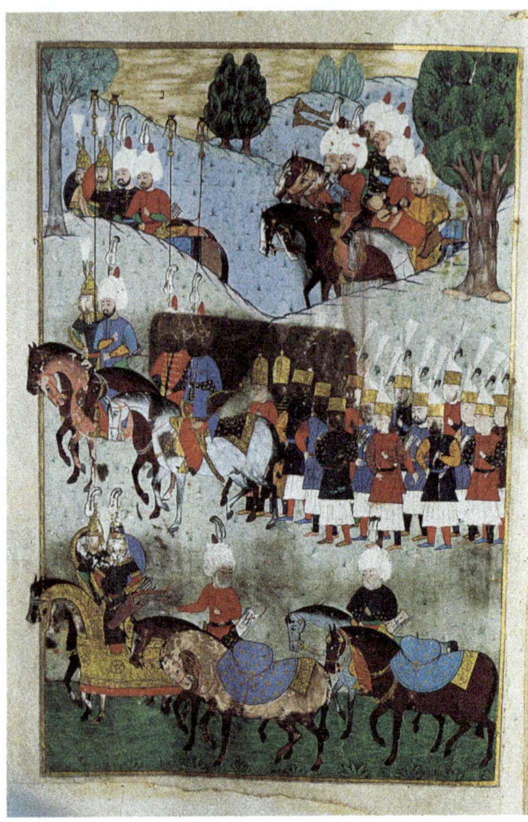

Ottoman Army on a campaign, Zigetvarname by Nakkaş Osman, 1568-59, H. 1339, fol.103b, Library of Topkapı Palace, İstanbul.

From the founding of the Ottoman State until 1402, the Ottomans continued to pursue an empire by conquering many countries between the Euphrates River in Anatolia and the Danube River in the Balkans. However, with the defeat they faced at the Battle of Ankara in 1402, they reached the very point of disintegration. What happened so that Bayezid I (r. 1389-1402), who was nicknamed Yıldırım –the Lightning– and had gone from victory to victory between Niğbolu (Nicopolis) on the Danube and Erzincan in mid-eastern Anatolia, was faced with an event that was so disastrous for his state that it led to his own enslavement?

Tamerlane's (r. 1370-1405) victory was the cause of a political crisis for the Ottoman State. Tamerlane, known by the title Uluğ Bey or "Magnificent Bey", acquired great political power in West Turkistan, which lies today within the boundaries of the Republic of Uzbekistan. Starting out from his own capital, Samarkand, and heading west, Tamerlane began occupying the Middle East. Having already occupied Persia, Azerbaijan, Iraq, and Northern Syria, he wanted to add Anatolia to his empire as well.

Throughout history, all the states that were founded on, or became rulers of, the Persian Highlands, wanted to take Anatolia, along with the Black Sea and the Mediterranean: the Medes, Persians, Parthians, Sassanids, Umayyads, Abbassids, and Mongols all followed this policy. It is also worth noting that, beginning with Alexander the Great (356-323 BC), all of the states founded in the West were also in pursuit of domination in the same regions: Rome's famous consuls and emperors occupied the Middle East except Persia; at the end of the 11th century, the Crusaders who were on their way to Jerusalem founded counties and kingdoms in Anatolia and Syria. After World War I (1914-1918), western states also wanted to divide up a large section of Anatolia.

There are many reasons why large states are attracted to Anatolia: Anatolia's important role in the world's trade routes; its strategic location due chiefly to the Istanbul (Bosphorus) and Çanakkale (Dardanelles) Straits; and its temperate climate that makes it suitable for cultivation of all kinds of plants, especially grains. During an era in which the wealth of a state was measured by its possession of bountiful lands and trade routes, it cannot be expected that Tamerlane would think or act any differently than the times dictated.

On a hot summer day, 28 July 1402, in the vicinity of Ankara, Tamerlane's forces, reinforced with 32 elephants, battled mercilessly with the forces of Ottoman Sultan Bayezid I that included soldiers of the Anatolian Emirates conquered by the Ottomans. These soldiers betrayed the Ottomans by joining the military ranks of their *Beys*, who had taken refuge behind Tamerlane. As a result of this betrayal, Bayezid I lost the battle and was taken prisoner.

After an extended period of captivity, Bayezid I heard that Tamerlane himself was going to take him to Samarkand. Because of this he became deeply distressed and most likely committed suicide by drinking the poison hidden under the stone in his ring (9 March 1403).

After Tamerlane departed from Anatolia in 1403, Bayezid I's sons Süleyman, İsa, Musa, and Mehmed began disputing the throne. In 1413, Mehmed I, also known as Çelebi Mehmed, took over the throne himself and thus put an end to the Interregnum; this event was all but a second founding of the Ottoman State.

Before leaving Anatolia and in return for their support, Tamerlane returned to those *Beys*, who had sought protection under him, the areas that they had formerly ruled. Thus Germiyan, Saruhan, Aydın, Menteşe, and Karamanid Emirates were founded anew; the Candar Dynasty also took back the land that they had lost. The Ottomans struggled for a period of over 50 years to erase these emirates from the map entirely.

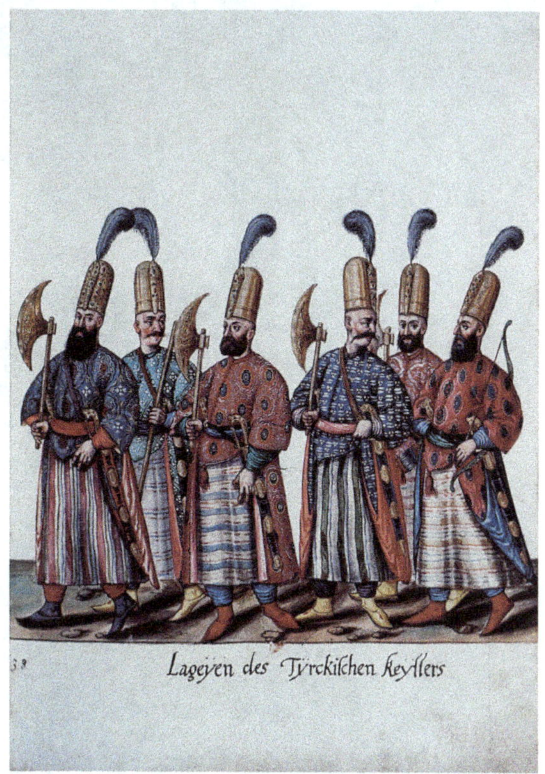

Ottoman Soldiers, Codex Vindobonensis, Cod. 8626, fol 38, Österreichische Nationalbibliothek, Vienna.

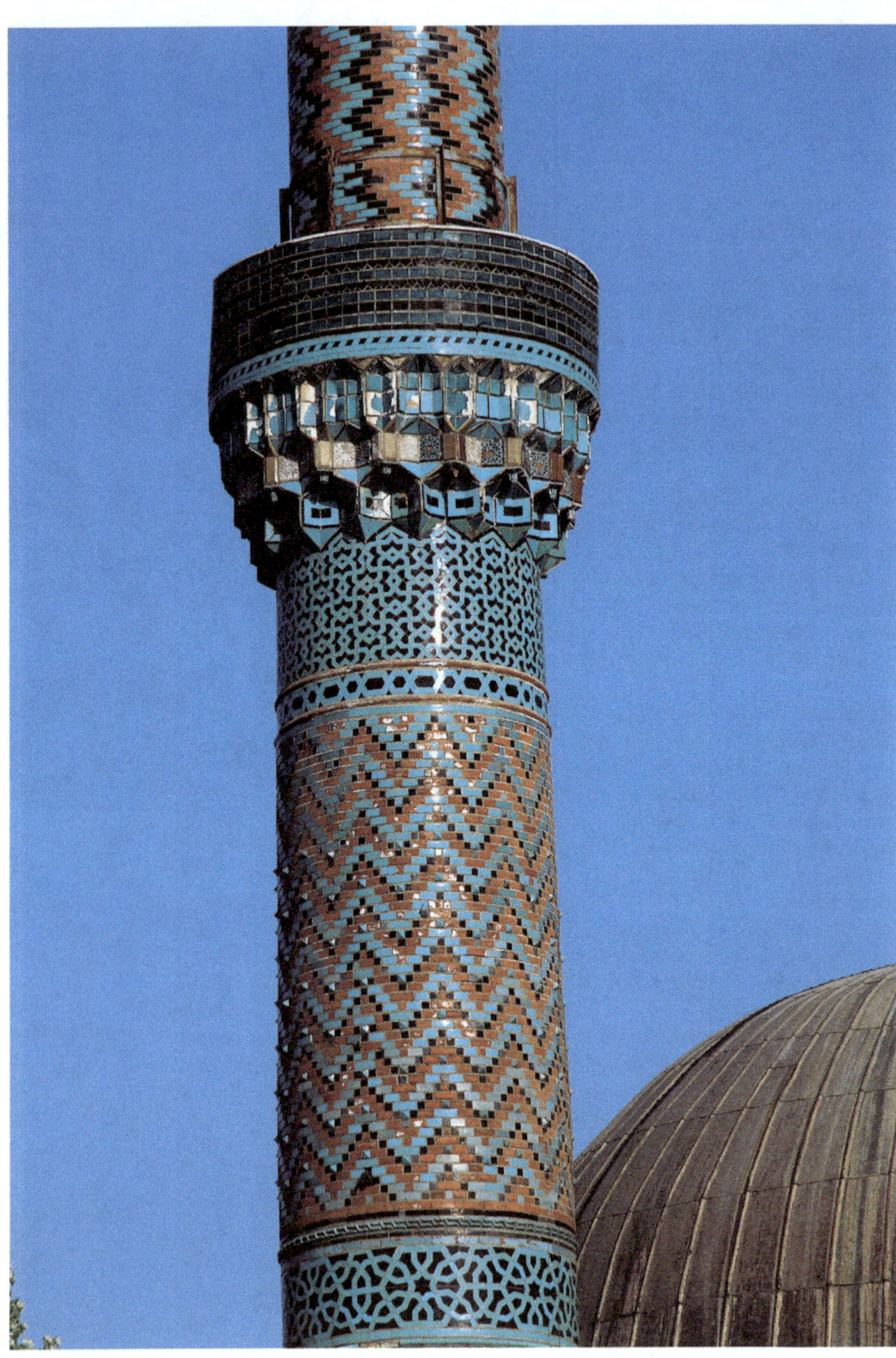

Orhan Gazi: Sultan of the People

Lale Bulut, Aydoğan Demir, Rahmi H. Ünal

V.I İZNİK

V.1.a Nilüfer Hatun İmaret (İznik Museum)
V.1.b Yeşil Mosque
V.1.c Süleyman Pasha Madrasa
V.1.d İsmail Bey Hammam
V.1.e Murad II Hammam
V.1.f Kırkkızlar Türbe

"Flowers that bloom in fire": 14th–and 15th–century Tile and Ceramic Art Administration in the Ottoman State

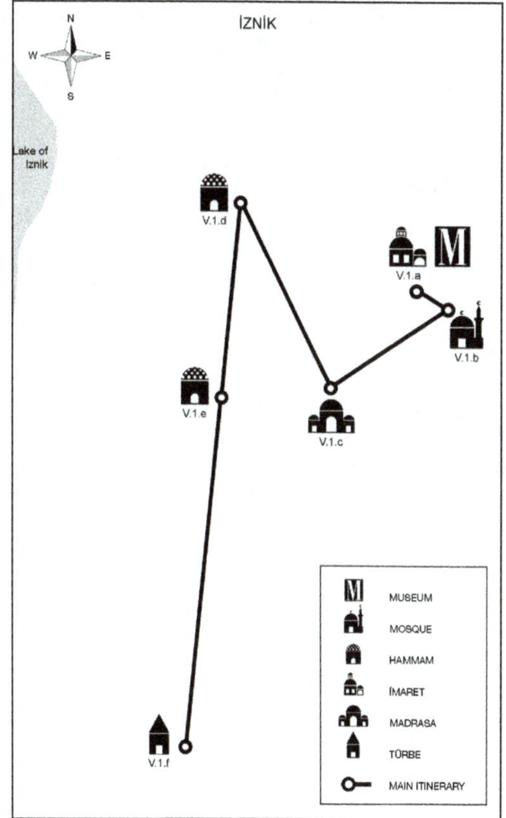

Yeşil Mosque, minaret, 1378-92, Halil Hayreddin Pasha, İznik.

Nilüfer Hatun imaret, portal, 1388, Murad I, İznik.

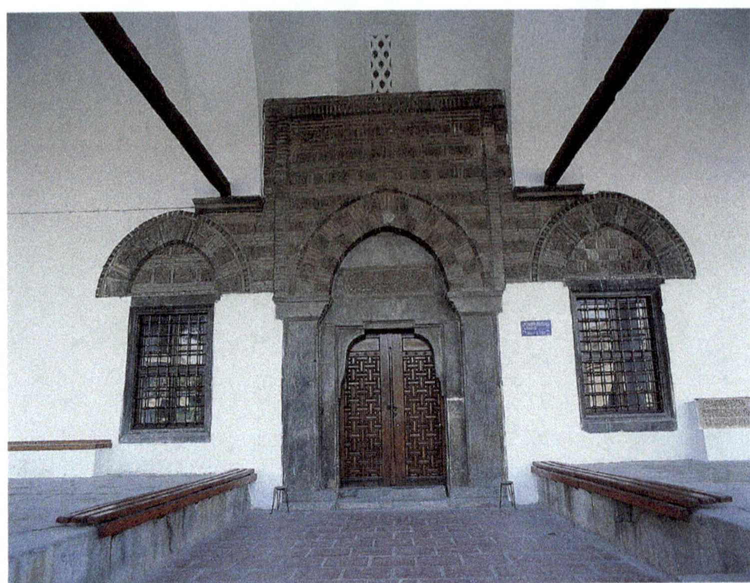

İznik (ancient Nicea), capital of the Anatolian Seljuq State between 1075 and 1097, came under Byzantine rule once again during the First Crusade. However, the second Ottoman ruler, Orhan Gazi, conquered İznik again in the year 1331. According to legend, as Orhan Gazi was entering the city, he asked his own soldiers to marry the widowed Rum women so that the women would not have to experience even more difficulties. One Ottoman writer tells the story as follows: "They carried out the command. The city had homes ready to be lived in, and they gave them to the married war veterans. A ready woman and a house for him too –who wouldn't accept the offer?"

İznik was adorned with various structures during the Ottoman period built by the sultans and many administrators. For example, Murad I had an *imaret* built in İznik in the name of his beloved mother, Nilüfer Hatun. Orhan Gazi himself picked up a ladle and distributed food in the *imaret* he had built, and the same sultan also lit the oil lamps with his own hands at the inauguration of the *madrasa* he commissioned in İznik; first Davud of Kayseri, and then Taceddin the Kurd was appointed as the *müderris* in this *madrasa*. The Ottoman sultans considered intelligence and skill important in the administration of the country, and they did not differentiate between races such as Turkish, Kurdish, Albanian, or Circassian.

The Çandarlıs, a distinguished family, played an important role in state services ever since the establishment of the Ottoman State. Çandarlı Halil Hayreddin Pasha, an *Ahi* and characteristically a good organiser, was İznik's first *kadı*. The Janissary corps initiated by Çandarlı Halil

Hayreddin Pasha formed an important part of the Ottoman Army. Several of Çandarlı Halil Hayreddin Pasha's sons and grandsons rose to the rank of Grand *Vizier* and some members of this family that were able to rise to a good position in the civil service did not forget their city of birth and thus decorated İznik with beautiful structures. For example, Yeşil Mosque which is a small, extremely fine and striking structure, was commissioned by Çandarlı Halil Hayreddin Pasha himself. Shaykh Bedreddin (d. 1419), whose identity and actions have been a topic for debate for centuries, was a government man acting as *kadıasker*, and also a learned man of religion and science who produced works in the field of "Sufism". In 1413 he was removed from his *kadıasker* duty and forced to live in İznik. Shaykh Bedreddin's disciples, Börklüce Mustafa and Torlak Kemal, started revolts in Karaburun close to İzmir, and Manisa respectively. Shaykh Bedreddin escaped from İznik and fled to the Balkans, where he started a people's rebellion in Deliorman. These revolts were suppressed by the Ottoman State (1419).
İznik's importance waned after the 15th century and it continued to exist as a small Ottoman town. It began to develop again in the Republican period, and is now one of the region's liveliest towns.

A. D.

İznik is reached from Bursa via a main road about 76 km. long. All the works on this itinerary are located in the city of İznik. Except for Kırkkızlar Türbe, which is a little outside the city centre, you can reach all the monuments on foot. For orientation: the town centre surrounded by two superb rings of walls has two main streets; one in a north-south direction, from Istanbul Gate to Yenişehir Gate; and the other in an east-west direction, from Lefke Gate to Göl Gate, respectively; at the junction, in the centre, is Ayasofya, the church where the First and the Seventh Ecumenical Councils were held.

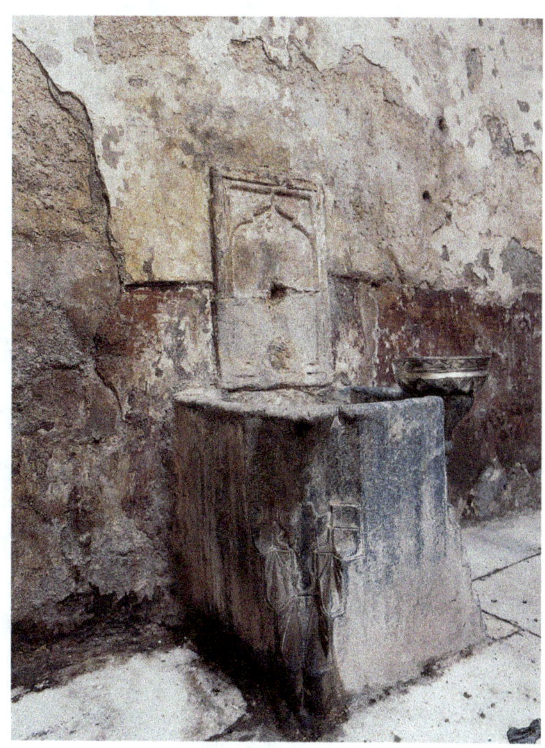

Murad II Hammam, basin in the sıcaklık of the women's section, 15th century, İznik.

V.1 İZNİK

The city was founded in 316 BC by Antigonus I Monophthalmos (380-301 BC), one of Alexander the Great's generals, and given the name Antigonia. Another of Alexander's generals, Lysimachus, captured the city in 301 BC, and named it after his

Nilüfer Hatun İmaret, general view from the southeast, 1388, Murad I, İznik.

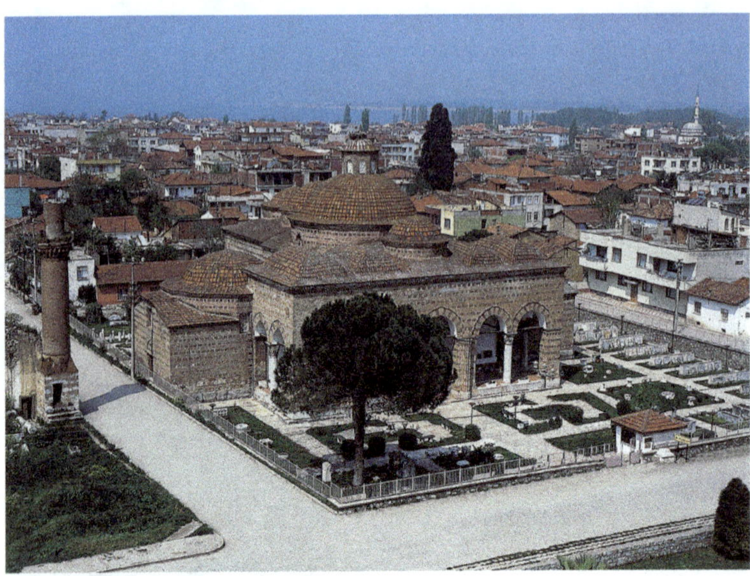

deceased wife (Nicea) and made it the capital of the region of Bithynia. After it came under the control of the Romans, the town became one of the most important cities of the Province of Asia. In 325 the First Ecumenical Council gathered in Nicea and laid the foundations of Orthodoxy. In 787, the Seventh Ecumenical Council ended up in moderation between iconodules and iconoclasts. In 1075 the Seljuqs captured Nicea and changed its name to İznik. At the same time, the town became the capital of the Rum Sultanate. However, it changed hands between the Byzantines and the Turks until Ottoman Sultan Orhan Gazi captured it for good in 1331.

V.1.a Nilüfer Hatun İmaret (İznik Museum)

In Eşrefzade District, on Museum Street. It is currently being used as the İznik Museum. The museum is open 08.00-12.00 and 13.00-16.30 in the winter and 08.30-12.30 and 13.30–17.00 in the summer. It is closed on Mondays. There is an entrance fee. You should inquire here about the keys for the İsmail Bey Hammam and Süleyman Pasha Madrasa.

Osman Gazi, the founder of the Ottoman Empire, remained a peripheral *Bey* all his life, bound to the Seljuqs and Ilkhanids. There is no inscription bearing his name as the founder of any structure. Holophira, the local Byzantine princess of Yarhisar, who married Osman Gazi's son Orhan Gazi, is said to have taken the name Nilüfer Hatun after converting to Islam. Although it is said that Bayalun Hatun, one of Osman Gazi's wives, whom the Arab traveller Ibn Bauta met in İznik, might have been Nilüfer Hatun, this rumour has not been confirmed. Sources speak of Nilüfer Hatun's taking an interest in philanthropic activities and giving many *sadaqa* or alms, to poor people. Likewise, because she had a bridge built across the creek that flows through the Bursa Plain, this creek is known today as Nilüfer Creek. Nilüfer Hatun, whose date of death is unknown, was buried in her husband Orhan Gazi's Türbe in Bursa. Shortly after Nilüfer Hatun's death, her son Sultan Murad I commissioned the building in İznik known today as Nilüfer Hatun İmaret. It is known that the word *imaret*, which later came to mean "a place where food is distributed to the poor", had a general meaning in the beginning, as "any type of building constructed for good deeds". For this reason, this and other structures called *imarets* belonging to the early period should not necessarily be defined as places where food was distributed to the poor. Some of these special structures called *imaret*, such as the one here, were constructed to shelter religious missionaries; we encounter many examples of such structures from the 14th and 15th centuries. In these structures, which give the impression of a mosque when viewed from the outside, only one of the areas was designated for communal worship and this area was accented with a *mihrab* niche.

Located 100 m. to the northwest of Yeşil Mosque, the building was recently renovated and is currently being used as the İznik Museum. In addition to rich finds of ceramics obtained during the ongoing excavations in İznik, Classical, Byzantine and a few ethnographic artefacts are displayed. The structure is striking with its exterior wall faced with brick rows alternating with courses of stone, and there are a few panels with brickwork decoration. Normally in this kind of structure, the majority of which are called mosques with *zawiya (tabhane)*, the five-bay portico extends completely along the facade, but here empty spaces were left at two ends; the piers flanking the middle arch are embellished with distinctive mouldings. The middle bay of the portico is surmounted by a small dome adorned with beautiful triangles and the rest are covered with vaults. According to the inscription above the entrance door, which is accented with brick-and-stone masonry on the top, the structure was completed on 8 April 1388. On entering, the visitor stands under a very large dome. The *tabhane* rooms to the right and left are used for exhibiting the ceramic finds of the Ottoman period. The prayer hall straight ahead, marked with a small *mihrab* niche on the left, houses the prehistoric artefacts. In such structures the prayer hall is usually covered with a dome but here the roof has been divided into two parts by a great arch; each part covered by a single small dome with elaborate transition zones.

R. H. Ü.

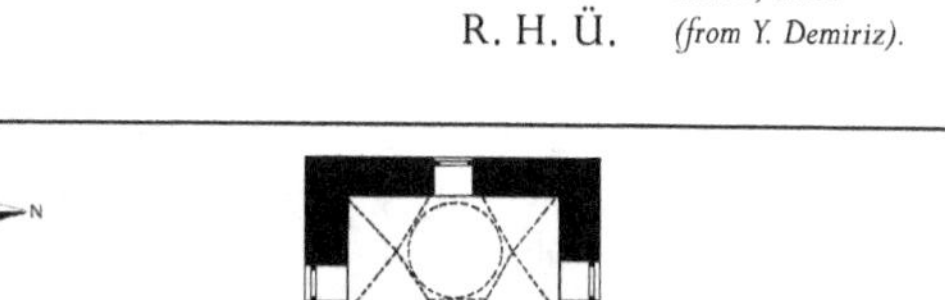

Plan of Nilüfer Hatun Imaret, İznik (from Y. Demiriz).

Ceramic plate, 15th century, Nilüfer Hatun İmaret (Inv. No. 1365), İznik.

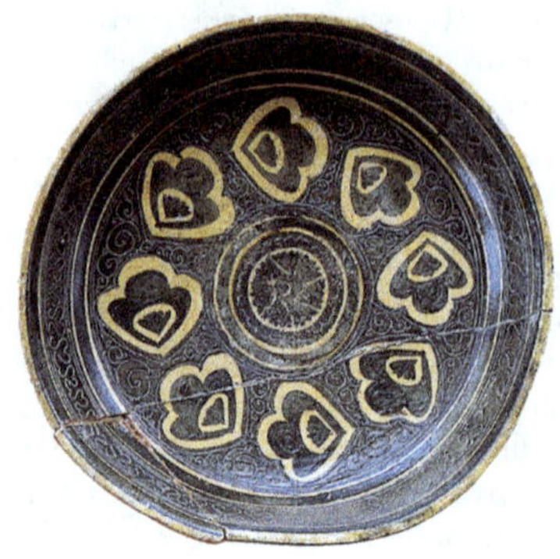

Ceramic Plate
(Inv. Num. 1365, 15th century)

This is one of the ceramics produced in İznik called "Miletus ware". First appearing in the 14th century, these red-clay ceramics are also known as "Emirates–Era Ceramics" and have a white background on which are blue designs. The kiln excavations in İznik revealed for certain that the production centre for this type of ceramic was not Miletus, but İznik. It was understood that these red-earth ceramics were produced for a long time as objects for daily use beginning in the 14th century. In this group, most of which are shallow bowls, there are also lamps, bowls, and plates. The inside of the red-clay base is completely lined with *engobe*; the external faces and base are usually not lined. The edges of this example are slightly raised. It was glazed after the designs had been drawn. The ornamentation applied in white upon the dark-blue background consists of concentric circles and stylised *palmette* motifs. Floral motifs were engraved on the blue-painted sections.

L. B.

Ceramic Mug
(Inv. Num. 4609, 15th century)

Produced in İznik, this "blue-white" ceramic mug is decorated in the under-glaze technique, which has been in use since the Seljuq period. The sun-dried ceramic clay was coated with *engobe* first; the decorations were created on top of this coating and the ceramic was baked; the ceramic taken out of the kiln was glazed and then fired again. In this way, the decorations are covered with a layer of shiny glaze. Numerous examples of ceramics in the under-glaze technique are found in many museums all over the world. The ceramic mug on display here has a cylindrical body that widens towards the top. The body is decorated with curling branches and stylised floral motifs drawn in blue, on a white background.

L. B.

Ceramic Plate
(Inv. Num. 5324, 15th century)

First the designs were drawn on this Miletus-type deep bowl and then it was glazed over. The cobalt-blue designs though

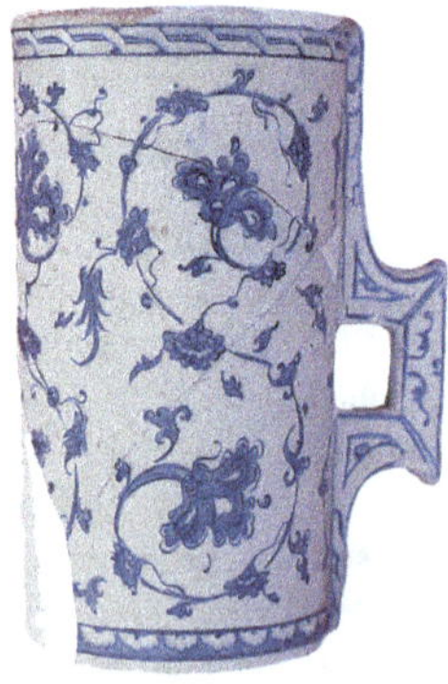

Ceramic mug, 15th century, Nilüfer Hatun İmaret, (Inv. No. 4609), İznik.

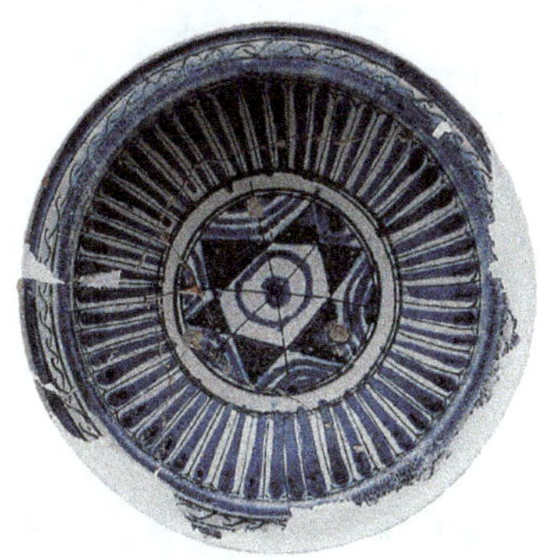

Ceramic plate, 15th century, Nilüfer Hatun İmaret, (Inv. No. 5324) İznik.

were applied on top of the white glaze. The star motif made up of triangles in the centre of the plate is enclosed in a medallion. Parallel lines drawn with brush strokes radiate from the centre to the edges.

L. B.

Ceramic Plate
(Inv. Num. 5304, 14th-15th century)

Produced in İznik, the designs on this bowl are done under the glaze using the slip technique. The slightly raised, beige-coloured large flower motifs placed on a brown background were drawn with slip. The stylised "moving" flowers completely cover the internal surface of the plate. The brown, yellow, and green glazes seen on this group of ceramics appear darker on a red background.

L. B.

Ceramic Plate
(Inv. Num. 5308, 14th-15th century)

Three different techniques were used on red-clay ceramics manufactured in İznik. "Lining décor" (slip) ceramics –one of three techniques– is also encountered during the Seljuq period. The decorative elements drawn on a red background are made of slip. The designs beneath the coloured transparent glaze layer are slightly raised. This bowl is ornamented with yellow *palmettes* and *rumis* placed on a dark-brown background; on the border there are yellow drop-shape dots.

L. B.

V.1.b **Yeşil Mosque**

Across the road and to the east of the Nilüfer Hatun İmaret (Museum).

Halil Hayreddin Pasha, of the Çandarlı family, is among the most famous civil servants to act as *vizier* during the century following the founding of the Ottoman State. In the first days after he was appointed *vizier* in the year 1372, he was awarded the duty of putting down a rebellion initiated by the governor of Selanik (Thessalonica); this is noteworthy because, before him the *viziers* did not interfere with military affairs. Contemporary local and foreign sources relate

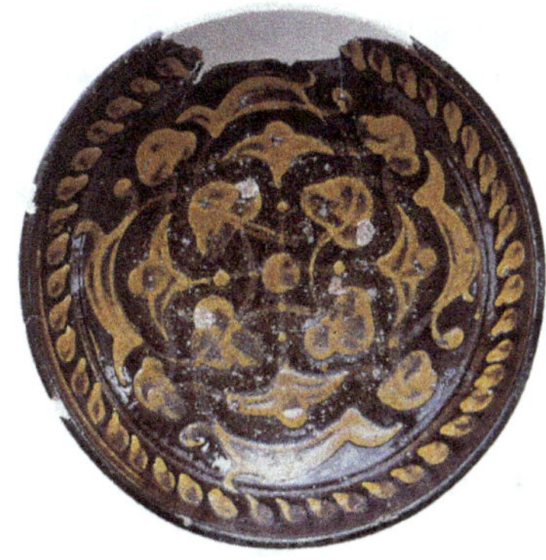

Ceramic plate, 14th-15th century, Nilüfer Hatun İmaret, (Inv. No. 5308) İznik.

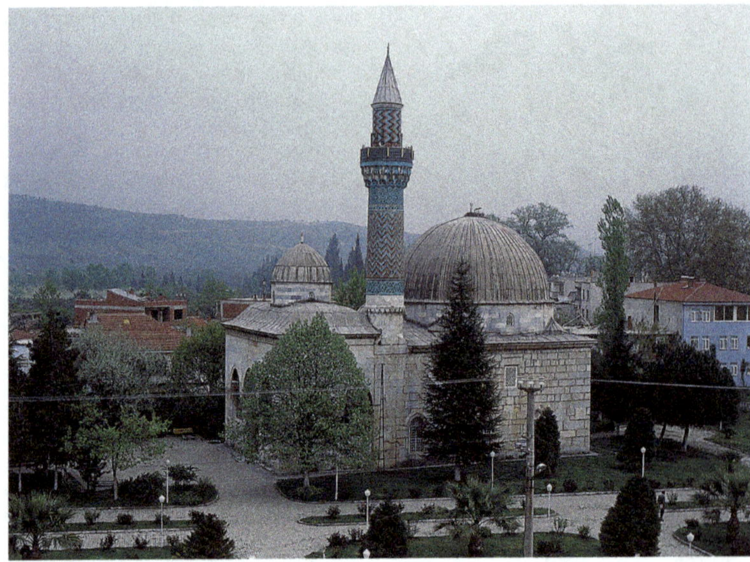

Yeşil Mosque, general view from the west, 1378-92, Halil Hayreddin Pasha, İznik.

that Halil Hayreddin Pasha had quite a lot of influence over Sultan Murad I. After Murad I had ascended to the throne, Halil Hayreddin Pasha was appointed *kadıasker* and he had a positive effect on the new arrangement of the army. Likewise, when not enough soldiers were found for the army, with Halil Hayreddin Pasha's recommendation, young Christian prisoners of war were first educated and then taken into the army. He proposed the establishment of a class of soldiers known as *Yeniçeri Ocağı*, Jannissary Corps, that constituted the Ottoman army's main striking forces for centuries thereafter.

Decoration on the portal of Yeşil Mosque, İznik (from Ş. Çakmak).

Halil Hayreddin Pasha, who received his education in a *madrasa*, initiated the protection of artists and scholars. He acted as *kadı* in Bilecik, İznik, and Bursa. Yeşil Mosque, which he started building in İznik in 1378, shows elaborate craftsmanship. It is understood that construction of the mosque continued for many years, although the reasons for the delay are not known. The inscription above the entrance of the prayer hall relates that the mosque was constructed by Çandarlı Halil Hayreddin in the year 1378 during the time of Sultan Murad I. However, another inscription above the entrance to the portico reads that the mosque built by the then deceased Hayreddin Pasha, was completed in 1392. This inscription also states that an architect by the name of Haci ibn Musa constructed the building.
Standing in a lovely and well-attended park, this beautiful structure with its

domes and coloured minaret is exhilarating. On the outside it is faced entirely with marble; the roof and domes are covered with lead sheets. The brick minaret resting on a prismatic marble base is decorated with zigzags formed by turquoise and dark-purple glazed and unglazed bricks, and bands of tile mosaic. The beautifully carved frieze along the eaves and the mouldings on the window frames reminds one of mouldings from ancient buildings. The portico's marble banisters, which suffered significant damage during the Greek occupation in 1919-1922, were replaced in the latest restorations. The columns bear wonderful capitals, with a decoration similar to the band along the eaves; and the frame of the unusual false door in the middle is striking. The central bay of the portico is covered with a fluted dome. On entering the prayer hall, the visitor is faced with two other columns and arches, beyond which is the main part surmounted with a dome rising above a cornice of Turkish triangles. This is a very interesting feature because with this additional three-bay area to the north, the square prayer hall is enlarged into a rectangle; it is, therefore, one of the first examples of an enlarged prayer hall. Yeşil Mosque has an important place in the history of Turkish architecture. In the 14th and 15th centuries, the majority of mosques were covered with either a single dome or multiple domes, and attempts were made to widen the prayer hall with additional areas placed on one, two, or three sides of the central dome. The walls of the prayer hall, which is otherwise very plain, but for the lovely marble *mihrab*, are faced with marble to a certain height.

R. H. Ü.

V.1.c **Süleyman Pasha Madrasa**

In Yeni District, on Süleymanpasha Street.

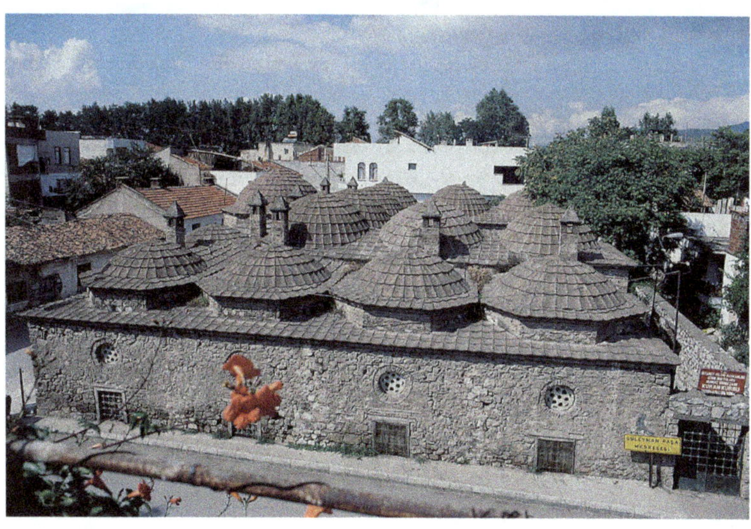

Süleyman Pasha Madrasa, general view from the south mid-14th century, Orhan Gazi, İznik.

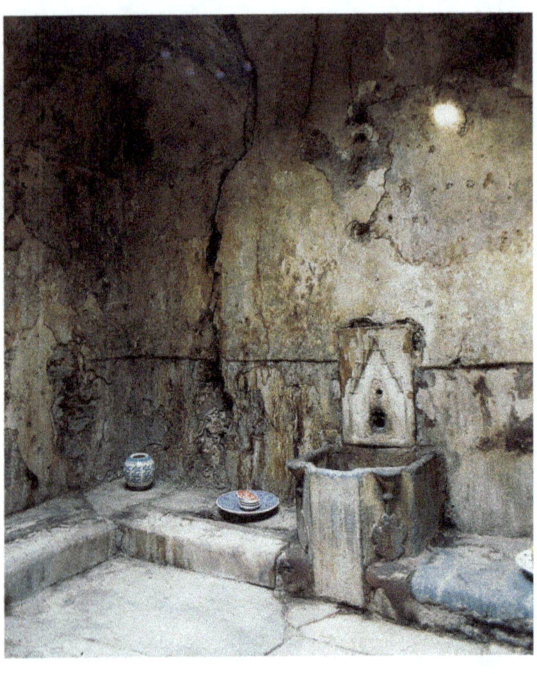

The *dershane* of the *madrasa* extends into the street to the west and is covered with a bigger dome than the rest. On the outside the upper row of round windows catches the eye. The simple entrance on the southeast opens onto the courtyard surrounded on three sides by domed porticoes rising on columns; beyond which are the cells and the *dershane* to the west. This is one of the first *madrasas* constructed during the Ottoman period. Nevertheless, it is quite different from the *madrasas* of the Seljuq period; here the domes replaced the vaults preferred in Seljuq *madrasas*. The use of columns in the porticoes instead of piers is also striking and seldom encountered in Seljuq *madrasas*. Although the definite date of construction is not known, Süleyman Pasha Madrasa probably dates to the mid-14th century. In 2000, the structure was abandoned but a restoration program is planned.

R. H. Ü.

Murad II Hamman, Sıcarlık of the women's section, 15th century, İznik.

Süleyman Pasha was the oldest son of the second Ottoman Sultan Orhan Gazi, born to Nilüfer Hatun. He lived in İznik until 1336, became a *vizier* from that date on, and took part in the conquest of Thrace. Researchers believe that this *madrasa* was built before Süleyman Pasha left İznik; however, Süleyman Pasha was only 20 years old when he left İznik in 1336. Following a fall from his horse, he passed away in 1360, and his father Orhan Gazi was deeply saddened and turned the property of Süleyman Pasha, together with the additional revenue from two villages in İznik, into a *waqf*; this brings to mind that this *madrasa* could have been built by Orhan Gazi in order that his beloved son's memeory live on.

V.1.d **İsmail Bey Hammam**

In Beyler District, on Yeni Street. From the Istanbul Gate to the south, turn east at Ziya Özbek Street. It is easily recognisable with the modern canopy soaring above it.

Turkish baths, like Roman baths, are structures open for public use. Palace and private residence *hammams*, very few examples of which have survived, are different from the traditional public baths because of their dimensions. The *soyunmalık*, *ılıklık*, and *sıcaklık* of the private *hammams* are of small dimensions. The fundamental bathing area –the *sıcaklık*– that consists of at least three or four connected units in the public *hammams*, usually consists of only one unit in these private ones. Large bathing areas in palaces and homes was not necessary since the number of people bathing at once did not generally exceed three to five.

In Islam, both women and men must remove pubic hair, the removal of which every Friday was considered to be *sevap* or grace begetting, as it was considered a non-obligatory yet meritorious good deed. It was deemed necessary to engage in this kind of cleaning at least once every 15 days, while it was seen as a sin if the time in between surpassed 40 days. In almost all *hammams*, there are private areas called *traşlık* where hair removal is done. Approaching from the street, the water tank with the collapsed vault to the right, is the first thing the visitor will see. The *külhan* to heat the water is underneath and opens outside. The main entrance is to the back of the path on the left. Being a residential bath dating to the late 14th-early 15th century, the İsmail Bey Hammam has only four small chambers, each one of which is covered by a single dome. The *soyunmalık* is the area the visitor first enters. Observe what remains of the beautiful transition zone. The chamber to the right is probably what was once the *traşlık*; the transition zone to the dome

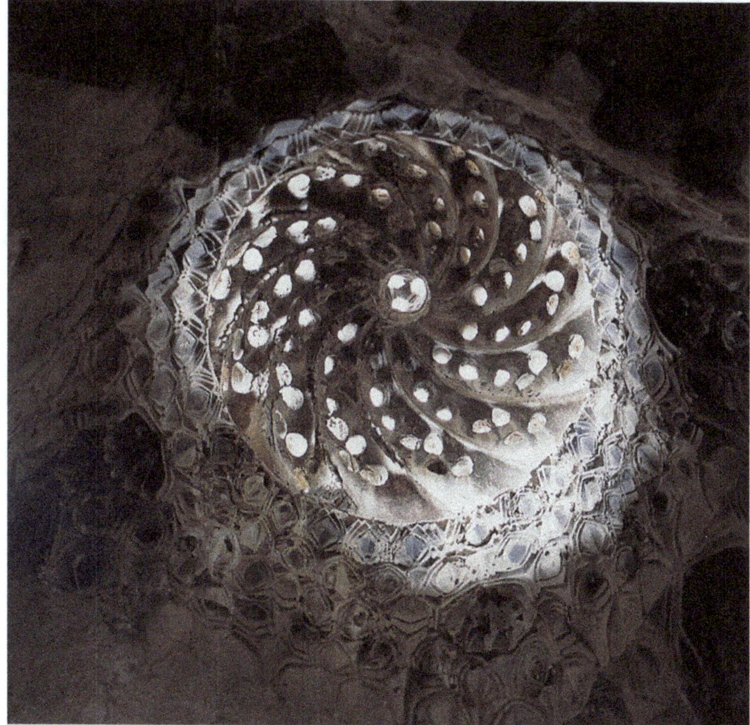

İsmail Bey Hammam, Dome of the ılıklık, late 14th–early 15th century, İznik.

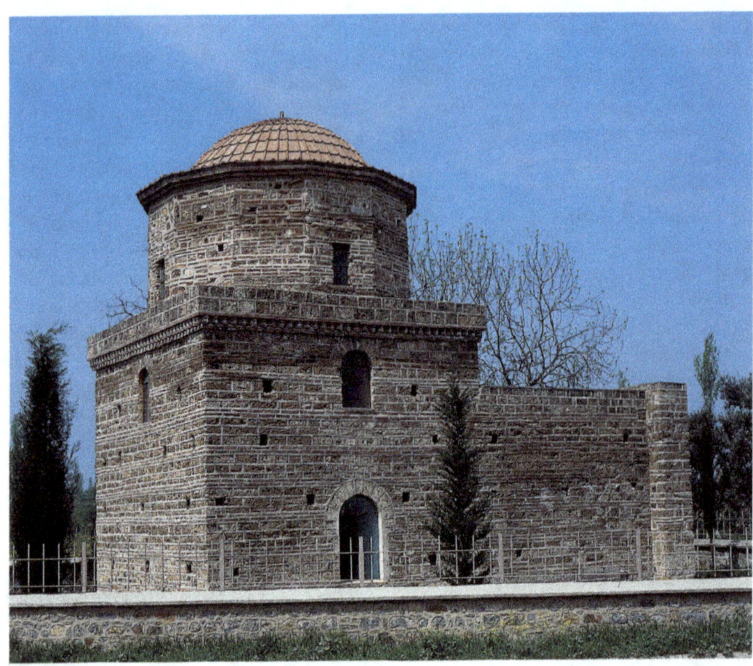

Kırkkızlar Türbe, general view from the southeast, 14th century, İznik.

consists of Turkish triangles. After the disrobing area, the first chamber is the *ılıklık*, the second is the *sıcaklık*, both of which have adorable whorled domes still in very good condition; observe the openings in the domes for glass jars which originally provided light into these chambers; the floors of both chambers are collapsed exposing the heating system under the floor. The *sıcaklık* adjoins the water tank and the furnace, the hot air and gases from the fire, which circulated under the floors and went up through the baked-clay pipes in the walls. All the chambers have remains of superb decorative plasterwork that must have made this *hammam* a delightful place to bathe.

R. H. Ü.

V.1.e **Murad II Hammam**

In Mahmut Çelebi District (Mahallesi). One block south of Ayasofya and to the extreme west of the tile-kiln excavation area. At the beginning of 2001, the men's part was fully restored and was still functioning; it can be visited with permission. The key to the ladies' section is at the Iznik Foundation.

While attending to the *Büyük Hammam* in Beçin in Itinerary I, we stated that some public baths were constructed as two separate *hammams* adjoining each other, and that one of these was designated for men, and the other for women. Murad II Hammam, also known as Hacı Hamza Hammam, is a double *hammam* like this.

Of these two *hammams*, the one in the north is quite a lot smaller in comparison to the other. Like most of the double *hammams*, the entrances open onto different streets. The *soyunmalık* of the *hammam* in the north for the use of women was built with a recess within so that its female users could comfortably enter and exit without attracting too much attention.
The men's bath consists a large disrobing area with beautiful squinches filled with *muqarnas*, an *ılıklık*, a *traşlık*, and a cruciform *sıcaklık* with *halvets* in the corners. The *soyunmalık* of the women's section, not in use at the time of writing, was employed as a display room by the İznik Foundation, which works on the revival of İznik tile and ceramic art. The ladies' bath has not been restored either, but the beautiful old water basins were still there to be seen. The Turkish traveller Evliya Çelebi writes that there were two double *hammams* in İznik: Tekioğlu Hamamı, and Yeni Hamam. Murad II Hamam (or Tekioğlu Hamamı?) dates to from the 15th century. The other double *hammam*, partially standing and known today as Büyük Hamam (Yeni Hamam?), was, however, constructed in the 15th or 16th century.

R. H. Ü.

V.1.f **Kırkkızlar Türbe**

In Selçuk District, about 150 m. south of Yenişehir Kapı.

Putting a dead body in a monumental grave to ensure regular visitors and help keep alive the memory of the person goes against Islamic belief. Considering that in some Orthodox Islamic sects such as the *Wahhabi* it is believed that even the location of the grave must not be obvious, the construction of a special monument for the dead person appears to be rather divergent behaviour. However, in the Islamic world, monumental tombs are closely related to the Turks. The earliest examples of these structures, which have a cubic, polygonal, or cylindrical body covered by a dome, are found in Iran.
Some scholars think that this tomb's name, which is *Kırkkızlar* (forty girls), must originally have been *Kırgızlar,* after the tribe of Kyrgyz Turks. In some sources, it is remembered as "Reyhan Türbe" or "Hacı Camasa Türbe". The structure has recently been completely restored. The masonry of brick rows alternating with stone courses is a characteristic that passed from Byzantine architecture to Ottoman architecture. The dodecagon dome drum was raised during later renovations. The structure consists of two rooms, the first of which was covered with a vault in the original construction and the main room is a square surmounted with a dome. The existing sarcophagus-shaped graves are plain and bear no inscriptions, and, therefore, they yield no information about the identity of the deceased. A window was altered and a niche was formed next to it in order to make room for graves built later. The decorative paintings on the inside have lovely floral and candlestick motifs. Although there is no record about the tomb and its owner, it is dated to the 14th-century. This dating is based upon its multi-sided drum, seen in other 14th-century structures such as Hacı Özbek Mosque and Yeşil Mosque in İznik, and also its decorative paintings, which have early Ottoman characteristics.

R.H.Ü.

"FLOWERS THAT BLOOM IN FIRE": 14th– and 15th–CENTURY TILE AND CERAMIC ART

Lale Bulut

The tile and ceramic arts experienced a long chain of developments in Anatolia. The tiles that decorated the walls in the Seljuq, Emirates and Ottoman periods are striking for their variety in both technique and design. Only a limited number of Anatolian Seljuq-period tiles have survived to the present day. However, examples that abound beginning in the 15th century, are as much the favoured pieces of domestic and foreign museums as they are of private collections. In Emirates-period structures dating to the 14th and 15th centuries, tile decoration is not frequently encountered. In the limited number of examples there are it is noticeable that the Anatolian Seljuq-period tradition continues without making significant changes. Glazed bricks are used along with tiles in the Birgi Great Mosque's (1312-13), Manisa Great Mosque's (1367), and İznik Yeşil Mosque's (1378-92) minarets.

The tile-mosaic technique –the favourite in the Anatolian Seljuq Period– was not much favoured in the Emirates and Early Ottoman periods; in tile-mosaic ornamentation of this period, which was arranged in larger compositions in comparison with those in the Seljuq period, white was also used in addition to blue, turquoise, purple, and black. The tile-mosaics seen on Birgi Grate Mosque's *mihrab* (1312-13) as well as on the transition zone of the dome before the *mihrab* in Selçuk İsa Bey Mosque (1375) are some rare examples of the period, while the ones in İznik Yeşil Mosque (1378-92), Bursa Yeşil Mosque, Yeşil Madrasa, and Yeşil Türbe (1419-24), and Bursa Muradiye Mosque (1426) are some rare examples from the Early Ottoman Period. The decreased use of tiles during the Emirates period did not prevent the appearance of new techniques in the 15th century. The "coloured glaze technique" (also known as *cuerda seca*) that we encounter for the first time during this period is not seen in Anatolian pottery; it was only applied to tiles. A variety of colours like blue, turquoise, deep–blue, black, white, yellow, gold-water, lilac, and pistachiogreen were used on the tiles produced in this technique which is seen particularly in structures at Bursa, Edirne, and Istanbul. The earliest examples of this type are found in Bursa Yeşil Mosque, Yeşil Türbe, and Yeşil Madrasa (1419-24) along with Edirne Muradiye Mosque (1426-27).

Konya, a tile production centre of the Anatolian Seljuq period, began to lose its importance at the beginning of the 15th century, and İznik and Kütahya became the new centres of the tile- and ceramic-art industry. İznik, an important settlement centre since the 4th century BC, was where the Early Ottoman Period's highest quality ceramics were produced. Its location on the route that connects Istanbul to Anatolia ensured its long-lived economic and cultural livelihood. According to various travellers' accounts, around

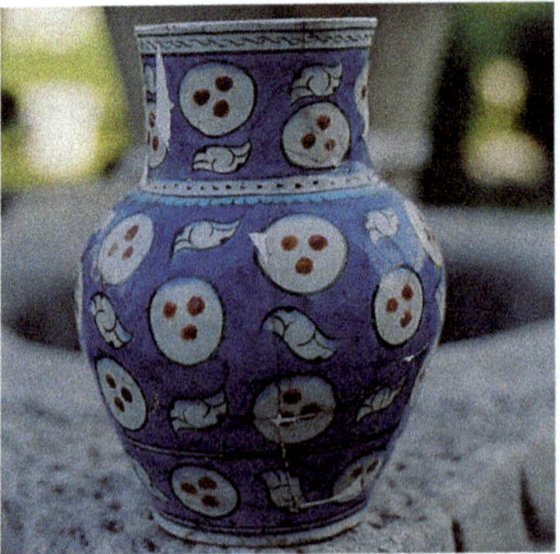

Ceramic Vase (Inv. no. 3373), Bursa Museum.

300 tile master-craftsmen were working in İznik. Although this may seem exaggerated for such a small town, the number of kilns revealed by excavations (for instance, there is an excavation site across the street to the east of Murad II Hammam) and research conducted in the last few years, are proving this rumour to be correct. Two types of kilns are found in İznik: one with a "rectangular firehouse" and the other with a "circular firehouse". In the rectangular kilns, the firehouse is covered with a cradle vault and the firing area has holes on its floor. The firing area of the circular kiln is covered with a dome. Higher temperatures could be reached in circular kilns than could be achieved in rectangular kilns.

The ceramics called "Miletus ware", produced with the under-glaze technique, have an important place among the 14th- and 15th-century ceramics. Because until recently it was supposed that they were produced in Miletus, these red-clay ceramics were known by this name, but now we know that they were actually manufactured in İznik. In the ceramics of this group, the colours: cobalt blue, dark purple, and turquoise were used, and in addition to decorations in a radial arrangement, decorations with floral and geometric motifs are also seen. For example, compositions consisting of leaves in a fan shape drawn with thin brush strokes coming out of a rosette in the centre are frequently encountered.

Ceramics that are called "blue-white" appeared after the Miletus type and are a higher quality product, closer to porcelain. These ceramics are the second innovation to appear in the Ottoman period after the coloured glaze technique. This under-glaze technique is rare on tiles, but frequently appears on ceramics for daily use. Produced in İznik until the beginning of the 16th century, in this group of tile and ceramics, the colours blue, turquoise, and deep-blue were applied on a white background; the most prized motifs on these tiles and ceramics, which are reminiscent of 15th-century Far Eastern Ming porcelain, are peonies, flowers, Chinese clouds, and dragons. On a group of blue-white ceramics mistakenly known as "Haliç ware" (Golden-Horn-ware), though, branches with curled leaves in a helical arrangement on a white background are seen.

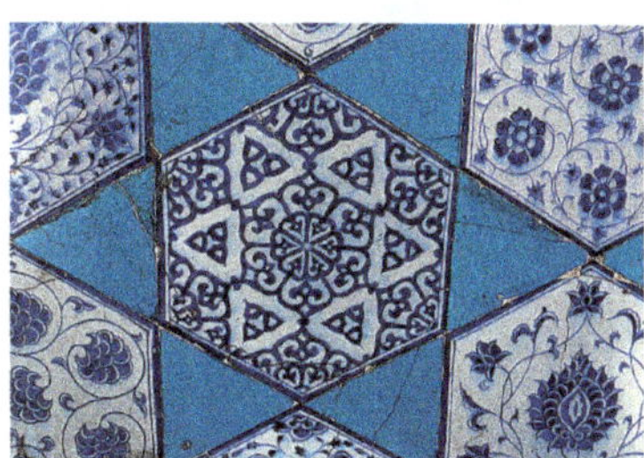

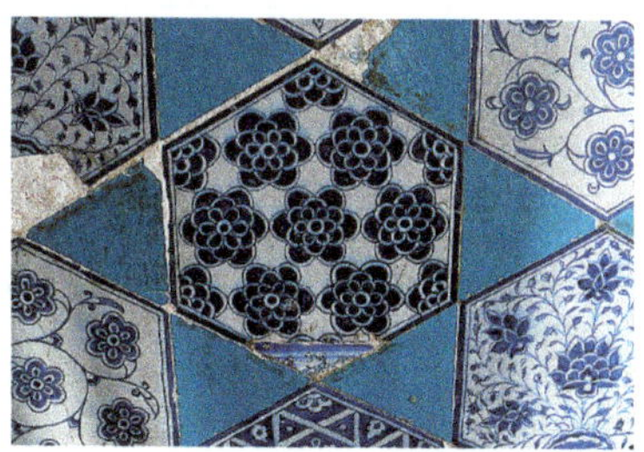

Details from the tile wall-panel, Muradiye Mosque, Edirne.

ADMINISTRATION IN THE OTTOMAN STATE

Aydoğan Demir

The Ottoman State administration underwent continuous development from the year it was founded until it finally evolved into a central bureaucratic structure. The tendency to administrate the state according to laws began in the time of Osman Gazi (r. 1281-1324) and continued throughout Ottoman history.

According to our current knowledge, the first Ottoman Sultan to gather the laws in a corpus, or, to put it another way, select and collect them, was Sultan Mehmed II (r. 1451-1481). Mehmed II's law proclamation or constitution of laws begins with these words: "This constitution of laws, is the constitution of my father and my forefathers, and my constitution too". This expression is proof that the Ottoman State had begun to be administered according to laws long before Sultan Mehmed II.

When the Ottoman State conquered a land, one of its first actions was to register every kind of information in deed registers about the region: the population living in the region who would be eligible for the payment of taxes, the fields, orchards, groves, mills, animals, mines, and so on, that would constitute sources of tax. At the very beginning of the register, the laws to which local people had to subscribe would be written. These laws were aimed at protecting the people. After the Ottoman city of Selanik (Thessalonica) had passed into Byzantine hands due to the Interregnum after the Battle of Ankara (1402), the new administrators were unable to lift the Ottoman laws and apply Byzantine laws because they were afraid that the Rum inhabitants would oppose the imposition of Byzantine laws. Although they had been under Ottoman administration for only a short period, they had got used to a lower, payable tax load.

The first thing that comes to mind when speaking of Ottoman State administration is the sultanate of the Osman dynasty. In the Ottoman State, for a period of more than 300 years, the sultanate passed from father to son, and between the years 1617-1922, it passed to the eldest member of the royal family. For a dynasty to manage a state for a period of over 600 years is something rarely seen in history. The Ottoman Sultan, equipped with very far-reaching authority, administered the state together with an assembly known as *Divan-ı Hümayun,* in which the *Grand Vizier*, *viziers*, *kadıasker*, *defterdar* and *nişancı* worked in their official capacities. When it was considered necessary, the *şeyhülislam* (shaykh al-islam), *yeniçeri ağası*, and the *kaptan-ı derya* were called to the meeting and consulted. Until the last days of Sultan Mehmed II's reign, the Sultans presided over the *divan* meetings, and after this date, the Grand *Viziers* presided.

At the *divan* meetings, all the country's issues were discussed; decisions were taken and submitted for the Sultan's approval. After national matters on the agenda had been discussed, a common Ottoman citizen had the right to enter the *divan*, explain his problems, and request a solution. For this reason the *divan*, in addition to governmental work, also functioned as a kind of high court.

The Ottoman central administration made its strength felt in the most remote corners of the empire. Local administrators (*beylerbeyi* and *sancak beyi*), *kadı*s, and *tımarlı sipahi*s would use their administrative, judicial and military authority as representatives of the Ottoman central administration everywhere from villages

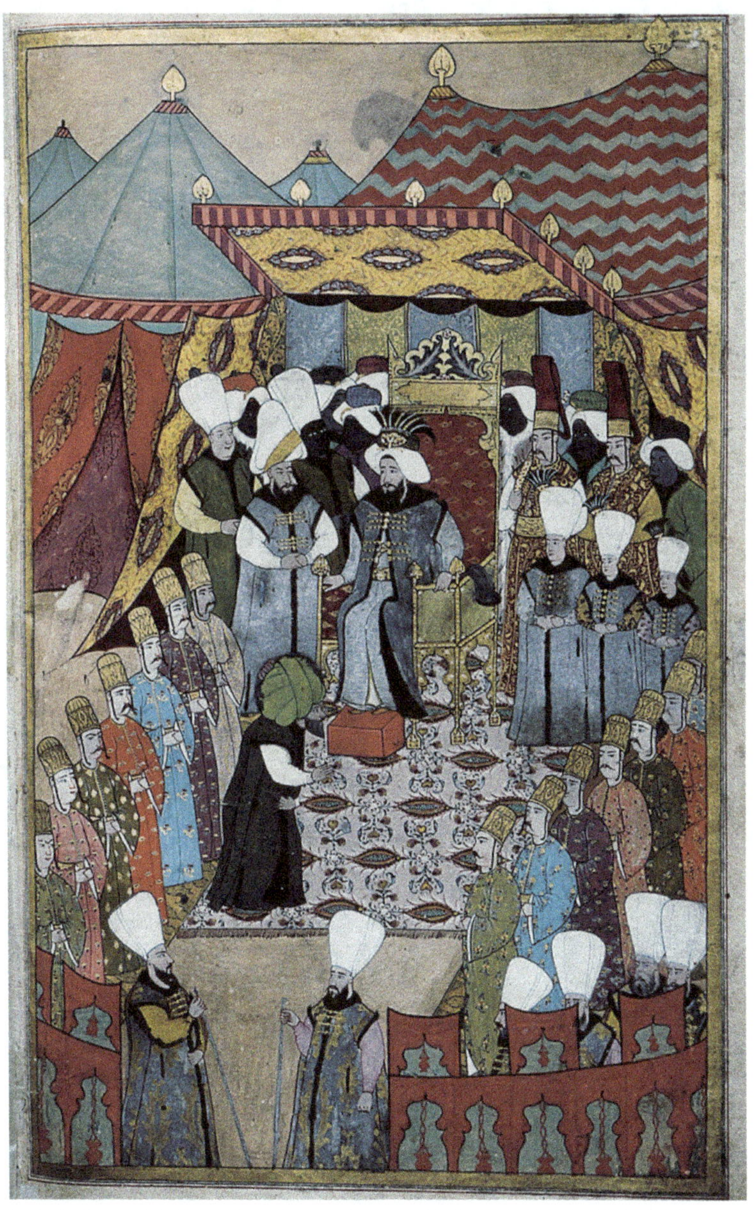

Divan meeting, Surname-i Vehbi, 3593, fol.176, by Levni, 1720, Library of Topkapı Palace, İstanbul.

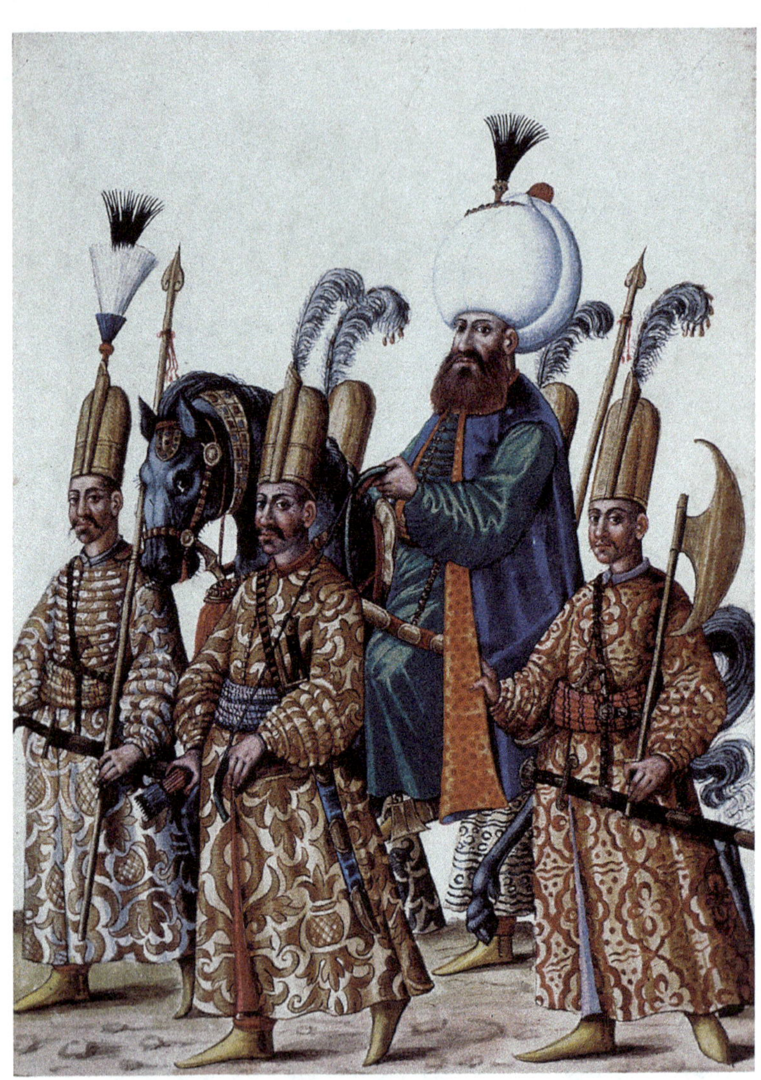

Vizier and the soldiers, Codex Vindobonensis, Cod. 8626, fol 46r, Österreichische Nationalbibliothek, Vienna.

to large provinces. The *kadı*s were not only busy with the judicial problems of the place in which they were located, but also with municipality services. In addition to the control of the shopping district and notary services, the city's public works services were also part of the *kadı*'s responsibility. During a judiciary decision, no one could interfere with the *kadıs*. However, those who were not pleased with their decisions could insist on their rights by applying to the *divan*. According to Ottoman State understanding, "the state cannot exist without a ruler; the ruler cannot exist without soldiers; the soldier cannot exist without money; the people cannot exist without justice". In short, the Ottoman administration appropriated and applied the principle "the state is founded on justice". Christians and Jews, the non-Muslim subjects of the Ottoman State, were able to worship and carry out their religions and traditions in comfort. When the Jews were expelled from Spain in 1492, they took refuge in the Ottoman country. "Escuchis Señor soldado" (Listen Sir Soldier), a Jewish folk song that explains those days, tells the story of a Jewish woman's search for her husband among the fugitives:

"Listen sir soldier
Are you returning from war?
- Yes ma'am, I am coming from war.
From the war with the Spaniards.
I wonder did you run into my husband?
Did you see him at all?
- The man you are speaking of may have died a month ago.
Or he may have found his freedom in Istanbul."

Those Ottoman subjects who did not follow Islam, or who had a different faith, and may have spoken a different language too, lived in peace for many centuries thanks to the Pax Ottomana.

The lake on the edge of the city of İznik known by the same name is Turkey's 5th largest lake. Its average depth is 30 m. A large part of the southern shore is beach and the lake is suitable for swimming.

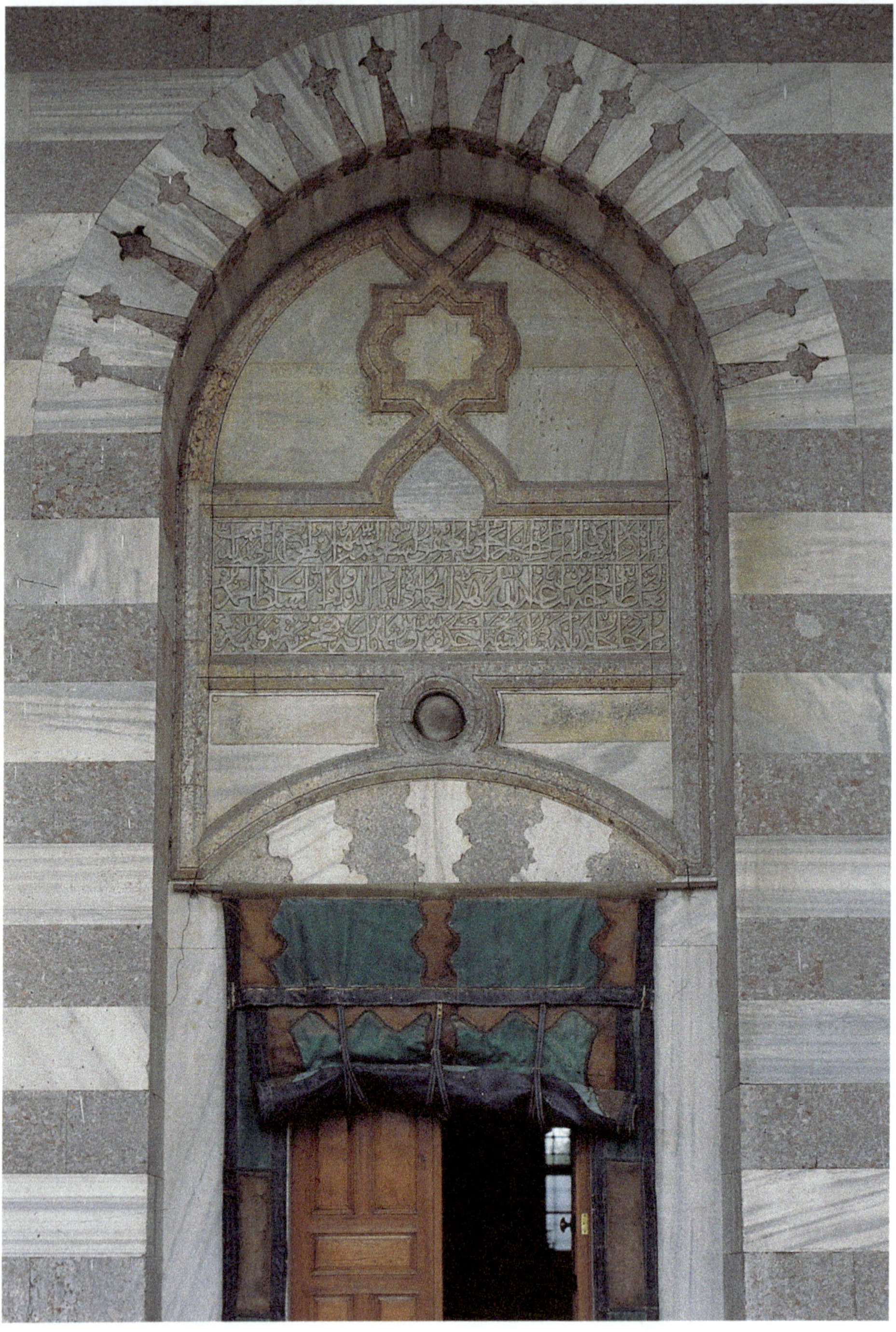

Social Solidarity

Şakir Çakmak, Aydoğan Demir, Rahmi H. Ünal

VI.1 YENİŞEHİR

VI.1.a Postinpuş Baba Zawiya

VI.2 İNEGÖL

VI.2.a İshak Pasha Complex

VI.3 KARACABEY

VI.3.a İmaret Mosque

Tabhanes, Zawiyas *and Itinerant Dervishes*

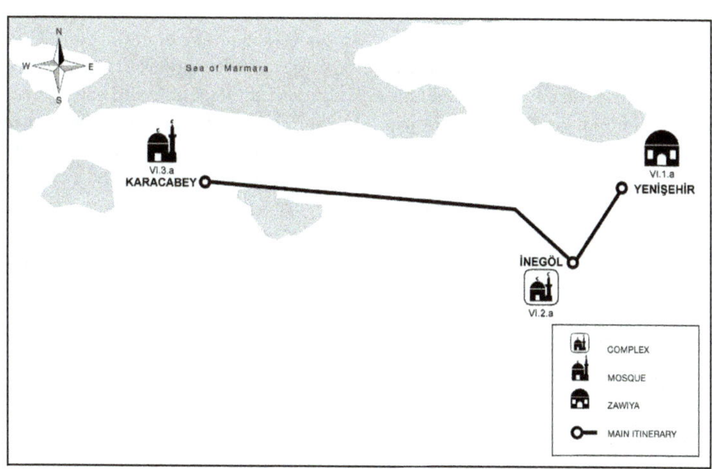

İmaret Mosque, portal, 1457, Karaca Pasha, Karacabey.

During the period when Osman Gazi was attempting to establish an emirate on the Söğüt Plateau, feudal Byzantine Rulers occupied the surrounding areas. Sometimes Osman Gazi engaged in battle with these rulers; at other times he attended weddings with them and shared their entertainment. At the wedding of the Byzantine Lord of Bilecik, they tried to trap him and take him prisoner. The Byzantine Lord of Harmankaya, Köse Mihail, informed Osman Gazi of the plot against him; Osman Gazi came to the wedding with his armed men disguised as women. With the help of his friend Köse Mihail, Osman Gazi acted first and destroyed the plot. One of the captives, Holophira, was given in marriage to Orhan Gazi, and the Ottoman dynasty was continued by a child of this marriage, Murad I. Holophira, a very charitable woman, who became a Muslim and took the name Nilüfer; in Bursa she had a bridge, a *masjid*, and a *dervish tekke* built; the stream over which Nilüfer had the bridge constructed is called today Nilüfer Çayı.

Osman Gazi's friend Köse Mihail also became a Muslim and entered the service of the state. Köse Mihail, his sons and his grandsons, known as the Mihailoğlu, offered valuable service to the Ottoman State for hundreds of years. İnegöl was among the cities that fell to Osman Gazi as a result of the spoiled wedding plot (1298-1299). İshak Pasha (d. 1485), one of the important statesmen of the 15th century, had a beautiful mosque, *madrasa*, and *türbe* built in İnegöl. Of slave origin, and possessed of intelligence and talent, İshak Pasha performed important duties under Sultans Murad II, Mehmed II, and Bayezid II, acting as governor, an army commander, and a *vizier*. Dedicating the property given to him by the sultans (as well as those bought from his own resources) to the *waqfs* of the institutions that he had established, he secured their continued existence for hundreds of years.

After Bilecik and İnegöl, the Ottoman Emirate also took Yenişehir, where Osman Gazi built new houses for his soldiers and thus the city became known as Yenişehir or "New City" (1299). Yenişehir served as the Ottoman capital until the capture of Bursa 27 years later (1326); for this reason 1299 is accepted as the year in which the Ottoman State was founded.

The first Ottoman sultans were very close to some heterodox religious personages, who performed important services for the state during the years of its foundation. Sultan Murad I had a *zawiya* built in Yenişehir for Postinpuş Baba, "who wore animal skins", and his *dervish*es. The town of Mihalıç (today Karacabey) came under Ottoman control in 1336. During the reigns of Sultans Murad II and Mehmed II, Karaca Pasha undertook important duties on behalf of the state and rose to the position of Beylerbeyi of Rumelia; he had an *imaret* established and endowed at Mihalıç. In the rooms of the *imaret* that stood apart from the prayer hall, *dervish*es and learned men were received as guests and were given food without charge. These costs, together with the expenses for the maintenance of the *imaret* and its personnel, were met by the *waqf*. Later Karaca Pasha died in the siege of Belgrade (1456) and the name of Mihalıç was changed to Karacabey in his honour.

A. D.

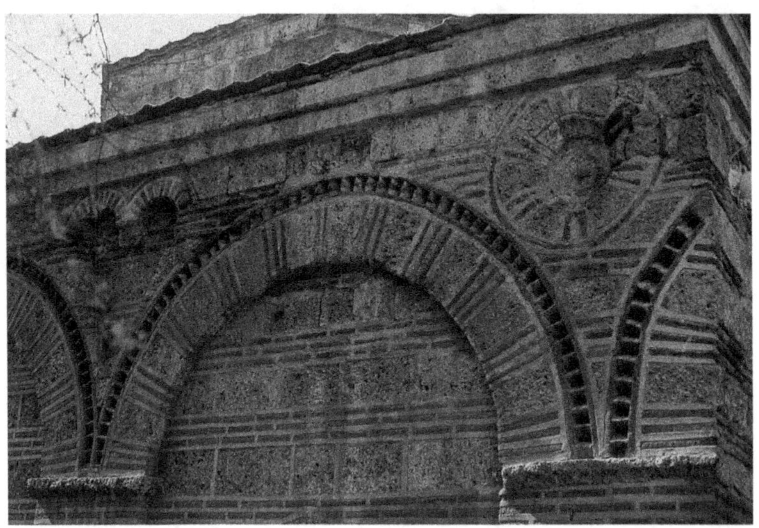

Postinpuş Baba Zawiya, detail from the south facade, 1362-89, Murad I, Yenişehir.

VI.1 YENİŞEHİR

VI.1.a **Postinpuş Baba Zawiya**

In Baba Sultan Park.

As mentioned above, Turkish chroniclers tell that Sultan Murad I (1362-1389) showed great interest in the *dervish*es and had the Postinpuş Baba Zawiya –also known as "Seyyid Mehmed Dede Zawiya" and "Baba Sultan Zawiya"– built in Yenişehir for Postinpuş Baba and his dervishes. It is said that, when this Muslim holy man who had come to Anatolia from Bukhara passed away in Yenişehir, Sultan Murad I built a *türbe* for him and a *zawiya* for his *dervish*es. In 1555, Hans Dernschwam, a German traveller –providing early written evidence for the structure since it does not have an inscription– briefly mentioned the building; at the beginning of the second half of the 17th century, the Turkish traveller Evliya Çelebi, who travelled around the Near East and Balkans and wrote his memoirs, said of this building that it was the grave of the Shaykh Postinpuş Pasha from Khorasan. In the 1920s the German researcher R. Hartmann wrote that the building was surrounded with a cemetery, of which nothing remains today. The building has recently been restored, but after the earthquake of 1999, it has been abandoned.

Set on a small hill, the structure today stands in solitude, accompanied by trees only. There is no evidence of any other building in the *zawiya*'s close vicinity –only the sad remains of a modern café. Constructed in alternating rows of stone and brick, it has beautiful brickwork panels and decoration on the tympana of the windows and the decoration on the spandrels of the blind arches on the south

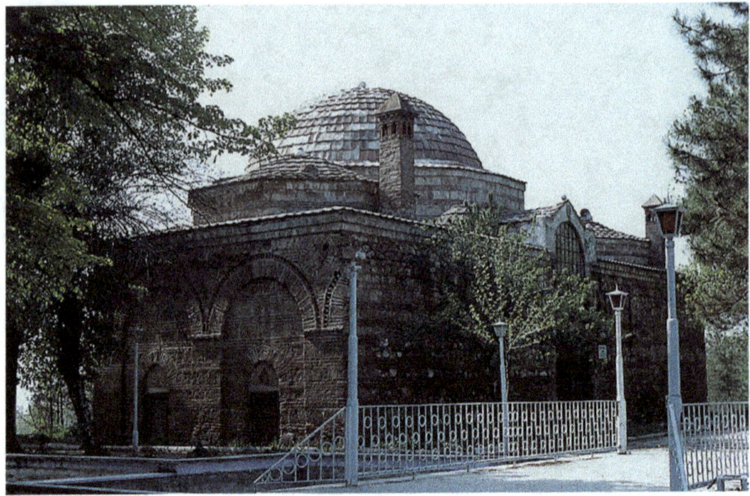

Postinpuş Baba Zawiya, view from the southeast, 1362-89, Murad I, Yenişehir.

front are especially noteworthy. The main facade on the east is totally blind other than the entrance way in the middle, now closed off with glass panes, and the portico that was once here has now disappeared; the traces of an arch on the eastern end of the south wall show that such an area once existed.

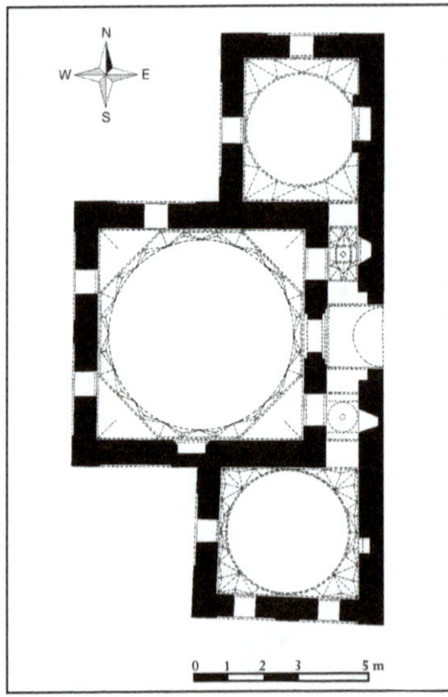

Plan of Postinpuş Baba Zawiya, Yenişehir (from S. Emir).

An example of "mosques with *zawiyas*," it was designed to offer hospitality to itinerant *dervish*es and other travellers. In these structures, built from the beginning of the 14th century through the middle of the 16th century, the prayer hall was distinctly separate from other areas in the building. For example, in this building the prayer hall is the large hall directly opposite the main entrance and is covered by a large dome; the square rooms on the north and south are reached by a corridor and served as *tabhane*s for guests. Another interesting feature is the building's orientation: in West Anatolia the *qibla* is towards the southeast, while in the East, it is towards the southwest. The main entrance is customarily located on the north, opposite the *mihrab* niche that indicates the direction of *Kaaba* in Mecca –the *qibla*. In the *zawiya* of Postinpuş Baba, however, the *mihrab* niche is not on the wall directly opposite the entrance, but on the wall to the left. As mentioned above, the area surrounding the building is now vacant. Although there is nothing to prevent the main entrance from being on the northern side of the building, there is no explanation for the unusual location of the *mihrab* and main entrance in this building.

The north and south *tabhanes* are surmounted by a dome and furnished with a fireplace on their east walls; they both have windows in their two outer walls but their east walls have been left blind; this must have been done in order to provide privacy for the guests staying overnight.

R. H. Ü.

VI.2 İNEGÖL

VI.2.a **İshak Pasha Complex**

In Cuma District (Mahallesi), on the Ankara Avenue by the Eski Belediye Square.

İshak Pasha was an important statesman in the time of Sultans Murad II (1421-1451) and Mehmed II (1451-1481). In the conquest of Istanbul he was an army commander, and later he acted as a governor and Grand *Vizier*. When he died in 1485 at Thessalonica, his body was brought to İnegöl and buried in the conventional cemetery to the south of the mosque he had built in his own name; in 1937 his grave was removed to the *türbe* to the southwest of the mosque. During his years in office he had many buildings

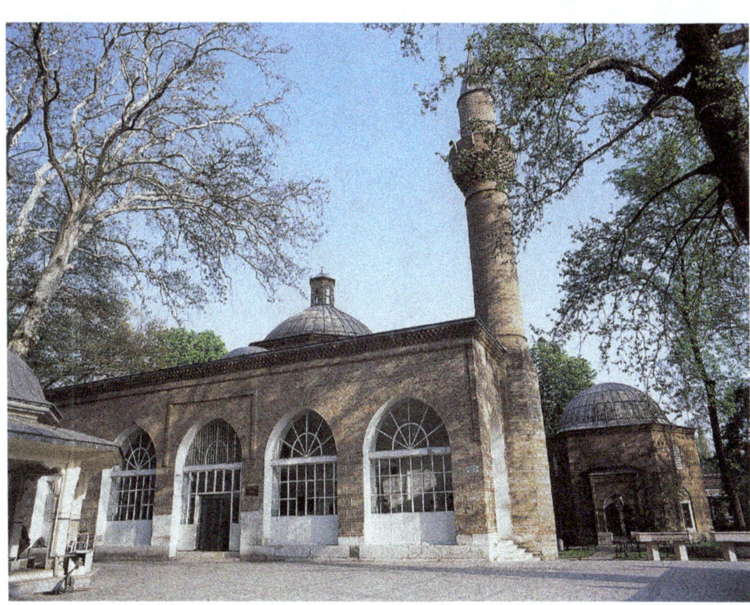

İshak Pasha Complex, View of mosque and türbe from the northwest, 1476, İshak Pasha, İnegöl.

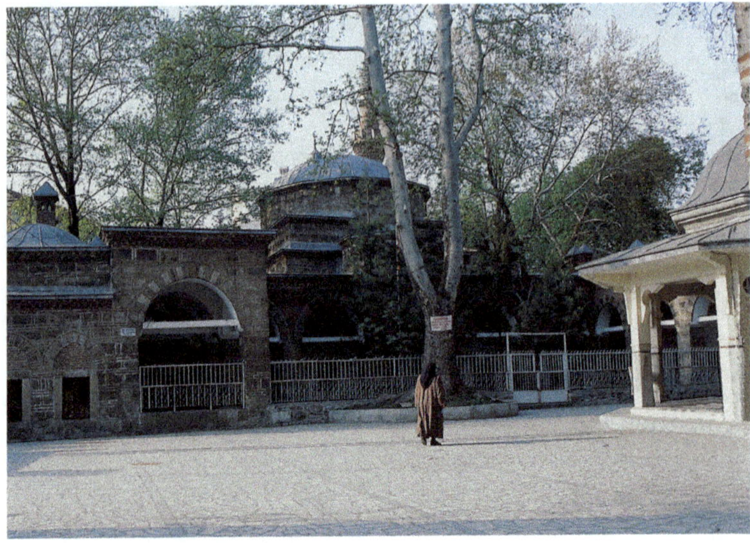

İshak Pasha Madrasa, view from the south, 1483, İshak Pasha, İnegöl.

constructed in several cities, such as Istanbul, Edirne, Kütahya, Bursa and, the income from several *hammams*, shops, mills, and land rental was dedicated to the *waqfs* for the maintenance of these buildings and to pay the salaries of the staff. The complex built by İshak Pasha in İnegöl consists of a mosque, a *madrasa*, and a *türbe*; although the *waqf* charter mentions a *han* there is no *han* present today.

İshak Pasha Mosque

This mosque built with alternating rows of stone and brick like the *madrasa* and the *türbe*, has some brickwork decoration and that on the spandrels of the portico is especially noteworthy. The plain portico –closed off with glass panes– has five domed bays separated with brick and stone piers. The single brick minaret rising on the northwest corner of the building is entered from the western end of the portico. The inscription on the plain portal tells of the repairs carried out in 1877 by Sultan Abdülhamid II. One enters an inner court flanked on the east and west with what were once the *tabhanes* but which are now joined together by removing the walls in between. The rectangular areas that are topped with a vault to the north of these lateral sections, seems to have once been the way leading into the *tabhanes*. The plain prayer hall is to the south. All the domes inside rise above beautiful Turkish triangles. Although there is no inscription, it is believed that the mosque was probably constructed in 1476, based upon the inscription of the *madrasa* and the date of the *waqf* charter established by İshak Pasha.

Madrasa

The *madrasa* is "U"-shaped opening towards the mosque; this layout reminds us of the Süleyman Pasha Madrasa in İznik. The *dershane* rising higher than the rest of the structure is covered by a dome and also protrudes out on the north. A total of 12 domed student cells flank the *dershane* on both sides; each cell is furnished with a fireplace and a niche for daily use. In front of the student cells is a portico with vaulted bays resting on piers surrounding the open courtyard. According to the construction inscription of the *madrasa*, it was built in 1483, that is, a little later than the mosque. Today (2000) the *madrasa* is used as a Koran school.

Türbe

The *türbe* to the southwest of the mosque is known to have been built by İshak Pasha for his wife Tacü'n-nisa (Taj al-nisa) Sultan. This hexagonal structure is covered by a dome and has a very plain portal on the north. Inside are three graves, one of which belongs to İshak Pasha; since there are no gravestones, it is not known for certain to whom the other two graves belong. However, taking into account historical documents, it is reasonable to assume that one grave belongs to Tacü'n-nisa. It is said that the third grave belongs to the Pasha's daughter, but this cannot be ascertained.

Ş. Ç.

İnegöl is famous for its köfte (meatballs). The Thursday market is lively and colourful. The Oylat Kaplıcaları (Spas) 20 km. from İnegöl is well worth a visit for the sulphurous water and the natural scenery. To reach Oylat, take the D200 towards Ankara after 10 km. turn right (south), then 5 km. later, turn right again.

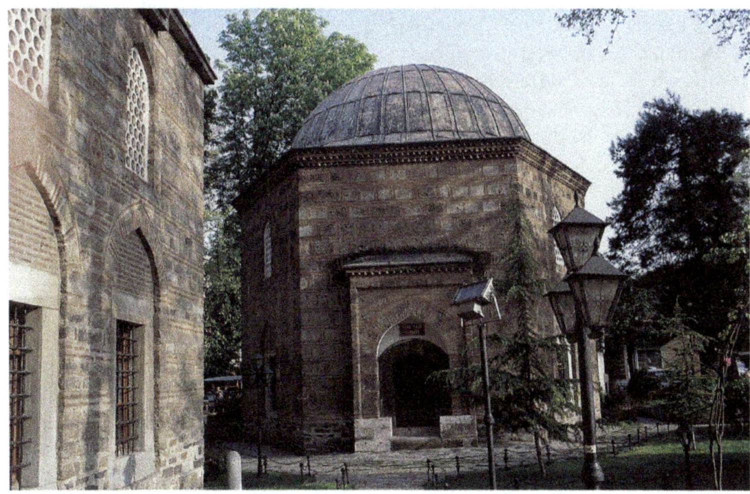

İshak Pasha Türbe, view from the north, end of 15th century, İnegöl.

İmaret Mosque, northern facade, 1457, Karaca Pasha, Karacabey.

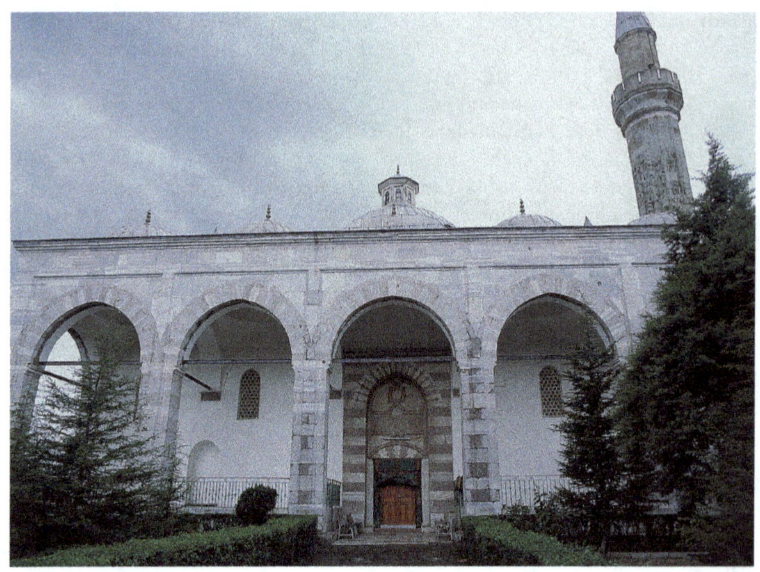

VI.3 KARACABEY

The former "Mihalıç" is known as "Karacabey" today in honour of the Beylerbeyi of Rumelia, Karaca Pasha, who had a complex built here. Karaca Pasha was a notable statesman at the time of Sultan Mehmed II and took part in the conquest of Istanbul. He died during the siege of Belgrade.

VI.3.a İmaret Mosque

Selimiye İmaret Avenue, 12, Karacabey.

In the 1920s, this building was in ruins and abandoned; only two large domes now remain. When restorations begun in the 1960s, the superstructure was completely missing. Open for worship today, the mosque has been reconstructed according to its original plan. Located in a lovely garden, the İmaret Mosque is accompanied by the cubic *türbe* to the west where Karaca Pasha's wife, Bülbül Hatun is buried, along with his brother. Approaching from the main street one notices the stone and brick construction on the mosque and *türbe*, then just going round, the main facade on the north is beautifully faced in marble with very soft colour contrasts. The portico in the front is divided into five bays by marble-faced piers and whereas the central bay is covered by a flat-topped cross vault, the other bays are covered with domes. The plain portal is also faced in marble but with stronger colour contrasts. The inscription explains that the mosque was completed in 1457, after the death of Karaca Pasha.

In the westernmost bay of the portico is the grave of Karaca Pasha himself. According to the inscription on the footstone, which is closer to the portal, he passed away on 20 July 1456. In Ottoman burial tradition, the name of the deceased is not recorded on the footstone, but on the headstone; and, according to Islamic law, the body is buried on its right side with the face turned in the direction of *qibla*; therefore, in this grave, the head is toward the west and the feet are toward the east; hence, the footstone is closer to the entrance of the prayer hall: as such, instead of being written on the headstone, the identity of the deceased was written on the footstone probably so as to be easily read by those passing by. Generally, wealthy individuals who established *waqfs*, set aside a room for their burial in a building they had constructed or they had a separate *türbe* erected. The purpose of this was to have visitors remember them with good prayers. Therefore, sometimes there is a window or a door connecting a *türbe* to an adjoining mosque, *madrasa* or other building, or the *türbe*'s entrance has been incorporated into the *madrasa*.

On entering the inner court one is struck by the rectangular somewhat elongated appearance, with a prayer hall to the south. Like most similar mosques, here too, the dome of the inner court is larger than that of the prayer hall. An indispensable component of a mosque with *tabhanes* is an area for visitors to spend the night; in this mosque, the *tabhanes* lie on either side of the inner court but separated from it by a wall; however, it is striking that here a corridor runs to the north providing access to the *tabhanes*, which are furnished with a fireplace and niches; the western corridor also leads to the minaret on the northwest corner, the other to a staircase for access to the roof.

R. H. Ü.

For those who wish to rest at the end of the day and enjoy the beauty of nature, do visit Manyas Gölü Kuş Cenneti or "Lake Manyas Bird Sanctuary". To get to the bird sanctuary, head for Çanakkale leaving Karacabey and 12 km. before reaching Bandırma turn onto the main road 565 in the direction of Balıkesir. Two km. later follow the road that turns to the right until you come to a small museum. Apart from an observation area and toilets there are no places to eat or spend the night in the sanctuary. Picnics are not permitted.

In ancient times Lake Manyas was known as Aphnitis or Daskylitis; it served as a hunting area for satraps when Anatolia was under Persian rule. The freshwater lake has an area of 166 km² and is at an altitude of 15 m. The lake is very shallow; towards the end of winter the water level rises and in the spring it reaches a depth of 10 m. at its deepest point. In the summer the water level falls to 1.5 m. White willow is the most common tree found on the shores of the lake, which is surrounded by villages, and large areas of farmland. The lake is a safe haven and a rich source of food for birds. Cormorants, pelicans, geese, ducks and herons take shelter here. The large number of fish, frogs, worms and seeds offer the birds ready access to an abundance of food. Vegetation is plentiful and healthy. One of the main reasons that birds gather here is that one of the migration paths passes over this lake. Here birds start to brood, pass the winter or just stop during their migration. 250 species of birds have been identified on the lake comprising between 2-3 million individual birds.

Şakir Çakmak

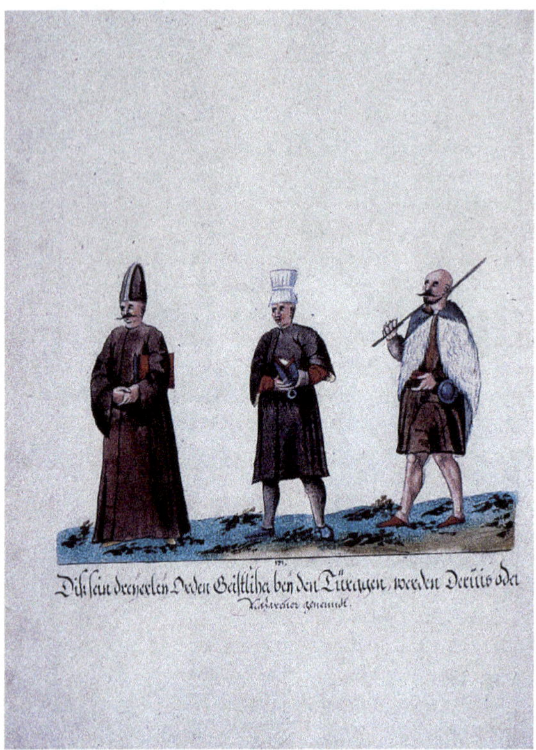

Dervishes, Codex Vindobonensis, Cod.8615, fol92r, Österreichische Nationalbibliothek, Vienna.

In Anatolia, beginning in Seljuq times, there were various social organisations influential in military, religious, social and economic affairs and playing an important role during the establishment of the Ottoman State. One of the most important was the *Ahiyan-ı Rum* (Anatolian *Ahi*s); it has been suggested that this organisation takes its name from either the Arabic word *akhi* for "brother" or from the Turkish word *akı* for "generous". The *Ahi* society is an extension of the *Futuwwa* supported by the Abbassid Caliph Nasir (1180-1225). Another famous organisation of the time was the *Abdalan-ı Rum* (Anatolian Abdals), a society of itinerant *dervish*es.

The Sultans, knowing the importance of the "Turkification" and economic development of conquered cities, and seeing the support these *Ahi*s and *dervish*es could lend in this process, patronised them. Some Sultans were even members of a society; and in order to facilitate their religious and vocational efforts, they had special buildings such as *zawiya*s, mosques with *zawiya*s and mosques with *tabhane*s built for the *Ahi*s and itinerant *dervish*es.

A 14th-century traveller by the name of Ibn Battuta gives valuable information on *Ahi zawiya*s that he encountered and was entertained in while travelling through some Anatolian cities. These *zawiya*s spread even to most remote villages and, along with giving education in religion, science and morality, they also gave training in various trades.

The mosques with *tabhanes*, which sultans and high-government officials had built for the *Ahi*s and itinerant dervishes, shed light on the social structures of the Early Ottoman period. The numerous examples of these mosques built from the 14th through to the 16th centuries in areas that fell under Ottoman rule are proof that the government considered such 'socialising' organisations important.

Mosques with *tabhane*s are different from regular mosques whose only function is to provide a place for prayer. In fact, these types of buildings are referred to as *zawiya*s or *imaret*s on building inscriptions, *waqf* charters, and other documents. Mosques with *tabhane*s were designed to meet the needs of the *Ahi*s and itinerant *dervish*es by providing them with a space for meetings, worship and lodgings. These buildings, also known as T-shaped mosques, are composed of three main sections: a meeting and transition area called the "central court" or "inner court" or "*sofa*"; a prayer hall; *tabhanes* functioning as guestrooms, whose number varies from two to six.

From the middle of the 15th century, the *Ahi* organisation began to assume the nature of a guild occupying itself in commercial affairs only. For this reason, the need for mosques with *tabhanes* diminished. The construction of this type of mosque continued until the beginning of the 16th century with a few alterations. From the 16th century on, *tabhanes* became separate buildings in a mosque complex and, as a result of this development, mosques with *tabhanes* were no longer constructed.

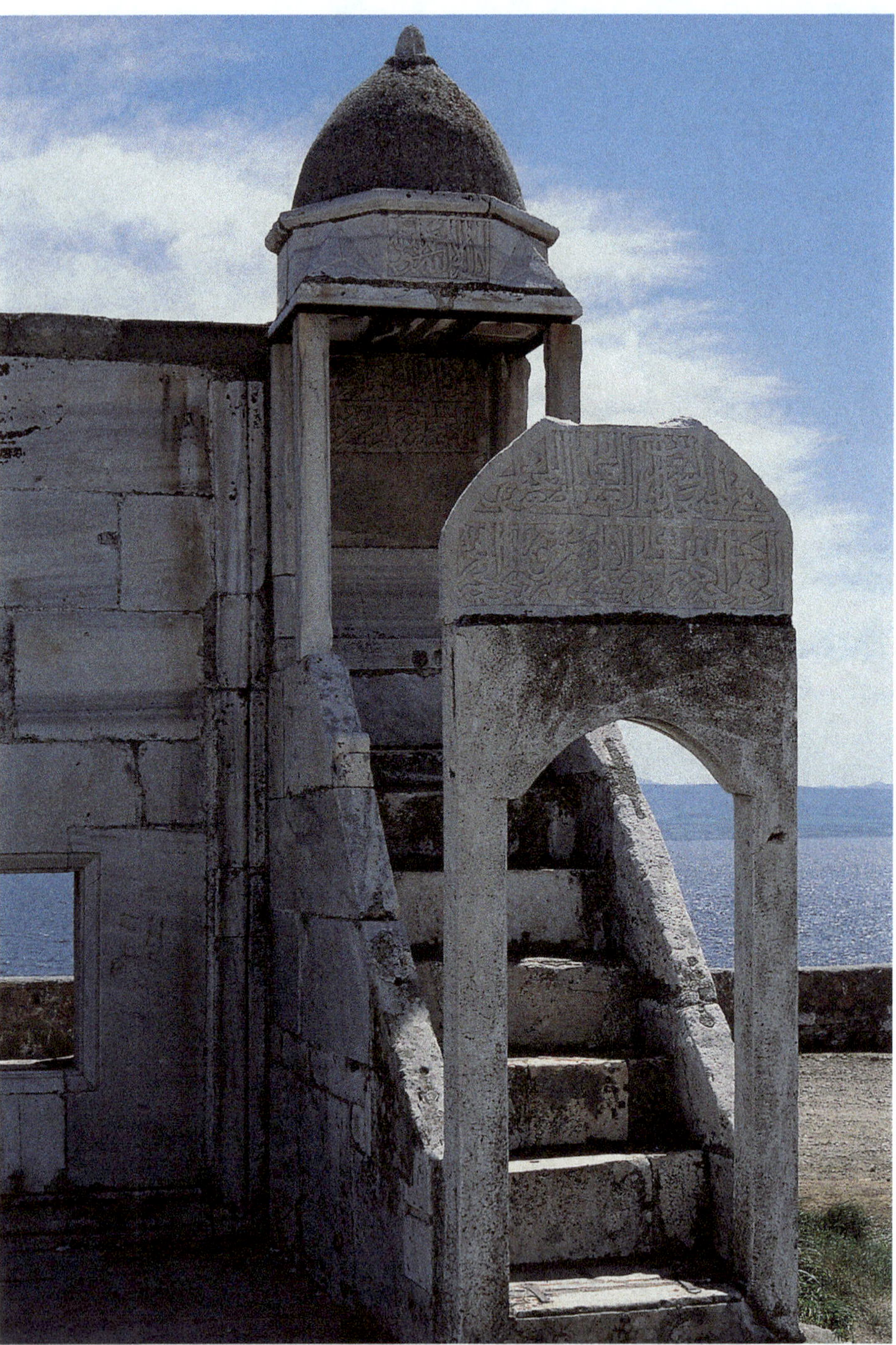

The Lock of the Sea

Şakir Çakmak, Aydoğan Demir

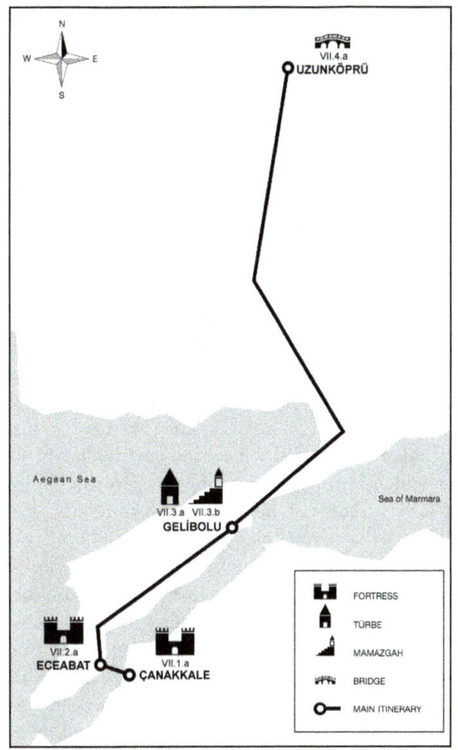

Azebler Namazgah, minbar, 1407, İskender Ibn Hacı Pasha, Gelibolu.

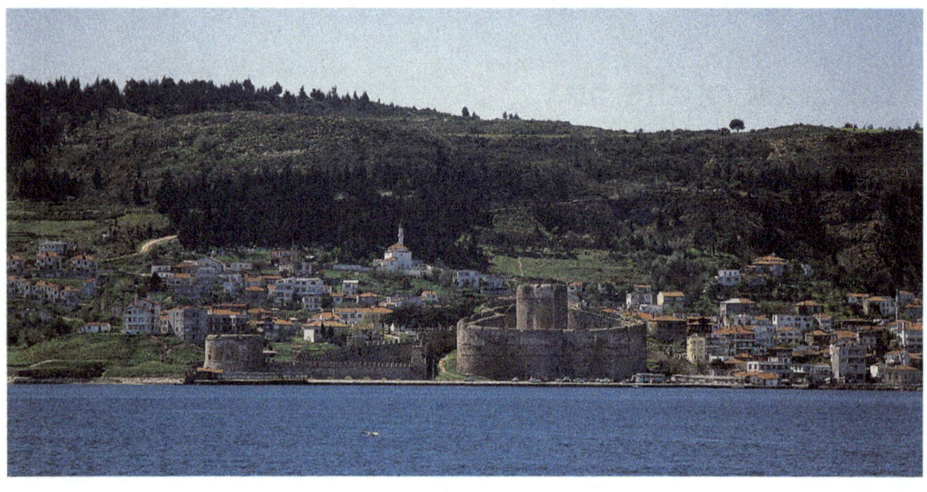

Kilitbahir Fortress, view from the east, 1463, Mehmed II, Eceabat.

A few kilometres away from the shore on the Anatolian side, at the entrance of the Çanakkale Strait (Dardanelles) that connects the Marmara Sea to the Aegean, on the spot known today as Hisarlık Hill, you can still see the remains of the ancient city of Troy. If you close your eyes for a minute and imagine ancient times, you will see King Priam standing on the city walls of Troy, his wife Hecabe, his famous son Paris, his daughter Cassandra, and his daughter in-law, the beautiful Helen watching with fearful eyes as two men fight. On the other side, there stands Agamemnon, the Achaean King, his brother Menelaus, the king of Sparta, and brave Odysseus, all observing the very same fight with some excitement. Those in battle are well known to both parties: invincible Achilles, son of a goddess and a mortal, and the other is the son of King Priam, namely brave Hector. Homer relates his glorified epic of the Iliad and immortalises the story of the Trojan War into a romantic love story: Paris's abduction of King Menelaus's wife, the beautiful Helen, was the cause of this long war. However, the real reason behind the war was the struggle to take over the Çanakkale Strait, a crucial trade and transportation route connecting the Black Sea with the Aegean Sea.

For many centuries, the Çanakkale and Istanbul (Bosphorus) Straits have been a major source of conflict between nations. At the beginning of the 14th century, the Anatolian shores of the Strait were under the sovereignty of the Karasi Emirate. When the Ottomans destroyed the Karasi Emirate around the middle of 14th century, they gained control over the shores of the area. At the same time, the Ottomans gained a base in Gelibolu, on the other side of the Çanakkale Strait in return for helping John VI Cantacuzenus, who at the time was struggling to acquire the Byzantine throne (1354). From this date on the Ottomans rapidly acquired all of Thrace. Gelibolu became a much-frequented place for people passing from

Anatolia to Thrace. Built on the Gelibolu-Edirne route, Uzunköprü, literally the Long Bridge, is one of the longest bridges of Thrace. This bridge indicates the importance given to the trade and conquest routes that tied Anatolia and Europe together in the first half of 15th century.

After Sultan Mehmed II conquered Istanbul in 1453, he followed an expansionary policy in the Aegean Sea and the Balkans, which meant great losses for the merchant communes of Venice and Genoa. Sultan Mehmed II became very popular in Italy, and many legends about him were passed on. In his *Essays*, Montaigne (1533-1592) says: "Muhammad the Conqueror believes himself to be a descendant of the Trojans, just like the Italians, and thus he is astonished that the Italians support the Greeks when they actually ought to work with him in order to take revenge for Hector". Since interstate relationships could not be resolved by such an approach of romanticism and kinship, Sultan Mehmed II had ordered the Sultaniye Fortress and Kilidü'l-Bahr Fortress to be built at the narrowest point of the Çanakkale Strait against possible Venetian and Genoese threats.

A. D.

This Itinerary starts on the Asian continent and ends on the European continent. With the ferryboat that you board at Çanakkale, you will reach Eceabat on the Gelibolu peninsula within 30 minutes. The Gelibolu peninsula occupies an important place in both world and Turkish history. In 1915, the Battle of Çanakkale –the so-called Battle of Gallipoli– took place here between the Allied Powers and the Ottoman Empire, and was one of the bloodiest wars in history. Today this area that witnessed the death of approximately 500,000 people is a National Park with monuments erected in various parts so that the painful experiences of the past will not be forgotten, and people will reflect on the great importance of peace. This route that proceeds through the fruitful land of Thrace is slightly rugged though the scenery is peaceful and relaxed. Following the main road D.550 north from Eceabat, you will first reach Gelibolu. This road continues across Uzunköprü via Keşan. To reach Edirne, you must turn onto the main road D.100 from Havsa.

VII.1 ÇANAKKALE

The city of Çanakkale situated on the Asian side of the Strait was founded around the middle of the 15th century,

Sultaniye Fortress, the inner court, 1463, Mehmed II, Çanakkale.

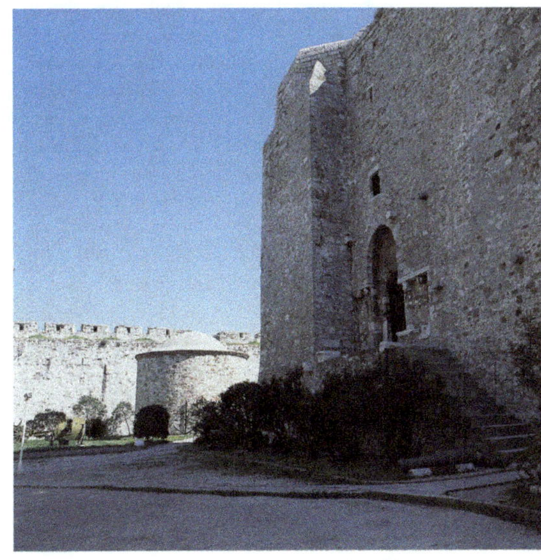

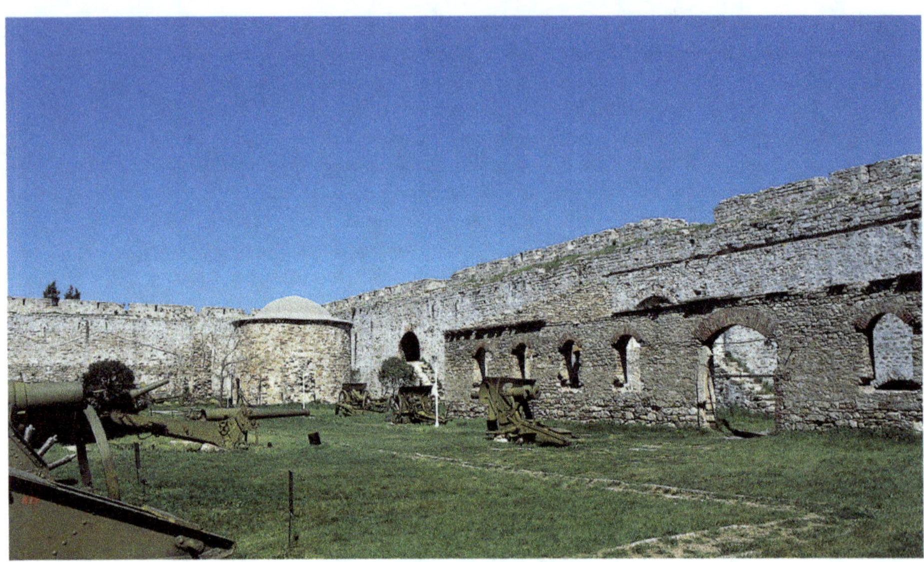

Sultaniye Fortress, the inner court and armoury, 1463, Mehmed II, Çanakkale.

with the building of the Sultaniye Fortress on the Anatolian shore by order of Mehmed II against potential Venetian and Genoese threats. Its citizens named the city Çanakkale because it was a centre of pottery production: in Turkish "Çanak" means earthenware pot and "Kale" means fortress. Pottery produced locally in Çanakkale was popular throughout the country.

The famous Troy is just half-an-hour's drive to the south of Çanakkale and some of the finds along with ancient objects from Assos, are on display in the Çanakkale Archaeological Museum.

VII.1.a **Sultaniye Fortress**

The fortress is located in the Kemalpaşa District (Mahallesi), on Yalı Avenue; 200 m. to the south of the ferry port. Today it is used as a Military (Navy) Museum. Open between the hours of 09.00-12.00 and 13.30-17.00, it is closed on Mondays and Thursdays. There is an entrance fee (plus an extra fee for the use of a camera).

Following the conquest of Istanbul, Sultan Mehmed II ordered the construction of two fortresses on the narrowest point in order to control the Dardanelles; these fortresses face each other, one on the Anatolian side, and the other on the Thracian side. Located today in Çanakkale's city centre, the fortress on the Anatolian side, Sultaniye Fortress, was built in 1463 under the supervision of Yakup Bey, one of Sultan Mehmed II's generals. The fortress has been restored recently and its surrounding area has been reorganised and turned into a museum.

Past the ticket office on the right is the Nusrat ship used for laying mines during the Battle of Çanakkale in 1915. The main entrance under a tower in the middle of the north side opens into the court. The Sultaniye Fortress, also known as Çimenlik Fortress, is composed of an outer fort, 110 x 160 m., and a three-storey inner castle of 30 x 42 m. and 20 m. high, along with two *masjids* and a circular armoury. The outer wall is fortified with several towers and bastions and supports battlements. On entering the court one faces the inner fort straight ahead, and the round armoury to the left in the distance. The first *masjid* adjoins the tower, under which is the entrance today, and the upper part of its short minaret is in ruins. In the court between the outer fort and the inner castle is an open-air display of cannons and artillery from the First World War. The second *masjid* stands by the southwest corner of the inner castle and according to the inscription, it was built during the reign of Sultan Abdülaziz (1861-1876). The redoubts in the west part of the outer fort were built in the same period. On the landing in front of the main door of the inner castle there is a broken marble seat, on which, according to legend, Sultan Mehmed II sat. This inner castle is a very secure building with walls more than 7 m. thick; according to the writings of researchers, a 38' cannon ball left only a small mark on its wall during the Battle of Çanakkale (1915); today it is used as an exhibition hall housing a display of weapons.
Grelot, a 17th-century traveller, describes Sultaniye Fortress in detail and records that there were 28 large cannons that could shoot cannon balls to the opposite shore, and that Çanakkale was a large village behind the castle, with a population of 3000.

Ş. Ç.

You can reach Eceabat by taking one of the Turkish Maritime Lines' ferries that leaves every hour from Çanakkale. Just to the south of the port, there are smaller private ferries going directly to Kilitbahir.

VII.2 ECEABAT

VII.2.a **Kilitbahir Fortress**

Kilitbahir Village, Eceabat. There is an entrance fee to the inner fort.

The fortress of Kilitbahir –or Kilidü'l-Bahr– is the second stronghold that Sultan Mehmed II built to control the Straits of Çanakkale. Built in 1463 along with the Sultaniye Fortress on the Asian side, it is named Kilidü'l-Bahr meaning "the lock of the sea" due to its strategic positioning; the village is also named after the fortress.
This fortress is unique among Turkish fortresses in terms of its architectural plan: the original fortress resembles the letter "D" and has a trefoil-shaped inner fort in the centre from which rises a trefoil-shaped tower. Coming from the ferry port one enters the outer fortress through the north gate; on the left is the shore with the walls now collapsed; and on the right stands the majestic inner fort with its bands of brickwork decoration high up to entice your eye upwards.

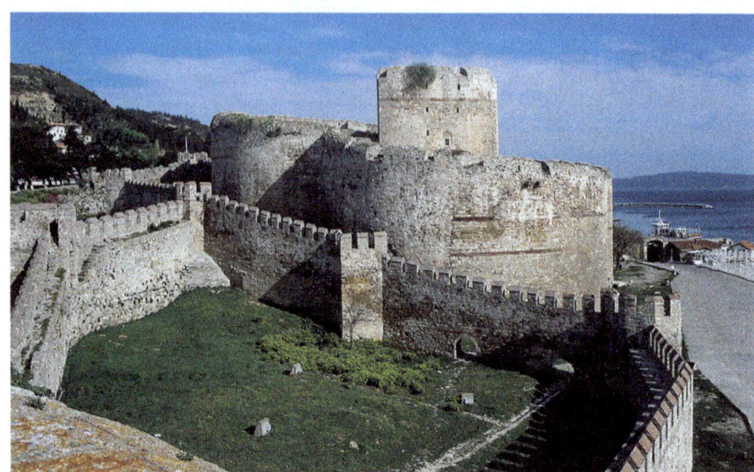

Kilitbahir Fortress, view from the south, 1463, Mehmed II, Eceabat.

The trefoil-shaped inner fortress, rising higher than the rest, consists of three courtyards separated from each other by gates. Its huge walls are 7 m. thick and 18 m. high. Two of the courtyards have monumental doors opening to the court of the outer fortress. A 30-m. high, seven-storied tower stands in the centre; the court in which this tower stands is not directly linked to the outer fortress. With this innovative architectural plan, the enemy forces that wanted to conquer the fortress would have had to pass through one courtyard to the other. Thus, it was rendered extremely difficult to reach the main tower in the centre. There are bands of brickwork with geometric designs on the upper parts of the tower walls. It is understood that the tower was divided by wooden flooring, and that wooden staircases built into the walls led to each of these floors. Unfortunately, neither the staircases nor the wooden floors have survived to the present day; only the first-floor level is accessible by the staircase in the wall.

The second fortress constructed in 1541 in the reign of Süleyman I adjoins the original one –forming an almost irregular figure-eight shape. A monumental tower of 21 m. in diameter stands in its southernmost corner. The outer circuits of the walls are 4 m. high, although the sections along the sea have not survived. It is known that wide moats existed around the fortress; the fortress was entered through two gates, one to the north and one to the south. There were suspended bridges over the moats to reach the gates; because the moats were filled in at some later date, they are no longer present today. Past the second fortress extend many emplacements and the remains of more 19th-century walls.

Ş. Ç.

Today the Gelibolu (known as Gallipoli in the West) Peninsula is a National Park full of monuments and cemeteries of Turkish and for-

eign soldiers who lost their lives in the Battle of Çanakkale. You can take a rather narrow main road to the southern end of the peninsula where there are Turkish, French and English monuments. In the direction of the town of Gelibolu to the north, you can reach Kabatepe, Anzac Bay and Conk Bayırı by heading north and then taking a road that curves to the left. There is a small museum at Kabatepe, where belongings recovered from the soldiers of the First World War are displayed.

You can reach Gelibolu by taking the main road D.550 north from Eceabat.

VII.3 GELİBOLU

Gelibolu is situated in a strategically important area, where the Dardanelles opens into the Sea of Marmara. The city, first founded by the Thracians, was called Kallipolis –the beautiful city– after the Greek colonisation. Alexander the Great then took the area in 334 BC. The Roman and Byzantine Empires later ruled the city, and the Byzantine Emperor Justinian I repaired the city walls. During the Third Crusade Friedrich I Barbarossa, the German Emperor, transported his armies from the port of Gelibolu to the Anatolian side.

Umur Bey of the Aydın Emirate besieged Gelibolu in 1332 and 1341, but did not succeed in conquering it. The Ottomans, who initially landed in Rumelia to help the Byzantines, later realised the strategic importance of the area and captured Gelibolu, whose fortress had been destroyed as a result of an earthquake. The town changed hands several times until 1367,

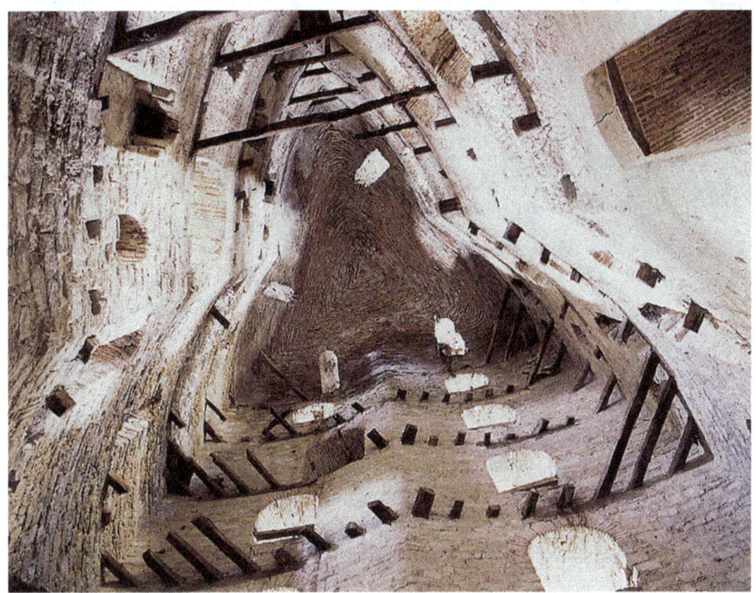

Kilitbahir Fortress, interior of the trefoil-shaped tower, 1463, Mehmed II, Eceabat.

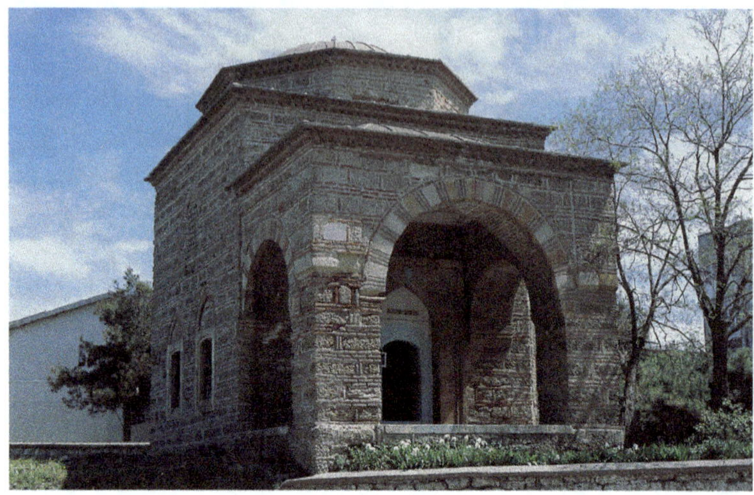

Türbe of Ahmet Bican Efendi (Hallacı Mansur), entrance facade, 15th century, Gelibolu.

when it finally became Ottoman territory. About the middle of the 15th century, Çanakkale took over surveillance of the strait, and Gelibolu thus lost its importance. In the city there are various works constructed in the reign of Murad II (1421-1451) in particular; most of these works have suffered from to neglect and have thus fallen into ruins.

VII.3.a Türbe of Ahmet Bican Efendi (Hallacı Mansur)

On Keşan Avenue.

The *türbe* of Ahmet Bican Efendi is one of the best-kept works in Gelibolu. Alhough it is assumed that it was built in the period of Murad II, it is not known for certain to whom it belongs. Some researchers argue that it belongs to Ahmet Bican Efendi, but some say it belongs to a person called Hallacı Mansur. Known to have died in the middle of the 15th century, Ahmet Bican Efendi was a wise man known for his works in the theology of Islam and Islamic geography. However, Hallacı Mansur is a Muslim saint who lived before the conquest of Gelibolu. Although the *türbe* was allegedly built in his memory, no evidence has been found to support this belief. A *hallaç* is a person who works cotton or wool with a bow and a mallet so that it is suitable for use in beds, covers, and pillows. The story goes that once upon a time, a bow and mallet used by *hallaçes* were found in the tomb. Thus, the belief that this *türbe* should be attributed to this person called Hallacı Mansur is based upon this legend.
Stones and bricks are used alternately on the walls of the domed *türbe*, which has a square plan. In front of the entrance is a single-bay portico covered with a flat-topped cross vault. Such porticoes located in front of the entrance of Anatolian *türbes* are observed to have started in the

early 15th century, as we have already seen in the *türbe* of Sultan Bayezid I (1406) in Bursa Yıldırım Complex.

There are two sarcophagi in the tomb. The richly ornamented one that is believed to belong to Ahmet Bican Efendi has no inscription on it. The other smaller sarcophagus is plain.

Ş. Ç.

VII.3.b **Azebler Namazgah**

It is on the road going east from the türbe *of Ahmet Bican Efendi, in the Fener District (Mahallesi).*

In Ottoman architecture, in addition to covered worship places such as mosques and *masjids*, there are also open-air prayer places built for use during the summer months. Called *namazgahs*, they are usually situated outside the city in recreation areas, suburbs, or on intercity roads. The term *namazgah* means "a large, open-air place, where prayer is performed". The *namazgahs* were not used only as venues for Friday or daily prayer times: people prayed together for those going into military service or taking part in a military campaign, or for those going on a pilgrimage to Mecca, that they may have a safe journey, and in times of drought people went to these places to pray for rain. Situated along routes between cities or suburbs, *namazgahs* also served as resting areas.

Namazgahs have rather simple architecture, the main elements of which are: a *mihrab* indicating the direction to Mecca, or a stone symbolising the *mihrab*; a small well or fountain for ablution; a clean and appropriate place for performing prayer and trees to protect the area from excess heat. There are also examples with a more ornamented and decorated *qibla* wall and a *minbar*.

Azebler Namazgah, view from the northeast, 1407, İskender Ibn Hacı Pasha, Gelibolu.

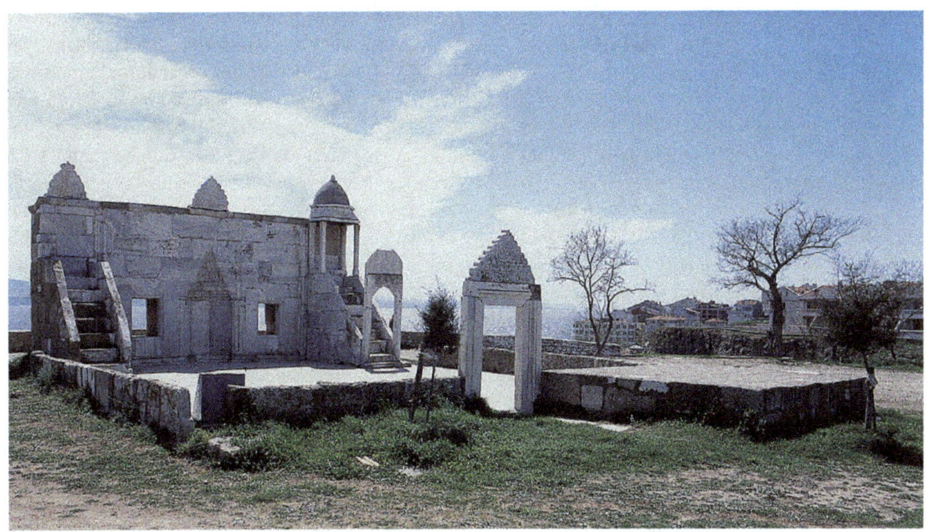

This *namazgah* in Gelibolu was built initially as a common prayer area for the soldiers in the Ottoman Navy, called *Azebs*, and is one of the most elaborate examples of such a structure. The *namazgah* is located on a flat area on top of a ridge, overlooking the Strait at the entrance to Dardanelles, southeast of the city. According to its inscription, it was built by the architect Aşık Ibn Süleyman for İskender Ibn Hacı Pasha in 1407.

The *namazgah* is surrounded by low walls on the east, west and north sides, and is entered through a false marble door on the north. There is a *mihrab* in the centre of the marble *qibla* wall along with two *minbars*, one at each end of the wall. Although it is a simple structure, it has a rich appearance with its fine decoration on the tympanum of the entrance and on the upper section of its *qibla* wall.

Ş. Ç.

VII.4 UZUNKÖPRÜ

VII.4.a **Uzunköprü Bridge**

Constructed over the Ergene River, the Uzunköprü (literally the long bridge) is positioned at the entrance to Uzunköprü town, formerly known as Ergene. It is one of the longest and most splendid historical Turkish bridges. In the 15th century, the inefficient roads and the strong- flowing rivers were major obstacles for the Ottoman army. Ergene River is one of the most intractable natural obstacles in Turkey. According to historical sources, the area where the bridge stands today used to be a swamp covered by trees; the wooden bridges over the river were insufficient to serve the needs and collapsed frequently when the river overflowed. Sultan Murad II built a new wooden bridge after another flood, but soon realised that it was not strong enough either and decided that a stone bridge should be built.

A mosque, a *han*, a *hammam* and an *imaret* were built near this 1400-m. long, 174-arched magnificent bridge. According to its inscription, which was later moved to a nearby fountain, the construction was completed in 1444. Historical sources state that Sultan Murad II himself attended the opening ceremony, which was followed by religious ceremonies, feasts and parades.

There are carvings of elephants, birds and lions on the bridge, as well as decorations with geometric and floral themes. The elephant figure, rarely seen in Turkish architectural decoration, has received much attention from scholars. There are various theories regarding the origin of this figure, the most remarkable of which is: Sultan Murad II had his son Mehmed married in 1449 in Edirne with a wedding lasting three months. In a manuscript that is known to have left Istanbul for the library in San Marco, Venice, Sitti Hatun –whose tombstone we will see at the Archaeological Museum in Edirne– the wife of Mehmed, is pictured sitting on a throne positioned on an elephant. Some researchers interpret this as follows: Sitti Hatun might have been brought to Edirne on an elephant passing over Uzunköprü. Thus, the elephant carving on the bridge may have been carried out in memory of this incident.

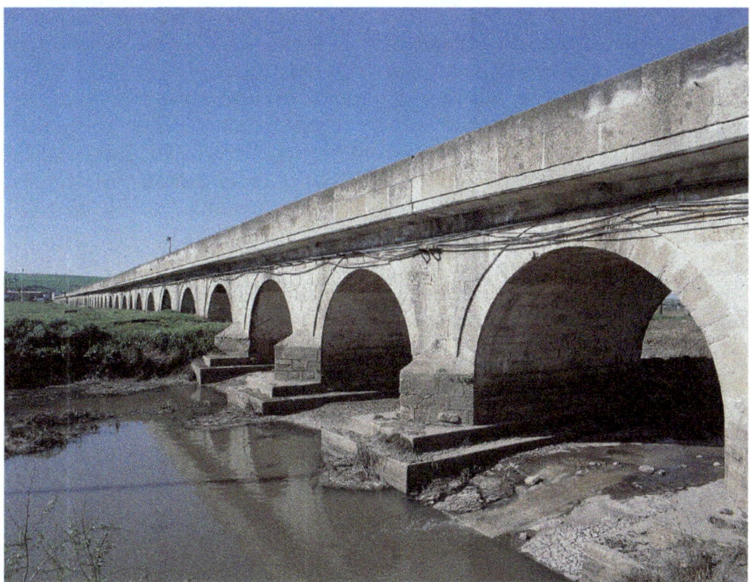

Uzunköprü Bridge, general view, 1444, Murad II, Uzunköprü.

Uzunköprü, attractive for its architecture and decoration, has undergone several renovations, the last one in 1970, and is still in use as part of the main road. Only the part directly above the river becomes hump-backed and has balconies with carvings at the top; the rest of the bridge extends flat over the marshy area. Today due to the alluvium brought by the river a large part of bridge's piers are buried underground.

Ş. Ç.

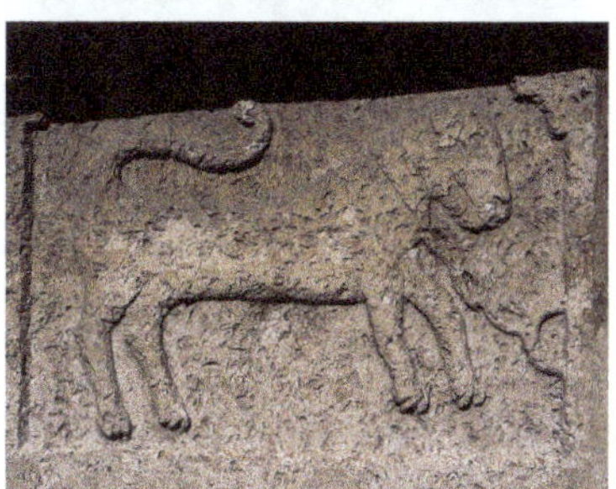

Uzunköprü Bridge, lion relief, 1444, Murad II, Uzunköprü.

Aydoğan Demir

Waqfs are pious foundations established to meet the construction and operating costs of non-profit structures like mosques, *madrasas*, hospitals, *imarets*, fountains, and so on, which an individual has built using his or her movable or real-estate property. In the Middle Ages, funds from the state treasury of Islamic countries were not allocated to the construction of public buildings. Buildings constructed by the rulers, bureaucrats and rich citizens of the town and funded by the *waqfs* embellished the splendid Islamic towns.

In Ottoman administration, a statesman that had such a building constructed determined in detail in the *waqf* charter exactly how the revenues of the foundation ought to be spent. For example:

1. It was determined, in detail, the qualifications and the number of people to be employed in these structures.
2. If there was a *madrasa*, the allowance of the students and the salaries of the staff were determined.
3. If there was an *imaret*, the types of food and the number of people to be served, as well as the specific details of the meals for certain days like religious holidays, were determined.
4. The regular maintenance, cleaning and renovation of the structures was organised.
5. Cash, farms, stores, houses, an ice-depot, blacksmith's shop, soap factory, *boza* factory, *hans*, *bedestens* and all other property that brings revenue to cover the costs of the service structures were listed one-by-one in the *waqf* charter.
6. The owner of the *waqf* bound the management of the *waqf* to himself as long as he was alive, and to one of his sons, or if he had no sons, to one of his daughters or grandsons.
7. All conditions regarding the management of the *waqf* were listed one-by-one in writing, and then signed by witnesses. The *waqf* charter then had to be approved by the court. Once the *waqf* charter was approved, as long as it followed the stated conditions, no one could interfere with the content of the *waqf*.

Waqfs were established for various purposes: some *waqfs* were to help poor girls prepare the necessary trousseau; some were to get indebted people out of prison; there were some that provided food for prisoners, or food and water for animals, and even some that took care of injured storks.

THE JANISSARY CORPS

Aydoğan Demir

The Ottoman State, founded in 1299, became a large empire within 150 years following its foundation. The organisation of the state in almost all areas, as well as its continuous legal reforms to protect its citizens, must have played an important role in the growth of the state.

Beginning with the founding of the state, military problems such as recruiting and training soldiers and protecting their futures were considered within a legal framework.

Osman Gazi (1281-1324) gathered volunteer and paid soldiers from his countrymen. However, soon these soldiers became insufficient as wars tended to last longer and took place farther away from the centre. During the reign of Orhan Gazi (1324-1362), an army was formed of cavalrymen and infantries, who lived not in the barracks but on the farms provided by the state when they were not away at war.

Besides soldiers that were half-farmer, half-infantry or half-cavalrymen, there were also those who owned a *tımar* fief allocated by the Sultan, through which they collected certain taxes in their administrative regions. These soldiers were called *Tımarlı Sipahi*s and constituted the main force of the Ottoman army until the end of the 16th century. The title *Tımarlı Sipahi* was usually passed from father to son.

Around the middle of the 14th century, during the reign of Murad I (1362-1389), a new group of infantries called *Yeniçeri* (Janissary) was formed, who were considered the court soldiers of the Sultan and were lodged in barracks in the capital. The cavalry formed around the same time as the Janissary corps reported directly to the Sultan himself. The

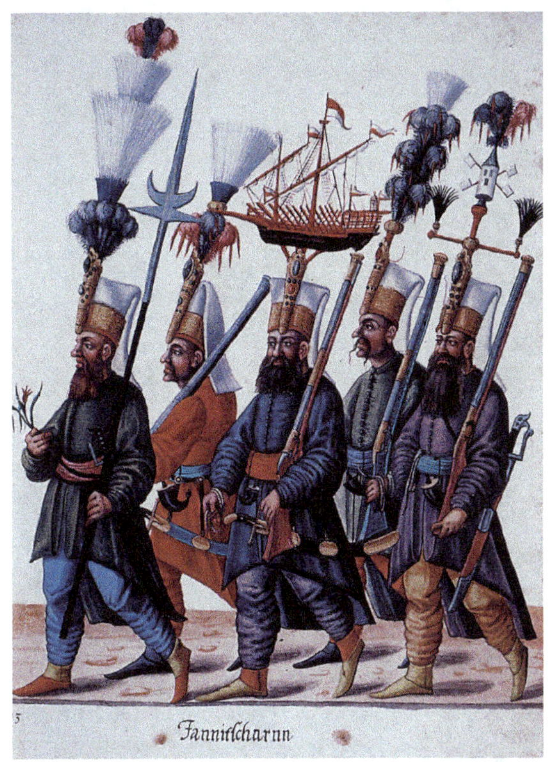

The Janissaries, Codex Vindobonensis, Cod. 8626, fol 13, Österreichische Nationalbibliothek, Vienna.

armourers to the military corps, sappers, artillerymen, caisson-drivers, Janissary corps and cavalrymen constituted the military personnel that were called the *kapıkulu*s meaning "the servant slaves of the Porte" since they waited upon the Gate of the Sultan.

Prisoners of war were the original source for the Janissary and cavalry corps. According to the laws in effect at that time, 1/5 of the spoils acquired in war was set aside for the state; since prisoners of war also qualified as part of the spoils, 1/5 of those captives between the ages of 10-20 who were potential war-

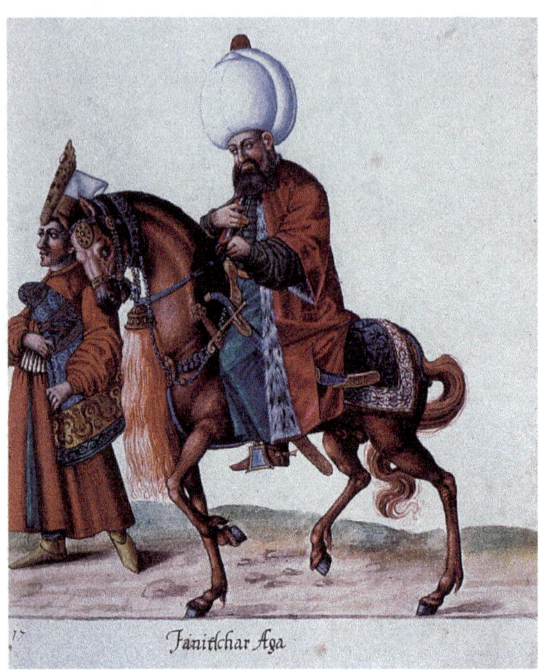

Janissary Ağası, Codex Vindobonensis, Cod. 8626, fol 17, Österreichische Nationalbibliothek, Vienna.

riors were educated for the state. The Janissary corps was originally formed using this system.

At the time of Sultan Bayezid I (1389-1402), some restrictions were imposed upon the training of war prisoners, and a new regulation was put into effect. According to the new *Devşirme* Law, once every three or seven years, male children were gathered from the Christian villages. It is known that certain procedural laws bound the gathering of these male children from only one out of every 40 households:

1. Only children of noble families or priests, between the ages of 8-20 were recruited.
2. Children were not taken from families with only one son.
3. The Ottomans were very fond of guessing people's characters by looking at their head, eyebrows, eyes, height, etc. This constituted "The Science of Personal Appearance". For example, according to the Science of Personal Appearance, it was believed that short people were clever but dishonest; people of middle height had good morals; and people with large heads were intelligent. Those who were charged with selecting individuals according to the Science of Personal Appearance would not choose bald or short people, but would choose beautiful, healthy children of average height. Tall children of appropriate build would also be taken for private education in the palace.
4. A child whose mother and father were deceased would not be taken.
5. The children of Jews dealing in trade would not be taken.

The most select of the recruited children would be set apart to be educated in the palace, while the rest would be given to Turkish farmer-families with children, with whom they were to spend three to eight years. These children who shared their environment with Turkish children and learned Turkish customs and traditions would join the *acemi ocağı* in Gelibolu. These young conscripted Janissaries would work on the construction of important social facilities and on ships, and then later, when their time came, they would become Janissaries.

During times of peace, the Janissaries would live as bachelors in barracks in the capital city; they were first given permission to marry at the beginning of the 16th century. The Janissaries were paid a salary once every three months. They fought in the middle section of the army alongside the Sultan, and for this they also received a special military expedition gratuity. They were also given a special gratuity when a new sultan ascended the throne.

To the janissaries and all the children receiving an education in the Palace School, all military and state positions were open; a Serb, Croat, Rum or Albanian farmer's child could become Grand *Vizier* if he was skilled enough.

With the sensibilities of our day, the idea of taking children from their families at a very young age might be approached with criticism. In his novel *The Drina Bridge*, Ivo Andrić tells the dramatic story of mothers in pursuit of their recruited children. However, it should be remembered that many families also tried in various ways to have their children recruited. There are concrete examples of this in Ottoman archival documents. In his work *L'Empire Ottoman*, the renowned Greek historian Dimitri Kitsikis points out that a process like gathering warriors from villagers was also practised under the Byzantine administration.

Beginning in the 17th century, as the recruitment system broke down and their training was neglected, the Janissaries participated in some revolts. Finally, in 1826, the Janissary corps as an institution was abandoned.

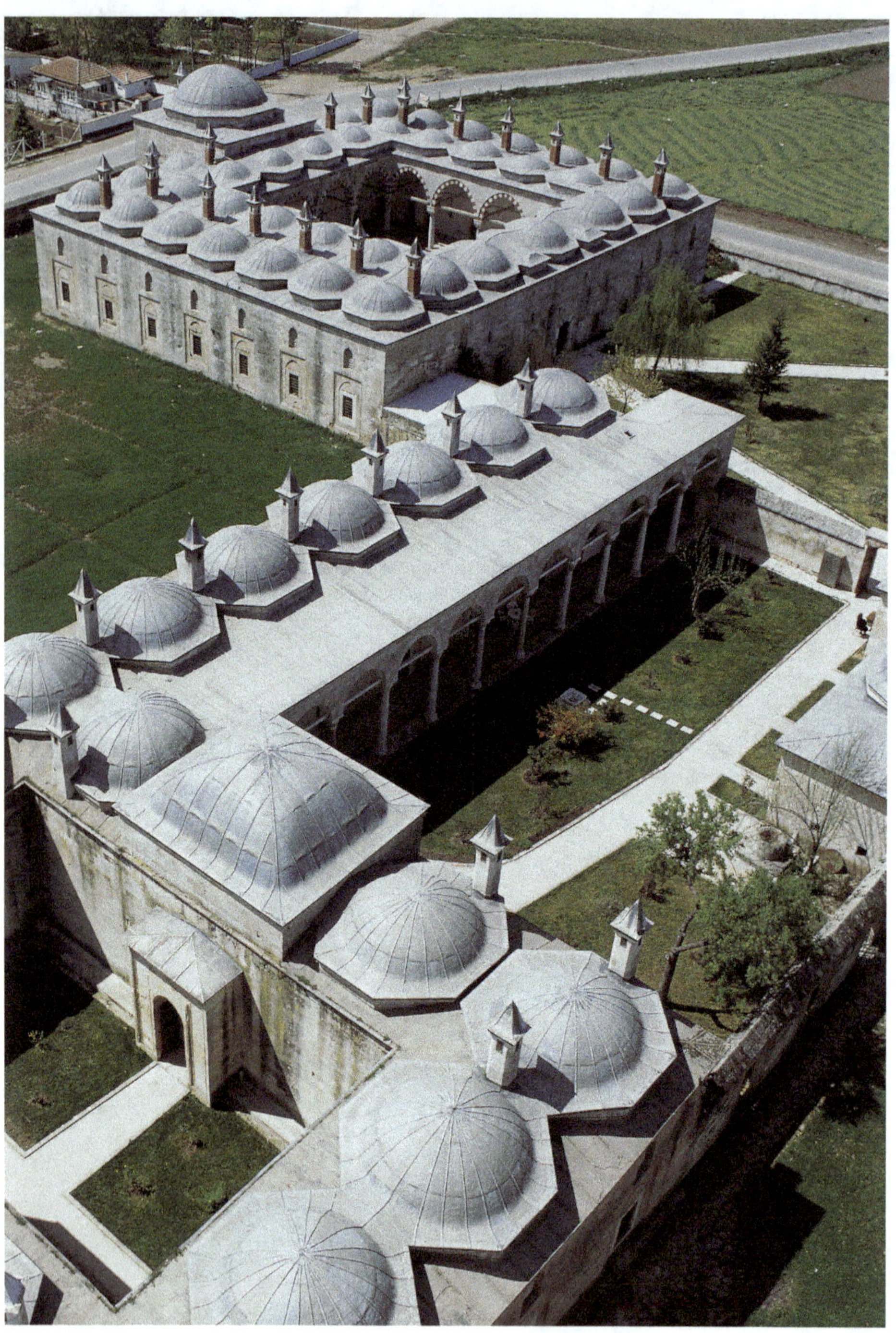

ITINERARY VIII

Music Therapy in the *Darüşşifa*

Lale Bulut, Aydoğan Demir, İnci Kuyulu

VIII.1 EDİRNE

- VIII.1.a Muradiye Mosque
- VIII.1.b Turkish and Islamic Arts Museum, and Archaeological Museum
- VIII.1.c Eski Mosque
- VIII.1.d Bedesten
- VIII.1.e Üç Şerefeli Mosque
- VIII.1.f Saatli Madrasa (option)
- VIII.1.g Peykler Madrasa (option)
- VIII.1.h Beylerbeyi Mosque
- VIII.1.i Bayezid II Complex
- VIII.1.j Yıldırım Mosque

Palaces

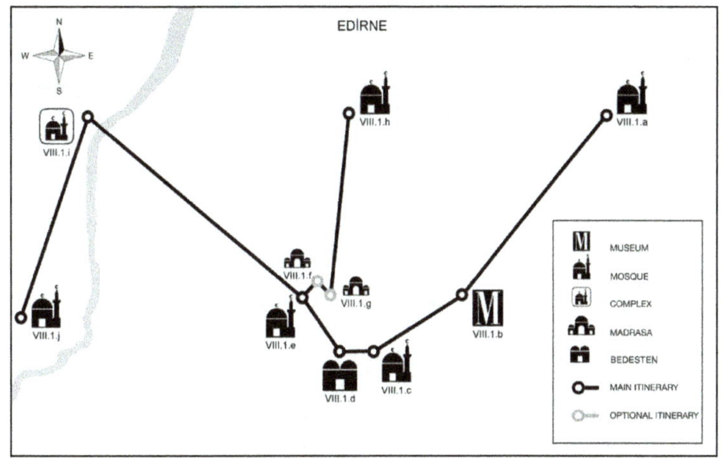

Bayezid II Complex Madrasa, view from the southeast, 1488, Bayezid II, Edirne.

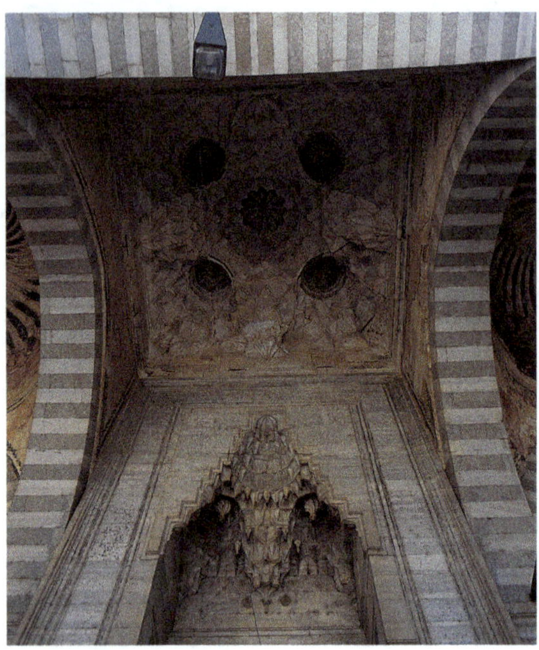

Bayezid II Complex, Mosque, dome in front of the prayer hall portal, 1488, Bayezid II, Edirne.

The city of Edirne is the crossroads for various routes that stretch across Anatolia to the Balkans. This city, the object of many military occupations, fell to the Ottomans in 1362 and became the capital in 1368. The city retained its importance even after Istanbul was conquered in 1453 and became the capital soon after; many Ottoman Sultans made additions to the Edirne Palace and resided occasionally in this palace on the shores of the Tunca River. However, after the Ottoman Sultans abandoned it in 1703, its days of glory became a part of the past; as a result of two large fires in the 19th century, the palace was heavily damaged and fell totally into ruins.

Edirne was the scene of great preparations made for military expeditions to the Balkans and Europe. When the preparations were complete, the Sultan headed off to battle from Edirne accompanied by great ceremony. Sultan Mehmed II accomplished all his preparations, including the casting of the cannons in Edirne before he embarked on the campaign in April 1453 to conquer Istanbul and to put an end to the Byzantine Empire on 29 May 1453.

The Ottoman Sultans and leading officials embellished Edirne with monuments. In Edirne, complexes hold an especially important place among the *waqf* buildings. Turkish towns enlarged and developed around such complexes, and the marvellous structures built by the Sultans Bayezid I, Mehmed I, Murad II, Mehmed II and Bayezid II are still the source of great admiration.

The *darüşşifa* of the Bayezid II Complex is a hospital with 50 beds. We learn from its *waqf* charter that one head doctor, two general practioners, two ophthalmologists, two surgeons, one pharmacist, five nurses, one clerk, one purchaser of merchandise, one store employee, two cooks, one cleaner, one launderer, one barber and one gatekeeper were employed. Two days a week, the outpatients were admitted for examination and given medication free of charge. The famous 17th-century Ottoman traveller, Evliya Çelebi, praises the attention paid to the patients, as well as the excellence of the beds and food. He also relates that music was used in the treatment of mental patients, saying that a group of 10 musicians gave concerts three times a week as part of music therapy.

Edirne was both an administrative city and a strategically located, lively commercial centre. For this reason, many *hans* and *bedestens*, which were an important source of income for the

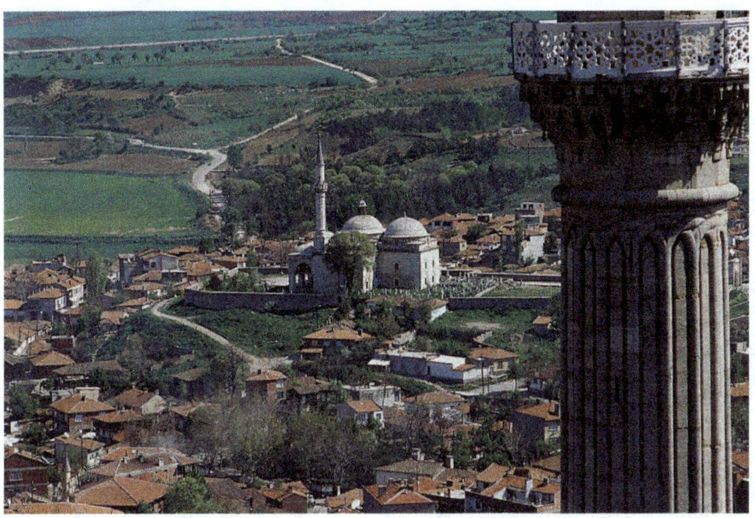

Muradiye Mosque, general view from the minaret of Selimiye Mosque, 1426-27, Murad II, Edirne.

social facilities of the *waqfs*, were built in the city.

A. D.

VIII.1 EDİRNE

This Itinerary covers the city of Edirne only. Most of the monuments are in the centre of town and within easy walking distance from one another. Muradiye Mosque, Yıldırım Mosque and Bayezid II Complex, however, are quite a long way from the centre, so transport is recommended.

Edirne was first founded by the Thracians and named Orestia. In the reign of the Roman Emperor Hadrian (117-138), it was given City status and took the name Hadrianople. The city developed as it reaped the blessings and advantages of the prosperous Roman Era.
When the Roman Empire was divided in 395, Hadrianople was left to the East Roman (Byzantine) Empire. Raids from the Balkans frequently threatened and destroyed the city.
After the Turks took the city, its name was corrupted to Edirne.

VIII.1.a **Muradiye Mosque**

On Kıyık Avenue, Furun Street. Follow Mimar Sinan Street from Selimiye Mosque; it can only be visited immediately after prayer times.

During the period of Sultan Murad II, construction work increased in Edirne; the complex bearing the name of this Sultan stands on a hill in the city's northeast. The story goes that Sultan Murad II dreamt that Mevlana Celaleddin Rumi, the head of the whirling *dervishes*, asked him to build a *tekke* in Edirne. At the time of its construction, the complex was comprised of a mosque, a *mektep*, an *imaret*, and a *tekke*, but only the mosque and graveyard have survived to the present day. It is known

Muradiye Mosque, tile wallpanel, 1426-27, Murad II, Edirne.

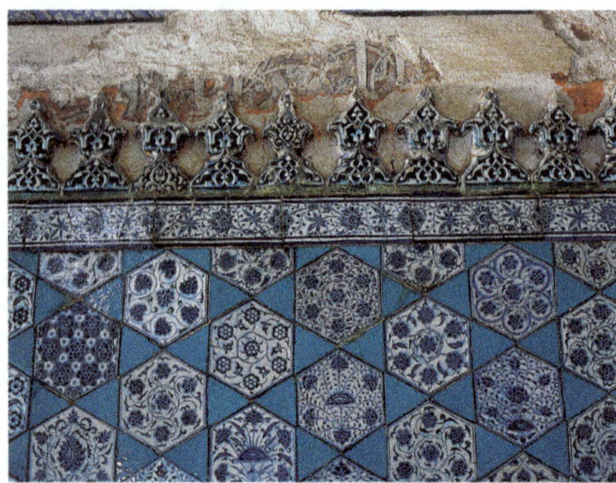

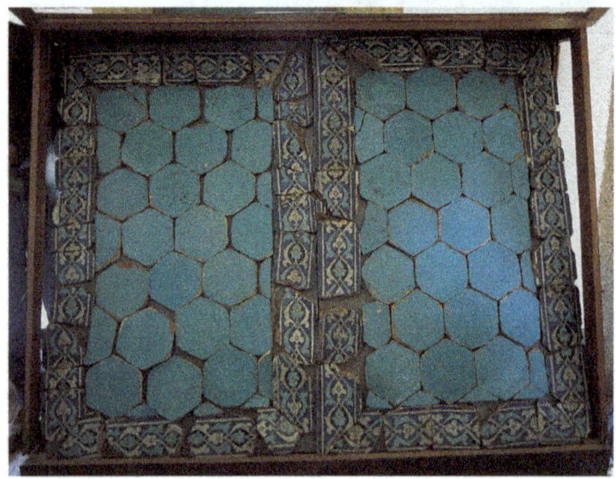

Tile wallpanel from Şahmelek Mosque, 1429, Turkish and Islamic Arts Museum, Edirne.

that the school was standing in the 1920s and that the *tekke* disappeared after 1935. The same sultan also built the Üç Şerefeli Mosque in Edirne and the Bursa Muradiye Complex, which we have already seen.

The Muradiye Mosque, standing all on its own on top of a hill, is completely faced with cut stone on the outside and the minaret stands on the northwest corner. On the north side of the mosque, there is a five-bayed portico, the central bay of which is covered by a dome, while the others are covered with flat-topped cross vaults. The inscription on the portal gives the name of Sultan Murad II but does not provide any date. The portal with a lovely *muqarnas* canopy opens into the central court covered with a dome and a lantern. Typical of mosques with *tabhanes* designed in order to meet the needs of itinerant *dervishes*, the central court is flanked with domed *tabhanes* to the east and west while the domed prayer hall lies to its south.

The Muradiye Mosque's wall paintings, tiles and wooden decorations are especially noteworthy. The walls of the prayer hall are covered with tiles up to a certain height. The hexagonal blue-white tiles are ornamented with naturalist floral motifs and among them are placed triangular tiles glazed in turquoise. The magnificent tile *mihrab* in *cuerda seca* and tile-mosaic techniques, like those at Bursa Yeşil Complex, is 3.65 m. wide and 6.35 m. high among the moulded tiles in yellow, white, blue and turquoise, the yellow is dominant; the geometric star motifs, *rumis*, *palmettes*, and peonies are especially striking. Above are traces of wall paintings with interlocking designs, *rumis*, and various floral motifs: in its day the interior must have looked as exuberant and glowing as the Green Mosque in Bursa.

İ. K.

VIII.1.b **Turkish and Islamic Arts Museum, and Archaeological Museum**

Today, the madrasa *situated to the southeast of Selimiye Mosque is used as the Turkish and Islamic Arts Museum with a good collection of hand–crafted artefacts. Just to the east, about 100 m. away is the Archaeological and Ethnographic Museum. Both museums are open between 08.00-12.00 and 13.00-16.30 during the winter and 08.30-12.30 and 13.30-17.00 during the summer. There is a separate entrance fee for each museum.*

Wall tiles

The Seljuqs brought with them to Anatolia the art of tile production and decoration, which developed in relationship to architecture. Various techniques were used in the production of Turkish tile art, examples of which span many centuries. The main raw material of tiles, which was an important decorative element in mosques, *masjids*, *madrasas*, *türbes*, and palaces, was clean and good-quality clay. Clay is cleaned of impurities and made into mud in pools; then it is transferred to a second pool and left to rest for a few days; later it is transported to a third pool. When the liquid-clay dough becomes thicker, it is shaped using moulds in the mould workshops and left to dry. Any rough parts are then cleaned using emery; then the tiles are baked in kilns. The hardened tiles are taken from the gradually cooling kiln and designs are drawn on them. They are then covered either with a transparent, coloured or colourless glaze and put back into the kiln.

The tiles on display here in one of the southern cells are from the Edirne Şahmelek Mosque and date back to 1429. They form two rectangular panels, which are filled with turquoise-coloured unornamented tiles and on the border bands are floral motifs applied in the coloured glaze (*cuerda seca*) technique.

L. B.

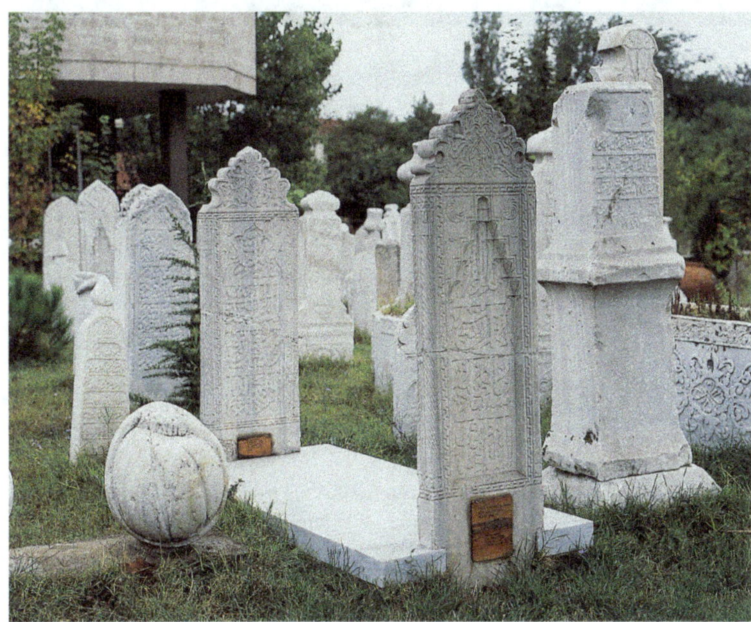

Gravestone of Sitti Hatun, 1486, Archaeological Museum, Edirne.

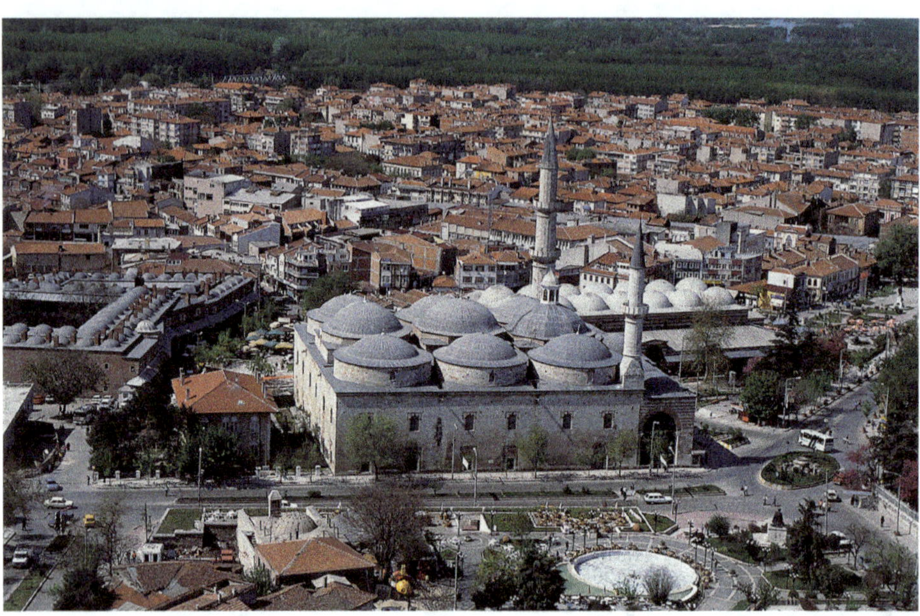

Eski Mosque, general view from the east, 1414, Mehmed I, Edirne.

Gravestones

Displayed in the yard of the Archaeological Museum, is the headstone of Sitti Hatun, daughter of Süleyman, son of Zülfikar; she was married to Sultan Mehmed II and passed away in June 1486. Usually, there is one gravestone at the head and one at the foot of Anatolian graves. In the Seljuq and Emirates periods, both the headstones and the footstones were ornamented with inscriptions. Beginning in the 17th century, figures like cypresses, date palms and grapevines replaced the scriptures on the footstones. In the Ottoman period, the pinnacle of most female graves ended in a triangular pediment, the inside of which was filled with geometric and floral motifs or depictions of mosques and other buildings. This rectangular gravestone has a top section shaped like, and ornamented with, *palmettes* and *rumis*. A carved niche resembling a *mihrab* is placed on the body of stone, and information about the deceased person is engraved in this niche; a single pinwheel and a rosette are carved in the corners of the niche; the niche is enclosed by a chain pattern.

L. B.

VIII.1.c **Eski Mosque**

In the centre, on Talat Pasha Boulevard, to the west of Selimiye Complex across the park.

After the tragic death of Sultan Bayezid I, his sons began fighting over the throne; their struggles calmed for a while when the eldest brother Süleyman Çelebi emerged victorious and ascended the throne. However, in 1411, his brother Musa seized the capital Edirne. Then in 1413, Mehmed I, also known as Çelebi Mehmed, took the city from his brother. The construction of Eski Mosque began in 1403 during the time of Süleyman Çelebi, it continued during the period of Musa and was finally finished in 1414 during the reign of Sultan Mehmed I. The inscription on top of the west entrance door tells us that the architect of this building was Hacı Alaaddin of Konya and his assistant was Omar Ibn Ibrahim. As the inscription above the false door of the portico informs us, the mosque was damaged in a fire of 1745 and then by an earthquake in 1752, and was thoroughly renovated by Sultan Mahmud I in 1753. Frequent renovations were also made in the 20th century, the latest being completed at the beginning of 2001.

Eski Mosque is the first monumental mosque in Edirne constructed in the Ottoman period. The minaret on the east was constructed at the same time as the mosque, while the one on the west is a later addition. The structure is completely faced with cut stone on the outside whereas both cut stone and brick were used in the portico. The central bay of the portico is emphasised with a dome and also has a false doorway. The mosque has nine domes and bears a great resemblance to the 20-domed Bursa Great Mosque, constructed by Sultan Bayezid I in 1400, continuing the Seljuq tradition of mosques with multiple bays of equal size. The domes, each with a diameter of 13.5 m., are supported with four colossal pillars. The three domes on the *mihrab* axis are higher than the others and the northernmost one has a lantern, under which there once used to stand the ablution fountain, as in Bursa Great Mosque. On the walls and pillars are religious inscriptions in very large and bold letters. The wall paintings on the top section of the walls, on the interior of the domes, and on the *mihrab* were probably added during an 18th-century renovation. There is intricate ornamentation on the side surfaces of the marble *minbar*.

İ. K.

VIII.1.d **Bedesten**

To the west of Eski Mosque, on Talat Paşa Boulevard.

The *bedesten* is a new building type that emerged in the 15th century as a result of the development of commercial life during the Emirates period. Originally constructed to gather fabric sellers called

Bedesten, interior, 1413-21, Mehmed I, Edirne.

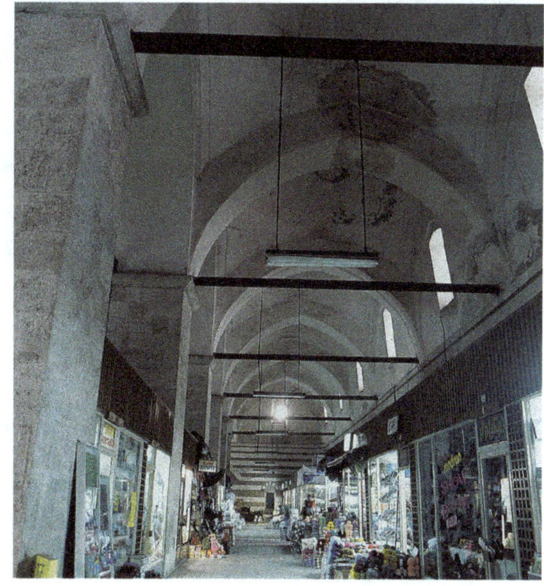

bezzaz under one roof, soon other goods began to be sold there as well. Valuable merchandise –like jewellery and money deposited by merchants– was stored and protected in the *bedestens*, which functioned like the banks of today. Goods were also priced and quality checked in the *bedestens*, whose officers, chosen among trustworthy persons, also acted as experts in commercial lawsuits.

In general, *bedestens* are rectangular structures closed to the outside; stores on all four sides completely surround the structure. A door is located in the centre of each front; the interior is divided into equal-size bays, each of which is covered with a dome; small cells adjoin the interior of the walls; the number of domed sections varies according to the size of the *bedesten*.

One of the most important *bedestens*, each of which was a *waqf* establishment, is the Edirne Bedesten constructed by Sultan Mehmed I. It is known that this *bedesten* belonged to the Eski Mosque's *waqf*. It has four *iwan*-shaped entrances, one in the middle of each front. Each of the windows on the upper section of the main-body walls has different stonework decoration to offer the observant; 14 lofty domes cover the main rectangular body of the structure; there are 56 stores on its exterior and 36 cells in its interior; the structure, which has been completely restored, is used as a bazaar today. According to a contemporary account by Evliya Çelebi, it was guarded by night by 60 Janissaries, with the four locked gates, for the goods inside were so valuable.

İ. K.

Üç Şerefeli Mosque, view from the southeast, 1445, Murad II, Edirne.

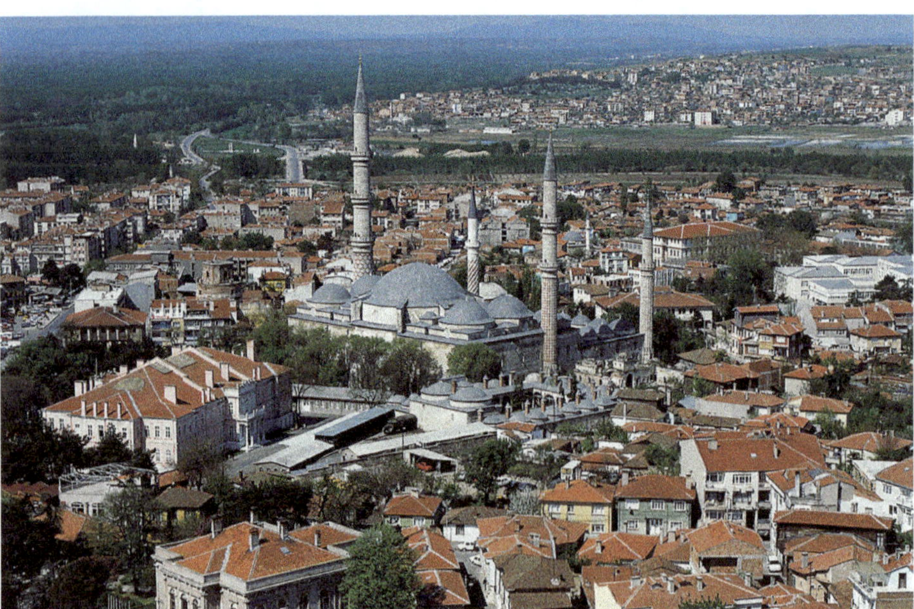

VIII.I.e **Üç Şerefeli Mosque**

In the centre, on Hükümet Avenue, to the north of Eski Mosque and bedesten *across the park.*

This very attractive mosque has four minarets, each of which is different from the other. At the time of its construction, the mosque was known as Cami-i Cedid (New Mosque) and Cami-i Kebir (Great Mosque) as well. However, the name Üç Şerefeli Mosque –Mosque with Three *Şerefes*– is also encountered in old documents from the very earliest periods. This name was most likely derived from the minaret with three *şerefe*s located on the southwest corner of the courtyard. The mosque has a total of four minarets, which makes it the earliest mosque with four minarets in Ottoman architecture. The minarets rising from the four corners of the courtyard have different ornamentation: the northeast minaret has parallel vertical mouldings whereas the northwest minaret has spiral mouldings; while the southeast one has smaller diamond designs executed in two colours of stone and the southwest minaret with three *şerefe*s is decorated with large chevrons; a separate staircase leads to each balcony of this minaret and with its height of 67.50 m. it is the second highest of the Ottoman mosques, after the minarets of the Selimiye Mosque (approximately 71 m.) constructed in Edirne by Sinan, the famous 16th-century Turkish architect. Approaching it, one notices that the lower windows are elaborately decorated, and all different from each other.

This courtyard, with a fountain in the centre, surrounded by porticoes on four sides and three portals opening outside –two on the sides and one on the *mihrab* axis– is the earliest example in Ottoman architecture of a courtyard with this layout, bringing to mind the courtyards of Manisa Great Mosque and Selçuk İsa Bey Mosque, both earlier in date and the work of the Emirates Period. This plan shall be employed repeatedly in numerous mosques built later; therefore, the Üç Şerefeli Mosque occupies an important place among the mosques of the Ottoman era. Two win-

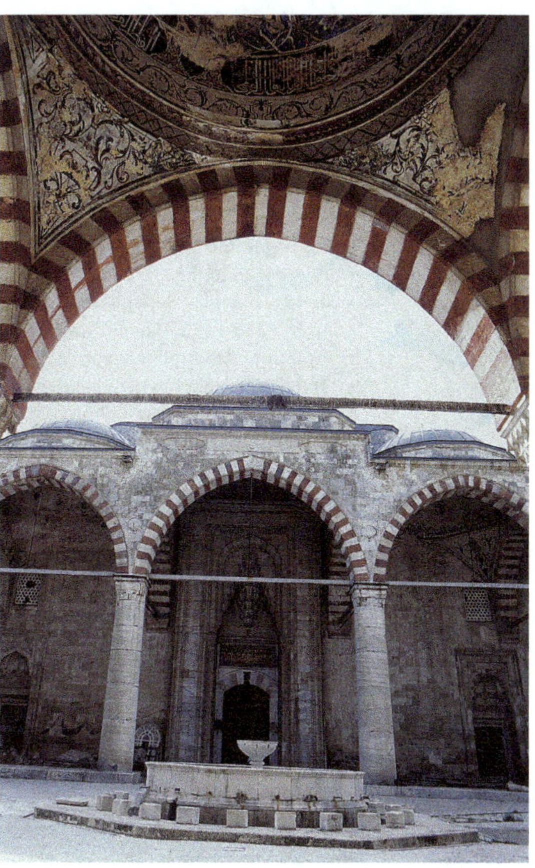

Üç Şerefeli Mosque, portico, 1445, Murad II, Edirne.

dows on the north wall, to the west of the central portal have lovely tile tympana with religious inscriptions; the domes covering the bays vary from each other in size and decoration; some of the painted ornamentation on the transitional elements and the portico domes were renovated during the restoration of 1763-1764.

According to the Arabic inscription on its elegant portal to the prayer hall, the construction of the Üç Şerefeli Mosque was completed in 1445. The beginning and completion dates of the construction given on some other inscriptions present in the mosque, however, indicate various dates with a couple of years difference; the reason for this discrepancy is not known exactly. According to legend, a master workman named "Muslihüddin" was put in charge of the mosque's construction in 1427 and 7000 bags of gold were spent on construction. The mosque, like most of the other structures, was damaged in the Thracian earthquake on 29 July 1752. According to the two inscriptions on both spandrels of the central arch of the portico, the mosque was completely restored in the reign of Sultan Mustafa II in 1763-64. As of beginning of 2001, the latest restoration to the inside that began in 1998 was completed and the courtyard was still under restoration.

The prayer hall opens into the courtyard with three portals, the central one of which is the most monumental; and also there is another doorway by the minaret with three *şerefe*s giving direct access to the outside. The central dome with a diameter of approximately 24 m. was the largest attempted by the Ottomans to that date and the Üç Şerefeli Mosque is the earliest example of a monumental Ottoman mosque with a central dome. This central dome stands on a hexagonal base supported by two self-standing pillars and four pillars embedded in the south and north walls. This hexagonal area is transformed into a square with the triangular areas in the corners covered by tiny domes and striking vaults. This central section is extended to the east and west, each covered with two domes of equal size separated from each other by an arch; all the domes have various painted decorations. The plain *mihrab* and *minbar* add to the beauty of this spacious mosque. According to legend, 70 camel-loads of dye were brought from Persia for the original 18th-century wall paintings, which is allegedly the work of a Persian artist.

İ. K.

VIII.1.f **Saatli Madrasa** (option)

Located at 14, Çamaşırcılar Street. Just to the east of the courtyard of Üç Şerefeli Mosque.

Two *madrasas* located side by side to the east of Üç Şerefeli Mosque are the Saatli Madrasa, which literally means Madrasa with Clock, and Peykler Madrasa, which means Madrasa of Running Footmen. However, there are doubts as to which one is Saatli, and which is Peykler. Neither of the two have construction inscriptions. Sources state that Sultan Murad II built Saatli Madrasa together with the Üç Şerefeli Mosque, while Sultan Mehmed II built the Peykler Madrasa. The similar architectural features of the two structures make them difficult to identify. However, since the *madrasa* on the north is located closer to the Üç Şerefeli Mosque, and the *madrasa* to the south is situated at a higher elevation than the mosque itself, it is believed that the one to the north is the Saatli Madrasa that was built at the same time as Üç Şerefeli Mosque. Therefore, the one located to the south, which is at a farther distance from the mosque, is most likely to be the Peykler Madrasa.

Today the Saatli Madrasa is largely in ruins. The west wall of the structure is faced with cut stone, while the rest of the walls are built with alternating rows of cut stone and brick. The inner surface of the dome that covers the entrance *iwan* behind the portal on the west is decorated with *muqarnas*. On one side of the courtyard is the summer *dershane iwan* along with the winter *dershane* area, and the student cells are found on the remaining sides of the courtyard; each chamber in the *madrasa* was covered with a dome.

İ. K.

VIII.1.g **Peykler Madrasa** (option)

Located on Çamaşırcılar Street, next to the Saatli Madrasa. As at 2000 the structure is closed and not in use. The key is at the Vakıflar (Waqfs) Directorate, which is just to the south of Eski Mosque on Talatpaşa Avenue.

Historical sources indicate that Sultan Mehmed II built the Peykler Madrasa. The structure is faced with cut stone on both the inside and outside. A dome decorated with *muqarnas* covers the entrance *iwan* located behind the portal on the west facing the Üç Şerefeli Mosque. However, today, the small doorway on the northeast on Çamaşırcılar Street is used as the entrance. The courtyard surrounded by porticoes on three sides, the arches of which are very attractive with low but pointed forms. The arch in front of the main portal is of the "Bursa" type. Located to the south is the summer *dershane iwan* protruding out together with a winter *dershane* to its east, while on the remaining three sides are the student cells. Both *dershanes* contain a *mihrab*, which suggests that they were also used as *masjids*. Each *dershane* is covered with a dome while each of the student cells is also covered either by a dome or vault.

İ. K.

VIII.1.h **Beylerbeyi Mosque**

On Hükümet Avenue. Continue about 150 m. further past the Üç Şerefeli Mosque, it is on the right, on a slope, behind a cemetery. It can be visited immediately after prayers.

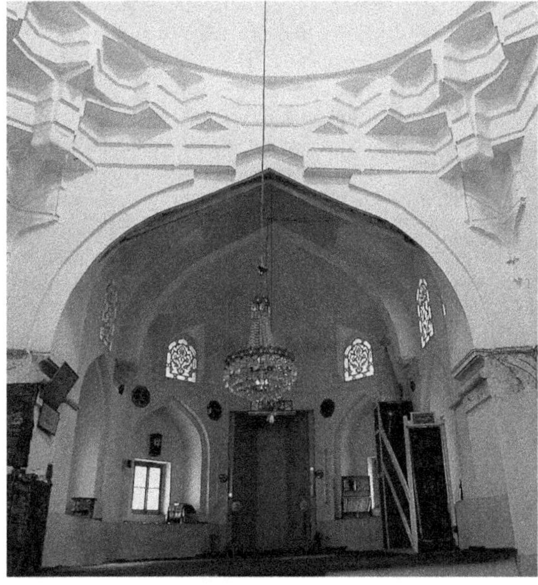

Beylerbeyi Mosque, prayer hall, 1429, Sinaneddin Yusuf Pasha, Edirne.

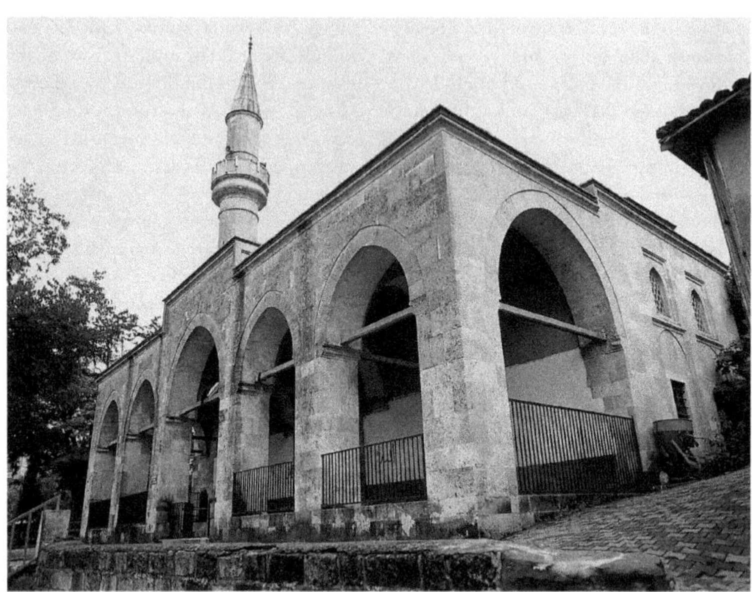

Beylerbeyi Mosque, view from the northwest, 1429, Sinaneddin Yusuf Pasha, Edirne.

Not only the sultans, but high-ranking officials, too, had various structures built for public use. The Beylerbeyi of Rumelia, Sinaneddin Yusuf Pasha, is among these high-ranking officials who commissioned buildings for public benefit. He also had the Beylerbeyi Mosque constructed in 1429, from whose *waqf* charter arranged in 1429 by Sinaneddin Yusuf Pasha, we learn that a *madrasa* and an *imaret* were also built in addition to the mosque, but they have not survived to the present day.
The structure stands on a high terrace behind the cemetery, within which are the ruins of a *türbe*. The mosque, faced entirely with cut-stone, has undergone various restorations and all the cut-stone facing and the minaret rising over the northeast corner have been renovated. The part of the minaret that lies between the *şerefe* and the spire collapsed in the mid-20th century and has been reconstructed. On the north, facing the cemetery is a five-bayed portico, the central bay of which is covered by a dome, while the others are vaulted. Past the plain portal with a fragment of the inscription remaining, one emerges into the central court covered with a dome of 7 m. in diameter, with a lantern at the centre. The prayer hall to the south is divided into two sections by an arch, just like the prayer hall of the Nilüfer Hatun İmaret in İznik. The northern section, planned in rectangular form, is covered with a small dome of 3 m. in diameter supported by stellar vaults, whereas the second section to the south containing the *mihrab* is covered with a half-dome, shaped like an oyster shell, reminiscent of the prayer hall of Yahşi Bey Mosque in Tire. There are traces of wall paintings, especially on the slanting arch

separating the prayer hall from the central court. The central court is flanked on the west and the east with a *tabhane,* each of which is covered by a dome and contains a single fireplace and four niches.

İ. K.

VIII.1.i **Bayezid II Complex**

It is on the other side of the river. It can be reached by either following the sign on Hükümet Avenue just 50 m. from the junction or by taking a dolmush *minibus to Y. İmaret, which leaves by the Sokollu Hammam 50 m. further on in Hükümet Avenue and passes by the Complex. There is an entrance fee for the Museum of Health and an extra charge for the hexagonal structure.*

Even after the Capital was moved to Istanbul, Edirne maintained its importance for a long time; the Bayezid II Complex, dating from the late 15th century, together with the Selimiye Mosque, a masterly work of Ottoman architecture completed in 1575, are the structures that emphasise the importance given to this city.

Sultan Bayezid II personally attended the ceremonies for the laying of foundations for his complex on 25 May 1484. During the ceremonies animals were sacrificed and their meat was distributed to the poor. The complex was completed in a short time; only four years, and then opened for service with great ceremony in 1488.

There are different opinions regarding the identity of the architect who built the complex. According to some researchers, the name of the architect is Hayreddin, while some others believe that it is Yakub Şah Ibn Sultan Şah.

The Complex of Bayezid II in Edirne, built after another complex of the same Sultan in Amasya, is a large group of buildings spread across an area of 22,000 m^2, and consisting of a mosque, *madrasa*, *darüşşifa*, *tabhane*, *hammam*, bridge, *imaret* and storerooms.

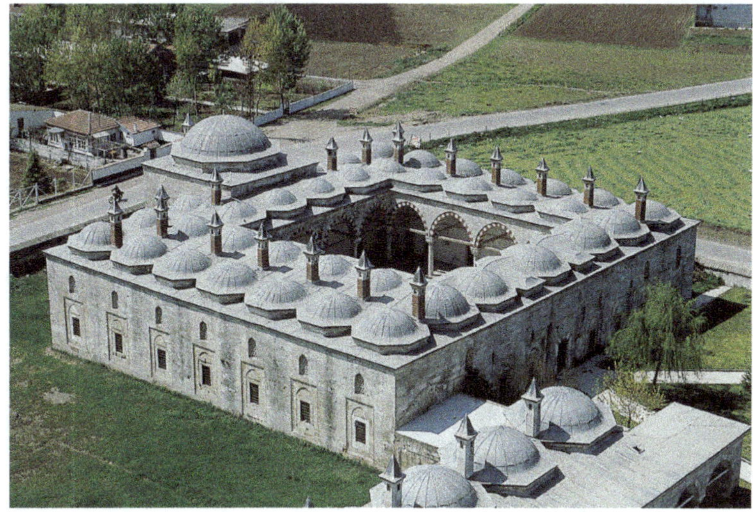

Bayezid II Complex, Madrasa, general view from the southeast, 1488, Bayezid II, Edirne.

Edirne

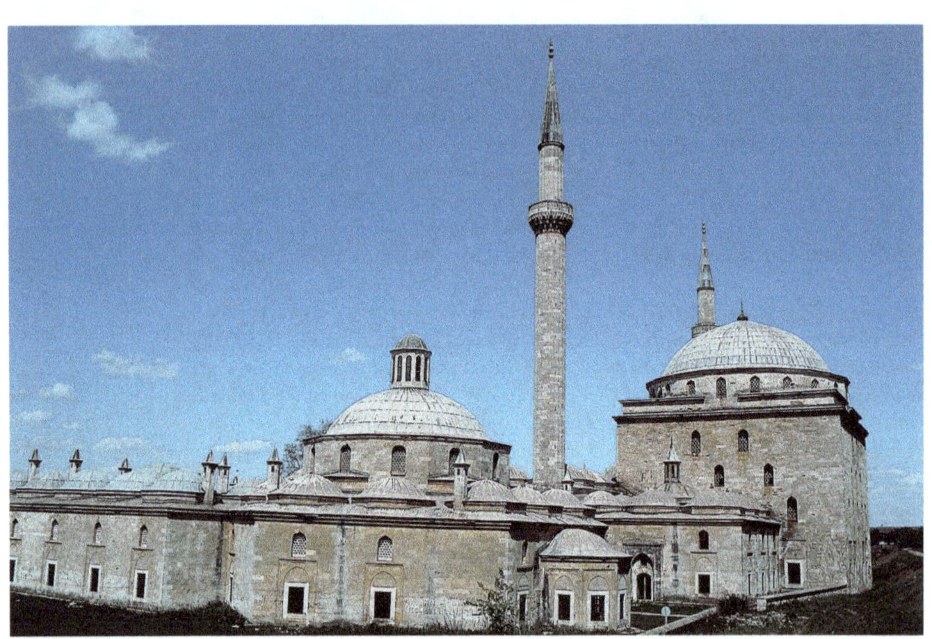

Bayezid II Complex, Darüşşifa, view from the west, 1488, Bayezid II, Edirne.

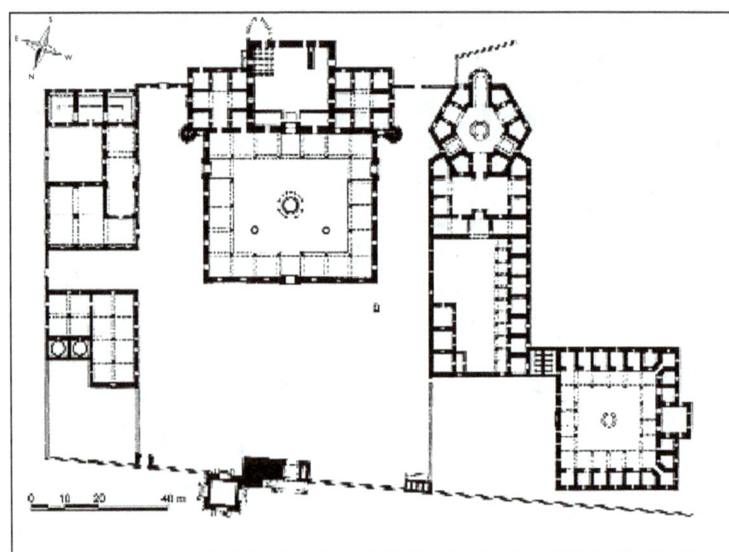

Plan of Bayezid II Complex, late 15th century, Edirne.

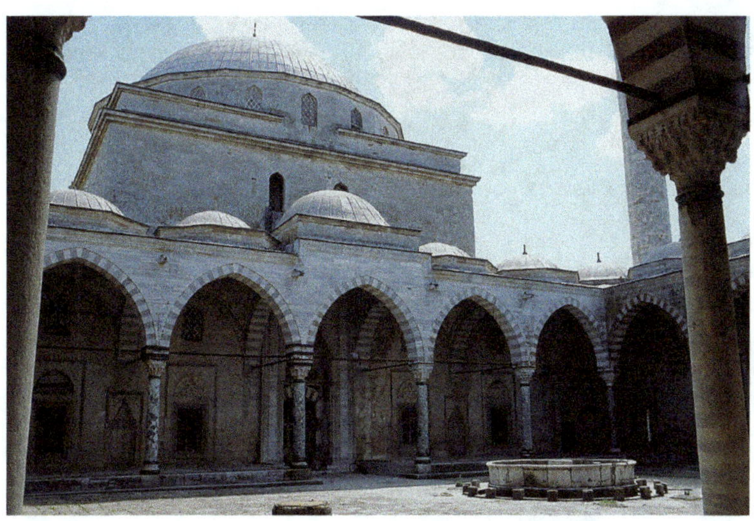

Bayezid II Complex Mosque, view from the courtyard, 1488, Bayezid II, Edirne.

The entrance to the common courtyard, which is surrounded by walls, is through the gates on the north, by the road; to the left of the main gate is the Sinan Ağa Fountain.
The mosque is located to the south of the common courtyard; the *darüşşifa* and the *madrasa* are to the west of the common courtyard, whereas to its east is the *imaret*, constructed as two blocks and consisting of a bakery with two ovens, a candle factory, refectory, a larder, and stables; the section containing the ovens and stoves is quite large. In addition to guests and the personnel of the complex, food was also distributed to the poor in the vicinity. Special meals were prepared during Ramadan, religious feasts, and on Fridays; upon the recommendation by a doctor, special food was also prepared for the sick in a separate kitchen.
To the southwest of the complex, outside the courtyard walls, lies the bridge over Tunca River, This was in order to make the mosque more accessible to those living nearby and thus enlarge the size of the mosque's congregation. The *hammam*, built on the same bank of the Tunca River as the rest of the complex near the bridge, does not exist today; according to historical sources, it was a double *hammam* comprising separate sections for women and men.

Bayezid II Complex Darüşşifa, view from the west, 1488, Bayezid II, Edirne.

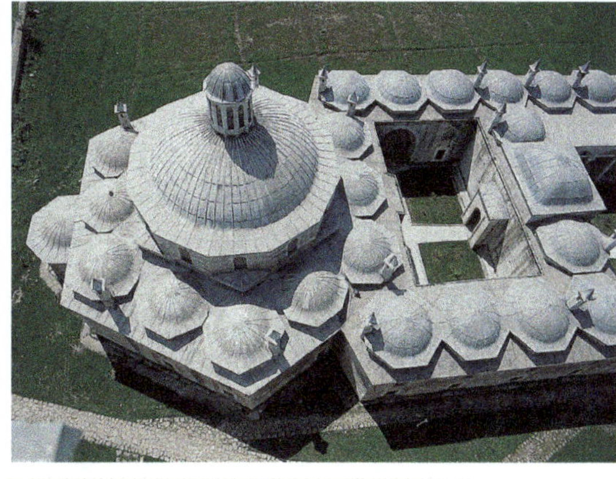

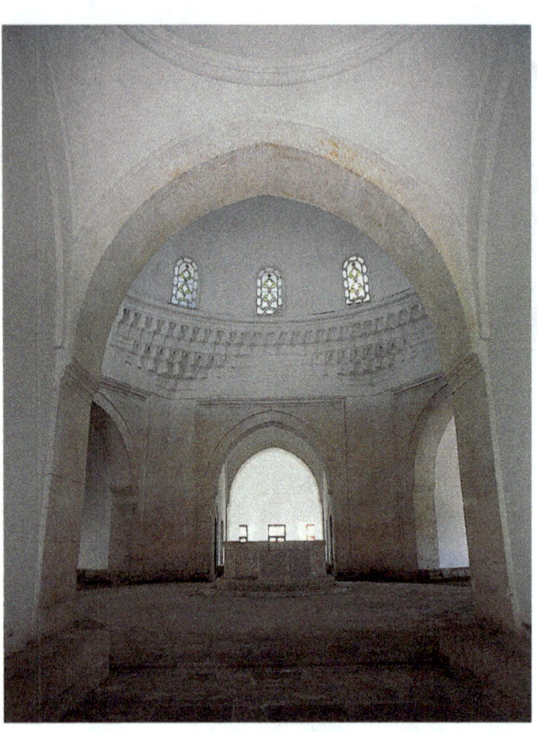

Bayezid II Complex, Darüşşifa, interior, 1488, Bayezid II, Edirne.

At the beginning of 2001, the imaret complex was closed and in a dilapidated state, while the mosque was closed for restoration, but the darüşşifa and the madrasa are in a very good state and in use by Trakya University as the Museum of Health, and a family health centre respectively.

Bayezid II Mosque

Three entrances lead from the common courtyard to the mosque courtyard: one is on the north, and the other two are on the sides. The courtyard is covered with marble plates and surrounded by domed porticoes on all four sides; at the centre of the rectangular courtyard is a marble fountain. In the seven-bayed portico in the front, the dome covering the central bay in front of the portal, is built higher to emphasise the entrance axis. There are also two outdoor *mihrabs* in the portico.
At the corners of the *tabhanes* adjoining the east and west of the prayer hall are elegant minarets 38 m. in height with a single *şerefe* and fluted bodies of 3.25 m. in diameter. Both *tabhanes* consist of nine bays, each of which is covered by a dome, with four *iwans* opening onto a central court and rooms in the corners. There is no direct connection between the *tabhanes* and the mosque: the windows in the walls between the *tabhanes* and the mosque are today blocked up.
From the courtyard a portal with an elegant and elaborate canopy filled with *muqarnas* opens into the prayer hall, which covers an area of about 500 m^2 and is covered with a dome of 20.55 m. in diameter rising upon a polygonal drum. The *mihrab* and the *minbar* are made of marble and the royal loge is noteworthy especially for the forest of reused small columns, on which it rests. The wooden door wings and the cupboard doors and window shutters are elaborately decorated.

Madrasa

According to most researchers who refer to the complex, the *madrasa* was a medical training institution. Some studies indicate that students who completed their education in the *madrasa* went on to study medicine in the adjoining hospital while continuing to reside in the *madrasa*. However, no clarifying evidence regarding this matter is known from historical sources or the known *waqf* charters of the complex.
The Bayezid II Madrasa is a single-storey rectangular structure with an open court-

yard. The entrance at the centre of the east front opens into the courtyard surrounded by domed porticoes on all four sides; there are traces of a fountain that was once located in the centre of this courtyard. The 18 student cells, each covered by a dome and each with a fireplace, were placed at the north, south, and west wings. The *dershane* in the middle of the western side, opposite the entrance, is a rectangular chamber protruding out and covered by a large dome, and on its east wall a stone staircase leads to an interesting balcony, which would probably have been used as a library.

Darüşşifa

To the west of the mosque and southeast of the *madrasa* lies the *darüşşifa* consisting of two courtyards and the main structure, all lined up along the north-south axis. The western side of the first rectangular courtyard is lined with domed cells behind a vaulted portico. On the northern part of the eastern side are domed chambers that had various functions and on the southern side two large double-domed chambers flank the *iwan* giving access to the second courtyard.

The second courtyard, which is entered through an *iwan* in the centre of the southern side of the first courtyard, is smaller and has two domed *iwans* on the sides, each flanked with two domed cells. The cells in the first courtyard and the eastern cells in the second courtyard are today used as exhibition halls by the Museum of Health.

The most attractive structure of the *darüşşifa* is the hexagonal main building: the central hexagonal hall is surrounded by an *iwan* in the centre of each side and

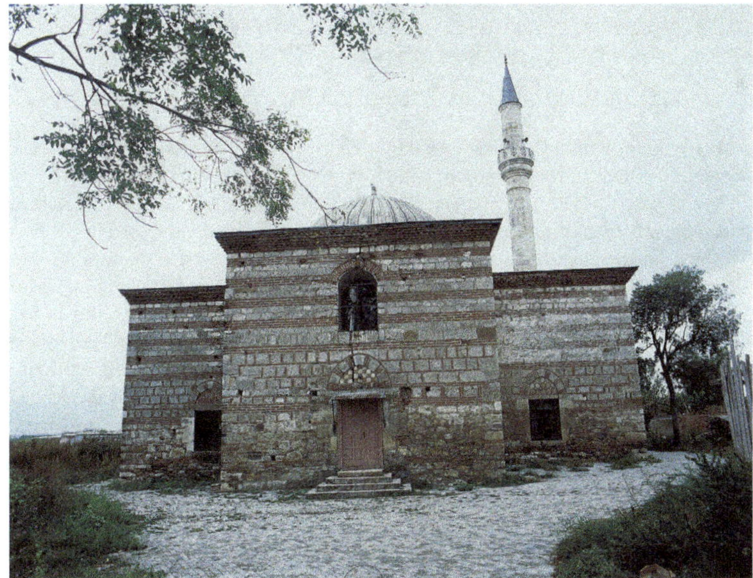

Yıldırım Mosque, view from the west, 1389-1402, Bayezid I, Edirne.

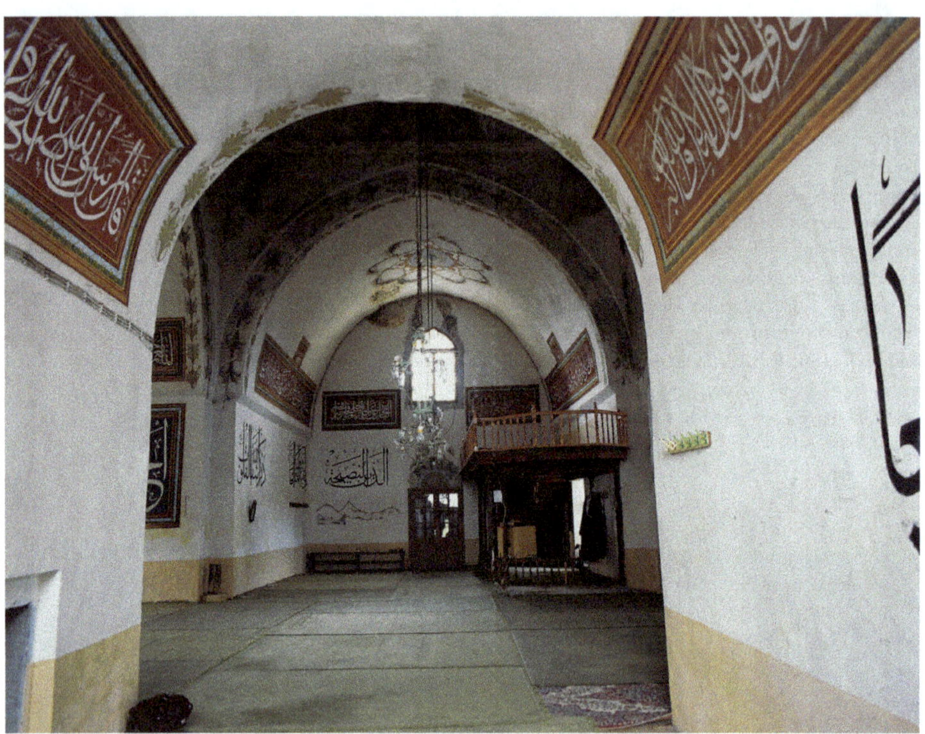

Yıldırım Mosque, prayer hall looking from east to the west, 1389-1402, Bayezid I, Edirne.

a square room with a fireplace on each corner. The *iwans* and chambers are each covered by an individual dome and the chambers are entered through the *iwans*. The hexagonal main hall also has a rather large dome rising on a cornice of *muqarnas*. The central lantern of the dome and the windows on the far walls of the *iwans* illuminate the main hall. A pool with a fountain is located in the centre of the main hall and the *iwan* opposite the entrance *iwan* is deeper than the rest of the structure and protrudes out. Today the structure is an exhibition hall where scenes of Ottoman daily life are excellently presented with mannequins.

There is some information in historical sources about the function of the various sections of the *darüşşifa*. For example, it is reported that the sections in the first courtyard were used as doctors' rooms, a pantry, a kitchen, isolation rooms for the mentally ill, a laundry and so on, while medicine was prepared and stored in the rooms that opened onto the two *iwans* opposite each other in the second courtyard. Again, based on historical records, it is known that on certain occasions musicians performed in the large *iwan* of the hexagonal main structure. According to legend, the sound of sprinkling water had a soothing effect on the mentally ill, and was helpful in their treatment.

İ. K.

VIII.1.j **Yıldırım Mosque**

If you are coming from the town centre follow Talatpaşa Avenue in the direction of Kapıkule and Bulgaria; 200 m. after passing over the Tunca River, take a right turn and pass over another small bridge, you will reach Yıldırım Mosque. From Bayezid II Complex, follow the embankment to the west and when you reach the main road turn right and 200 m. later turn right again, and past the small bridge is the mosque.

Edirne, conquered by Sultan Murad I in 1362, became the capital of the Ottoman State in 1368. Most of the structures built during the years following the conquest have not survived to the present day. In Edirne, the oldest mosque still standing is the one built by and named after Sultan Bayezid I (1389-1402), who is also known as Yıldırım –the Lightning. According to many sources, the Yıldırım Mosque was constructed on the foundations of a church. The noticeable errors in the design of the structure and the placement of the *mihrab* seem to verify this. However, some researchers argue that the mosque was not built upon the foundations of a church, but was actually designed and constructed as a mosque. It is a well-known fact that in the early times of Islam, churches in conquered cities were converted into mosques and used as such. Moreover, it is known that before the construction of the Great Mosque in Damascus, Muslims worshipped together with the Christians under the same roof for a while. For this reason, it is quite possible that the Yıldırım Mosque may have been converted from a church, and there is no reason why this should be regarded as odd.

Some sources refer to the Yıldırım Mosque as the Küpeli Mosque, literally Mosque with Earrings. According to one legend, the latter name was attached to the mosque due to the rings and the chandeliers hanging in the structure, while according to another story, the second name was given to it because Sultan Bayezid I's daughter Küpeli Sultan sold her diamond earrings and used the money for the mosque.

The structure, built with alternating rows of brick and stone, has charming brick– and stone– decoration on the tympana of the windows. The western part of the building protrudes out and has a door opening into the prayer hall. Today the portico, which originally had a wooden roof and was located on the eastern side of the mosque, is in ruins; the door to the right opens into a *tabhane,* which is also in ruins but has some lovely stucco decoration above the fireplace. Passing through the main doorway on the east, one enters an *iwan* with a tiny doorway on the left opening into the second *tabhane,* which is used as a storeroom for funeral materials today. This entrance *iwan* opens into a domed area in the centre, which is flanked with three more *iwans* on the north, south, and west, thus, giving the prayer hall a cruciform shape. The *mihrab* has been placed in a corner of the southern *iwan*. All four *iwans* have barrel vaults whereas the central area is covered with a dome rising directly above a cornice of Turkish triangles. The wall paintings derive from a 19th-century renovation.

İ. K.

İnci Kuyulu

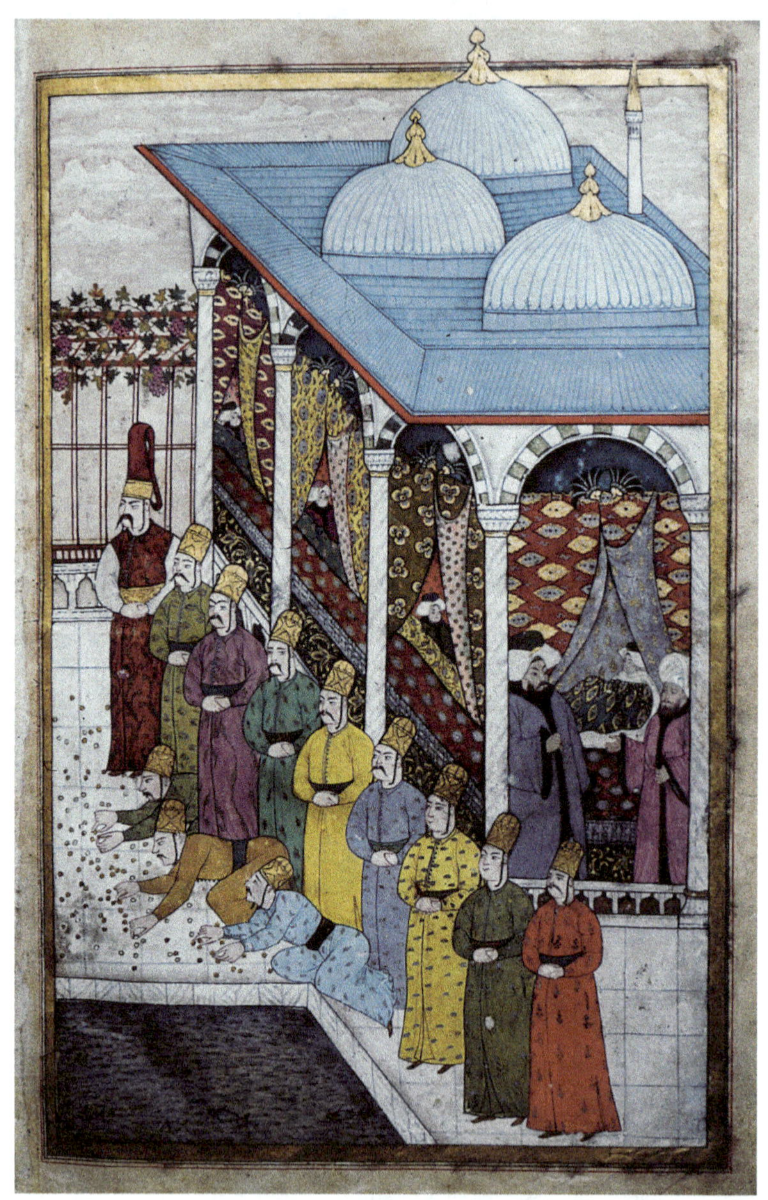

Life in the palace, Surname-i Vehbi, 3593, fol.170a, Levni, 1720, Library of Topkapı Palace, İstanbul.

Palaces (*saray* in Turkish) played an important role in reflecting the political, social, and cultural character of the periods in which they were built. Palace complexes were where sultans lived and handled affairs of the state. During the Emirates period when Anatolia was politically and economically weak, palaces were generally small and far from monumental. Even so, palaces, being both residential and administrative edifices, had to be built with more care than other structures.

İbn Batuta, a North African traveller who toured Anatolia in the 14th century, provides information about palaces in the Emirate period, although none of these palaces have survived to the present day. Apart from the Aydın Emirate's palace at Birgi, each of the Bey mansions in Alanya, Eğirdir, Antalya, Beçin, Ladik, and Bursa were apparently modest palaces. Sadly, none of these structures have survived.

Osman Gazi built the first known Ottoman palace in Yenişehir, which was conquered in 1299 and subsequently became the scene of an extensive construction operation. Of these structures only the remains of a *hammam* have survived to the present day. Another palace known from sources was situated in Bursa and dates to the period of Orhan Gazi; this structure, enlarged with various additions since the time of its construction, has not survived either. Located inside the citadel, the Bursa Palace was completely abandoned after Edirne became the capital.

Two palaces were constructed in Edirne, which came under Turkish rule in 1362. The first was known as Saray-ı Atik, literally the Old Palace, in which Sultans Bayezid I and Murad II lived. This palace was constructed by Sultan Murad I, who conquered Edirne. The 17th-century Turkish traveller Evliya Çelebi recounts that this palace, located somewhere near the Selimiye Mosque, was built between the years 1365-1368 and that several structures were added subsequently.

Sultan Murad II initiated the construction of the second palace in Edirne and his son Sultan Mehmed II had the structure enlarged and completed. The Yeni Saray (New Palace), also known variously as Saray-ı Cedid-i Amire (New Royal Palace), Tunca Palace (named after the river) and Hünkar Bahçesi Palace (Royal Garden Palace), Edirne Saray-ı Hümayunu (Edirne Royal Palace), was located in the district presently known as Sarayiçi. In the 1870s the basement of the palace was used as a storehouse for ammunition and in 1876 the palace exploded when the storehouse was set on fire. Only some remains of the palace have survived.

The New Edirne Palace consisted of five large courtyards with buildings located around them. Housing about 6000 people, it maintained its importance even after the capital was moved to Istanbul. It is known that sultans resided here temporarily from time to time. The palace, spread across a wide area, continuously underwent expansion and became a source of inspiration for palaces built in Istanbul.

Sultan Mehmed II, also known as Mehmed the Conqueror for he added Istanbul to Ottoman territory in 1453, immediately ordered the construction of a palace. We know of this palace called the Saray-ı Atik (Old Palace) where Mehmed II lived for some years (1454-1478), through information provided by

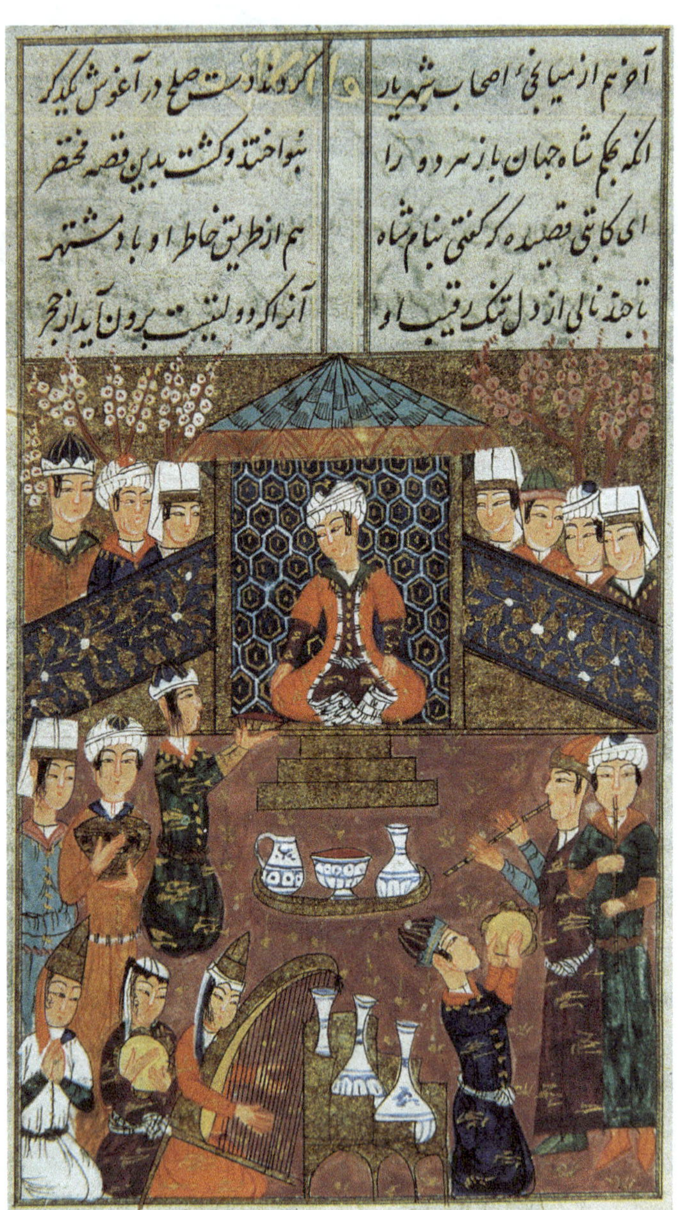

Entertainment in the palace, Külliyat-ı Katibi, 1450-80, R.989, 93a, Library of Topkapı Palace, İstanbul.

Evliya Çelebi and from manuscript miniatures. Saray-ı Atik was established where Istanbul University stands today, and it is known that the palace was spread across a large area and was surrounded by a circuit of two walls.

Shortly after the first one, Sultan Mehmed II ordered the construction of a second palace. The Saray-ı Cedid (New Palace), known as the Topkapı Palace today, was constructed at Sarayburnu (Seraglio Point), overlooking the Marmara Sea, the entrance of the Bosphorus and the Golden Horn. The Topkapı Palace covers an area of about 700,000 m^2 and is a large complex of buildings, resembling the Old Palace of Edirne with regard to its design and the names of some of its pavilions and kiosks. For a while after the construction of the Topkapı Palace, the sultans continued to live in the Old Palace with their families and children, while carrying out the state affairs from the Topkapı Palace. In 1578, Murad III completed the moving of his *harem* to the Topkapı Palace. Thus, when the Old Palace lost its important status, it became a place of exile or a prison for the children, women and the *cariyes* and especially the mother of the deceased or dethroned sultans –the ex-*Valide Sultan*.

Topkapı Palace comprises three sections: the *Birun*, the *Enderun* and the *Mabeyn*. The section that attracts Westerners the most is the *Harem* inside the *Enderun*. Many *cariyes* were housed in this Ottoman palace, having either been bought or taken as slaves and they were kept at hand for private service to the sultan. It is known, however, that when the Ottoman Empire was established the word *harem* had a different meaning than that fancied by most people today: The *harem* consisted of private apartments for the reigning Sultan, apartments for the *Valide Sultan*, other apartments for the use of women, for the Sultan's *ikbals*, the princes and princesses of the imperial house, the *ustas*, the *kalfas* and the *cariyes*. The men chosen among those who were either enslaved during conquests or who were bought, were educated in the *Enderun* to serve the state, while the healthy women were given reading, writing, and courtesy lessons in preparation for special services to the Sultan. Although the captives had the status of slaves, they were in a different position from those bought or sold as property.

The palaces are important because of their architectural design; they are also important as buildings that reflect the lifestyles of the Ottoman sultans. The abandonment of the Topkapı Palace and the move to Dolmabahçe Palace in 1853 is the best example of these changes in the lifestyles of Ottoman sultans: the Dolmabahçe Palace and the other palaces are single massive structures built in one stage like European Palaces.

According to legend, at one time during the 1350s, some Ottoman soldiers stopped to rest on a meadow while crossing from Anatolia to Rumelia. Some 40 of these soldiers paired up to wrestle with each other. Some days after, arriving at the place known as Kırkpınar, they took up wrestling once again. Finally, two of the wrestlers became finalists. When these two wrestled with each other, neither was able to emerge victorious, and eventually both died of exhaustion. They were then buried at the place where they died. Years later, the soldiers who returned to the place to visit the graves of their friends saw that a spring had surfaced where they were buried and named the place Kırkların Pınarı (Spring of the Forty). Ever since then, wrestling competitions, originally among soldiers but later among wrestlers in general, have been organised at this location, whose name with time has changed to Kırkpınar, literally Forty Springs.

The wrestlers of Kırkpınar rub oil all over their bodies prior to wrestling. They wear trousers called kıspet, *the waist and lower parts of the legs of which are tightly bound.* Kıspet *is usually made of calfskin, and is held around the waist by a thin leather cord or string instead of elastic. The wrestling continues until one of the wrestlers gives up or one of them becomes the winner.*

Kırkpınar wrestling matches take place at Sarayiçi every year at the end of June and the beginning of July. The Hükümet Avenue, Sarayiçi is across the river at the end of the Avenue.

The city of Edirne is embellished with many edifices, the most remarkable of which is the Selimiye Complex in the city centre, to the east of the Eski Mosque, rising on a slope dominating the skyline with its four minarets. Built for Sultan Selim II by the great architect Sinan in the latter half of the 16th century, it was considered the masterpiece of his career by Sinan himself.

The area to the west of Eski Mosque is known as Kaleiçi (Citadel). This area was totally rebuilt after a devastating fire in 1905. It is a very pleasant area for a stroll with its old houses and traces of Jewish, Christian and Muslim culture and mosaics.

There are several bridges over the Tunca River, all of them built by the Ottomans. They are all beautiful and worth visiting.

GLOSSARY

Abdalan-ı Rum	The itinerant heterodox dervishes in Anatolia.
Acemi ocağı	The barracks where conscripts for Janissary Corps were trained.
Ahi	A trade guild organization established by tradesmen and artisans. The members of the organization were called the same.
Ahiyan-ı Rum	The *Ahi*s of Anatolia.
Akritoi	The Byzantine frontier troops.
Aralık	The passageway between the *soyunmalık* and *ılıklık* in a Turkish *hammam*.
Arasta	A row of shops aligned along an (un)covered street.
Ayet	Verses in the Koran.
Balbal	The engraved stone pillars in a human shape that are put on some tombs and tumuli by Turks.
Bedesten	A commercial building with two aisles and covered with domes of equal size. The most precious merchandise was kept in the *bedestens*, which functioned like banks do today.
Bey	The ruler of an independent emirate; the governor of a *sanjak;* a title of respect for the men of the upper classes.
Beylerbey	The *bey* of the *beys*: the highest rank in the provincial government of the Ottoman Empire.
Beylik	Any district ruled by a *Bey,* so the Emirates are called *Beylik* in Turkish.
Bezzaz	Sellers of fabrics.
Birun	The public section of the sultan's palace, which includes the administration.
Boza	A viscous drink made from fermented barley, maize or wheat.
Caliph	From Arabic *Khalifa*, meaning the supreme head of the Muslim community in the line of the Porphet's successors.
Cami	Mosque in Turkish. Also transliterated as *jami'*.
Caravanserai	Hostel along main travelling routes to accommodate travellers and safeguard their goods.
Cariye	"Slave girl", the lowest degree in the hierarchy of the palace harem.
Çelebi	A title of respect, given to men of the upper classes; the epithet of Sultan Mehmed I.
Cuerda seca	A decorative process used for ceramics. Before firing and imprinting the desired decorative motifs, a dark line of manganese is drawn around them to separate the various colours of the enamel or glaze.
Darülhadis	A *madrasa* for studying the *hadith* (*hadis* in Turkish).
Darülhuffaz	A *madrasa* for training of memorising the Koran.
Darüşşifa	A hospital, sometimes with an asylum for the insane.

Darüttıb	A *madrasa* where the medical sciences were taught.
Defterdar	Head of the Treasury.
Dershane	A classroom (especially in a *madrasa*).
Dervish	A member of a Muslim religious order noted for devotional exercises.
Devşirme	The boys recruited from Christian families to be trained as janissary, or officials for the palace; the system for recruiting these boys.
Divan-ı Hümayun	The Imperial Council, chaired by the Grand *vizier* (*vezir* in Turkish), forming the central organ of the Ottoman government.
Emir	Governor, Prince, dignitary. The ruler of an emirate or principality.
Enderun	The inner section of the sultan's palace containing the *harem,* the Sultan's private apartments, and the Palace School for the education of high-ranking state and palace officials.
Engobe	A mixture of non-vitrifiable earth, applied to all or part of a piece of pottery to cover, decorate or outline drawings on it.
Ferman	An edict of the sultan.
Fiqh	Muslim canonical jurisprudence.
Funduq	In Northern Africa, a hostel for merchants and their pack animals; store for merchandise and a commercial centre, equivalent of a *caravanserai* or *khan* in Oriental Islam (*Han* in Turkey).
Futuwwa	A semi-religious fraternity that originated during the Abbasid Empire and spread across the Muslim lands though the Middle Ages.
Gazi	A warrior fighting on behalf of Islam.
Hacı	In Turkish a Muslim who has been on a pilgrimage to Mecca
Hadis	(*Hadith* in Arabic and Lit. "sayings".) Tradition related to acts, sayings and attitudes of the Prophet Muhammad and his companions.
Halvet	The private chambers in a public bath.
Hammam	Public or private bathhouse.
Han	(*Khan* in Arabic) Inn, lodgings for travellers and merchants on the main caravan routes: Store and hostel in large centres. (See also *funduq* and *caravanserai*).
Hanikah	A structure built for hosting itinerant *dervishes,* scholars etc. during the Anatolian Seljuq period.
Harem	The women's apartments in a Muslim household.
Hatun	A title of respect, for women of the upper classes.
Hodja	A Muslim teacher.
Ibn	Son of (Arabic).

İkbal	Favourite women of a sultan; the second highest degree in the hierarchy of the palace *harem.*
Ilıklık	*Tepidarium*/lukewarm-bath area in a Turkish hammam where bathers would rest after bathing.
Imam	One who presides Islamic prayer. A guide, chief, spiritual model or cleric, and sometimes also a politician, in a Muslim society.
İmaret	A complex of buildings and institutions supported by a *waqf;* after the 16th century the word was used to mean a soup kitchen for the poor.
Iwan	Vaulted hall, walled on three sides with a large opening arch and vaulted recess.
Jami'	Main mosque where daily prayer is celebrated and that of Friday.
Janissary Corps	(*Yeniçeri Ocağı* in Turkish.) The sultan's standing infantry corps, recruited from the devşirme and paid from the Treasury.
Ka'ba	(Litterally. "cube".) Temple in Mecca. Centre of Islamic religion.
Kadı	Judge of Islamic canon law and Ottoman law and the governor of a township called *kadılık.*
Kadıasker	The highest judicial authority of the empire after the *Shaykh al-Islam.* There were two *Kadıasker,* one for Rumelia and one for Anatolia. Also known as *kazasker.*
Kalemişi	The colourful decoration done with a *kalem* (pen) on a plastered surface.
Kalfa	The second lowest degree in the hierarchy of the palace harem.
Kapıkulu	"Slave of the Porte", a *devşirme* or slave employed in military, administrative or Palace service.
Kaplıca	Spas, hot springs used for therapeutic purposes, and facilities on such springs.
Kaptan-ı Derya	Grand Admiral of the Ottoman fleet.
Katı' technique	A technique which can be described as "paper inlay". The pattern is drawn on either paper or leather then the closed spaces are cut out with a knife. It is then stuck onto paper, leather or glass.
Kese	A coarse, cloth bath glove; a small bag or pouch.
Khanqa	Monastery or hostel for *sufis* or *derviches.*
Koran	(From the Arabic root qr', "to recite, to read".) Sacred text of the Islamic revelation, transmitted by the Archangel Gabriel to the Prophet Muhammad.
Külhan	A stoking hole in a *hammam.*
Külliye	A complex of several buildings where the mosque is at the centre. The other buildings were the *madrasa, imaret, han, hammam, darüşşifa*, etc.
Kümbet	A monumental tomb, usually covered with a dome hidden under a spire.

Kündekari and Fake Kündekari	A woodwork technique. Polygonal pieces decorated with carved floral motifs are held together with rods and mortise without the use of glue or nails. When nails or glue are used it is fake *kündekari*.
Mabeyn	A section in an Ottoman palace where the sultan received ambassadors, envoys and the viziers.
Madrasa	(*Medrese* in Turkish.) Islamic school of sciences (theology, law, Koran, etc.) and lodgings for students.
Masjid	A mosque without a *minbar.* The Friday Service cannot take place in a *masjid* due to the absence of a *minbar.*
Mektep	Primary School, also known as *sıbyan mektebi.*
Menzil han	A *han* at a day's journey.
Mevlevihane	A place for the Mevlevi Order dervishes, also known as whirling *dervishes.*
Mihrab	Niche in a *qibla* wall indicating the direction of Mecca towards which worshippers faced when praying.
Minbar	Pulpit in a mosque where the *imam* preaches his sermon *(khutba)* to the faithful.
Müderris	The chief teacher and administrator of a *madrasa.*
Müezzin	Religious Muslim administrator, in charge of announcing the five daily prayers from the top of the mosque's minaret.
Mu'id	A tutor in a *madrasa,* who assisted the *müderris.*
Muqarnas	Stalactite or honeycomb ornament which adorns cupolas or corbels of a building.
Muvakkithane	Clock room equipped with the necessary apparatus to calculate the time for prayer, also where horoscopes were read.
Müzehhip	An illuminator of manuscripts.
Namaz	Muslim ritual prayers exercised five times a day.
Namazgah	An open-air place on inter-city roads or recreation areas for performing the *namaz.*
Naskhi	(Lit. "coppied".) One of the most widespread styles of calligraphy used in Arabic script.
Nişancı	The secretary of the Imperial Council who checked the *tuğra* to be attached to official orders and letters.
Ocak	A fireplace, hearth; a household; any institution for training recruits.
-oğlu	"Son of" in Turkish, or "- oğulları" plural.
Opus sectile	Stone and/or marble mosaic, in which the pieces are cut in different shapes and sizes and fit side by side forming generally geometric designs.

Qibla	Direction of *Ka'ba*, towards which believers turn to face for prayer. Wall of mosque in which the *mihrab* is situated.
Qubba	Dome. By extension, monument erected upon the grave of a saint.
Ribat	Fortified enclosure for religious warriors (North Africa); a hospice for pilgrims (Mamluk Egypt, Palestine and Syria).
Rumi	Stylised leaf motif; half-cut palmette motif.
Sadaqa	Alms.
Şadırvan	Fountain with taps and a pool for ritual ablutions.
Sancak Bey	The governor of a Sanjak, subdivision of a beylerbeyilik.
Şehzade	Prince.
Şemse	Sunburst motif.
Şerefe	Balcony of a minaret.
Sevap	Meritorious in God's sight.
Sgraffito	A technique of scratching through one layer so as to reveal another of contrasting colour.
Shaykh al-Islam	(*Şeyhülislam* in Turkish.) The head in the hierarchy of the doctors of Muslim canon law, tradition and theology.
Sherbet	Sweet fruit drink; a medicinal drink.
Sıbyan mektebi	See *mektep*.
Sıcaklık	Caldarium/hot-bath area in a Turkish hammam.
Şifahane	Hospital; lunatic asylum.
Slip	A creamy diluted clay, used for decorating pottery.
Solomon's knot	A motif of interlocking broken or curving lines, like a David's star.
Soyunmalık	The apoditerium/disrobing hall in a Turkish *hammam*.
Spandrel	The triangular area between two arches, or between the outer curve of an arch and the horizontal line from its apex and the vertical line from the pillar supporting it.
Squinch	An arch placed diagonally at each corner of a square and filled decoratively with a variety of methods, providing the transition from the cubical walls to the sphere of the dome.
Sufi	Mystical or ascetic order in Islam. Mystic, a devotee.
Sunna	(Literally "tradition".) For Orthodox Islam, group of traditions of the Prophet in which legal advisers and theologians find support and foundations to establish the content of Islamic Law arising from the Koran.
Sunni	Follower of *Sunna*. "Sunnism", a political and religious system opposed to "shi'ism". Sunnites are divided into 4 schools: *maliki, hanbali, hanafi, shafi'i*.
Suq	Market place.
Sura	Chapter of the Koran.

Tabhane	Guestroom at a mosque for itinerant *dervishes* and other travellers.
Tandır	Heating arrangement consisting of a brazier which is put under a table which is covered with a blanket; or in the *hans* of Seljuq period, clay-lined pit or earthenware jar buried in the ground and used for cooking and heating.
Tekke	A centre for *dervishes,* where they could gather, worship and live.
Tezhip	Art of illuminating the borders of scriptures in a manuscript.
Tile Mosaic	Pieces of different colour tile pieces cut in certain shapes and placed in plaster to form a composition.
Tımar	Small military fief with an annual value of less than 20,000 akches.
Tımarlı Sipahi	Man-at-arms holding a *tımar* fief.
Traşlık	A small room in a Turkish *hammam* used the removal of body hair.
Tuğra	The sultan's official monogram, attached to state documents to confirm their legality.
Türbe	A monumental tomb, sometimes with a crypt downstairs.
Turkish triangles	A form of transitional with triangles and chevrons from the cubical walls to the dome.
Usta	The third highest degree in the hierarchy of harem women.
Valide Sultan	The mother of the reigning Sultan, therefore the most powerful woman in the Empire.
Vezir	(Vizier.) Minister. The highest vezir was called the Grand Vezir or Sadrazam.
Yeniçeri Ağası	Chief officer of the Janissary Corps.
Wahhabi	A sect of Islam, which forbids any mediator like a prophet, saints, veneration of the dead or of their tombs, or votive offerings and supports the belief that the worship to God must be direct.
Waqf	(*Vakıf* in Turkish.) Endowment in perpetuity, usually land or property, from which the revenue was reserved for the upkeep of religious foundations.
Waqf charter	(Vakfiye in Turkish.) The deed of endowment of a *waqf.*
Zawiya	Small *tekke*; a hospice for *dervishes* and travellers. Establishment reserved for religious teaching designed for training *shaykhs*; includes mausoleum of a saint, built on the site where he lived.
Zellij	Small enamelled ceramic tiles used to decorate monuments or interiors.

HISTORICAL PERSONALITIES

Name	Born-Died	Information
Abdülaziz	1830-1876	Ottoman Sultan
Abdülhamid II	1842-1918	Ottoman Sultan
Abu Bakr	c. 570-634	First caliph after Muhammad
Ahmet Gazi	?-1391	Emir of Menteşe
Ahmet Paşa	?-1497	*Müderris*, *kadı* and poet
Ahmet Vefik Pasha	19th c.	Governor of Bursa
Ahmeti	?-1413	Poet and author on Ottoman History
Ahmet Bican Efendi	15th c.	Ottoman *sufi* and scholar
Alaaddin Ali	?-?	Son of Sultan Murad II
Alâeddin Keykubad I	?-1237	Anatolian Seljuq Sultan (1220-37)
Alem Şah	1466-1503	Son of Bayezid II
Andrić, Ivo	1892-1975	Yugoslavian author, who won the Nobel Prize
Aziza Hatun	14th -15th c.	Wife of İsa Bey of Aydın Emirate
Babinger, Franz	1891-1967	German Turkologist and historian
Bartolomeu Dias	1450-1500	Portugese sailor
Bayalun Hatun	13th-14th c.	Wife of Osman Gazi (?) or another name for Nilüfer Hatun
Bayezid I	1360-1403	Ottoman Sultan, also known as Yıldırım Bayezid, The father of Sultan Mehmed I, and Süleyman Çelebi, İsa Çelebi and Musa Çelebi
Bayezid II	1447-1512	Ottoman Sultan, the father of Selim I
Bayezid Paşa	?-1421	Grand *Vizier*
Bellini, Gentile	1429-1507	Venetian painter
Bellini, Giovanni	1430-1516	Venetian painter
Börklüce Mustafa	?-1416-19	Ottoman rebel
Bülbül Hatun	15th c.	Wife of Karaca Pasha
Cantacuzenus	?-1383	Epithet of Byzantine Emperor John VI, ruled 1341-54
Cem Sultan	1459-1495	Son of Sultan Mehmed II
Charles VIII	1470-1498	King of France
Cüneyd	?-?	Aydın Bey
Davud of Kayseri	14th c.	*Müderris*
Dernschwamm, Hans	1494-1568	German traveller
Devlet Hatun	?-1414	Devletşah Hatun, the wife of Sultan Bayezid I
Ducas	1400-1470	Byzantine chronicler
Emir Süleyman Çelebi	?-1411	Son of Mehmed I

Emir Sultan	1368/69-1429/30	Ottoman *sufi* and son-in-law of Bayezid I
Ertuğrul Bey	?-1281	Father of Osman Gazi
Evliya Çelebi	1611-1681	Ottoman traveller
Firuz Bey (Hoca)	?-1402	Ottoman Commander
Friedrich I Barbarossa	c. 1122-1190	German Emperor, who passed through the Balkans and Anatolia on the Third Crusade and drowned in the Tarsus River.
Gazi Umur Bey	?-1348	Aydın bey, also known as Bahaeddin
Geyikli Baba	14th c.	Heterodox Islamic religious man during the reign of Orhan Gazi
Gıyaseddin Keyhusrev II	1221/22-1246	Anatolian Seljuq Sultan
Grelot	?17th c.	Traveller
Gülşah Hatun	?-1487	Wife of Sultan Mehmed II; buried at Bursa
Hacı İvaz Paşa	?-1429	Son of Ahi Bayezid, second *vizier* to Sultan Murad II, supervised the construction of Yeşil Türbe
Hacı Umur bin Menteşe	?-1400	Member of Menteşe dynasty
Hafsa Hatun	14th c.	Daughter of İsa Bey of Aydın Emirate, wife of Bayezid I
Hafsa Sultan	?-1534	Wife of Sultan Selim I
Halil Hayreddin Paşa (Çandarlı)	? -1389	Grand *Vizier*, founder of the Janissary Corps
Halil Yahşi Bey	15th c.	Governor of Aydın Sanjak
Hallacı Mansur	857-922	Heterodox Islamic religious man
Hartmann, R.	?-?	German scholar
Hızır Bey	14th c.	Son of Mehmed and Aydın Bey (1348-60)
Hızırşah	?-1410	Last Saruhan Bey (1388-90 and 1403-10)
Holbein, Hans	1460-1524	Known as "the Elder", German painter
Holophira	14th c.	Also Nilüfer Hatun, wife of Orhan Gazi
Hüsnüşah Hatun	15th-beginning of 16th c.	Wife of Bayezid II
Ibn Battuta	1304-1369	Traveller from al-Andalus
İlyas Bey	?-1421	Menteşe Bey, son of Mehmed

İne Bey (Eyne Bey)	14th c.	Ottoman officer
İsa Bey	?-?	Aydın Bey (1360-90), son of Mehmed Bey
İshak Çelebi (Muzaffereddin)	?-1388	Saruhan Bey (1366-88)
İshak Paşa	?-1485	Grand *Vizier*
John III Ducas Vatatzes	1193-1254	Nicean Byzantine Emperor (1222-54)
Justinian I	482-565	Byzantine Emperor (527-65)
Karaca Pasha	?-1456	Beylerbey of Rumelia, also known as Karaca Bey
Kazanoğlu Mehmed Bey	15th c.	A local potentate from Tire
Kılıç Arslan II	?-1192	Anatolian Seljuq Sultan
Kitsikis, Dimitri	1935-	Contemporary Greek historian
Köse Mihail	14th c.	Ottoman army commander
Küpeli Sultan	15th c.	Daughter of Bayezid I
Lotto, Lorenzo	1480-1556	Venetian painter
Mahmud I	1696-1754	Ottoman Sultan (1730-54)
Mehmed Bey	?-1334	Son of Aydın, Aydın Bey (1308-34)
Mehmed I	c. 1389 -1421	Ottoman Sultan also known as Çelebi Mehmed, father of Murad II
Mehmed II	?-1423	Karamanid Bey
Mehmed II	1432-1481	Ottoman Sultan also known as Mehmed the Conqueror
Menteşe Bey	?-1296	Originally an admiral of Anatolian Seljuqs who founded the Menteşe Emirate in 1282
Mesut Bey	?-1319	Menteşe Bey
Mevlana Celaleddin Rumi	?-1273	Founder of the Mevlevi order of the whirling dervishes
Michael Ducas	14th c.-?	Byzantine scientist and doctor
Michael VIII Palaeologus	1224-1282	Byzantine Emperor
Molla Şemseddin Fenari	1350-1430	Ottoman Sheikh-al-Islam and scholar
Montaigne	1533-1592	French author
Murad I	c. 1326-1389	Ottoman Sultan also known as Hüdavendigar, the father of Bayezid I
Murad II	1403/4-1451	Ottoman Sultan, the father of Mehmed II
Musa Bey	?-?	Aydın Bey
Musa Çelebi	?-1413	Son of Bayezid I
Mustafa II	1664-1703	Ottoman Sultan (1695-1703)
Mutasım	776-842	Abbasid Caliph

Nilüfer Hatun	14th c.	Originally Holophira, the wife of Orhan Gazi, also known as Bayalun Hatun (?)
Nizam al-Mulk	1018-1092	Grand *Vizier* of the Great Seljuq Empire
Orhan Bey	?- before 1344	Menteşe Bey
Orhan Gazi	c. 1281-1362	Also known as Orhan Bey, second Ottoman Sultan, father of Murad I
Osman Gazi	c. 1258-1326	Also known as Osman Bey, founder of the Ottoman Empire
Parvillé, Léon	19th c.	French architect, employed for the restoration of Bursa monuments destroyed in the earthquake of 1855
Postinpuş Baba	14th c.	Heterodox religious man of Khorasan
Saruhan Bey	?-1345	Founder of Saruhan Emirate
Savcı Bey	14th c.	Son of Sultan Murad I
Şehinşah	1461-1511	Son of Bayezid II
Selim I	1467-1520	Ottoman Sultan (1512-20) also known as Yavuz Selim, father of Süleyman the Magnificent
Şemseddin	15th c.	Kadı of Bursa
Sheikh Bedreddin	1359-1419	Ottoman minister of justice and education - rebel
Sinaneddin Yusuf Paşa	?-?	Beylerbeyi of Rumelia
Sitti Hatun	1435-1486	Wife of Mehmed II and daughter of Süleyman, from Dulkadir Emirate in southeast Anatolia
Şücaeddin İlyas Bey	?-1421	MenteşeBey
Süleyman Çelebi	?-1411	Son of Bayezid I
Süleyman I	1495-1566	Ottoman Sultan (1520-66) also known as Süleyman the Lawgiver or Süleyman the Magnificent
Süleyman Paşa	1316-1360	Son of Orhan Gazi
Süleyman Şah	?-?	Son of Mehmed of Aydın Emirate
Sultan Abdullah	?-1481	Son of Bayezid II
Sultan Mustafa	1451-1474	Son of Mehmed II, brother of Cem Sultan
Sultan Şah Hatun	?-?	Sister of Mehmed, son of Aydın
Taceddin the Kurd	14th c.	*Müderris*
Tacü'n-nisa or Taj al-Nisa Hatun	15th c.	Wife of Murad II first, then of İshak Paşa

Tamerlane	1336-1405	Timur Lenk: Mongol Conqueror of Asia
Theodora	c. 500-548	Byzantine Empress (527-48), wife of Justinian I
Torlak Kemal	14th c. -1416-19	rebel
Yakup Bey	?-after 1483	commander of Mehmed II and teacher of Cem Sultan
Yakup Çelebi	?-1389	Son of Murad I, brother of Bayezid I
Yavukluoğlu (Yoğurtluoğlu) Mehmed Bey	15th c.	A local potentate at Tire

FURTHER READING

AKURGAL, E., *The Art and Architecture of Turkey*, Oxford, 1980.

ALDERSON, A. D., *The Structure of the Ottoman Dynasty*, Oxford, 1956.

ANHEGGER, R., *Beiträge zur frühosmanischen Baugeschichte*, İstanbul, 1953.

ARIK, O., *Turkish Art and Architecture*, Ankara, 1985.

ASLANAPA, O., *Türkische Fliesen und Keramik in Anatolien*, İstanbul, 1965.

ASLANAPA, O., *Turkish Art and Architecture,* London, 1971.

ASLANAPA, O., *İznik Tile Kiln Excavations Part I*, Istanbul, 2000.

ATASOY, N.; RABY, J., *Iznik, The Pottery of Ottoman Turkey*, London, 1994.

BABİNGER, F., *Mehmet the Conqueror and His Time* (tr. From German by R. Manheim), Princeton, 1978.

BRANDENBURG, D., *Die Madrasa, Ursprung, Entwicklung, Ausbreitung und künstlerische Gestaltung der Islamischen Moschee-Hochschule*, Graz,1978.

CAHEN, Cl., Pre-Ottoman Turkey, New York, 1968.

CAHEN, Cl., *La Turquie pré-Ottomane*, 1988.

CARSWELL, J., *Iznik Pottery*, London, 1998.

ÇAĞMAN, F.; ATASOY, N., *Turkish Miniature Painting*, Istanbul, 1974.

DEMİRALP, Y., *Erken Dönem Osmanlı Medreseleri (1300-1500)*, Ankara, 1999.

DEMİRİZ, Y., *Osmanlı Mimarisinde Süsleme I (Erken Devir 1300-1453)*, Istanbul, 1973.

EVLİYA EFENDİ (EVLİYA ÇELEBİ), *Narrative of Travels in Europe, Asia and Africa in the 17th Century (tr. By J. Von Hammer-Purgstall),* 3 vols. London, 1834, 1846 & 1850.

DERMAN, U., *The Art of Calligraphy in the Islamic Heritage*, Istanbul, 1998.

FRISHMAN, M.; KHAN, H., *The Mosque, History, Architectural Development and Regional Diversity*, London, 1997.

GABRIEL, A., *Une Capitale Turque, Brousse (Bursa)*, Paris, 1958.

GİBBONS, H. A., *The Foundations of the Ottoman Empire*, Oxford, 1916.

GOODWİN, G., *A History of Ottoman Architecture*, London, 1971.

GOODWİN, G., *The Janissaries*, London, 1994.

GOODWİN, G., *A Guide to Edirne*, Istanbul, 1995.

HAMMER-PURGSTALL, J. Von, *Histoire de l'Empire Ottoman* (tr. From German by J.J. Hellert), 18 vols. Paris, 1835-43.

HİLLENBRAND, R., *Islamic Architecture*, Edinburgh, 1994.

IBN BATTUTA, *Travels in Asia and Africa 1325-54* (tr. And selected by H.A.R. Gibb) London, 1983.

IMBER, C., *The Ottoman Empire*, 1300-1481, 1990.

İNALCIK, O.E. -Pitcher, D., *An Historical Geography of the Ottoman Empire*, 1972.

İNALCIK, H., *The Ottoman Empire, The Classical Age 1300-1600*, London, 1973.

İNALCIK, H., *An Economic and Social History of the Ottoman Empire, 1300-1600*, 2 vols., Cambridge, 1994.

JANSSENS, H. F., *I. Batouta, 'Le Voyageur de l'Islam' 1304-63*, 1948.

KRİTOVOULOS, M., *The History of Mehmet the Conqueror* (tr. By C. T. Riggs), Princeton, 1954.

KURAN, A., *The Mosque in Early Ottoman Architecture*, Chicago, 1968.

KURAN, A.; SÖZEN, M., *Anadolu Medreseleri*, 2 vols., 1969-1972.

KÜHNEL, E., *Die Moschee*, Graz, 1974.

LEMERLE, P., *L'Emirat d'Aydın*, Paris, 1957.

LEVEY, M., *The World of Ottoman Art*, London, 1975.

ÖNEY, G., *Turkish Tile Art*, İstanbul, 1976.

ÖNEY, G., *Anadolu Selçuklu Mimarisinde Süsleme ve El Sanatları*, Ankara, 1978.

ÖNEY, G., *Beylikler Devri Sanatı XIV-XV Yüzyıl (1300-1453)*, Ankara, 1989.

OTTODORN, K., *Das Islamische Iznik*, Berlin, 1941.

ÖZEL, M., ed., *Traditional Turkish Arts*, Istanbul, 1992.

PETERSEN, A., *Dictionary of Islamic Architecture*, London, 1996.

REİNDL, H., *Männer um Bayezid. Eine Prosopographische Studie über die Epoche Sultan Bayezids II (1481-1512)*, 1985.

RESTLE, M., *Istanbul - Bursa, Edirne, İznik*, 1976.

SÖNMEZ, Z., *Başlangıçtan 16. yy'a Kadar Anadolu Türk-İslam Mimarisinde Sanatçılar*, Ankara, 1989.

TAESCHNER, F., *Zünfte und Bruderschaften in Islam*, 1979.

UZUNÇARŞILI, İ. H., *Anadolu Beylikleri*, Ankara, 1998.

ÜNAL, R. H., ed., *Birgi (Tarihi, Tarihi Coğrafyası ve Türk Dönemi Anıtları)*, 2001.

ÜNSAL, B., *Turkish Islamic Architecture in Seljuk and Ottoman Times 1071-1923*, London, 1959.

WİTTEK, P., *Das Fürstentum Mentesche*, 1934.

WİTTEK, P., *The Rise of the Ottoman Empire*, 1938.

WULZİNGER, K.; WİTTEK, P.; SARRE, F., *Das Islamische Milet*, Berlin, 1935.

YETKİN, S. K., *L'architecture Turque en Turquie*, Paris, 1962.

YETKİN, S. K.; ÖZGÜÇ, T., et al, *Turkish Architecture*, Ankara, 1965.

YETKİN, Ş., *Historical Turkish Carpets*, İstanbul, 1981.

ZACHARİADOU, E.A., *Trade and Crusade, Venetian Crete and the Emirates of Menteshe and Aydın (1300-1415)*, Venice, 1983.

AUTHORS

Gönül Öney

Gönül Öney graduated from the Faculty of Languages, History and Geography at the University of Ankara in 1955. She joined the academic staff of the same university in 1957. After getting her Ph.D. in History of Art in 1961, she became assistant professor in 1967. She was awarded full professorship in 1972 and she served as professor in the History of Art Department from 1972 to1981.

After 1981, Professor Öney continued her academic career in Ege University in Izmir. She was named Dean of the Faculty of Letters in 1982 and served in that capacity until 1993 when she became Deputy Rector of Ege University, a position that she presently holds.

Professor Öney specializes in Turkish-Islamic art and architecture. Her publications include numerous articles and books published abroad in English or German.

She is a member of the "Group of Specialists on Heritage Education" of the Council of Europe and ICOMOS.

Rahmi H. Ünal

Born in 1937, Professor. Ünal graduated from the Faculty of Letters at Istanbul University in 1959. He joined the academic staff in the History of Art Department of Atatürk University in Erzurum as assistant in 1961. He went to France as a scholar in 1963 to continue his studies in the History of Turkish-Islamic Architectural History. After receiving his Ph.D. from the Faculty of Letters of Sorbonne University, he returned to his previous position at Atatürk University in 1965. He became Associate Professor in 1968 and Full Professor in 1976. Since 1978 he has been Professor of the Faculty of Letters, Ege University. He has written various books and articles on Turkish History and Turkish-Islamic Architectural History. He is currently Head of the History of Art Department.

Aydoğan Demir

A Lecturer in History, he was born in İzmir in 1938. He graduated from the History Department of the Faculty of Letters at İstanbul University in 1960. He worked as a teacher in Salihli High School from 1960 until 1963 and between 1963 and 1980 he taught in the Institute of Education. He has been working as lecturer in History in Ege University, Faculty of Letters, History and History of Art Departments since 1980. He has published several articles on Ottoman archive documents and on Ottoman tombstones.

İnci Kuyulu

Born in 1957, she graduated from Hacettepe University, Social and Administrative Sciences Faculty, Department of History of Art in 1980. She received her M.A. degree in 1982 and Ph.D. in 1989. She has since been serving as an assistant professor at the History of Art Department of the Faculty of Letters, Ege University. Her work has been published widely on Turkish and Islamic Art and Architectural Decoration.

Lale Bulut

Born in 1960, she graduated from Ankara University, Faculty of Languages, History and Geography, Department of History of Art in 1983. She received her M.A. degree in 1987 and Ph.D. in 1991. She has since been serving as an assistant professor at the History of Art and Archaeology Department of the Faculty of Letters, Ege University. Her work has been reproduced in various publications on Turkish Minor Arts.

Yekta Demiralp

Born in 1959, he graduated from the Faculty of Languages, History and Geography of the University of Ankara, Department of History of Art in 1980. He worked as an art history teacher in Samsun from1981 to1984. He received his M.A. degree in 1990 and Ph.D. in 1997. He is currently serving as an assistant professor at the History of Art Department of the Faculty of Letters, Ege University. He has been involved in various publications on the History of Turkish and Islamic Art and Architecture.

Şakir Çakmak

Born in 1964, he graduated from Ege University Faculty of Letters, Department of Archaeology and Art History in 1986. He received his M.A. degree in 1991 and his Ph.D. in 1998. He is now a research assistant at the Faculty of Letters, Ege University. He has been involved in various publications on Turkish-Islamic Art and Architectural History.

Ertan Daş

Born in 1963, he graduated from Ege University, Faculty of Letters, Archaeology and History of Art Department in 1986. He received his M.A. degree in 1998. He is a research assistant in the same department. He is also a professional photographer and is responsible for the photography in this volume.

ISLAMIC ART IN THE MEDITERRANEAN

This cycle of Museum With No Frontiers Exhibition Trails permits the discovery of secrets in Islamic Art, its history, construction techniques and religious inspiration.

ALGERIA

*LEGACY OF ISLAM IN ALGERIA: The Art and Architecture of Light** introduces the varied and richest forms Islamic art assumed in Central Maghreb (Algeria), an important artistic heritage related to crucial events that marked the country's history, from the rise of dissident religious movements to the influence of great dynasties, and the roles played by trade and pilgrimage routes and by the Ottomans in the Mediterranean cities. The synthesis of Arab and Berber, African, Andalusian and Eastern influences shaped the artistic and architectural models, the purity and harmony of Ibadid architecture, Almoravid mosques, Ziyanid monuments and Ottoman palaces on the Mediterranean shore.

Five itineraries invite you to discover 70 museums, monuments and sites in Biskra, Ghardaia, Bani Isguen, Algiers, Tlemcen, Nedroma and Tamentit (among others).

EGYPT

MAMLUK ART: The Splendour and Magic of the Sultans tells the story of almost three centuries of political security and economic stability achieved by the sultans' successful defence against Mongol and Crusader threats. The intellectual, scientific and artistic currents that flourished then are manifest in Mamluk architecture and decorative arts, almost modern in their elegant and lively simplicity, bearing witness to the vitality of Mamluk trade, to their cultural exuberance and to their military and religious strength.

Eight itineraries invite you to discover 51 museums, monuments and sites in Cairo, Alexandria and the Nile Delta.

ITALY

SICULO-NORMAN ART: Islamic Culture in Medieval Sicily illustrates how the great artistic and cultural heritage of the Arabs who ruled the island in the 10th and 11th centuries was assimilated and reinterpreted during the Norman reign that followed, achieving its acme in the resplendent age of Ruggero II in the 12th century. Spectacular coastal and mountain landscapes provide the backdrop for visits to villages, castles, gardens, churches and Christianised old mosques.

Ten itineraries invite you to discover 91 museums, monuments and sites in Palermo, Monreale, Mazara del Vallo, Salemi, Segesta, Erice, Cefalù and Catania (among others).

JORDAN

THE UMAYYADS: The Rise of Islamic Art presents a journey through the great artistic and cultural flourishing that gave birth to the formative phase of Islamic art during the 7th and 8th centuries. The Umayyads unified the Mediterranean and Persian cultures and developed an innovative artistic synthesis that incorporated and immortalised Classical, Byzantine and Sassanid heritage. The elegant architecture of desert castles and the frescoes, mosaics and masterpieces of figurative and decorative art still evoke the strong sense of realism and the great cultural, artistic and social vitality of the centres of the Umayyad Caliphate.

Five itineraries invite you to discover 43 museums, monuments and sites in Amman, Madaba, Al-Badiya, Jerash, Umm Qays, Aqaba and Humayma (among others).

MOROCCO

ANDALUSIAN MOROCCO: Discovery in Living Art tells the story of the exchanges between the furthest frontier of the Maghreb and Al-Andalus for more than five centuries. Political and social circumstances gave birth to a crossroads of cultures, techniques and artistic styles revealed by the splendour of Idrisid, Almoravid, Almohad and Marinid mosques, minarets and madrasas. The influence of Cordoban architecture and Andalusian decorative models, horseshoe arches, floral and geometric motifs and the use of stucco, wood and polychromatic tiles, display the continuous interchange that made Morocco one of the most brilliant homes of Islamic civilisation.

Eight itineraries invite you to discover 89 museums, monuments and sites in Rabat, Meknès, Fez, Chefchaouen,Tétouan and Tangier (among others).

PALESTINIAN TERRITORIES

PILGRIMAGE, SCIENCE AND SUFISM: Islamic Art in the West Bank and Gaza explores a period during the reigns of the Ayyubid, Mamluk and Ottoman dynasties when numerous pilgrims and scholars from all quarters of the Muslim world came to Palestine. The great dynasties commissioned architectural and artistic masterpieces in the most important religious centres. Attracting the most learned scholars, many centres enjoyed considerable prestige and encouraged the spread of a rarefied art that still fascinates today. The Islamic monuments and architecture of this Exhibition Trail clearly reflect the connections between dynastic patronage, intellectual activity and the rich expression of people's devotion, rooted in this land for centuries.

Nine itineraries invite you to discover 70 museums, monuments and sites in Jerusalem, Jericho, Nablus, Bethlehem, Hebron and Gaza (among others).

PORTUGAL

IN THE LANDS OF THE ENCHANTED MOORISH MAIDEN: Islamic Art in Portugal uncovers five inspired centuries of Islamic civilisation that shaped the people of the former Gharb al-Andalus. From Coimbra to the furthest reaches of the Algarve there are palaces, Christianised mosques, fortifications and urban centres, all of which bear witness to the splendour of a glorious past. This artistic recollection is the expression of a very delicate symbiosis that determined the particularities of vernacular architecture and still permeates the cultural identity of Portugal.

Ten itineraries invite you to discover 76 museums, monuments and sites in Lisbon, Sintra, Coimbra, Evora, Mertola, Faro and Sesimbra (among others).

SPAIN

MUDEJAR ART: Islamic Aesthetics in Christian Art uncovers the fascinating richness of a genuinely Hispanic cultural and artistic symbiosis that became a distinctive element of Christian Spain after the end of Arab rule. Mudejars were Muslims who were allowed to stay in the reconquered territories and Mudejar artists and craftsmen strongly influenced the culture and art of the new Christian kingdoms. Beautifully decorated brick-built churches, monasteries and palaces in Aragona, Castile, Estremadura and Andalusia provide a unique example of the creative preservation of Islamic forms within Christian art in Spain between the 11th and 16th centuries.

Thirteen itineraries invite you to discover 124 museums, monuments and sites in Madrid, Guadalajara, Saragossa, Tordesillas, Toledo, Guadalupe and Seville (among others).

SYRIA

*THE AYYUBID ERA: Art and Architecture in Medieval Syria** focuses on the unique artistic and architectural development in 12th–13th century Syria, when Atabeg and Ayyubid military resistance to the Crusaders coincided with a great cultural and artistic revival in the most important Syrian cities. The Ayyubid patrons provided educative, religious and charitable institutions; their intense activity left its mark in the sober elegance of mosques, madrasas, citadels, mausoleums and hospitals, embellished with Eastern architectural and decorative motifs, muqarnas, Kufic inscriptions, carved stucco and wooden minbars, beautifully illuminated manuscripts, pottery, metalwork and textiles.

Eight itineraries invite you to discover 95 museums, monuments and sites in Damascus, Bosra, Homs, Hama,Tartus,Aleppo and Raqqa (among others).

TUNISIA

IFRIQIYA: Thirteen Centuries of Art and Architecture in Tunisia is a voyage through the history of the Islamic architecture of the Maghreb, to uncover a millenary civilisation that made works of art of its most important spaces. The great Islamic dynasties – Abbasids, Aghlabids, Fatimids, Zirids, Almohads, Hafsids, Ottomans – and Islamic religious schools and movements left the mark of their artistic expression over the centuries. Islamic art in Tunisia is a cultural crossroads, widely influenced by local artistic customs, by Andalusian and eastern architectural and decorative elements, by Arab, Roman and Berber traditions and by the variety of its natural landscape.

Eleven itineraries invite you to discover 108 museums, monuments and sites in Tunis, Sidi Bou Saïd, Bizerte, Testour, Al-Kef, Kairouan, Mahdia, Sfax, Tozeur and Gabès (among others).

TURKEY

EARLY OTTOMAN ART: The Legacy of the Emirates presents the artistic and architectural expressions in Western Anatolia and the emergence of the Ottoman dynasty in the 14th and 15th centuries. The Turkish Emirates developed a new stylistic synthesis by blending Central Asian and Seljuq traditions and the legacy of the Greek, Roman and Byzantine past.The architectural schemes of mosques, hammams, hospitals, madrasas, mausoleums and the great religious complexes, columns and domes, floral and calligraphic decoration, ceramics and illumination testify to the richness of styles.The cultural and artistic flourishing that matched the rise of the Ottoman Empire was deeply marked by the distinctive legacy of the Emirates.

Eight itineraries invite you to discover 61 museums, monuments and sites in Milas, Selçuk, Manisa, Bursa, İznik, Karacabey, Çanakkale, Gelibolu and Edirne (among others).

* Under preparation.

www.ingramcontent.com/pod-product-compliance
Lightning Source LLC
LaVergne TN
LVHW010858110826
845149LV00005B/1420